The Civil War
A Narrative

ALL THESE WERE HONOURED IN THEIR GENERATIONS

AND WERE THE GLORY OF THEIR TIMES

THERE BE OF THEM

THAT HAVE LEFT A NAME BEHIND THEM

THAT THEIR PRAISES MIGHT BE REPORTED

AND SOME THERE BE WHICH HAVE NO MEMORIAL

WHO ARE PERISHED AS THOUGH THEY HAD NEVER BEEN

AND ARE BECOME AS THOUGH THEY HAD NEVER BEEN BORN

AND THEIR CHILDREN AFTER THEM

BUT THESE WERE MERCIFUL MEN

WHOSE RIGHTEOUSNESS HATH NOT BEEN FORGOTTEN

WITH THEIR SEED SHALL CONTINUALLY REMAIN

A GOOD INHERITANCE

AND THEIR CHILDREN ARE WITHIN THE COVENANT

THEIR SEED STANDETH FAST

AND THEIR CHILDREN FOR THEIR SAKES

THEIR SEED SHALL REMAIN FOR EVER

AND THEIR GLORY SHALL NOT BE BLOTTED OUT

THEIR BODIES ARE BURIED IN PEACE

BUT THEIR NAME LIVETH FOR EVERMORE

Ecclesiasticus xliv

THE
Civil War

A Narrative

★ ★

PETERSBURG
to SAVANNAH

★ ★

War Is Cruelty—You Cannot Refine It

By SHELBY FOOTE

RANDOM HOUSE · NEW YORK

Library of Congress Cataloging in Publication Data
Foote, Shelby.
The Civil War.
CONTENTS.—1.   Fort Sumter to Perryville.—
2.   Fredericksburg to Meridian.—3.   Red River to
Appomattox.
1.   United States—History—Civil War.
E468.F7 973.7 58-988
ISBN 0-307-29030-1
Manufactured in the United States of America
10 9 8 7 6 5 4 3 2 1

CONTENTS

★ ✗ ☆

☆

Petersburg
to
Savannah

☆

War Is Cruelty . . .

★ ✗ ☆

EASTWARD, WITH LEE AT LAST OUT-FOXED,
the blue tide ran swift and steady, apparently inexorable as it surged
toward the gates of the capital close in his rear. But then, at the
full, the outlying Richmond bulwarks held; Beauregard, as he had been
wont to do from the outset — first at Sumter, three years back, then
again two years ago at Corinth, and once more last year in Charleston
harbor — made the most of still another "finest hour" by holding Petersburg against the longest odds ever faced by a major commander on either
side in this lengthening, long-odds war.

Grant's crossing of James River went like clockwork, and the
clock itself was enormous. Preceded in the withdrawal by Baldy Smith,
whose corps took ship at White House Landing on June 13 for the
roundabout journey to rejoin Butler at Bermuda Hundred, Hancock
reached Wilcox Landing by noon of the following day, completing a
thirty-mile hike from Cold Harbor to the north bank of the James,
and began at once the ferrying operation that would put his corps on
Windmill Point, across the way, by dawn of June 15. While he crossed,
the engineers got to work on the pontoon bridge, two miles downriver,
by which the other three corps of the Army of the Potomac were to
march in order to reinforce Smith and Hancock in their convergence
on Petersburg, the rail hub whose loss, combined with the loss of the
Virginia Central — Hunter and Sheridan were presumed to be moving
down that critical Shendandoah Valley supply line even now — would
mean that Richmond's defenders, north as well as south of the James,
would have to abandon the city for lack of subsistence, or else choose
between starvation and surrender. In high spirits at the prospect, Grant
was delighted to recover the mobility that had characterized the opening
of the final phase of his Vicksburg campaign, which the current operation so much resembled. Now as then, he was crossing a river miles
downstream from his objective in order to sever its lines of supply and
come upon it from the rear. Whether it crumpled under a sudden as-

sault, as he intended, or crumbled under a siege, which he hoped to avoid, the result would be the same; Richmond was doomed, if he could only achieve here in Virginia the concert of action he had enjoyed last year in Mississippi.

By way of ensuring that this would obtain, he did not tarry long on the north bank of the James, which he reached on the morning of June 14 to find the head of Hancock's column arriving and the engineers already hard at work corduroying approaches to the bridge the pontoniers would presently throw across the nearly half-mile width of river to Windmill Point. Instead, wanting to make certain that Butler understood his part in the double-pronged maneuver, Grant got aboard a steamer for a fast ride up to Bermuda Hundred and a conference with the cock-eyed general. Butler not only understood; he was putting the final touches to the preliminary details, laying a pontoon bridge near Broadway Landing, where Smith would cross the Appomattox tonight for a quick descent on Petersburg next morning, and preparing to sink five stone-laden vessels in the channel of the James at Trent's Reach, within cannon range of his bottled-up right, to block the descent below that point of rebel gunboats which might otherwise make a suicidal attempt to disrupt the main crossing, some thirty winding miles downstream. Satisfied that no hitch was likely to develop in this direction, either from neglect or misconception, Grant prepared to return to Wilcox Landing for a follow-up meeting with Meade, but before he left he got off a wire to Halleck, who had opposed the movement from the outset in the belief that the scattered segments of both armies, Meade's and Butler's, would be exposed to piecemeal destruction by Lee while it was in progress. "Our forces will commence crossing the James today," Grant informed him. "The enemy show no signs yet of having brought troops to the south side of Richmond. I will have Petersburg secured, if possible, before they get there in much force. Our movement from Cold Harbor to the James River has been made with great celerity and so far without loss or accident."

The answer came next morning, not from Old Brains, who was not to be dissuaded from taking counsel of his fears, but from the highest authority of all:

> Have just read your dispatch of 1 p.m. yesterday. I begin to see it. You will succeed. God bless you all.
>
> A. LINCOLN

By that time Smith was over the Appomattox and moving directly on Petersburg, whose outer defenses lay within six miles of Broadway Landing. He had 16,000 men in his three infantry divisions, including one that joined him from City Point at daybreak — a Negro outfit under Brigadier General Edward Hincks, which had been left behind when the rest of the corps shifted northside for a share in the Cold Harbor

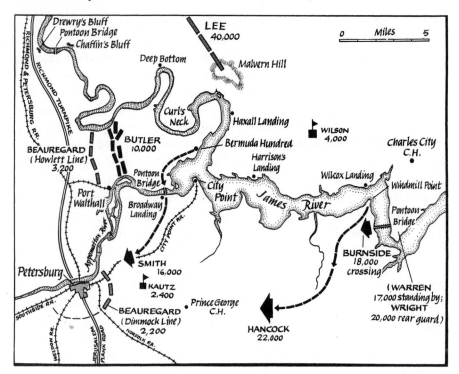

nightmare — plus Kautz's 2400 wide-ranging troopers, over toward the City Point Railroad, where they covered the exposed southeast flank of the column on the march. Four miles from the river, after receiving long-range shots from rebel vedettes who scampered when threatened, the marchers came upon a fast-firing section of artillery posted atop an outlying hill with butternut infantry in support. Hincks, on the left, sent his unblooded soldiers forward at a run. One gun got away, but they took the other, along with its crew, and staged a jubilation around the captured piece, elated at having made the most of a chance to discredit the doubts that had denied them a role in the heavy fighting two weeks ago. Baldy too was delighted, despite the delay, as he got the celebrants back into column, left and right, and resumed the march; for this was the route by which he believed Petersburg could have been taken in the first place, back in early May, and he had said as much, repeatedly though without avail, to Butler at the time. Another mile down the road, however, he came upon a sobering view, spirit-chilling despite the noonday heat, and called a halt for study and deployment.

What he saw, dead ahead down the tracks of the railroad, might well have given anyone pause, let alone a man who had just returned from playing a leading role in Grant's (and Lee's) Cold Harbor demonstration of what could happen to troops, whatever their numerical advantage, who delivered a hair-trigger all-out attack on a prepared position, however scantly it might be defended. Moreover, this one had been under construction and improvement not for two days, as had been the case beyond the Chickahominy, but for nearly two years, ever since August 1862, when Richmond's defenders learned that McClellan had wanted to make just such a southside thrust, as a sequel to *his* Peninsular "change of base," only to be overruled by Halleck, who had favored the maneuver no more then, when he had the veto, than he did now that he lacked any final say-so in the matter. Called the "Dimmock Line" for Captain Charles H. Dimmock, the engineer who laid them out, the Petersburg fortifications were ten miles in length, a half oval tied at its ends to the Appomattox above and below the town, and contained in all some 55 redans, square forts bristling with batteries and connected by six-foot breastworks, twenty feet thick at the base and rimmed by a continuous ditch, another six feet deep and fifteen wide. In front of this dusty moat, trees had been felled, their branches sharpened and interlaced to discourage attackers, and on beyond a line of rifle pits for skirmishers, who could fall back through narrow gaps in the abatis, the ground had been cleared for half a mile to afford the defenders an unobstructed field of fire that would have to be crossed, naked to whatever lead might fly, by whatever moved against them. Confronting the eastward bulge of this bristly, hard-shelled oval, Smith gulped and then got down to figuring how to crack it. First there was reconnoitering to be done; a risky business, and he did much of it himself, drawing sniper fire whenever he ventured out of the woods in which he concealed his three divisions while he searched for some apparently nonexistent weak point to assault.

Despite a superfluity of guns frowning from all those embrasures, there seemed to be a scarcity of infantry in the connecting works. Accordingly, he decided to try for a breakthrough with a succession of reinforced skirmish lines, strong enough to overwhelm the defenders when they came to grips, yet not so thickly massed as to suffer unbearable losses in the course of their naked advance across the slashings. All this took time, however. It was past 4 o'clock when Smith wound up his reconnaissance and completed the formulation of his plan. Aware that the defenders were in telegraphic contact with Richmond, from which reinforcements could be rushed by rail — the track distance was only twenty-three miles — he set 5 o'clock as the jump-off hour for a coördinated attack by elements from all three divisions, with every piece of Federal artillery firing its fastest to keep the heads of the defenders down while his troops were making their half-mile sprint from the woods, where they now were masked, to the long slow curve of breastworks in their front.

It was then that the first organic hitch developed. Unaware that an attack was pending (for the simple reason that no one had thought to inform him) the corps artillery chief had just sent all the horses off for water; which meant that there could be no support fire for the attackers until the teams returned to haul the guns into position along the western fringe of the woods. Angered, Baldy delayed the jump-off until 7. While he and his 18,000 waited, and the sun drew near the landline, word came that Hancock, after a similar hitch on Windmill Point this morning, was on the way but would not arrive till after dark. For a moment Smith considered another postponement; Hancock's was the largest corps in Meade's army, and the notion of more than doubling the Petersburg attack force to 40,000 was attractive. But the thought of Confederate reinforcements, perhaps racing southward in untold thousands even now, jam-packed into and onto every railway car available in this section of Virginia — plus the companion thought that Hancock outranked him and might therefore hog the glory — provoked a rejection of any further delay. The revised order stood, and at 7 o'clock the blue skirmishers stepped from the woods, supported by fire from the just-arrived guns, and started forward to where friendly shells were bursting over and around the rebel fortifications, half a mile ahead.

Once more Hincks and his green black troops showed the veterans how to do the thing in style. Swarming over the cleared ground and into the red after-glory of the sunset, they pursued the grayback skirmishers through the tangled abatis, across the ditch, and up and over the breastworks just beyond. Formidable as they had been to the eye, the fortifications collapsed at a touch; no less than seven of the individual bastions fell within the hour, five of them to the jubilant Negro soldiers, who took twelve of the sixteen captured guns and better than half of the 300 prisoners. Astride and south of the railroad, the blue attackers occupied more than a mile of intrenchments, and Hincks, elated at the ease with which his men had bashed in the eastern nose of the rebel oval, wanted to continue the drive right into the streets of Petersburg, asking only that the other two divisions support him in the effort. Smith demurred. It was night now, crowding 9 o'clock, and his mind was on Lee, who was reported to have detached a considerable portion of his army for a crossing of the James that afternoon; they had probably arrived by now, in which case the Federals might be counterattacked at any moment by superior numbers of hornet-mad Confederate veterans. The thing to do, he told Hincks, was brace for the shock and prepare to hold the captured works until Hancock arrived to even or perhaps reverse the odds. Then they would see.

Hancock arrived something over an hour later; two of his three divisions, he said, were a mile behind him on the road from Prince George Courthouse. This had been a trying day for him and his dusty marchers, beginning at dawn, when he received orders to wait on Windmill Point for 60,000 rations supposedly on the way from Butler. He had no use for them, having brought his own, but he waited as ordered until 10.30 and then set out without them. That was the cause of the first delay, a matter of some five hours. The second, equally wasteful of time, was caused by an inadequate map, which misled him badly — with the result that the distance to Petersburg by the direct route, sixteen miles, was nearly doubled by the various countermarches he was obliged to make when he found that the roads on the ground ran in different directions from those inked on paper — and faulty instructions, which identified as his destination a point that later turned out to lie within the enemy lines. "I spent the best hours of the day," he would complain in his report, "marching by an incorrect map in search of a designated position which, as described, was not in existence."

Nor was that the worst of the oversights and errors that developed in the course of this long hot June 15, from which so much had been expected and of which some ten critical hours thus were thrown away. Approaching Prince George Courthouse about sunset, Hancock met a courier from Baldy Smith, who gave him a dispatch headed 4 p.m. and including the words: "If the II Corps can come up in time to make an assault tonight after dark, in the vicinity of Norfolk & Petersburg Railroad, I think we can be successful." This was the first he had heard that he and his 22,000 were intended to have any part in today's action; no one on Grant's staff had thought to tell Meade, who could scarcely be expected to pass along orders he himself had not received. Hancock hastened his march and rode ahead to join Smith at about 10.30, two miles east of Petersburg, only to find that the Vermonter had changed his mind about a night attack. He requested, rather, that Hancock relieve Hincks's troops — whether as a restful reward for all they had done today, or out of a continuing mistrust of their fighting qualities, he did not say — in occupation of the solid mile of rebel works they had taken when they charged into the sunset.

It was done, though Hincks continued to insist that he could march into Petersburg if his chief would only unleash and support him. Hancock rather agreed, though he declined to assume command, being unfamiliar with the ground and partly incapacitated by his Gettysburg wound, which had reopened under the strain of the fretful march. Smith — suffering too, as he said, "from the effects of bad water, and malaria brought from Cold Harbor" — was willing, even glad, to bide his time; his mind was still on all those probable grayback reinforcements coming down from Richmond in multi-thousand-man relays. The 40,000 Federals on hand would be about doubled tomorrow by the arrival of Burnside, who was over the James by now, and Warren, who had just begun to cross. Wilson and Wright would bring the total to roughly 100,000 the following morning; which would surely be enough for practically anything, Smith figured, especially since they had only to expand the gains already made today.

"Unless I misapprehend the topography," he wired Butler before turning in at midnight, "I hold the key to Petersburg."

Beauregard agreed that Baldy held the key. What was more, he also agreed with Hincks that the key was in the lock, that all the blue-coats had to do at this point was give the thing a turn and the gate would swing ajar. "Petersburg was clearly at the mercy of the Federal commander, who had all but captured it," he said later, looking back on that time of strain and near despair.

He had in all, this June 15, some 5400 troops in his department: 3200 with Bushrod Johnson, corking the bottle in which Butler was confined on Bermuda Hundred, and 2200 with Brigadier General Henry A. Wise at Petersburg. The rest — Hoke's division and the brigades of Ransom and Gracie; about 9000 in all — were beyond the James, detached to Lee or posted in the Richmond fortifications. Wise, it was true, had held his own last week in the "Battle of the Patients and the Penitents," which turned back a similar southside thrust, but the Creole identified this recent probe by Butler as no more than "a reconnaissance connected with Grant's future operations." Heavier blows were being prepared by a sterner commander, and he had been doing all he could for the past five days to persuade the War Department to return the rest of his little army to him before they landed. Smith had no sooner been spotted moving in transports up the James the day before, June 14, than Beauregard redoubled his efforts, insisting, now that the crisis he had predicted was at hand, that Hoke and the others be sent without delay. Next morning — today — with Smith bearing ponderously down on him from Broadway Landing and his detached units still unreleased by Richmond, he warned Bragg that even when these were returned, as he was at last assured they would be, he probably would have to choose which of his two critical southside positions to abandon, the Howlett Line above the Appomattox or the Dimmock Line below, if he was to scrape together enough defenders to make a fight for the other. While Wise shifted his few troops into the eastern nose of the intrenchments ringing Petersburg, thus to confront the enemy approaching down the City Point Railroad, Beauregard put the case bluntly in a wire to Richmond: "We must now elect between lines of Bermuda Hundred and Petersburg. We can not hold both. Please answer at once." Evading the question, Bragg merely replied that Hoke was on the way and should be used to the best advantage. Old Bory lost patience entirely. "I did not ask your advice with regard to the movement of troops," he wired back, "but wished to know preference between Petersburg and lines across Bermuda Hundred Neck, for my guidance, as I fear my present force may prove unequal to hold both."

Bragg made no reply at all to this, and while Wise and his 2200, outnumbered eight-to-one by the blue host assembling in front of their works, made enough of a false show of strength to delay through the long afternoon an assault that could scarcely fail, the Creole general fumed and fretted.

Smith's sunset attack was about as successful as had been expected, though fortunately it was not pressed home; Hoke came up in time to assist in work on the secondary defenses, to which Wise and his survivors had fallen back when more than a mile of the main line caved in. Beauregard's strength was now about 8000 for the close-up defense of the town, but this growth was inconsiderable in the light of information that a second Federal column, as large as the first, was approaching from Prince George Courthouse. Dawn would no doubt bring a repetition of the sunset assault, which was sure to be as crumpling since it could be made with twice the strength. Alone in the darkness, ignored by his superiors, and convinced that Wise and Hoke were about to be swamped unless they could be reinforced, the southside commander, who had joined them by then from his headquarters north of the Appomattox, notified Richmond that he had decided to risk uncorking Butler so as to reinforce Petersburg, even though this was likely to mean the loss of its vital rail and telegraph connections with the capital beyond the James. "I shall order Johnson to this point," he wired Bragg. "General Lee must look to the defenses of Drewry's Bluff and Bermuda Hundred, if practicable."

Notified of this development two hours past midnight, Lee reacted promptly. He had suspected from the outset that Grant would do as he had done; "I think the enemy must be preparing to move south of James River," he warned Davis at noon on June 14, before the first blue soldier crossed to Windmill Point. Still, that did not mean that he could act on the supposition. Responsible for the security of Richmond, he had his two remaining corps disposed along a north-south line from White Oak Swamp to Malvern Hill, where he covered the direct approach to the capital twelve miles in his rear, and he could not abandon or even weaken this line until he was certain that the Federals did not intend to come this way. Information that Smith was back at Bermuda Hundred, and then that he had crossed the Appomattox for an attack on Petersburg, was no real indication of what *Meade* would do; Smith was only returning to the command from which he had been detached two weeks ago. Nor was the report that a corps from the Army of the Potomac was on the march beyond the James conclusive evidence of what Grant had in mind for the rest of that army. Butler had reinforced Meade for the northside strike at Lee: so might Meade be reinforcing Butler for the southside strike at Beauregard — who, in point of fact, had yet to identify or take prisoners from any unit except Smith's; all he had really said, so far, was that he had an awesome number of bluecoats in his front, and that was by no means an unusual claim for any general to make, let alone the histrionic Creole.

However, when Lee was wakened at 2 o'clock in the morning to learn that the Howlett Line had been stripped of all but a skeleton force of skirmishers ("Cannot these lines be occupied by your troops?" Beauregard inquired. "The safety of our communications requires it") he no longer had any choice about what to do if he was to save the capital in his rear. A breakout by Butler, westward from Bermuda Hundred, would give the Federals control of the one railroad leading north from Petersburg, and that would have the same effect as if the three railroads leading south had been cut; Richmond would totter, for lack of food, and fall. Accordingly, Lee had Pickett's division on the march by 3 a.m. and told Anderson to follow promptly with one of his other two divisions, Field's, and direct the action against Butler, who almost certainly would have overrun the Howlett Line by the time he got there. Moreover, leaving instructions for A. P. Hill to continue shielding Richmond from a northside attack by Meade — whose army, even with one corps detached, was still better than twice as large as the Army of Northern Virginia, depleted by Early's departure three days ago — Lee struck his tent at Riddell's Shop, while it still was dark, and mounted Traveller for the headquarters shift to Chaffin's Bluff, where Anderson's troops would cross by a pontoon bridge to recover the critical southside works Beauregard had abandoned the night before.

Sure enough, when Lee reached Chaffin's around 9.30 this June 16 and crossed the James behind Pickett, just ahead of Field, the nearby popping of rifles and the distant rumble of guns informed him, simultaneously, that Butler had indeed overrun the scantly manned Bermuda works, whose northern anchor was six miles downriver, and that Beauregard was fighting to hang onto Petersburg, a dozen miles to the south. Presently word came from Anderson that Butler's uncorked troops had advanced westward to Port Walthall Junction, where they were tearing up track and digging in to prevent the movement of reinforcements beyond that point, either by rail or turnpike. Lee replied that they must be driven off, and by nightfall they were, though only as far as the abandoned Howlett Line, which they held in reverse, firing west. All this time, Beauregard's guns had kept growling and messages from him ranged in tone from urgent to laconic, beginning with a cry for help — to which Lee replied, pointedly, that he could not strip the north bank of the James without evidence that more than one of Meade's corps had crossed — and winding up proudly, yet rather mild withal: "We may have force sufficient to hold Petersburg." In response to queries about Grant, whose whereabouts might indicate his intentions, Old Bory could only say at the end of the long day's fight: "No satisfactory information yet received of Grant's crossing James River. Hancock's and Smith's corps are however in our front."

Lee already knew this last. What he did not know, because Beauregard did not know it to pass it along to him, was that Burnside had been in front of Petersburg since midmorning (in fact, his was the corps responsible for such limited gains as the Federals made today) and that Warren was arriving even then, bringing the blue total to more than 75,000, with still another 25,000 on the way. Wilson, who had served Grant well in Sheridan's absence with the other two mounted divisions, was riding hard through the twilight from Windmill Point, and Wright would finish crossing the pontoon bridge by midnight with the final elements of Meade's army. Beauregard, whose strength had been raised in the course of the day to just over 14,000 by the arrival of Johnson from Bermuda Hundred and Ransom and Gracie from Richmond, might find the odds he had faced yesterday and today stretched unbearably tomorrow, despite the various oversights and hitches that had disrupted the Union effort south of the James for the past two days.

In all that time, hamstrung by conflicting orders and inadequate maps — and rendered cautious, moreover, by remembrance of Cold Harbor, fought two weeks ago tomorrow — the attackers had not managed to bring their preponderance of numbers to bear in a single concerted assault on the cracked and creaking Dimmock Line. Yet Grant, for one, was not inclined to be critical at this juncture. As he prepared for bed tonight in his tent at City Point, where he had transferred his headquarters the day before, he said with a smile, sitting half undressed on the edge of his cot: "I think it is pretty well, to get across a great river and come up here and attack Lee in the rear before he is ready for us."

So he said, and so it was; "pretty well," indeed. But June 17, even though all of Meade's army was over the James before it dawned and had been committed to some kind of action before it ended, turned out to be little different. Today, as yesterday, the pressure built numerically beyond what should have been the rebel breaking point — better than 80,000 opposed by fewer than 15,000 — yet was never brought decisively to bear. From the outset, things again went wrong: beginning with Warren, who came up the previous night. Instructed to extend the left beyond the Jerusalem Plank Road for a sunrise attack up that well-defined thoroughfare, he encountered skirmishers on the approach march and turned astride the Norfolk Railroad to drive them back, thus missing a chance (which neither he nor his superiors knew existed) to strike beyond the occupied portion of the Dimmock Line. If this had not happened, if Warren had brushed the skirmishers aside and continued his march as instructed, Beauregard later said, "I would have been compelled to evacuate Petersburg without much resistance." As it was, the conflict here at the south end of the line amounted to little more than an all-day long-range demonstration.

Northward along the center, where Burnside's and Hancock's corps were posted, the fighting was a good deal bloodier, although not much more productive in the end. One of Burnside's divisions started things off by seizing a critical hill, yet could not exploit the advantage because he failed to alert his other two divisions to move up quickly in support. The Confederates had time to shore up their crumbling defenses, both here and just to the north where Hancock's three divisions were

lying idle; Hancock having been obliged by his reopened wound to
turn the command over to Birney — a good man, but no Hancock —
they too had failed to get the word, with the result that they were
about as much out of things as were Wright's three divisions, one of

which was used to bolster the
fought-out Smith, inactive on
the right, while the other two
were sent in response to Butler's urgent plea for reinforcements to keep Lee from driving
him back into the bottle he had
popped out of yesterday.
Wright went, but failed to arrive in time to do anything
more than join the Bermuda
Hundred soldiers in captivity.
By midafternoon, Pickett and
Field had retaken the Howlett

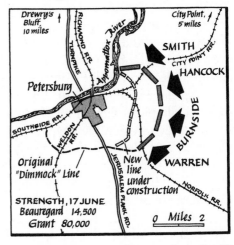

Line from end to end; Butler was recorked, this time for good, and still
more troops were reported to be on the march from Lee's position east of
Richmond.

　　If they got there, if Petersburg was heavily reinforced, the Army
of the Potomac would simply have exchanged one stalemate for another, twice the distance from the rebel capital and on the far side of a
major river. There still was time to avoid this, however. None of Lee's
veterans was yet across the Appomattox, and most of them were still
beyond the James. With the railroad severed at Walthall Junction, even
the closest were unlikely to reach the field by first light tomorrow;
which left plenty of time for delivering the coördinated attack the
Federals had been trying for all along, without success.

　　Happily, near sunset, at least a portion of the army recovered a
measure of its old élan. Burnside and Birney, suddenly meshing gears,
surged forward to seize another mile of works along the enemy center,
together with a dozen guns and about 500 prisoners. A savage counterattack (by Gracie's brigade, it later developed, though at the time the
force had seemed considerably larger) forestalled any rapid enlarge-
ment of the breakthrough, either in width or depth. Dusk deepened
into darkness, and though the moon, only two nights short of the full,
soon came out to flood the landscape with its golden light, Meade —
'ike Smith before him, two dusks ago — declined to follow through
by continuing the advance. Instead, he issued orders for a mass assault
to be launched all along the line at the first wink of dawn.

　　Beauregard said afterwards that at this point, with his center
pierced and Petersburg once more up for grabs, it seemed to him that
"the last hour of the Confederacy had arrived." In fact, he had been ex-

pecting his patched-up line to crack all day, and he had begun at noon the laying out of a new defensive position, the better part of a mile in rear of the present one, to fall back on when the time came. He had no engineers, and indeed no reserves of any kind for digging; all he could do was mark the proposed line with white stakes, easily seen at night, and hope the old intrenchments would hold long enough for darkness to cover the withdrawal of his soldiers, who would do the digging when they got there. The old works, or what was left of them, did hold; or anyhow they nearly did, and Gracie's desperate counterattack delayed a farther blue advance until nightfall stopped the fighting. Old Bory ordered campfires lighted all along the front and sentinels posted well forward; then at midnight, behind this curtain of light and the fitful spatter of picket fire, the rest of his weary men fell back through the moon-drenched gloom to the site of their new line, which they then began to dig, using bayonets and tin cans for tools and getting what little sleep they could between shifts.

At 12.40 a.m. their commander got off his final dispatch of the day to Lee. "All quiet at present. I expect renewal of attack in morning. My troops are becoming much exhausted. Without immediate and strong reinforcements results may be unfavorable. Prisoners report Grant on the field with his whole army."

Lee now had a definite statement, the first in five days, not only that Meade's army was no longer in his front, but also that it was in Beauregard's, and he reacted accordingly. In point of fact, he had begun to act on this premise in response to a dispatch written six hours earlier, in which the southside commander informed him that increasing pressure along his "already much extended lines" would compel him to retire to a shorter line, midway between his original works and the vital rail hub in his rear. "This I shall hold as long as practicable," he added, "but without reinforcements I may have to evacuate the city very shortly." Petersburg's fate was Richmond's; Lee moved, as he had done two nights ago when the Creole stripped the Howlett Line, to forestall disaster — or anyhow to be in a better position to forestall it — by ordering Anderson's third division to proceed to Bermuda Neck and A. P. Hill to cross the James at Chaffin's Bluff and await instructions for a march in either direction, back north or farther south down the Petersburg Turnpike, depending on developments.

So much he had done already, and now that Beauregard's 12.40 message was at hand, stating flatly that Grant was "on the field with his whole army," he followed through by telling Anderson to send his third division on to Petersburg at once and follow with the second. A. P. Hill would go as well, leaving one of his three divisions north of the Appomattox in case Richmond came under attack. This last seemed highly unlikely, however; for a report came in, about this time, that cavalry had ridden down the Peninsula the previous afternoon, as far as Wilcox Landing, and found that all four of Meade's corps had crossed to Windmill Point in the course of the past three days. Beauregard's information, gathered from prisoners, thus was confirmed beyond all doubt. It was now past 3.30 in the morning, June 18; Lee's whole army, except for one division left holding the Howlett Line against Butler — and of course Early, who made contact with Hunter at Lynchburg that same day — would be on the march for Petersburg within the hour.

Two staff officers arrived just then from beyond the Appomattox, sent by their chief to lend verbal weight to his written pleas for help. "Unless reinforcements are sent before forty-eight hours," one of them told Lee he had heard Old Bory declare, "God Almighty alone can save Petersburg and Richmond." Normally, Lee did not approve of such talk; it seemed to him tinged with irreverence. But this was no normal time. "I hope God Almighty will," he said.

For the first time since the crossing of the James, Meade's army gave him on schedule all he asked for. In line before dawn, the troops went forward before sunrise, under orders to take the Confederate works "at all costs." They took them, in fact, at practically no cost at all; for they were deserted, covered only by a handful of pickets who got off a shot or two, then scampered rearward or surrendered. The result was about as disruptive to the attackers, however, as if they had met the stiffest kind of resistance. First, there was the confusion of calling a halt in the abandoned trenches, which had to be occupied for defense against a tricky counterstroke, and then there followed the testy business of groping about to locate the vanished rebels. All this took time. It was midmorning before they found them, nearly a mile to the west, and presently they had cause to wish they hadn't. Beauregard had established a new and shorter line, due south from the Appomattox to a connection with the old works beyond the Jerusalem Plank Road, and was dug in all along it, guns clustered thicker than ever. A noon assault, spearheaded by Birney, was bloodily repulsed: so bloodily and decisively, indeed, that old-timers among the survivors — who had encountered this kind of fire only too often throughout six weeks of crablike sidling from the Rapidan to the Chickahominy — sent back word that Old Bory had been reinforced: by Lee.

It was true. Anderson's lead division had arrived at 7.30 and the second marched in two hours later, followed at 11 o'clock by Lee himself, who rode out to confer with Beauregard, now second-in-command, his lonely ordeal ended. As fast as the lean, dusty marchers came up they were put into line alongside the nearly fought-out defenders, some of whom tried to raise a feeble cheer of welcome, while others wept from exhaustion at the sudden release from tension. They were pleased to hear that A. P. Hill would also be up by nightfall to reduce the all-but-unbearable odds to the accustomed two-to-one, but as far as they were concerned the situation was stabilized already; they had considered their line unbreakable from the time the first of the First Corps veterans arrived to slide their rifles across the newly dug earth of the parapets and sight down them in the direction from which the Yankees would have to come when they attacked.

Across the way, the men who would be expected to do the coming flatly agreed. Remembering one Cold Harbor, they saw here the makings of another, and they wanted no part of it. The result, after the costly noon repulse, was a breakdown of the command system, so complete that Meade got hopping mad and retired, in effect, from any further participation in the effort. "I find it useless to appoint an hour to effect coöperation.... What additional orders to attack you require I cannot imagine," he complained in a message sent to all corps commanders. His solution, if it could be called such, was for them "to attack at all hazards and without reference to each other."

Under these circumstances, the army was spared another Cold Harbor only because its members, for the most part, declined to obey such orders as would have brought on a restaging of that fiasco. Hancock's troops had come up in high spirits, three days ago; "We knew that we had outmarched Lee's veterans and that our reward was at hand," one would recall. These expectations had died since then, however, along with a great many of the men who shared them. "Are you going to charge those works?" a cannoneer asked as a column of infantry passed his battery, headed for the front, and was told by a foot soldier: "No, we are not going to charge. We are going to run toward the Confederate earthworks and then we are going to run back. We have had enough of assaulting earthworks."

As the afternoon wore on, many declined to do even that much. Around 4 o'clock, for example, Birney massed a brigade for an all-out attack on the rebel center. He formed the troops in four lines, the front two made up of half a dozen veteran units, the rear two of a pair of outsized heavy-artillery regiments, 1st Massachusetts and 1st Maine. All four lines were under instructions to remain prone until the order came to rise and charge; but when it was given, the men in the front ranks continued to hug the ground, paying no attention to the shouts and exhortations of their saber-waving officers. They looked back and saw that the rear-rank heavies had risen and were preparing to go forward. "Lay down, you damn fools! You can't take them works!" they cried over their shoulders. For all their greenness, the Bay State troops knew sound advice when they heard it. They lay back down. But the Maine men were rugged. They stepped through and over the prone ranks of veterans and moved at the double against the enemy intrenchments, which broke into flame at their approach. None of them made

it up to the clattering rebel line, and few of them made it back to their
own. Of the 850 who went forward, 632 fell in less than half an hour.
That was just over 74 percent, the severest loss suffered in a single
engagement by any Union regiment in the whole course of the war.

This could not continue, nor did it. Before sunset Meade wired
Grant that he believed nothing more could be accomplished here today.
"Our men are tired," he informed his chief, "and the attacks have not
been made with the vigor and force which characterized our fighting
in the Wilderness; if they had been," he added, "I think we should have
been more successful." Grant — who had maintained a curious hands-
off attitude throughout the southside contest, even as he watched his
well-laid plan being frustrated by inept staff work and the bone-deep
disconsolation of the troops — invoked no ifs and leveled no reproaches.
Declaring that he was "perfectly satisfied that all has been done that
could be done," he agreed that the time had come to call a halt. "Now
we will rest the men," he said, "and use the spade for their protection
until a new vein can be struck."

A new vein might be struck, in time, but not by the old army,
which had suffered a further subtraction of 11,386 killed, wounded, or
captured from its ranks since it crossed the James. That brought the
grand total of Grant's losses, including Butler's, to nearly 75,000 men —
more than Lee and Beauregard had had in both their armies at the start of
the campaign. Of these, a precisely tabulated 66,315 were from the five
corps under Meade (including Smith's, such time as it was with him)
and that was only part of the basis for the statement by its historian,
William Swinton, that at this juncture "the Army of the Potomac,
shaken in its structure, its valor quenched in blood, and thousands of its
ablest officers killed and wounded, was the Army of the Potomac no
more."

Much the same thing could be said of the army in the Petersburg
intrenchments. Though its valor was by no means "quenched," it was
no longer the Army of Northern Virginia in the old aggressive sense,
ready to lash out at the first glimpse of a chance to strike an unwary
adversary; nor would it see again that part of the Old Dominion where
its proudest victories had been won and from which it took its name.
When Lee arrived that morning, hard on the heels of one corps and a
few hours in advance of the other, Beauregard was in such a state of
elation ("He was at last where I had, for the past three days, so anxiously
hoped to see him," the Creole later wrote) that he proposed an all-out
attack on the Union flank and rear, as soon as A. P. Hill came up. Lee
rejected the notion out of hand, in the conviction that his troops were
far too weary for any such exertion and that Hill's corps would be
needed to extend the present line westward to cover the two remaining
railroads, the Weldon and the Southside, upon which Richmond — and
perhaps, for that matter, the Confederacy itself — depended for sur-

vival. He did not add, as he might have done, that he foresaw the need for conserving, not expending in futile counterstrokes, the life of every soldier he could muster if he was to maintain, through the months ahead, the stalemate he had achieved at the price of his old mobility. "We must destroy this army of Grant's before he gets to James River," he had told Early three weeks ago, in the course of the shift from the Totopotomoy. "If he gets there it will become a siege, and then it will be a mere question of time." It was not that yet; Richmond was not under direct pressure, north of the James, and Petersburg was no more than semi-beleaguered; but that too, he knew, was only a "question of time."

Grant agreed, knowing that the length of time in question would depend on the rate of his success in reaching around Lee's right for control of the two railroads in his rear. First, though, there was the need for making the hastily occupied Federal line secure against dislodgment. The following day, June 19, was a Sunday (it was also the summer solstice; *Kearsarge* and *Alabama* were engaged off Cherbourg, firing at each other across the narrowing circles they described in the choppy waters of the Channel, and Sherman was maneuvering, down in Georgia, for ground from which to launch his Kennesaw assault); Meade's troops kept busy constructing bombproofs and hauling up heavy guns and mortars that would make life edgy, not only for the grayback soldiers just across the way, but also for the civilians in Petersburg, whose downtown streets were so little distance away that the blue gun crews could hear its public clocks strike the hours when all but the pickets of both armies were rolled in blankets. Grant had it in mind, however, to try one more sudden lunge — a two-corps strike beyond the Jerusalem Plank Road — before settling down to "gradual approaches."

Warning orders went out Monday to Wright, whose three divisions would be reunited by bringing the detached two from Bermuda Hundred, and to Birney, whose corps would pull back out of line for the westward march, and on Tuesday, June 21, the movement got under way. Simultaneously, while still waiting for Sheridan to return from his failure to link up with Hunter near the Blue Ridge, Wilson, reinforced by Kautz, was sent on a wide-ranging strike at both the Petersburg & Weldon and the Southside railroads, with instructions to rip up sizeable stretches of both before returning. Grant had settled down at his City Point headquarters that afternoon to await the outcome of this double effort by half of Meade's infantry and all of the cavalry on hand, when "there appeared very suddenly before us," a staff colonel wrote his wife, "a long, lank-looking personage, dressed all in black and looking very much like a boss undertaker."

It was Lincoln. After sending his "I begin to see it" telegram to Grant on the 15th, he had gone up to Philadelphia for his speech next day at the Sanitary Fair; after which he returned to Washington, fidgeted through another three days while the Petersburg struggle mounted to climax, and finally, this morning, boarded a steamer for a cruise down the Potomac and a first-hand look at the war up the James. "I just thought I would jump aboard a boat and come down and see you," he said, after shaking hands all round. "I don't expect I can do any good, and in fact I'm afraid I may do harm, but I'll just put myself under your orders and if you find me doing anything wrong just send me right away."

Grant replied, not altogether jokingly, that he would do that, and the group settled down for talk. By way of reassurance as to the outcome of the campaign, which now had entered a new phase — one that opened with his army twice as far from the rebel capital as it had been the week before — the general took occasion to remark that his present course was certain to lead to victory. "You will never hear of me farther from Richmond than now, till I have taken it," he declared. "I am just as sure of going into Richmond as I am of any future event. It may take a long summer day, as they say in the rebel papers, but I will do it."

Lincoln was glad to hear that; but he had been watching the casualty lists, along with the public reaction they provoked. "I cannot pretend to advise," he said, somewhat hesitantly, "but I do sincerely hope that all may be accomplished with as little bloodshed as possible."

Aside from this, which was as close to an admonition as he came, he kept the conversation light. "The old fellow remained with us till the next day, and told stories all the time," the staff colonel informed his wife, adding: "On the whole he behaved very well."

One feature of the holiday was a horseback visit to Hincks's division, where news of Lincoln's coming gathered around him a throng of black soldiers ("grinning from ear to ear," the staffer wrote, "and displaying an amount of ivory terrible to behold") anxious for a chance to touch the Great Emancipator or his horse in passing. Tears in his eyes, he took off his hat in salute to them, and his voice broke when he thanked them for their cheers. This done, he rode back to City Point for the night, then reboarded the steamer next morning for an extension of his trip upriver to pay a courtesy call on Ben Butler, whose views on politics were as helpful, in their way, as were Grant's on army matters. He returned to Washington overnight, refreshed in spirit and apparently reinforced in the determination he had expressed a week ago at the Sanitary Fair: "We accepted this war for an object, a worthy object, and the war will end when that object is attained. Under God, I hope it never will until that time."

Helpful though the two-day outing was for Lincoln, by way of providing relaxation and lifting his morale, the events of that brief span around Petersburg had an altogether different effect on Grant, or at any rate on the troops involved in his intended probe around Lee's right. After moving up, as ordered, on the night of June 21, Wright and Birney (Hancock was still incapacitated, sloughing fragments of bone from the reopened wound in his thigh) lost contact as they advanced next morning through the woods just west of the Jerusalem Plank Road, under instructions to extend the Federal left to the Weldon Railroad. Suddenly, without warning, both were struck from within the gap created by their loss of contact. Lee had unleashed A. P. Hill, who attacked with his old fire and savagery, using one division to hold Wright's three in check while mauling Birney's three with the other two. The result was not only a repulse; it was also a humiliation. Though his loss in killed and wounded was comparatively light, no fewer than 1700 of Birney's men — including those in a six-gun battery of field artillery, who then stood by and watched their former weapons being used against their former comrades — surrendered rather than risk their lives in what he called "this most unfortunate and disgraceful affair." Hardest hit of all was Gibbon's division, which had crossed the Rapidan seven weeks ago with 6799 men and had suffered, including heavy reinforcements, a total of 7970 casualties, forty of them regimental commanders. Such losses, Gibbon declared in his formal report, "show why it is that troops, which at the commencement of the campaign were equal to almost any undertaking, became toward the end of it unfit for almost any."

Wilson, after a heartening beginning, fared even worse than the infantry in the end. Reinforced by Kautz to a strength of about 5000 horsemen and twelve guns, he struck and wrecked a section of the Weldon Railroad above Reams Station, nine miles south of Petersburg, then plunged on to administer the same treatment to the Southside and the Richmond & Danville, which crossed at Burkeville, fifty miles to the west. Near the Staunton River, eighty miles southwest of Petersburg, with close to sixty miles of track ripped up on the three roads, he turned and started back for his own lines, having been informed that they would have been extended by then to the Petersburg & Weldon. On the way there, he was harried by ever-increasing numbers of gray cavalry, and when he approached Reams Station he found it held, not by Wright or Birney, who he had been told would be there, but by A. P. Hill. Moreover, the mounted rebels, pressing him by now from all directions, turned out to be members of Hampton's other two divisions, returned ahead of Sheridan from the fight at Trevilian Station. Outnumbered and all but surrounded, Wilson set fire to his wagons, spiked his artillery, and fled southward in considerable disorder to the Nottoway River, which he succeeded in putting between him and his pursuers for a getaway east and north. He had accomplished most of what he was sent out to do, but at a cruel cost, including 1500 of his troopers killed or captured, his entire train burned, and all twelve of his guns abandoned.

Grant had the news of these two near fiascos to absorb, and simultaneously there came word of still a third, one hundred air-line miles to the west, potentially far graver than anything that had happened close at hand. Wright and Birney at least had extended the Federal left beyond the Jerusalem Road, and Wilson and Kautz had played at least temporary havoc with no less than three of Lee's critical rail supply lines. But David Hunter, aside from his easy victory two weeks ago at Piedmont and a good deal of incidental burning of civilian property since, accomplished little more, in the end, than the creation of just such a military vacuum as Lee specialized in filling.

Descending on Lynchburg late in the day, June 17, Hunter found Breckinridge drawn up to meet him with less than half as many troops. He paused overnight, preparing to stage another Piedmont in the morning, only to find, when it broke, that Jubal Early had arrived by rail from Charlottesville to even the odds with three veteran divisions: whereupon Hunter (for lack of ammunition, he later explained) went over to the defensive and fell back that night, under cover of darkness, to the shelter of the Blue Ridge. Early came on after him, and Hunter decided that, under the circumstances, his best course would be to return to West Virginia without delay. For three days Early pursued him, with small profit, then gave it up and on June 22 — while A. P. Hill was mauling Birney, south of Petersburg — marched for Staunton and the head of the Shenandoah Valley, that classic route for Confederate invasion which Lee had used so effectively in the past to play on Halleck's and Lincoln's fears.

These last were likely to be enlarged just now, and not without cause. With Hunter removed from all tactical calculations, nothing blue stood between Early and the Potomac, and with the capital defenses stripped of their garrisons to provide reinforcements and replacements for Meade, little remained with which to contest a gray advance from the Potomac into Washington itself. Lincoln had come up the James this week for a first-hand look at the war, but now it began to appear that he needed only to have waited a few days in the White House for the war to come to him.

So much was possible; Halleck's worst fears as to the consequences of the southside shift for the failed assault might now be proved only too valid. But Grant was not given to intensive speculation on possible future disasters; he preferred to meet them when they came, having long since discovered that few of them ever did. Instead, in writing to Old Brains on June 23 he stressed his need for still more soldiers, as a way of forestalling requests (or, in Lincoln's case, orders) for detachments northward from those he had on hand. "The siege of Richmond bids fair to be tedious," he informed him, "and in consequence of the very extended lines we must have, a much larger force will be necessary than would be required in ordinary sieges against the same force that now opposes us." Two days later, in passing along the news that Hunter was indeed in full retreat, he added that Sheridan had at last returned, though with his horses too worn down to be of any help to Wilson, who was fighting his way back east against lengthening odds. "I shall try to give the army a few days' rest, which they now stand much in need of," Grant concluded, rather blandly.

★ ★ ★

After frightening Hunter's 18,000 away from Lynchburg, westward beyond the Blue Ridge, and enjoying a day's rest from the three-day Allegheny chase that followed, the 14,000 Confederates took up the march for Staunton via Lexington, where on June 25 part of the column filed past Stonewall Jackson's grave, heads uncovered, arms reversed, bands intoning a dirge with muted horns and muffled drums. This salute to the fallen hero was altogether fitting as an invocation of the spirit it was hoped would guide the resurrected Army of the Valley through the campaign about to be undertaken by his old Second Corps, now led by Jubal Early. "Strike as quick as you can," Lee had telegraphed a week ago, as soon as he learned that Meade's whole army was south of the James, "and, if circumstances authorize, carry out the original plan, or move upon Petersburg without delay."

The original plan, explained to Early on the eve of his departure from Cold Harbor, June 13, was for him to follow the slash at Hunter with a fast march down the Valley, then cross the Potomac near Harpers Ferry and head east and south, through western Maryland, for a menacing descent on the Federal capital itself. Lee's hope was that this would produce one of two highly desirable results. Either it would alarm Lincoln into ordering heavy detachments northward from the Army of the Potomac, which might give Richmond's defenders a chance to lash out at the weakened attackers and drive them back from the city's gates, or else it would provoke Grant into staging a desperate assault, Cold Harbor style, that would serve even better to bleed him down for being disposed of by the counterattack that would follow his repulse. Given his choice, Early stuck to the original plan. After driving Hunter beyond the mountains, which removed him from all immediate tactical calculations, the gray pursuers rested briefly, then passed for the last time in review by their great captain's grave in battered Lexington and continued on to Staunton, where their hike down the Valley Turnpike would begin.

Early got there next day, ahead of his troops, and reorganized the 10,000 foot soldiers into two corps while awaiting their arrival. By assigning Gordon's division to Breckinridge, who coupled it with his own, he gave the former Vice President a post befitting his dignity and put thirty-five-year-old Robert Rodes — a native of Lynchburg, which he had just helped to save from Hunter's firebrands, and a graduate and one-time professor at V.M.I., whose scorched ruins he viewed sadly, and no doubt angrily as well, after marching his veterans past that other V.M.I. professor's grave — in charge of the remaining corps, composed of his own and Dodson Ramseur's divisions; Ramseur, a North Carolinian, promoted to major general the day after his twenty-seventh birthday early this month, was the youngest West Pointer to achieve that rank in Lee's army. The remaining 4000 effectives were cavalry and artillery, and these too were included in the shakeup designed to promote efficiency in battle and on the march. Robert Ransom, sent from Richmond for the purpose, was given command of the three mounted brigades ("buttermilk rangers," Early disaffectionately styled these horsemen, riled by their failure to bring Hunter to bay the week before) along with instructions to infuse some badly needed discipline into their ranks. As for the long arm, it was not so much reshuffled as it was stripped by weeding out the less serviceable guns and using only the best of teams to draw the surviving forty, supplemented by ten lighter pieces the cavalry would bring along. Recalling his predecessor Ewell's dictum, "The road to glory cannot be followed with much baggage," Early stipulated that one four-horse "skillet wagon" would have to suffice for transporting the cooking utensils for each 500 men, and he even warned that "regimental and company officers must carry for themselves such underclothing as they need for the present expedition." One major problem remained unsolved: a lack of shoes for half the army. This would not matter greatly in Virginia, but experience had shown that barefoot men suffered cruelly on the stony Maryland roads. Assured by the Quartermaster General that a shipment of shoes would overtake him before he crossed the Potomac, Early put the column in motion at first light June 28. Already beyond New Market two days later, some fifty miles down the turnpike, he informed Lee that his troops were "in fine condition and spirits, their health greatly improved. . . . If you can continue to threaten Grant," he added, "I hope to be able to do something for your relief and the success of our cause shortly. I shall lose no time."

True to his word, he reached Winchester on July 2, the Gettysburg anniversary, and there divided his army, sending one corps north, through Martinsburg, and the other east toward Harpers Ferry, where they were to converge two days later; Franz Sigel was at the former place with a force of about 5,000, while the latter contained a garrison roughly half that size, and Early wanted them both, if possible, together with all their equipment and supplies. It was not possible. Sigel — who by now had been dubbed "The Flying Dutchman" — was too nimble for him, scuttling eastward to join the Ferry garrison before the rebel

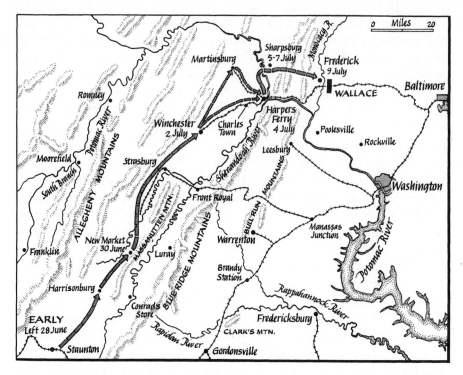

jaws could close and then taking sanctuary on Maryland Heights, which Early found too stout for storming when he came up on Independence Day. While one brigade maneuvered on Bolivar Heights to keep up the scare across the way, the rest of the Valley army settled down to feasting on the good things the Federals had left behind, here and at Martinsburg as well. Two days were spent preparing to cross the Potomac at Boteler's Ford, just upstream near Shepherdstown, and distributing the shipment of shoes that arrived on schedule from Richmond. On July 6 the crossing began in earnest; a third gray invasion was under way. No bands played "My Maryland," as before, but there was a chance for some of the veterans to revisit Sharpsburg, where they had fought McClellan, two Septembers back, from dawn to dusk along Antietam Creek. On they trudged, across South Mountain on July 8, breaking in their new shoes, and entered Frederick next morning in brilliant sunlight. East and southeast, beyond the glittering Monocacy River, the highway forked toward Baltimore and Washington, their goal.

Certain adjunctive matters had been or were being attended to by the time the infantry cleared Frederick. Coincident with the Potomac crossing, Imboden's cavalry had been sent westward, out the Baltimore & Ohio, to wreck a considerable stretch of that line and thus prevent a rapid return by Hunter's numerically superior force from beyond the Alleghenies, and simultaneously, by way of securing reparation for Hunter's recent excesses in the Old Dominion, a second mounted brigade, under Brigadier General John McCausland — another V.M.I.

graduate and professor — was sent to Hagerstown with instructions to exact an assessment of $200,000, cash down, under penalty of otherwise having the torch put to its business district. En route, McCausland somehow dropped a digit, and the Hagerstown merchants, knowing a bargain when they saw one, were prompt in their payment of $20,000 for deliverance from the flames. No such arithmetical error was made at Frederick, where McCausland rejoined in time to see the full $200,000 demanded and paid in retaliation for what had been done, four weeks ago in Lexington, to Washington College and his alma mater. No sooner had he returned than the third brigade of horsemen, under Colonel Bradley Johnson, was detached. Hearing from Lee, in a sealed dispatch brought north by his son Robert, that a combined operation by naval elements and undercover agents was planned for the liberation of 17,000 Confederate prisoners at Point Lookout, down Chesapeake Bay at the mouth of the Potomac, Early sent for Johnson — a native of Frederick, familiar with the region to be traversed — and told him to take his troopers eastward, cut telegraph wires and burn railroad bridges north and south of Baltimore in order to prevent the flow of information and reinforcements through that city when the gray main body closed on Washington, and then be at or near Point Lookout on the night of July 12, in time to assist in setting free what would amount to a full new corps for the Army of Northern Virginia. If things worked out just right, for them and for Early, the uncaged veterans might even return south armed with weapons taken from various arsenals, ordnance shops, and armories in the Federal capital, just over forty miles from Frederick, at the end of a two-day march down the broad turnpike.

Two days, that is, provided there was no delay en route: a battle, say, or even a sizeable skirmish, anything that would oblige a major portion of the army to deploy, engage, and then get back into march formation on the pike — always a time-consuming business, even for veterans such as these. And sure enough, Early had no sooner ridden southeast out of Frederick, down the spur track of the B. & O. toward its junction with the main line near the Monocacy, than he saw, drawn up to meet him on the far side of the river, with bridgeheads occupied to defend the crossings — the railroad itself and the two macadamized turnpikes, upstream and down — a considerable enemy force, perhaps as large as his own, with sunlight glinting from the polished tubes of guns emplaced from point to point along the line. Its disposition looked professional (which might signify that Grant had hurried reinforcements north from the Army of the Potomac, under orders from Lincoln to cover the threatened capital) but Early's first task, in any case, was to find out how to come to grips with this new blue assemblage and thereby learn its identity and size, preferably without a costly assault on one of the bridgeheads. McCausland promptly gave him the answer by plunging across a shallow ford, half a mile to the right of the Washington road, and launching a dismounted charge that overran a Federal battery. Counterattacked in force, the troopers withdrew, remounted, and splashed back across the river. Though they were unable to hold the guns they had seized, they brought with them something far more valuable: the key to the enemy's undoing. So Early thought at any rate.

By now it was noon, and he wasted no time in fitting the key to the lock. Rodes and Ramseur would feint respectively down the Baltimore pike and the railroad, while the main effort was being made downstream by Gordon, who would cross by the newly discovered ford for a flank assault, with Breckinridge in support. "No buttermilk rangers after you now, damn you!" Old Jube had shouted three weeks ago at Lynchburg, shaking his fist at the bluecoats as they backpedaled under pressure from his infantry, just off the cars from Charlottesville. He repeated this gesture today on the Monocacy, confident that victory was within his grasp whether the troops across the way were veterans, up from Petersburg, or hundred-day militia, hastily assembled from roundabout the Yankee capital and dropped in his path as a tub to the invading rebel whale.

They were both, but mostly they were veterans detached from the Army of the Potomac three days ago, on July 6, just as Early began crossing into Maryland. Warned by Halleck that Hunter had skittered westward, off the tactical margin of the map, and that Sigel too had removed his troops from contention with the 20,000 to 30,000 Confederates reported to be about to descend on Washington — which had nothing to defend it but militia, and not much of that — Grant loaded Ricketts' 4700-man VI Corps division onto transports bound for Baltimore, along with some 3000 of Sheridan's troopers, dismounted by the breakdown of their horses on the recent grueling raids beyond Burkeville and Louisa. Three days later, with Early across South Mountain and Washington approaching a state of panic, if not of siege, he not only followed through by ordering Wright to steam north in the wake of Ricketts with his other two divisions; he also informed Old Brains that he would be sending the XIX Corps, whose leading elements were due about now at Fortress Monroe, en route from New Orleans and the fiasco up Red River. This last came hard, badly needed as these farwestern reinforcements were as a transfusion for Meade's bled-down army, straining to keep up the pressure south of the James. Yet Grant was willing to do even more, if need be, to meet the rapidly developing crisis north of the Potomac.

"If the President thinks it advisable that I should go to Washington in person," he wired Halleck that evening from City Point, while the last of Wright's men were filing aboard transports for the trip up Chesapeake Bay, "I can start in an hour after receiving notice, leaving everything here on the defensive."

Meantime Ricketts had landed at Baltimore, headquarters of Major

General Lew Wallace's Middle Department, including Maryland, Delaware, and the Eastern Shore of Virginia. Wallace was not there, however. He had left two days ago, on July 5, after learning that the rebels were at Harpers Ferry in considerable strength, their outriders already on the loose in western Maryland as an indication of where they would be headed next. A former Illinois lawyer, now thirty-seven years old, he had been at the time of Shiloh the youngest major general in the Union army, but his showing there had soured Grant on him; the brilliant future predicted for him was blighted; he was shifted, in time, to this quiet backwater of the war. Quiet, that is, until an estimated 30,000 graybacks appeared this week on the banks of the Potomac, with nothing substantially blue between them and the national capital. Wallace said later that when he pondered the consequences of such a move by Early, "they grouped themselves into a kind of horrible schedule." If Washington fell, even temporarily, he foresaw the torch being put in rapid sequence to the Navy Yard, the Treasury, and the Quartermaster Depot, whose six acres of warehouses were stocked with $11,000,000 in equipment and supplies; "the war must halt, if not stop for good and all." Accordingly, having decided to meet the danger near the rim of his department — though at considerable personal risk, for while he knew that Halleck was keeping tabs on him for Grant, watching sharply for some infraction that would justify dismissal, he could not inform his superiors of what he was about to do, since he was convinced that they would forbid it as too risky — he got aboard a train for Monocacy Junction, where the roads from nearby Frederick branched toward Baltimore and Washington. There he would assemble whatever troops he could lay hands on, from all quarters, and thus cover, from that one position, the approaches to both cities: not so much in hope of winning the resultant battle, he afterwards explained, as in hope of slowing the rebel advance by fighting the battle at all. Whatever the outcome, the delaying action on the Monocacy would perhaps afford the authorities time to brace for the approaching shock, not only by assembling all the available militia from roundabout states, but also by summoning from Grant, down in Virginia, a substantial number of battle-seasoned veterans to throw in the path of the invaders.

Sure enough, after managing to scrape together in two days, July 6–7, a piecemeal force of 2300 of all arms, he learned that this last had in fact been done, or at least was in the process of being done. Troops from the Army of the Potomac were debarking at Baltimore even then, hard-handed men in weathered blue who had taken the measure of Lee's touted veterans down the country and were no doubt willing and able to do the same up here. Greatly encouraged, Wallace sent for Ricketts to bring his division to Monocacy Junction without delay, leaving Sheridan's unhorsed troopers — more than a third of whom lacked arms as well as mounts — to man the Baltimore or Washington defenses, and thereby help, perhaps, to reduce the civilian panic reported to be swelling in both places. Ricketts arrived by rail next day, and none too soon; Early came over South Mountain that afternoon, July 8, and on into Frederick next morning. By noon he had his army moving by all the available roads down to the Monocacy, where Wallace had disposed his now 7000-man force to contest a crossing, posting Ricketts on the left, astride the Washington pike, where he figured the rebels would launch their main attack.

He figured right, but not right enough to forestall an end-on blow that soon resulted in a rout. Gordon struck from beyond the capital pike, not astride it, coming up from the ford downstream for an attack that Ricketts saw would roll up his line unless he effected a rapid change of front. He tried and nearly succeeded in getting his soldiers parallel to the turnpike, facing south, before they were hit. They gave ground, uncovering the unburnable iron railroad bridge for a crossing by Ramseur, who together with Breckinridge added the pressure that ended all resistance on this flank. Rickett's two brigades, or what was left of them by now — the second, made up of veterans long known as "Milroy's weary boys," had been through this kind of thing before — scrambled northward for the Baltimore road, the designated avenue of retreat, and there lost all semblance of order in their haste to get out of range of the whooping rebels, one of whom afterwards called this hot little Battle of the Monocacy "the most exciting time I witnessed during the war."

By 4 o'clock it was over, and though Wallace (with 1880 casualties, including more than a thousand captured or otherwise missing, as compared to fewer than 700 killed or wounded on the other side) managed to piece together a rear guard not far east of the lost field, there was no real pursuit; Early did not want to be encumbered with more prisoners than he had already taken, more or less against his will. Nor did he want to move eastward, in the direction of Baltimore. His route was southeast, down the Washington pike, which Gordon's attack had cleared for his use in continuing the march begun that morning out of Frederick.

In any case he knew now, from interrogating captives with the canted VI Corps cross on the flat tops of their caps, that troops had arrived from the Army of the Potomac, and though he had whipped them rather easily — as well he might have expected to do, with the odds at two-to-one — he knew only too well that others were probably on the way, if indeed they were not already on hand in the capital defenses. If this was a source of satisfaction, knowing that he had fulfilled a considerable measure of Lee's purpose by obliging Grant to reduce the pressure on Petersburg and Richmond, it also recommended caution. Additional blue detachments might have arrived or be arriving from down the country in such numbers that his small army, cut off from the few available fords across the Potomac as he advanced, would be swamped and abolished. As it was, he had only to turn southwest, down the B. & O. to Point of Rocks, for a crossing that would gain him the security of the Virginia Piedmont, after which he could move south or west, unmolested, for a return to Lee or the Shenandoah Valley. Either course had its attractions, but Early dwelt on neither. He would move as he had intended from the outset, against Washington itself, and deal with events as they developed, knowing from past service under Jackson that audacity often brought its own rewards. Today was too far gone for resumption of the march, but he passed the word for his men to bed down for a good night's rest, here on the field where they had fought today, and be ready to move at "early dawn."

Sunday, July 10, was hot and dusty. By noon, the cumulative effect of all those twenty-mile hikes since the army left Staunton twelve days ago had begun to tell. Straggling increased as the day wore on, until finally the head of the column went into bivouac short of Rockville, just over twenty miles from the Monocacy and less than ten from the District of Columbia. Rear elements did not come up till after midnight, barely three hours before Early, hopeful of storming the Washington defenses before sundown, ordered the march resumed in the predawn darkness. Aware that he might be engaged in a race with reinforcements on the way there, he could afford to show his weary men no mercy, though he sought to encourage them, as he doubled the column on his lathered horse, with promises of rest and a high feast when the prize was won. Beyond Rockville, he had Mc-Causland's troopers hold to the main pike for a feint along the Tenallytown approaches, while the infantry forked left for Silver Spring, half a dozen miles from the heart of the city by way of the main-traveled Seventh Street Road.

Heat and dust continued to take their toll; "Our division was stretched out almost like skirmishers," one of Gordon's veterans, tottering white-faced with fatigue near the tail of the column, would recall. Then, close to 1 o'clock, the heavy, ground-thumping boom-bam-*boom* of loud explosions — guns: siege guns! — carried back from the front, where the head of the column had come within range of the outlying capital works.

Early rode fast toward the sound of firing, beyond the District line, and drew rein in time to watch his advance cavalry elements dismount and fan out to confront a large earthwork on rising ground to the right of the road, two miles below Silver Spring. Identified on the map as Fort Stevens, a major installation, it lay just over a thousand yards away, and when he studied it through his binoculars he saw a few figures on the parapet; by no means enough, it seemed to him, to indicate that the work was heavily, even adequately, manned. He had won his race with Grant. All he had to do, apparently, was bring up his men and put them in attack formation, then move forward and take it, along with much that lay beyond, including the Capitol itself, whose new dome he could see plainly in the distance, six miles south of where he stood.

Just now, though, his troops were in no condition for even the slightest exertion, whatever prize gleamed on the horizon. Diminished by cavalry detachments, by their losses in battle two days ago, and by stragglers who had fallen out of the column yesterday and today, they scarcely totaled 10,000 now, and of these no more than a third were fit for offensive action without a rest. All the same, he told Rodes, whose division was in the lead, to see what he could accomplish along those lines, and while Rodes did his best — which wasn't much; his men were leaden-legged, short of wind and spitting cotton — Early continued to study the objective just ahead. Beyond it, around 1.30, he saw a long low cloud of dust approaching from the rear, up the Seventh Street Road. Reinforcements, most likely; but how many? and what kind? Then he spotted them in his glass, the ones at the head of the fast-stepping column at any rate, and saw that they were dressed not in linen dusters and high-crowned hats, after the manner of home guardsmen or militia, but in the weathered blue tunics and kepis he had last encountered two days ago, when he found Ricketts' VI Corps veterans drawn up to meet him on the Monocacy.

Veterans they were, all right, and VI Corps veterans at that; Wright and the first of his other two divisions, the second relay of reinforcements ordered north from the Army of the Potomac, had begun debarking at the Sixth Street docks a little after noon and were summoned at once to the point of danger, out the Seventh Street Road. Grant himself might be on the way by now, moreover, for Lincoln — under increasing pressure as the rebel column, having knocked Wallace out of its path, drew closer to Washington hour by hour — had responded approvingly to the general's offer to come up and take charge "in person," adding that it might be well if he brought still more of his soldiers along with him. "What I think," he told Grant, "is that you should provide to retain your hold where you are, certainly, and bring the rest with you personally and make a vigorous effort to destroy the enemy's force in this vicinity. I think there is really a fair chance to do this if the movement is prompt." In other words, hurry. But then, mindful once more of his resolution not to interfere in military matters, even with the graybacks practically at the gate, he closed by saying: "This is what I think, upon your suggestion, and it is not an order."

If he was jarred momentarily from his purpose — and, after all, the notion was Grant's in the first place; Lincoln merely concurred —

it was small wonder, what with Hunter fled beyond recall up the Kanawah, Sigel holed up at Harpers Ferry, out of touch since July 4, and Washington panicked by rumors of Armageddon. Wallace, falling back down the Baltimore pike from his sudden drubbing on July 9, reported that Early had hit him with 20,000 of all arms, and though this was 10,000 fewer than Sigel had reported before the wire went dead in his direction, it still was 10,000 more than had been mustered, including War Department clerks and green militia, to man the capital defenses. Sheridan's dismounted troopers arrived about that time, a rather straggly lot who did less to bolster confidence here than their removal from Baltimore had done to provoke resentment there. When a group of that city's leading citizens telegraphed Lincoln that Sunday evening, July 10, protesting that they had been abandoned to their fate, he did what he could to reassure them. "Let us be vigilant, but keep cool," he replied. "I hope neither Baltimore nor Washington will be taken."

They remained disgruntled, wanting something more substantial. By next morning things looked better, however, at least in their direction. Returning with Ricketts, Wallace assured them that Early was headed for Washington, not Baltimore just yet. And even in the capital there was encouraging news to balance against reports that the rebel column had cleared Rockville soon after sunrise; Wright was expected hourly from Virginia with his other two divisions, and an advance detachment of 600 troops was already on hand from the XIX Corps, fine-looking men with skin tanned to mahogany by the Louisiana sun. Even Henry Halleck — who, according to an associate, had spent the past week "in a perfect maze, bewildered, without intelligent decision or self-reliance" — recovered his spirits enough to reply with acid humor to a telegram from an unattached brigadier at the Fifth Avenue Hotel, New York City, offering his services in the crisis now at hand. "We have five times as many generals here as we want," Old Brains informed him, "but are greatly in need of privates. Anyone volunteering in that capacity will be thankfully received." Then at noon the transports arrived at the Sixth Street docks (near which the Navy had a warship berthed with steam up, ready to whisk the President downriver in case the city fell); Wright's lead division came ashore and marched smartly through the heart of town to meet Early, who was reported to be approaching by way of Silver Spring. Presently the boom of guns from that direction made it clear how close the race had been, and was.

Lincoln, having ridden down to the docks to greet them from his carriage, also rode out the Seventh Street Road to watch them reinforce Fort Stevens; he may have been one of the figures — surely, if so, the tallest — Early saw etched against the sky when he focussed his binoculars on the parapet of the works just over a thousand yards ahead. Watching the dusty blue stream of veterans flow into position in the course of the next hour, Old Jube — or "Jubilee," as soldiers often styled him — knew there could be no successful assault by his weary men today. A good night's rest might make a difference, though, depending on how heavily the defenses had been reinforced by morning, either here or elsewhere along the thirty-seven miles of interconnected redans, forts, and palisades ringing the city and bristling with heavy guns at every point. What remained of daylight could be used for reconnaissance (and was; "Examination showed what might have been expected," Early would report, "that every application of science and unlimited means had been used to render the fortifications around Washington as strong as possible") but the thing to do now, he saw, was put the troops into bivouac, then feed and get them bedded down, while he and his chief lieutenants planned for tomorrow. He and they had come too far, and Lee had risked too much, he felt, for the Army of the Valley to retire from the gates of the enemy capital without testing to see how stoutly they were hung.

Accordingly, he turned his horse and rode back toward Silver Spring, where his staff had set up headquarters, just beyond the District line, in the handsome country house of Francis P. Blair, who had decamped to avoid an awkward meeting with one-time friends among the invaders. A member of Andrew Jackson's "kitchen cabinet" and an adviser to most of the Presidents since, Old Man Blair had two sons in high Union places: Montgomery, Lincoln's Postmaster General, whose own home was only a short walk up the road, and Frank Junior, the former Missouri congressman, now a corps commander with Sherman.

Guards had been posted to protect the property; especially the wine cellar, which contributed to the festive spirit that opened the council of war with recollections by Breckinridge, as the toasts went round, of the good times he had had here in the days when he was Vice President under Buchanan. Someone remarked that tomorrow might give him the chance to revisit other scenes of former glory, such as the U.S. Senate, where he had presided until Lincoln's inauguration and then had sat as a member until he left, eight months later, to throw in with other Confederate-minded Kentuckians for secession. This brought up the question Early had called his lieutenants together to consider: Was an attack on Washington tomorrow worth the risk? Time was short and getting shorter; Hunter and Sigel could be expected to come up from the rear, eventually, and Grant was known to have sent what seemed to be most of a corps already. Doubtless other reinforcements were on the way, from other directions, and though the prize itself was the richest of all — perhaps even yielding foreign recognition, at long last, not to mention supplying the final straw that might break the Federal home-front camel's back — was it worth the risk of losing one fourth of Lee's army in the effort?

Early considered, with the help of his four division commanders, and decided that it was. He would launch an assault at dawn, he told them, "unless some information should be received before that time showing its impracticability."

Such information was not long in coming. The council of war had scarcely ended when a courier arrived from Bradley Johnson, whose brigade was still on its way to Point Lookout. After wrecking railroad bridges and tearing down telegraph lines around Baltimore he had sent scouts into the city to confer with Confederate agents, and from these he learned that not one but *two* Federal corps, the VI and the XIX, were steaming up Chesapeake Bay and the Potomac to bolster the Washington defenses. In the light of this intelligence that tomorrow might find him outnumbered better than two to one by the bluecoats in the capital intrenchments, Early countermanded his orders for a dawn assault. This came hard. Just thirty days ago tomorrow he had received instructions from Lee to attempt what he was on the verge of doing. Now though — as a result, he perceived, of the victory Wallace had obliged him to win on the Monocacy, at the cost of a twenty-hour delay — it began to appear that the verge was as close as he was likely to get. Daylight would give him the chance to reconnoiter the Union works and thus determine the weight of this new unwelcome information, but he could see already that an attack was probably beyond his means and a good deal worse than risky.

Dawn broke, July 12, over a Washington in some ways even more distraught than it had been the morning before, with the rebels bearing down on its undermanned defenses. Overnight the shortage had been considerably repaired; Wright's third division followed the second out the Seventh Street Road at dusk, and soon after dark the first of the two XIX Corps divisions landed. But as these 20,000 stalwarts arrived to join about the same number of militiamen, galvanized clerks, and dismounted cavalry in the outworks, so did a host of rumors, given unlimited opportunity for expansion by the fact that the city was cut off from all communication northward, either by rail or wire, newspapers or telegrams, speech or letters. Known secessionists did not trouble to mask broad smiles, implying that they knew secrets they weren't sharing. One that leaked out by hearsay was that Lee had given Meade the slip, down around Richmond, and was crossing the Potomac, close at hand, with an army of 100,000 firebrands yelling for vengeance for what had been done, these past three years, in the way of destruction to their homeland.

Lincoln rose early, despite a warning from Stanton that an assassination plot was afoot, and rode with Seward to visit several of the fortifications out on the rim of town, believing that the sight of him and the Secretary of State, unfled and on hand to face the crisis unperturbed, would help to reduce the panic in the streets through which their carriage passed. His main hope, now that he knew Grant would not be coming — "I think, on reflection, it would have a bad effect for me to leave here," the general had replied from City Point to the suggestion that he come north without delay — was in Horatio Wright, who had helped to drive these same gray veterans southward, down in Virginia, throughout the forty days of battle in May and June. Lincoln's belief was that the Connecticut general, now that he had the means, could do the same up here.

Wright rather thought so too. Taking Early's failure to attack this morning as a sign that the rebels were preparing to withdraw, probably after nightfall, he wanted to hit them before they got away unscathed. In particular he wanted to drive off their skirmishers, who had crept to within rifle range of Fort Stevens and were sniping at whatever showed above the parapet. However, when he requested permission, first of the fort commander and then of the district commander, Major Generals Alexander McCook and C. C. Augur — both of whom outranked him, although neither had seen any action for nearly a year, having been retired from field service as a result of their poor showings, respectively, at Chickamauga and Port Hudson — they declined, saying that they did not "consider it advisable to make any advance until our lines are better established."

By midafternoon this objection no longer applied; McCook, bearded in his command post deep in the bowels of the fort, agreed at last to permit a sortie by units from one of the VI Corps divisions. Wright started topside for a last-minute study of the terrain, and as he stepped out of the underground office he nearly bumped into Abraham Lincoln, who had returned from a cabinet meeting at the White House to continue his tour of the fortifications. Informed of what was about to be done, he expressed approval, and when the general asked, rather casually, whether he would care to take a look at the field — "without for a moment supposing he would accept," Wright later explained — Lincoln replied that he would indeed. Six feet four, conspicuous in his frock coat and a stovepipe hat that added another eight inches to his height, he presently stood on the parapet, gazing intently at puffs of smoke from the rifles of snipers across the way. Horrified, wishing fervently that he could revoke his thoughtless invitation, Wright tried to persuade the President to retire; but Lincoln seemed not to hear him amid the twittering bullets, one of which struck and dropped an officer within three feet of him. From down below, a young staff captain — twenty-three-year-old Oliver Wendell Holmes, Junior, whose combat experience had long since taught him to take shelter whenever possible under fire — looked up at the lanky top-hatted civilian and called out to him, without recognition: "Get down, you damn fool, before you get shot!"

This got through. Lincoln not only heard and reacted with amusement to the irreverent admonition, he also obeyed it by climbing down and taking a seat in the shade, his back to the parapet, safe at last from the bullets that continued to twang and nicker overhead.

Relieved of the worst of his concerns, Wright turned now to the interrupted business of clearing his front. Deployment of the brigade assigned the task required more time than had been thought, however, with the result that it was close to 6 o'clock before the signal could be given to move out. The firing swelled, and Lincoln, popping up from time to time to peer over the parapet, had his first look at men reeling and falling in combat and being brought past him on stretchers, groaning or screaming from pain, leaking blood and calling on God or Mamma, in shock and out of fear. Presently the racket stepped up tremendously, and the brigade commander sent back for reinforcements, explaining that he had encountered, beyond the retiring screen of pickets, a full-fledged rebel line of battle. Supporting regiments moved up in the twilight and the attack resumed, though with small success against stiffened resistance. Gunflashes winked and twinkled along the slope ahead until about 10 o'clock, when they diminished fitfully and finally died away. The cost to Wright had been 280 killed and wounded in what one of his veterans called "a pretty and well-conducted little fight."

Across the way, the Confederates considered it something worse: especially at the outset, when it erupted in the midst of their preparations to depart. Early had needed no more than a cursory look at the enemy works that morning to confirm last night's report that they would be substantially reinforced by dawn. Permanently canceling the deferred assault, he ordered skirmishers deployed along a line that stretched for a mile to the left and a mile to the right of the Seventh Street Road to confront Forts Reno, Stevens, and De Russy, while behind this he had Rodes and Gordon form their divisions, in case the Federals tried a sortie, and sent word for McCausland to keep up the feint on the far right, astride the Georgetown pike. Here they would stay, bristling as if about to strike, until night came down to cover the withdrawal, back through Silver Spring to Rockville, then due west for a recrossing of the Potomac. Fortunately, the Yankees seemed content to remain within their works, and Early, having learned that the amphibious raid on Point Lookout had been called off because the prison authorities had been warned of it, had time to send a courier after Johnson, whose horsemen were beyond Baltimore by then, instructing him to turn back for the Confederate lines by whatever route seemed best now that the capture of Washington was no longer a part of the invasion plan. Preparations for the retirement were complete — were, in fact, about to be placed in execution — when Wright's attack exploded northward from Fort Stevens, flinging butternut skirmishers back on the main body, which then was struck by the rapid-firing Federals coming up in apparently endless numbers through the gathering dusk. The thing had the look of an all-out battle that would hold the Army of the Valley in position for slaughter tomorrow by preventing it from taking up its planned retreat tonight. Major Kyd Douglas, formerly of Jackson's staff and now of Early's, said quite frankly that he thought "we were gone up."

Presently though, to everyone's relief, the fireworks sputtered into darkness; the field grew still, except for the occasional jarring explosion of a shell from one of the outsized siege guns in the forts, and Early, resuming his preparations for withdrawal, summoned to headquarters Breckinridge and Gordon, whose divisions would respectively head and tail the column, for last-minute orders on the conduct of the march. They arrived to find him instructing Douglas to take charge of a rear-guard detail of 200 men and with them hold the present position until midnight, at which time he too was to pull out for Rockville: provided, of course, the bluecoats had not gotten wind of what was up, beforehand, and obliterated him. When the handsome young Marylander left to assume this forlorn assignment, Early called after him, apparently in an attempt to lift his spirits: "Major, we haven't taken Washington, but we've scared Abe Lincoln like hell!"

Douglas stopped and turned. "Yes, General," he said, as if to set the record straight, "but this afternoon when that Yankee line moved out against us, I think some other people were scared blue as hell's brimstone."

"How about that, General?" Breckinridge broke in, smiling broadly beneath his broad mustache.

"That's true. But it won't appear in history," Early replied, thereby assuring the exchange a place in all the accounts that were to follow down the years.

It turned out there were no further losses, even for the rear-guard handful under Douglas, who took up the march on schedule without a parting shot being fired in his direction. He saw, as he went past it after midnight, that except for the depletion of its wine cellar and linen closets — all the bedclothes had been ripped into strips for bandages — Old Man Blair's mansion had suffered no damage from the occupation, but that his son Montgomery's house, just up the road, had been reduced to bricks and ashes by some vengeance-minded incendiary. Although the act perhaps was justified by Hunter's burning of Former Governor Letcher's home the month before, Early's regret that this had been done was increased when he learned that Bradley Johnson, off on his own, had also indulged in retaliation by setting fire to Governor A. W. Bradford's house near Baltimore. Such exactions, he knew, were unlikely to encourage pro-Confederate feelings, either here in Maryland or elsewhere. In any case, dawn of July 13 — thirty days, to the hour, since the re-created Army of the Valley pulled out of Cold Harbor, bound for Lynchburg and points north — found the column slogging through Rockville, where it turned left for Poolesville and the Potomac. At White's Ford by midnight, just upstream from Ball's Bluff and thirty miles from its starting point on the outskirts of Washington, the army crossed the river in good order next morning, still unmolested, to make camp near Leesburg for a much needed two-day rest; after which it shifted west, July 16, beyond the Blue Ridge. Back once more in the Lower Valley, within an easy day's march of Harpers Ferry, Early began preparing for further adventures designed to disrupt the plans of the Union high command.

This recent thirty-day excursion had accomplished a great deal in that direction, as well as much else of a positive nature, including the recovery of the grain-rich Shenandoah region from Hunter and Sigel, just in time for the harvesting of its richest crop in years, and the return from beyond the Potomac with a large supply of commandeered horses and cattle, not to mention $220,000 in greenbacks for the hard-up Treasury and close to a thousand prisoners, most of them captured on the Monocacy, the one full-scale battle of the campaign. In fact, aside from his two main hopes — and hopes were all they were — that he could occupy Washington, even for a day, and that he could provoke Grant into making a suicidal assault on Lee's intrenchments, Early had accomplished everything that could have been expected of him. Best of all, he had obliged Grant to ease the pressure on Petersburg by sending large detachments north, and still had managed, despite the smallness of his force, if not to reverse the tide of the war, then anyhow to strike fear in the hearts of the citizens of Washington and Baltimore, both of which saw gray-clad infantry at closer range than any Federal had come, so far, to Richmond. This was much; yet there was more. For in the process Early had won the admiration not only of his fellow countrymen, whose spirits were lifted by the raid, but also of foreign observers, who still might somehow determine the outcome of this apparently otherwise endless conflict.

"The Confederacy is more formidable than ever," the London *Times* remarked when news of this latest rebel exploit crossed the ocean the following week. And closer at hand, on July 12 — even as Early and his veterans bristled along the rim of the northern capital, quite as if they were about to assail and overrun the ramparts in a screaming rush — the *New York World* asked its readers: "Who shall revive the withered hopes that bloomed on the opening of Grant's campaign?"

★ ★ ★

Who indeed. The task was Lincoln's, as the national leader, but evidence piled higher every day that it would be his no longer than early March, when the outcome of the presidential election, less than four months off, was confirmed on the steps of the lately threatened Capitol. Despite setbacks, such as Cold Harbor, Petersburg, and this recent gray eruption on the near bank of the Potomac, he was convinced that he had found in U. S. Grant the man to win the war. But that was somewhat beside the point, which was whether or not the people could be persuaded, between now and November, to believe it, too — and whether or not, believing it, they would agree that the prize was worth the additional blood, the additional money, the additional drawn-out anguish it was clearly going to cost. They, like Grant, would have to "face the arithmetic," and keep on facing it, to the indeterminate end.

One of the things that made this difficult was that the arithmetic kept changing, not only in the lengthening casualty lists, but also in the value fluctuations of what men carried in their wallets, a region where their threshold of pain was notoriously low. Gold opened the year at 152 on the New York market. By April it had risen to 175, by mid-June to 197, and by the end of that month to an astronomical 250. Reassurances from money men that the dollar was "settling down" brought the wry response that it was "settling down out of sight." Sure enough, on July 11, as Early descended on Washington, gold soared to 285, reducing the value of the paper dollar to forty cents. Moreover, Lincoln faced this crisis without the help of the man who had advised him in such matters from the outset: Salmon Chase.

In late June, with the office of assistant treasurer of New York about to be vacated, the Secretary recommended a successor unacceptable to Senator Edwin D. Morgan of that state, who suggested three alternates for the post. "It will really oblige me if you will make a choice among these three," Lincoln wrote Chase, explaining the political ramifications of a tiff with Morgan at this time. Chase then requested a personal interview, which Lincoln refused "because the difficulty does not, in the main part, lie within the range of a conversation between you and me." In reaction to this snub, the Secretary went home and, as was his custom in such matters, "endeavored to seek God in prayer." So he wrote in his diary that night, adding: "Oh, for more faith and clearer sight! How stable is the City of God! How disordered the City of Man!" Mulling it over he reached a decision. His resignation was on the presidential desk next morning. "I shall regard it as a real relief if you think proper to accept it," he declared in a covering letter.

Lincoln read this fourth of the Ohioan's petulant resignations, and accepted it forthwith. "Of all I have said in commendation of your ability and fidelity, I have nothing to unsay," he replied, "and yet you and I have reached a point of mutual embarrassment in our official relationship which it seems cannot be overcome or longer sustained consistently with the public service." Ohio's Governor John Brough, who happened to be in town, went to the White House in an attempt to "close the breach," as he had done in one of the other instances of a threatened resignation, only to find that he could perform no such healing service here today. "You doctored the business up once," Lincoln told him, "but on the whole, Brough, I reckon you had better let it alone this time." Chase departed, still in something of a state of shock from the unexpected thunderclap, and retired to think things over, for a time, in the hills of his native New Hampshire.

A replacement was not far to seek. Next morning, July 1, when William Pitt Fessenden of Maine, chairman of the Senate Finance Committee, called on the President to recommend someone else for the Treasury post, Lincoln smiled and informed him that his nomination had just been sent for approval by his colleagues on the Hill. Fessenden's dismay was plain. "You must withdraw it. I cannot accept," he protested. His health was poor; Congress was to adjourn tomorrow, and he looked forward to a vacation away from the heat and bustle of the capital. "If you decline, you must do it in open day," Lincoln told him, "for I shall not recall the nomination." Fessenden hurried over to the Senate in an attempt to block the move, only to find that he had been unanimously confirmed in about one minute. Regretfully, with congratulations pouring in from all quarters — even Chase's — he agreed to serve, at least through the adjournment. A soft-money man like his predecessor, he was sworn in on July 5, and it was observed that no appointment by the President, except perhaps the elevation of Grant four months before, had met with such widespread approval by the public and the press. "Men went about with smiling faces at the news," one paper noted.

Lincoln himself was not smiling by then. His trouble with Chase — whom he described as a man "never perfectly happy unless he is thoroughly miserable, and able to make everyone else just as uncomfortable as he is" — had been personal; Chase irked him and he got rid of him. But on the day after Fessenden's appointment he found himself in an even more irksome predicament, one that was susceptible to no such resolution because the men involved were not subject to dismissal; not by him, at any rate. On the morning of July 2, last day of the congressional session that was scheduled to adjourn at noon, Lincoln sat in the President's room at the Capitol, signing last-minute bills, including one that repealed the Fugitive Slave Law and another that struck the $300 commutation clause from the Draft Act. Both of these he signed gladly, along with others, but as he did so there was thrust upon him the so-called Wade-Davis bill, passed two months ago by the House and by the Senate within the hour. He set it aside to go on with the rest, and when an interested observer asked if he intended to sign it, he replied that the bill was "a matter of too much importance to be swallowed in that way."

He found it hard, in fact, to swallow the bill in any way at all, since what it represented was an attempt by Congress — more specifically, by the radicals in his party — to establish the premise that the legislative, not the executive, branch of government had the right and duty to define the terms for readmission to the Union by states now claiming to have left it; in other words, to set the tone of Reconstruction. Sponsored by Benjamin Wade in the Senate and Henry Winter Davis in the House, the bill proceeded from Senator Charles Sumner's thesis that secession, though of course not legally valid, nonetheless amounted to "State suicide," and it set forth certain requirements that would have to be met before the resurrected corpse could be readmitted to the family it had disgraced by putting a bullet through its head. Lincoln had done much the same thing in his Proclamation of Amnesty and Reconstruction, back in December, but this new bill, designed not so much to pave as to bar the path to reunion, was considerably more stringent. Where he had required that ten percent of the qualified voters take a loyalty oath, the Wade-Davis measure required a majority. In addition, all persons who had held state or Confederate offices, or who had voluntarily borne arms against the United States, were forbidden to vote for or serve as delegates to state constitutional conventions; the rebel debt was to be repudiated, and slavery outlawed, in each instance. Moreover, this was no more than a precedent-setting first step; harsher requirements would come later, once the bill had established the fact that Congress, not the President, was the rightful agency to handle all matters pertaining to reconstruction of the South. Sumner and Zachariah Chandler in the Senate, Thaddeus Stevens and George W. Julian in the House — Jacobins all and accomplished haters, out for vengeance at any price — were strong in their support of the measure and were instrumental in ramming it through on this final day of the session.

Gideon Welles saw clearly enough what they were after, and put what he saw in his diary. "In getting up this law, it was as much an object of Mr. Henry Winter Davis and some others to pull down the Administration as to reconstruct the Union. I think they had the former more directly in view than the latter." Lincoln thought so, too, and was determined to keep it from happening, if he could only find a way to do so without bringing on the bitterest kind of fight inside his party.

The fact was, he had already found what he perceived might be the beginning of a way when he set the bill aside to go on signing others. Zachariah Chandler, who had asked him whether he intended to endorse it and had then been told that it was "too important to be swallowed in that way," warned him sternly, in reference to the pending election: "If it is vetoed, it will damage us fearfully in the Northwest. The important point is the one prohibiting slavery in the reconstructed states." "That is the point on which I doubt the authority of Congress to act." "It is no more than you have done yourself." "I conceive that I may, in an emergency, do things on military grounds which cannot be done constitutionally by Congress," Lincoln replied, and Chandler stalked out, deeply chagrined.

His chagrin, and that of his fellow radicals, was converted to pure rage the following week — July 8; Early was crossing South Mountain to descend on Frederick — when Lincoln, having declined either to sign or to veto the bill, issued a public proclamation defending his action (or nonaction) on grounds that, while he was "fully satisfied" with some portions of the bill, he was "unprepared" to give his approval of certain others. "What an infamous proclamation!" Thaddeus Stevens protested. "The idea of pocketing a bill and then issuing a proclamation as to how far he will conform to it!"

By means of the "pocket veto," as the maneuver came to be called, Lincoln managed to avoid, at least for a season, being removed from all connection with setting the guidelines for Reconstruction; but he had not managed to avoid a fight. Indeed, according to proponents of the bill now lodged in limbo, he had precipitated one. Convinced, as one of them declared, that his proposed course was "timid and almost pro-slavery," they took up the challenge of his proclamation, which they defined as "a grave Executive usurpation," and responded in more than kind, early the following month in the New York *Tribune*, with what became known as the Wade-Davis Manifesto. Seeking "to check the encroachments of the Executive on the authority of Congress, and to require it to confine itself to its proper sphere," bluff Ben Wade and vehement Henry Davis charged that "a more studied outrage on the legislative authority of the people has never been perpetrated," and they warned that Lincoln "must understand that our support is of a cause and not of a man," especially not of a man who would connive to procure electoral votes at the cost of his country's welfare.

All this the manifesto set forth, along with much else of a highly personal nature from the pens of these Republican leaders, just three months before the presidential election. Lincoln declined to read or discuss it, not wanting to be provoked any worse than he was already, but he remarked in this connection: "To be wounded in the house of one's friends is perhaps the most grievous affliction that can befall a man."

Horace Greeley, editor of the paper in which the radical manifesto made its appearance, had been involved for the past month in an affair that added to Lincoln's difficulties in presenting himself as a man of war who longed for peace. Hearing privately in early July that Confederate emissaries were waiting on the Canadian side of Niagara Falls with full authority to arrange an armistice, Greeley referred the matter to the President and urged in a long, high-strung letter that he seize the opportunity this presented to end the fighting. "Confederates everywhere [are] for peace. So much is beyond doubt," he declared. "And therefore I venture to remind you that our bleeding, bankrupt, almost dying country also longs for peace — shudders at the prospect of fresh conscription, of further wholesale devastations, and of new rivers of human blood." Placed thus in the position of having to investigate this reported gleam of sunlight (which he suspected would prove to be moonshine) Lincoln was prompt with an answer. "If you can find any person anywhere professing to have any proposition of Jefferson Davis in writing, for peace, embracing the restoration of the Union and the abandonment of slavery, whatever else it embraces, say to him he may come to me with you." The editor, aware of the risk of ridicule, had not counted on being personally involved. He responded with a protest that the rebel agents "would decline to exhibit their credentials to me, much more to open their budget and give me their best terms." Lincoln replied: "I was not expecting you to send me a letter, but to bring me a man, or men." He also told Greeley, in a message carried by John Hay, who was to accompany him on the mission, "I not only intend a sincere effort for peace, but I intend that you shall be a personal witness that it is made."

Being thus coerced, Greeley went with Hay to Niagara, where he discovered, amid the thunder and through the mist, what Lincoln had suspected from the start: that the "emissaries" not only had no authority to negotiate, either with him or with anyone else, but seemed to be in Canada for the purpose of influencing, by the rejection of their empty overtures, the upcoming elections in the North. He retreated hastily, though not in time to prevent a rash of Copperhead rumors that the President, through him, had scorned to entertain decent proposals for ending the bloodshed. Lincoln wanted to offset the effect of this by publishing his and Greeley's correspondence, omitting of course the editor's references to "our bleeding, bankrupt, almost dying country," as well as his gloomy prediction of a Democratic victory in November. Greeley said no; he would consent to no suppression; either print their exchange in full or not at all. Obliged thereby to let the matter drop, Lincoln explained to his cabinet that it was better to withhold the letters, and abide the damaging propaganda, than "to subject the country to the consequences of their discouraging and injurious parts."

Simultaneously, in the opposite direction — down in Richmond itself — another peace feeler was in progress, put forth by Federal emissaries who had no more official sanction than their Confederate counterparts in Canada. Still, Lincoln had better hopes for this one, not so much because he believed that it would end the conflict, but rather, as he remarked, because he felt that it would "show the country I didn't fight shy of Greeley's Niagara business without a reason." What he wanted was for the northern public to become acquainted with Jefferson Davis's terms for an armistice, which he was sure would prove unacceptable to many voters who had been lured, in the absence of specifics, by the siren song of orators claiming that peace could be his for the asking, practically without rebel strings. Moreover, he got what he wanted, and he got it expressed in words as strong and specific as any he himself might have chosen for his purpose.

Colonel James F. Jaquess, a Methodist minister who had raised and led a regiment of Illinois volunteers, had become so increasingly shocked by the sight of fellow Christians killing each other wholesale — especially at Chickamauga, where he lost more than two hundred of his officers and men — that he obtained an extended leave of absence to see what he could do, on his own, to prepare the groundwork for negotiations. He had no success until he was joined in the effort by J. R. Gilmore, who enjoyed important Washington connections. A New York businessman, Gilmore had traveled widely in the South before the war, writing of his experiences under the pen name Edmund Kirke, and he managed to secure Lincoln's approval of an unofficial visit to Richmond by Jaquess and himself, under a flag of truce, for the purpose of talking with southern leaders about the possibility of arriving at terms that might lead to a formal armistice. On Saturday, July 16, the two men were conducted past one of Ben Butler's outposts and were met between the lines by Judge Robert Ould, head of the Confederate commission for prisoner exchange. By nightfall they were lodged in the Spotswood Hotel, in the heart of the rebel capital, Jaquess wearing a long linen duster over his blue uniform. Next morning, amid the pealing of church bells, they conferred with Judah Benjamin, who promised to arrange a meeting for them that evening, here in his State Department office, with the President himself. They returned at the appointed time, and there — as Gilmore later described the encounter — at the table, alongside the plump and smiling Benjamin, "sat a spare, thin-featured man with iron-gray hair and beard, and a clear, gray eye full of life and vigor." Jefferson Davis rose and extended his hand. "I am glad to see you, gentlemen," he said. "You are very welcome to Richmond."

Although he neither mentioned the fact nor showed the strain it cost him, he had not been able to receive them earlier this Sunday because of the lengthy cabinet meeting that had resulted in the dismissal telegram Joe Johnston was reading now, on the outskirts of Atlanta. "His face was emaciated, and much wrinkled," Gilmore observed from across the table, "but his features were good, especially his eyes, though one of them bore a scar, apparently made by some sharp instrument. He wore a suit of grayish brown, evidently of foreign manufacture. . . . His manners were simple, easy and quite fascinating, and he threw an indescribable charm into his voice."

Jaquess opened the interview by saying that he had sought it in the hope that Davis, wanting peace as much as he did, might suggest some way to stop the fighting. "In a very simple way," the Mississippian replied. "Withdraw your armies from our territory, and peace will come of itself." When the colonel remarked that Lincoln's recent Proclamation of Amnesty perhaps afforded a basis for proceeding, Davis cut him short. "Amnesty, Sir, applies to criminals. We have commited no crime." Gilmore suggested that both sides lay down their arms, then let the issue be decided by a popular referendum. But Davis, thinking no doubt of the North's more than twenty millions and the South's less than ten, was having no part of that either. "That the *majority* shall decide it, you mean. We seceded to rid ourselves of the rule of the majority, and this would subject us to it again." It seemed to Gilmore that the dispute narrowed down to "Union or Disunion," and the Confederate President agreed, though he added that he preferred the terms "Independence or Subjugation." Despairing of semantics and the profitless exchange of opposite views that had brought on the war in the first place, the New Yorker made an appeal on personal grounds. "Can you, Mr Davis, as a Christian man, leave untried any means that may lead to peace?" Davis shook his head. "No, I cannot," he replied. "I desire peace as much as you do; I deplore bloodshed as much as you do." He spoke with fervor, but seemed to choose his words with care. "I tried in all my power to avert this war. I saw it coming, and for twelve years I worked night and day to prevent it, but I could not. And now it must go on till the last man of this generation falls in his tracks, and his children seize his musket and fight his battle, *unless you acknowledge our right to self-government.* . . . We are fighting for Independence — and that, or extermination, we will have."

Additional matters were discussed or mentioned, including the military situation, which Davis saw as favorable to the South, and slavery, which he maintained was never "an essential element" in the contest, "only a means of bringing other conflicting elements to an earlier culmination." But always the talk came back to that one prerequisite. Whether it was called Self-Government or Disunion, all future discussion between the two parties would have to proceed from that beginning if there was to be any hope of ending the carnage they both deplored. The Confederate leader made this clear as he rose to see his visitors to the door, shook their hands, and spoke his final words. "Say to Mr Lincoln, from me, that I shall at any time be pleased to receive proposals for peace on the basis of our Independence. It will be useless to approach me with any other."

Whatever sadness he felt on hearing this evidence that the war
was unlikely to end through negotiation, Lincoln perceived that the
closing message, along with much that preceded it, would serve quite
well to further his other purpose, which was to demonstrate his adversary's intransigence in the face of an earnest search for peace. He asked
Gilmore, who had stopped by Washington on his return journey from
Richmond, what he proposed to do with the transcript he had made of
the interview. "Put a beginning and an end to it, Sir, on my way home,"
the New Yorker said, "and hand it to the *Tribune*." Lincoln demurred.
He had had enough of Horace Greeley for a while. "Can't you get it
into the *Atlantic Monthly*? It would have less of a partisan look there."
Gilmore was sure he could; but first, by way of counteracting what
Lincoln called "Greeley's Niagara business," it was decided to release
a shorter version in the Boston *Evening Transcript* the following week,
while the full *Atlantic* text was being set in type and proofed for review
by Lincoln. "Don't let it appear till I return the proof," he cautioned.
"Some day all this will come out, but just now we must use discretion."
The *Transcript* piece appeared July 22, followed a month later by the
one in the *Atlantic*, from which the President had deleted a few hundred
words mainly having to do with terms he had found acceptable off the
record. Both received much attention, especially the longer version.
Indeed, so widely was it reprinted, at home and abroad, that another
distinguished contributor — Oliver Wendell Holmes, whose son had
lately cursed Lincoln off the parapet at Fort Stevens — soon told
Gilmore that it had attracted more readers than any magazine article
ever written.

Meantime (as always) Lincoln had kept busy with other problems,
military as well as political. Often they overlapped, as in the case of
facing up to the need for replacing the troops whose fall or discharge
left gaps in the ranks of the two main armies: especially Meade's, which
had a lower reënlistment quotient and had been further reduced, moreover, by detachments northward to shield Washington from attack by
Early, still hovering nearby. On Sunday, July 17, while Jaquess and
Gilmore talked in Richmond with Jefferson Davis — who had just
put a message on the wire to Atlanta that presaged a step-up in the
fighting there — Lincoln telegraphed Grant: "In your dispatch of
yesterday to General Sherman I find the following, to wit: 'I shall make
a desperate effort to get a position here which will hold the enemy
without the necessity of so many men.' Pressed as we are by lapse of
time, I am glad to hear you say this; and yet I do hope you may find
a way that the effort shall not be desperate in the sense of a great loss
of life." He sent this by way of preparation for a proclamation, issued
next day, calling for 500,000 volunteers and ordering a draft to take
place immediately after September 5 for any unfilled quotas.

This must surely be the last before November, he was saying, although there were already those who believed, despite the recent removal of the $300 exemption clause, that the results would not suffice even for the present. "We are not now receiving one half as many [troops] as we are discharging," Halleck complained to Grant the following day. "Volunteering has virtually ceased, and I do not anticipate much from the President's new call, which has the disadvantage of again postponing the draft for fifty days. Unless our government and people will come square up to the adoption of an efficient and thorough draft, we cannot supply the waste of our army."

Coming square up was easily said, but it left out factors that could not be ignored, including the reaction to this latest call for volunteers, which was seen as a velvet glove encasing the iron hand of a new draft. "Only half a million more! Oh that is nothing," one angry Wisconsin editor fumed, and followed through by saying: "Continue this Administration in power and we can all go to war, Canada, or to hell before 1868."

Now that the year moved into the dog days, with the fall elections looming just beyond, there was need for caution, if not in the military, then certainly in the political arena. Yet even caution might not serve, so portentous were the signs that a defeat was in the making. Frémont was something of a joke as an opponent, though not as a siphon for drawing off the Radical votes that would be needed if Lincoln was to prevail against the Democrats, who were scheduled to convene in Chicago in late August to adopt a platform and select a candidate for November. The platform would be strong for peace, and the candidate, it was believed, would be George McClellan: a formidable combination, one that might well snare both the anti-war and the soldier vote, not to mention the votes of the disaffected, likely to go to almost any rival of the present national leader. Indeed, the prospect so thoroughly alarmed a number of members of the Republican hierarchy that a secret call went out for a convention to meet in Cincinnati in September "to consider the state of the nation and to concentrate the Union strength on some one candidate who commands the confidence of the country, even by a new nomination if necessary."

For the present this was circulated privately, with the intention of bringing it out in the open when the time was ripe. In point of fact, however, the time seemed ripe enough already, to judge by the immediate response. Dissatisfaction with Lincoln had grown by now to include even close friends: Orville Browning, for example, who confessed he had long suspected that his fellow Illinoisan could not measure up to the task required. "I thought he might get through, as many a boy has got through college, without disgrace; but I fear he is a failure." Others agreeing were the eminent lawyer David Dudley Field, whose brother Lincoln had recently appointed to the Supreme Court, and

Schuyler Colfax, Speaker of the House. Chase expressed interest in the supersession, of course, and Ben Butler lent encouragement from down on Bermuda Hundred. Henry Davis was vehemently for it, but Wade and Sumner remained aloof for the time being, the former because he preferred to wait till after the Democratic convention, the latter because he thought it would make less trouble for the party if they gave Lincoln a chance to withdraw voluntarily. Many prominent editors favored the maneuver, including Parke Godwin of the New York *Evening Post* and Whitelaw Reid of the *Cincinnati Gazette*. But the most vociferous of them all was Horace Greeley, whose expression was cherubic but whose spirit had lately been strained beyond forbearance. "Mr Lincoln is already beaten," he declared. "He cannot be elected. And we must have another ticket to save us from overthrow."

Lincoln knew little or nothing yet of this plan by his friends and associates for a midstream swap, but he saw as clearly as they did that the drift was toward defeat and was likely to remain so unless some way could be found, between now and November, to turn the tide. A military victory would help, even one on a fairly modest scale — the more modest the better, in fact, so far as bloodshed was concerned — just so it encouraged the belief that things were looking up for one or another of the armies. But that was mainly up to Grant, locked in a stalemate below Richmond, and Sherman, apparently no better off in front of Atlanta. The other possibility was politics, Lincoln's field, and he was prepared to do all he could in that direction. His native Kentucky would be the first state to hold an election since his nomination; August 1 was the balloting date, and though only some county offices and an appellate judgeship were at stake, the contest was certain to be regarded as a bellwether for the rest, which were to follow in September. Consequently, he took off the gloves for this one. Declaring martial law, he suspended the writ of habeas corpus on July 5, continued the suspension through election day, and gave a free rein to Stephen Burbridge, who, having recently disposed of John Morgan at Cynthiana, proposed to move in a similar aggressive manner against all foes of the Administration throughout his Department of Kentucky. As a result, prominent Democrats were arrested wholesale for "disloyalty," and the name of their candidate for the judgeship was ordered stricken from the ballot on the same vague charge, obliging the survivors to make a last-minute substitute nomination for the post. Lincoln awaited the outcome with much interest, only to find on August 1 that all his pains had gone for nothing. The Democratic candidates swept the state.

There would be other contests; Maine, for instance, was coming up next, to be followed by Vermont. Although the snub just given him in his native state did not augur well for the result, he had no intention of doing anything less than his best to win in all of them, with the help of whatever devices he thought might help and despite the clamor of his critics, left and right, in his own party or the other. "The pilots on our western rivers steer from point to point, as they call it," he told a caller one of these days, "setting the course of the boat no farther than they can see. And that is all I propose to do in the great problems that are before us." One such point now was Atlanta; or anyhow it seemed to him it might be. Events that followed hard on the rebel change of commanders there had brought the fighting to a pitch of intensity, throughout the last two weeks in July, that matched the savagery of the struggle here in the East before it subsided into stalemate. The same thing might happen there — for that seemed to be the pattern: alternate fury and exhaustion — but Lincoln kept peering in that direction, seeking a point to steer by in his effort to land the boat in his charge before it split and sank.

✕   2   ✕

"The appointment has but one meaning," the Richmond *Examiner* declared on July 19, in reference to Johnston's supersession down in Georgia the day before, "and that is to give battle to the foe." Because John Bell Hood, in contrast to his predecessor, was "young, dashing, and lucky," the rival *Whig* informed its readers that same day, "the army and the people all have confidence in his ability and inclination to fight, and will look to him to drive back Sherman and save Atlanta." Thus the two papers were in agreement on the matter, not only with each other, but also, for once, with the new western leader's red-haired adversary, who rarely subscribed to any journalist's opinion, North or South. "I inferred that the change of commanders meant fight," Sherman remarked after conferring with subordinates who had known Hood in the days before the war. But he added, in contrast to the inference the two Confederate editors drew, five hundred miles away: "This was just what we wanted, viz., to fight in open ground, on anything like equal terms, instead of being forced to run up against pre-pared intrenchments."

He was about to get what he said he wanted. Hood — whose recent association with Johnston, he later explained, had made him "a still more ardent advocate of the Lee and Jackson school" — needed only one full day at his post before he resolved to go over to the offensive. By then, moreover, though he had had to spend a good part of the time discovering where his own troops were, he not only had decided to lash out at the encircling Federal host; he also had determined just when and where and how he would do so, with a minimal adjustment of the lines now held by his three corps. Accordingly, on the evening of July 19, he summoned Hardee and Stewart to headquarters along with Ben Cheatham, his temporary successor as corps commander, and gave them face-to-face instructions for an attack to be launched soon after midday tomorrow in order to take advantage of an opportunity Sherman was affording them, apparently out of overweening contempt or unconcern, to accomplish his piecemeal destruction. In the execution of what he termed "a general right wheel" from the near bank of the Chattahoochee, with Thomas inching the pivot forward across Peachtree Creek to close down on Atlanta from the north, and McPherson and Schofield swinging wide to come in from the east along the Georgia Railroad, the Ohioan had in effect divided his army and developed a better than two-mile gap between the inner edges of its widespread wings. It was Hood's intention, expressed in detail at his first council of war tonight on the outskirts of the city in his charge, not to plunge into but rather to preserve this gap, and thus keep the two blue wings divided while he crushed them in furious sequence, left and right.

Cheatham, with the help of Wheeler's troopers and some 5000 Georgia militia, would confront McPherson and Schofield from his present intrenchments east of Atlanta, taking care to mass artillery on his left and thus prevent the bluecoats in front from crossing the gap between them and Thomas, who meantime would be receiving the full attention of the other two corps. The Union-loyal Virginian's infantry strength was just above 50,000 — about the number Hood had in all — but the intention was to catch him half over Peachtree Creek, which he had begun to bridge today, and hit him before he could intrench or bring up reinforcements. Hardee on the right and Stewart on the left, disposed along a jump-off line roughly four miles north of the city, were to attack in echelon, east to west, each holding a division in reserve for immediate exploitation of any advantage that developed, "the effort to be to drive the enemy back to the creek, and then toward the river, into the narrow space formed by the river and creek." Once Thomas had been tamped into that watery pocket and ground up, the two gray corps would shift rapidly eastward to assist Cheatham in mangling Schofield and McPherson, with Wheeler's free-swinging horsemen standing by to carry out the roundup that would follow. Hood explained all this to his chief lieutenants "by direct interrogatory," having long since learned "that no measure is more important, upon the eve of battle, than to make certain in the presence of commanders that each thoroughly comprehends his orders."

His concern in this regard was not unfounded. Remembering, as he must have done, the Army of Tennessee's latest — and indeed, under Johnston, only — contemplated full-scale offensive at Cassville two months ago today, midway down the doleful road from Tunnel Hill to Atlanta, Hood knew only too well the dangers that lurked in tactical iotas. Nothing had come of the Cassville design, largely because of his own reaction to finding a misplaced blue column approaching his flank,

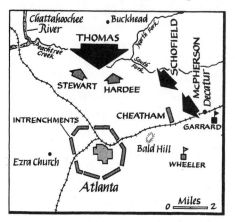

and presently on July 20, with all his troops in position and the 1 o'clock jump-off hour at hand, there were signs that a repetition was in the making. Cheatham sent word before noon that he would have to shift his line southward to keep McPherson from overlapping his right, beyond the railroad. Hood could only approve, and issue simultaneous instructions for Hardee and Stewart to conform by side-stepping half a division-front to their right, thus to prevent too wide an interval from developing between them and Cheatham, through which Schofield might plunge when he came up alongside McPherson. Hardee then had a difficult choice to make. Sidestepping as ordered, he found the interval wider than Hood had supposed, which left him with the decision whether to continue the sidling movement, at the cost of delaying his jump-off, or go forward on schedule — it was 1 o'clock by now — with a mile-wide gap yawning empty on his right. He chose the former course, Stewart conforming on his left, and thus delayed the attack for better than two hours. Shortly after 3 o'clock he sent three of his four divisions plunging northward into the valley of Peachtree Creek.

George Thomas was there, in strength and largely braced. Though the attack achieved the desired surprise, those extra two hours had given him time, not only to get nearly all of his combat elements over the creek, but also to get started on the construction of intrenchments. Hardee struck them and rebounded as if from contact with a red-hot stove, followed by Stewart, who drove harder against the enemy right with no better luck. The Federals either stood firm or hurried reinforcements to shore up threatened portions of their line. Moreover, in the unexpected emergency, Thomas abandoned his accustomed role of Old Slow Trot. Urging his guns forward to "relieve the hitch," he used the point of his sword on the rumps of laggard battery horses, then crossed the stream to direct in person the close-up defense of the bridgehead. An Indiana officer judged the progress of the fighting by the way Old Tom fiddled with his short, thick, gray-shot whiskers. "When satisfied he smoothes them down; when troubled he works them all out of shape." They were badly tousled now, and presently, when he saw the attackers falling back from the blast of fire that met them, he moved even further out of character in the opposite direction. "Hurrah!" he shouted, and took off his hat and slammed it on the ground in pure exuberance. "His whiskers were soon in good shape again," the Hoosier captain noted.

They might have been worse ruffled shortly thereafter; Hardee was about to throw Cleburne's reserve division into the melee, and in fact had just summoned him forward, when an urgent dispatch from Hood directed that troops be sent at once to the far right, where Cheatham's flank was under heavy pressure from McPherson. Cleburne arrived after nightfall, in time to confront a piece of high, cleared ground known as Bald Hill, two miles east of Atlanta and a mile south of the Georgia Railroad; Wheeler's dismounted troopers, after being pushed back all morning, had managed to hang on there through most of the afternoon. Northward, the battle raged along Peachtree Creek, but with decreasing fury, until about 6 o'clock, when it sputtered out. At a cost of 2500 casualties suffered, and 1600 inflicted, Hood's plan for crushing first Thomas, then the other two Union armies, had failed because the Rock of Chickamauga declined, as usual, to be budged or flustered. The southern commander had only praise for Cheatham and Wheeler, who fought hard all day against long odds, and especially for Stewart, who, though his losses were close to two thirds of the Confederate total, "carried out his instructions to the letter." He put the blame for his lack of success on Hardee — his former senior, known since Shiloh as Old Reliable — whose corps, "although composed of the best troops in the army, virtually accomplished nothing" and in fact, as a comparison of casualties would show, "did nothing more than skirmish with the enemy."

So Hood would report afterwards, when he got around to distributing blame for the failure of his first offensive action; the Battle of Peachtree Creek, it was called, or "Hood's First Sortie." But that did not keep him from choosing Hardee to deliver the main effort, two days later, in what would be referred to as "Hood's Second Sortie" or the Battle of Atlanta.

While Cleburne struggled the following day to prevent a blue advance past Bald Hill — the fighting on this third anniversary of First Manassas, he said, was "the bitterest" of his life — Wheeler moved still farther to the right, another mile beyond the railroad, to forestall another Federal flanking effort. What he found instead was an invitation for just such a movement by the Confederate defenders. McPherson, apparently with his full attention drawn to the day-long contest with Cleburne, had his left flank "in the air," unprotected by cavalry and wide open to assault. Informed of the situation early that morning, Hood grasped eagerly at this chance to turn the tables on the attackers. It was one of the chief regrets of his career that he had missed Chancellorsville, having been on detached service with Longstreet around

Suffolk while the Lee-Jackson masterpiece was being forged in the smoky, vine-choked Wilderness a hundred miles away. Now here was a God-given once-in-a-lifetime opportunity to stage a Chancellorsville of his own, down in the piny woods of Georgia, within a scant five days of his appointment to command the hard-luck Army of Tennessee.

In preparation for exploiting this advantage — and also because both ends of his present line were gravely threatened, Thomas having begun to build up pressure against the left about as heavy as McPherson had been exerting on the right — Hood directed that all three corps begin a withdrawal at nightfall to the works rimming the city in their rear, already laid out by Johnston the month before. These were to be held by Stewart and Cheatham, on the north and east, while Hardee marched south, then southeast, six miles down the McDonough Road to Cobb's Mill, where he would turn northeast and continue for the same distance up the Fayetteville Road to the Widow Parker's farm, south of the railroad about midway between Atlanta and Decatur. This would put his four divisions (including Cleburne's, which would join him on his way through town) in position for an all-out assault on McPherson's left rear. Though the route was as circuitous and long as Stonewall's flanking march had been, fourteen months ago in Virginia, an early start this evening should enable Old Reliable to launch a dawn

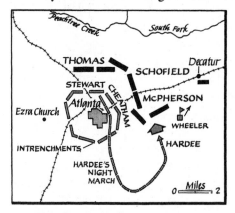

attack, and a dawn attack would give him a full day in which to accomplish McPherson's destruction, whereas Jackson had had only the few hours between sunset and dusk to serve Hooker in that fashion. Moreover, by way of increasing the blue confusion and distress, Wheeler's troopers, after serving as guides and outriders for the infantry column, would continue eastward to Decatur for a strike at McPherson's wagon train, known to be parked in the town square with all his reserve supplies and munitions. Hood explained further that once the flank attack got rolling he would send Cheatham forward to assail McPherson's front and keep Schofield from sending reinforcements to the hardpressed Union left, while Stewart, around to the north, engaged Thomas for the same purpose. Now, as before the Peachtree venture, he assembled a council of war to make certain that each of his lieutenants understood exactly what was required of him, and why. This was all the more advisable here, because of the greater complexity of what he was asking them to do. "To transfer after dark our entire line from the immediate presence of the enemy to another line around Atlanta, and to throw Hardee, the same night, entirely to the rear and flank of McPherson — as Jackson was thrown, in a similar movement, at Chancellorsville and Second Manassas — and to initiate the offensive at daylight, required no small effort on the part of the men and officers. I hoped, however, that the assault would result not only in a general battle, but in a signal victory to our arms."

Such hope was furthered by the secrecy and speed of the night-time withdrawal to Atlanta's "inner line," which Stewart and Cheatham then began improving with picks and shovels while Hardee set out on his march around the Federal south flank. Almost at once the first hitch developed. Two miles to the east, confronting the enemy on Bald Hill, Cleburne had trouble breaking contact without giving away the move-ment or inviting an attack; it was crowding midnight before Hardee solved the problem by instructing him to leave his skirmishers in position and fall in behind W. H. T. Walker's men, marking time in rear of the other two divisions under Bate and George Maney, Cheatham's senior brigadier. Cleburne managed this by 1 a.m. of the projected day of battle — Friday, July 22 — but it was 3 o'clock in the morning before the final elements of the corps filed out of the unoccupied intrenchments south of town.

That was the first delay. Another was caused by the weariness of the marchers, still unrested from Wednesday's bloody work and Thurs-day's fitful skirmishing under the burning summer sun. Strung out on the single, narrow road, which had to be cleared from time to time when Wheeler's dusty horsemen clattered up or down it, the head of the column did not reach Cobb's Mill until dawn, the supposed jump-off hour. Disgruntled, Hardee turned northeast for the Widow Parker's, another half dozen miles up the troop-choked road. It was close to noon by the time he got there, evidently unsuspected by the enemy in the woods across the way, and 12.30 before the corps was formed for assault, Maney and Cleburne on the left, astride the Flat Shoals Road, which ran northwest past Bald Hill, where McPherson's flank was anchored — Cleburne thus had nearly come full circle — and Walker and Bate on the right, on opposite sides of Sugar Creek, which also led northwest, directly into McPherson's rear. Old Reliable could take pride in being just where he was meant to be, in position to duplicate Jackson's famous end-on strike at Hooker, but he was also uncom-fortably aware that he was more than six hours behind schedule.

This made him testy: as anyone near him could see in these final minutes before he gave the order to go forward. When Wheeler sent word that a sizeable column of blue troopers had passed this way a while ago, apparently headed southward on a raid, and requested permission to take out after them, Hardee was quick to say no; "We must attack, as we arranged, with all our force." So Wheeler, disappointed at being denied the chance to cross sabers with the intruders, set out eastward for Decatur and McPherson's unsuspecting and perhaps unguarded wagon train. Then Walker came to headquarters to report that he had dis-covered in his immediate front a giant brier patch, which he asked to be allowed to skirt when he advanced, despite the probable derange-ment of his line and the loss of still more time. Normally courteous, Hardee was emphatic in refusal. "No, sir!" he said roughly, not bother-ing to disguise his anger. "This movement has been delayed too long already. Go and obey my orders!"

Walker, a year younger at forty-seven than his chief, who had finished a year behind him at West Point—a veteran of the Seminole and Mexican wars, heavily bearded, with stern eyes, he was one of three West Pointers among the eight Confederate generals named Walker—then demonstrated a difficulty commanders risked with high-strung subordinates in this war, particularly on the southern side. He took offense at his fellow Georgian's tone, and he said as much to an aide who rode with him on the way back to his division. "Major, did you hear that?" he asked, fuming. The staffer admitted he had; "General Hardee forgot himself," he suggested. Walker was not to be put off, however. "I shall make him remember this insult. If I survive this battle, he shall answer me for it." Just then an officer from Hardee's staff overtook them with the corps commander's regrets for "his hasty and discourteous language" and assurance that he would have "come in person to apologize, but that his presence was required elsewhere, and would do so at the first opportunity." So the envoy informed Walker, whose companion remarked soothingly, after they had ridden on: "Now that makes it all right." But Walker's blood was up. He was by no means satisfied. "No, it does not," he said hotly. "He must answer me for this."

As it turned out, no one on this earth was going to answer to W. H. T. Walker for anything. Ordered forward shortly thereafter, he and his three brigades clawed their way through the brier patch, hearing Maney's and Cleburne's attack explode on the left as it struck McPherson's flank, and then emerged from a stand of pines into what was to have been the Union rear, only to find a nearly mile-long triple line of bluecoats confronting them on ground that had been empty when it was reconnoitered, half an hour before. Walker had little chance to react to this discovery, however, for as he and his men emerged from the trees, sunlight glinting on his drawn saber and their rifles, a Federal picket took careful aim and shot him off his horse.

Hood, who had waited and watched impatiently for the past six hours in a high-sited observation post on the outskirts of Atlanta, was dismayed by what he saw no more than a mile away across the treetops. Plunging northwest, on the far left of the Confederate assault, Maney overlapped the Union flank and had to swing hard right as he went past it, which threw his division head-on against the enemy intrenchments facing west. This caused Hood to assume — and later charge — that

Hardee's attack had been launched, not into the rear of the blue left flank, as directed, but against its front, with predictable results; Maney rebounded, then lunged forward again, and again rebounded. Beyond him, out of sight from Hood's lookout tower, Cleburne was doing better, having struck the Federals endwise, and was driving them head-long up the Flat Shoals Road, which ran just in rear of their works below Bald Hill. Still farther to the east, however, Bate and Walker's successor, Brigadier General Hugh Mercer, were having the hardest time of all. In this direction, the element of surprise was with the de-fenders, whose presence was as unexpected, here on the right, as the appearance of the attackers had been at the opposite end of the line.

Advancing westward yesterday and this morning, under instruc-tions "not to extend any farther to the left" beyond the railroad, lest his troops be spread too thin, McPherson's front had contracted so much that he could detach one of his three corps, led by Major General Grenville M. Dodge, to carry out an order from Sherman to "destroy every rail and tie of the railroad, from Decatur up to your skirmish line." Dodge completed this assignment before midday and was moving up to take a position in support of Blair, whose corps was on the left, when he learned that a heavy force of graybacks was approaching from the southeast, up both banks of Sugar Creek. Under the circumstances, all he had to do was halt and face his two divisions to the left, still in march formation on an east-west road, to establish the triple line of defense whose existence Walker and Bate had not suspected until they emerged from the screen of pines and found it bristling in their front. If they had come up half an hour earlier they would have stepped into a military vacuum, with little or nothing between them and the rear of Blair and Logan, whose corps was on Blair's right, connecting McPher-son and Schofield. Now, instead, Walker was dead and Bate and Mercer were involved in a desperate fight that stopped them in their tracks, much as Maney had been stopped on the left, under different circum-stances. Thus, of the four gray divisions involved in the attack from which so much had been expected, only Cleburne's was performing as intended. Yet he and his fellow Arkansans made the most of their ad-vantage, including the killing of the commander of the Army of the Tennessee.

McPherson was not with his troops when Hardee's attack exploded on his flank. He was up in rear of Schofield's left, just over half a mile north of the railroad, conferring with Sherman in the yard of a two-story frame house that had been taken over for general headquarters, about midway of the line confronting Atlanta from the east. What he wanted was permission to open fire with a battery of long-range 32-pounders on a foundry whose tall smokestack he could see beyond the rebel works from a gun position he had selected and already had under construction on Bald Hill — or Leggett's Hill, as it was called

on the Federal side, for Brigadier General Mortimer Leggett, whose
division of Blair's corps occupied it. McPherson's notion was that if
he could "knock down that foundry," along with other buildings inside
Atlanta, he would hasten the fall of the city. Moreover, he had personal
reasons for wanting to accomplish this in the shortest possible time,
since what he was counting on, in the way of reward, was a leave of
absence that would permit him to go to Baltimore and marry a young
lady to whom he had been engaged since his last leave, just after the
fall of Vicksburg. He had tried his best to get away in March and April,
but Sherman had been unwilling, protesting that there was too much
to be done before the drive through Georgia opened in early May. So
the thirty-five-year-old Ohioan had had to bide his time; though only
by the hardest. Just last week he had asked his friend Schofield when he
supposed his prayers would be answered. "After the capture of Atlanta,
I guess," Schofield replied, and McPherson had taken that as his preliminary objective, immediately preceding the real objective, which was
Baltimore and a union that had little to do with the one he and more
than a hundred thousand others would die fighting to preserve.

Sherman readily assented to the shelling of the city, and ordered
it to begin as soon as the guns were in position. His first impression, on
finding the rebel trenches empty in his front this morning, had been
that Hood had evacuated Atlanta overnight; but that had lasted only until he relocated the enemy in occupation of the city's inner line, as
bristly as ever, if not more so, and now he took the occasion of Mc-
Pherson's midday visit to show him, on the headquarters map, his plan
for shifting all three armies around to the west for the purpose of cutting Hood's remaining rail connections with Macon and Mobile, which
would surely bring on the fall of Atlanta if the proposed bombardment
failed. It was by then around 12.30, and as they talked, bent over the
map, the sound of conflict suddenly swelled to a roar: particularly
southward, where things had been quiet all morning. Sherman whipped
out his pocket compass, trained it by earshot, and "became satisfied that
the firing was too far to our left rear to be explained by known facts."
McPherson quickly called for his horse and rode off to investigate,
trailed by members of his staff. Sherman stood and watched him go,
curly bearded, six feet tall, with lights of laughter often twinkling in his
eyes; "a very handsome man in every way," according to his chief,
who thought of his fellow Ohioan as something more than a protégé or
younger brother. He thought of him in fact as a successor — and not
only to himself, as he would tell another friend that night. "I expected
something to happen to Grant and me; either the rebels or the newspapers would kill us both, and I looked to McPherson as the man to
follow us and finish the war."

From a ridge in rear of the road on which Dodge had been marching until he stopped and faced his two divisions left to meet the assault

by Bate and Walker, McPherson could see that the situation here was less desperate than he had feared; Dodge was plainly holding his own, although the boom of guns from the east gave warning that a brigade he had posted at Decatur to guard the train in the cavalry's absence was also under attack. Sending the available members of his staff in both directions, with instructions for all units to stand firm at whatever cost, the army commander turned his attention westward to Blair's position, where the threat seemed gravest.

In point of fact it was graver than he knew. Cleburne by now had driven Blair's flank division back on Leggett, whose troops were fighting to hold the hill that bore his name, and numbers of enemy skirmishers had already worked their way around in its rear to seize the wooded ground between there and Dodge's position. That was how it happened that McPherson, who had sent away all of his staff except an orderly, encountered graybacks while trotting along a road that led across to Leggett's Hill. Indeed, he was practically on top of one group of Confederates before he suspected they were there. An Arkansas captain, raising his sword as a signal for the two riders to surrender, was surprised by the young general's response ("He checked his horse slightly, raised his hat as politely as if he were saluting a lady, wheeled his horse's head directly to the right, and dashed off to the rear in a full gallop") but not for long. "Shoot him," the gray-clad officer told a corporal standing by, and the corporal did.

McPherson was bent over his mount's withers to keep from being swept from the saddle by the drooping limbs of trees along the road. He fell heavily to the ground, struck low in the back by a bullet that ranged upward through or near his heart. His companion, unhorsed and momentarily stunned by a low-hanging branch, recovered consciousness to find the general lying beside him, clutching his breast in pain, and the butternut soldiers hurrying toward them. He bent over him and asked if he was hurt. "Oh, orderly, I am," McPherson said, and with that he put his face in the dust of the road, quivered briefly, and died. The orderly felt himself being snatched back and up by his revolver belt; "Git to the rear, you Yankee son of a bitch," he heard the rebel who had grabbed him say. Then the captain got there and stood looking down at the polished boots and buff gauntlets, the ornate sash about the waist, and the stars of a major general on both dead shoulders. "Who is this lying here?" he asked. The orderly had trouble answering. Sudden grief had constricted his throat and tears stood in his eyes. "Sir, it is General McPherson," he said. "You have killed the best man in our army."

Sherman's grief was as great, and a good deal more effusive. "I yield to no one but yourself the right to exceed me in lamentations for our dead hero," he presently wrote the Baltimore fiancée. "Though the cannon booms now, and the angry rattle of musketry tells me that

I also will likely pay the same penalty, yet while life lasts I will delight in the memory of that bright particular star which has gone before to prepare the way for us more hardened sinners who must struggle to the end."

But that was later, when he could spare the time. Just now he responded to the news that McPherson's horse had come riderless out of the woods in back of Leggett's Hill by ordering John Logan, the senior corps commander, to take charge of the army and counterattack at once to recover the ground on which his chief might be lying wounded. Logan did so, and within the hour McPherson's body was brought to headquarters in an ambulance. Someone wrenched a door off its hinges and propped it on two chairs for a catafalque, and Sherman went on directing the battle from the room where his fellow Ohioan was laid out. Already he had sent a brigade from Schofield to support the one Dodge had defending Decatur from Wheeler's attack, but aside from this he sent no reinforcements to help resist the assault on his left flank and rear. "I purposely allowed the Army of the Tennessee to fight this battle almost unaided," he later explained, partly because he wanted to leave to McPherson's veterans the honor of avenging his fall, and also because he believed that "if any assistance were rendered by either of the other armies, the Army of the Tennessee would be jealous."

His confidence in his old army — it had also once been Grant's, and had yet to come out loser when the smoke of battle cleared — was justified largely today because of Logan, who exercised his new command in style. Dubbed "Black Jack" by his soldiers, the former Illinois politician knew how to translate stump oratory into rousing military terms. Clutching his flop-brim hat in one hand so that his long raven hair streamed behind him in the wind, he spurred from point to embattled point and bellowed: "Will you hold this line with me? Will you hold this line?" The veterans showed they would. "Black Jack! Black Jack!" they chanted as they beat off attacks that soon were coming from all directions: particularly on Leggett's Hill, which Hood by now had ordered Cheatham to assault from the west while Cleburne kept up pressure from the south and east. Brigadier General Manning Force's brigade, menaced front and rear, was obliged at times to fight on alternate sides of its breastworks. At one critical point he called for a flag, and a young lieutenant, assuming from the look of things that the time had come to surrender, began a frantic search for a white handkerchief or shirt. "Damn you, sir!" Force shouted. "I don't want a flag of truce; I want the *American* flag!" Shot in the face shortly thereafter, he lost the use of his voice and fell back on conducting the hilltop defense with gestures, which were no less flamboyant and seemed to work as well. The hill was held, though at a cost of ten guns — including the four McPherson had planned to use against Atlanta at long range — fifteen stands of colors, and better than a thousand prisoners, mostly from Blair's other division under Brigadier General Giles A. Smith (one of an even dozen Federal generals with that name, including one who spelled it Smyth) which had given way at the outset, badly rattled by Cleburne's unexpected flank-and-rear assault.

Although there were no other outright surprises, the issue continued to swing in doubt from time to time and place to place. Sherman watched with interest from his headquarters on the central ridge, and when Cheatham scored a breakthrough around 4 o'clock, just north of the railroad, he had Schofield mass the fire of several batteries to help restore Logan's punctured right. Word came then from Decatur that the two brigades of infantry had managed to keep Wheeler's troopers out of the town square, where the train was parked, and from Dodge that he was confident of holding against weakening attacks on the left rear. Mercurial as always, despite the tears that trickled into his stub red beard whenever he thought of McPherson laid out on his improvised bier inside the house, Sherman was in high spirits as a result of these reports, which reached him as he paced about the yard and watched the progress of the fighting in all directions. Presently the headquarters came under long-range fire, obliging him and his attendants to take cover in an adjoining grove of trees. Sheltered behind one of these, he noticed a terrified soldier crouched nearby in back of another, moaning: "Lord, Lord, if I once get home," and: "Oh, I'll be killed!" Sherman grinned and picked up a handful of stones, which he then began to toss in that direction. Every pebble that struck the tree brought a howl or a groan from behind it. "That's hard firing, my man," he called to the unstrung soldier, who replied without opening his tight-shut eyes: "Hard? It's fearful! I think thirty shells have hit this tree while I was here." The fire subsided, and the general stepped into the open. "It's all over now; come out," he told the man, who emerged trembling. When he saw who had been taunting him, he took off running through the woods, pursued by the sound of Sherman's laughter.

From end to end, the Federal line was held or restored, except where Smith's unfortunates had been driven back across the lower slopes of Leggett's Hill, and though the fighting was sometimes hand-to-hand and desperate, on past sundown into twilight, there was by then no doubt that Hood's Second Sortie — aside, that is, from the capture of a dozen guns and an assortment of Union colors — had been no less a failure than his First, two days ago. It was, however, considerably more expensive; for this time the Confederate leader held almost nothing back, including the Georgia militia, which he used in a fruitless attack on Schofield that had no effect on the battle except to swell the list of southern casualties. In the end, Hood's loss was around 8000 killed, wounded, and missing, as compared to Sherman's 3700.

All next day the contending armies remained in position, licking their wounds, until Hardee withdrew unimpeded the following night into the Atlanta works. Saddened by the loss of Walker, who had called at headquarters on the eve of battle to assure him of his understanding and support, as well as by the news about McPherson — "No soldier fell in the enemy's ranks whose death caused me equal regret," he later said of his West Point friend and classmate — Hood was profoundly disappointed by the failure of his two sorties to accomplish the end for which they had been designed; but he was by no means so discouraged that he did not intend to attempt a third, if his adversary presented him with still another opportunity. He knew only too well how close he had come, except for the unlucky appearance of Dodge's corps in exactly the wrong place at the wrong time, to wrecking the encircling Union host entirely.

Frank Blair, for one, concurred in this belief. Hood's flanking movement, he afterwards declared, "was a very bold and a very brilliant one, and was very near being successful. The position taken up accidentally by [Dodge's] corps prevented the full force of the blow from falling where it was intended to fall. If my command had been driven from its position at the time that [Logan's] corps was forced back from its intrenchments, there must have been a general rout of all the troops of the Army of the Tennessee . . . and, possibly, the panic might have been communicated to the balance of the army."

Sherman was not much given to speculation on the might-have-beens of combat, and in any case he no more agreed with this assessment than he did with subsequent criticism that, in leaving Schofield and Thomas standing comparatively idle on the sidelines while Logan battled for survival, he had missed a prime chance to break Atlanta's inner line, weakened as it was by the withdrawal of a major portion of its defenders for the attack on his south flank. What he mainly concluded, once the smoke had cleared, was that in staging two all-out sorties in as many days — both of them not only unsuccessful but also highly expensive in energy, blood, and ingenuity — Hood had shot his wad. And from this Sherman concluded further that he was unlikely to be molested in his execution of the maneuver he had described to McPherson at their final interview; that is, "to withdraw from the left flank and add to the right," thereby shifting his whole force counterclockwise, around to the west of the city, in order to probe for its rail supply lines to the south.

First, though, there was the problem of finding a permanent replacement for his fallen star, McPherson. On the face of it, Logan having performed spectacularly under worse than trying conditions, the solution should have been simple. But it turned out to be extremely complicated, involving the exacerbation of some tender feelings and, in the end, nothing less than the reorganization of the command structure of two of the three armies in his charge.

Thomas came promptly to headquarters to advise against keeping

Logan at his temporary post. Although there was bad blood between them, dating back to Chattanooga, basically his objection was that Black Jack, like all the other corps and division leaders in the Army of the Tennessee — not one of them was a West Pointer, whereas two thirds of his own and half of Schofield's were Academy graduates — was a nonprofessional. "He is brave enough and a good officer," the Virginian admitted, "but if he had an army I am afraid he would edge over on both sides and annoy Schofield and me. Even as a corps commander he is given to edging out beyond his jurisdiction." Sherman agreed in principle that volunteers from civilian life, especially politicians, "looked to personal fame and glory as auxiliary and secondary to their political ambition. . . . I wanted to succeed in taking Atlanta," he later explained, "and needed commanders who were purely and technically soldiers, men who would obey orders and execute them promptly and on time." That ruled out Logan, along with Blair. Who then? he asked Thomas, who replied: "You cannot do better than put Howard in command of that army." Sherman protested that this would make Logan "terribly mad" and might also create "a rumpus among those volunteers," but then agreed. One-armed and two years younger even than McPherson, O. O. Howard, West Point '54, a Maine-born recent eastern import to the western theater, was then announced as the new commander of the army that had once been Sherman's own.

Returned to his corps, Logan managed to live with the burning aroused in his breast by this disappointment. But the same could not be said for Old Tom's ranking corps commander, the altogether professional Joe Hooker. Outraged at having been passed over in favor of the man he largely blamed for his defeat at Chancellorsville, Fighting Joe characterized the action as "an insult to my rank and services" and submitted at once a request to be relieved of his present duties. Thomas "approved and *heartily* recommended" acceptance of this application, which Sherman was quick to grant, remarking incidentally that the former commander of the Army of the Potomac had not even been considered for the post that now was Howard's, since "we on the spot did not rate his fighting qualities as high as he did." Hooker departed for an inactive assignment in the Northern Department, where he spent the rest of the war, further embittered by the news that his successor was Major General Henry W. Slocum, another enemy, who had been sent to Vicksburg on the eve of the present campaign to avoid personality clashes between them. Pending Slocum's arrival from Mississippi, Alpheus Williams would lead the corps as senior division commander, much as Major General David S. Stanley had succeeded to the command of Howard's corps, though on a permanent basis.

By July 25, within five days of the Peachtree crossing, when work on it began, the railroad bridge over the Chattahoochee — 760 feet long and 90 high — was completed and track relaid to a forward base immediately in Thomas's rear. Sherman, his supplies replenished and generals reshuffled, was ready within another two days to begin the counterclockwise western slide designed to bring on the fall of Atlanta by severing its rail connection with the world outside. Already this had been accomplished up to the final step; for of the four lines in and out of the city all but one had been seized or wrecked by now, beginning with the Western & Atlantic, down which the Federals had been moving ever since they chevied Johnston out of Dalton. Then Schofield and McPherson had put the Georgia Railroad out of commission by dismantling it as they moved westward from Stone Mountain and Decatur. Of the remaining two — the Atlanta & West Point and the Macon & Western, which shared the same track until they branched southwest and southeast at East Point, five miles south of the city — the former, connecting with Montgomery and Mobile, had been severely damaged the week before by Major General Lovell Rousseau, who raided southward through Alabama with 2500 troopers, practically unopposed, and tore up close to thirty miles of the line between Montgomery and Opelika, where it branched northeast for West Point and Atlanta. That left only the Macon road, connecting eastward with Savannah, for Hood's use in supplying his army and for Sherman to destroy. He began his large-scale semicircular maneuver to accomplish this on July 27, ordering Howard to swing north, then west — in rear of Schofield and Thomas, who would follow him in turn — for a southward march down the near bank of the Chattahoochee, which would serve as an artery for supplies, to descend as soon as possible on that one railroad still in operation out of a place that once had boasted of being "the turntable of the Confederacy."

Simultaneously, by way of putting two strings to his bow, he turned 10,000 horsemen loose on the same objective in an all-out double strike around both rebel flanks. Brigadier General Edward McCook, his division reinforced to a strength of 3500 by the addition of a brigade from Rousseau — who, it was hoped, had established the model for the current operation, over in Alabama the week before — would ride down the north bank of the Chattahoochee for a crossing at Campbelltown, under orders to proceed eastward and hit the Macon & Western at or below Jonesboro, just under twenty miles on the far side of Atlanta. This was also the goal of the second mounted column, 6500 strong, which would set out from Decatur under Stoneman, who had Garrard's division attached to his own for a southward lunge around the enemy right. Both columns were to start on July 27, the day the infantry slide began; Sherman expected them back within three days at the most. But when Stoneman asked permission to press on, once the railroad had been wrecked, to Macon and Andersonville for the purpose of freeing the prisoners held in their thousands at both places, he readily agreed to this hundred-mile extension of the raid, on condition that Garrard head back as soon as the Macon road was smashed, to work with McCook in covering the infantry's left wheel around Atlanta. The redhead's hopes were high, but not for long: mainly because of Joe Wheeler, who, though outnumbered three-to-two by the blue troopers, did not neglect this opportunity to deal with them in detail.

Right and left, at Campbelltown and Decatur, both of them closer to Jonesboro than they were to each other at the outset, the two columns took off on schedule, though not altogether in the manner Sherman intended. Stoneman's mind was fixed so firmly on his ultimate goal — Andersonville and its 30,000 inmates, whose liberation would be nothing less than the top cavalry exploit of the war — that he no longer had any discernible interest in the limited purpose for which the two-pronged strike had been conceived. Accordingly, without notifying anyone above him, he sent Garrard's 4300 troopers pounding due south to draw off the enemy horsemen while he and his 2200 rode east for Covington, which Garrard had raided five days ago during the Battle of Atlanta. In this he was successful; he reached Covington undetected and turned south, down the east bank of the Ocmulgee River, for Macon, the first of his two prison-camp objectives. Garrard meantime had been no less successful in carrying out his part of the revised design, which was to attract the attention of the rebels in his direction. On Snapfinger Creek that afternoon, barely ten miles out of Decatur, he ran into mounted graybacks whose number increased so rapidly overnight that at Flatrock Bridge next morning, another five miles down the road, he had to turn and ride hard, back to Decatur, to keep from losing everything he had. His nimbleness kept down his losses; yet even so these would have been much heavier if Wheeler, about to give chase with eight brigades — just over 6000 sabers in all — had not received word that McCook had crossed the Chattahoochee, en route for the Macon & Western, and that Stoneman was beyond the Ocmulgee, apparently headed for Macon itself. The Georgia-born Alabamian, two months short of his twenty-eighth birthday, left one brigade to keep up the pressure on Garrard and turned with the other seven to meet these rearward threats, sending three brigades to deal with Stoneman while he himself set out with the rest to intercept McCook.

As it turned out, the interception came after, not before, McCook struck the railroad at Lovejoy Station, seven miles beyond Jonesboro. He got there four hours ahead of Wheeler, which gave him time to burn the depot, tear up a mile and a half of track, and destroy a sizeable wagon train, along with its 800 mules, before the graybacks arrived to drive him off and pursue him all the way to the Chattahoochee. Overtaken at Newnan, due west on the West Point road, McCook lost 950 troopers killed and captured, along with his pack train and two guns, between there and the river, which he crossed to safety on July 30, reduced in strength by nearly a third and much the worse for wear.

By that time Stoneman had reached the outskirts of Macon, only to find it defended by local militia. While he engaged in a long-range duel across the Ocmulgee with these part-time soldiers, hoping to cover his search for a downstream ford, the three brigades sent after him by Wheeler came up in his rear. He tried for a getaway, back the way he had come, then found himself involved in a running fight that ended next day near Hillsboro, twenty-five miles to the north, when he was all but surrounded at a place called Sunshine Church. He chose one brigade to make a stand and told the other two to escape as best they could; which they did, while he and his chosen 700 were being overrun and rounded up. One of the two surviving brigades made it back to Decatur two days later, but the other, unable to turn west because of the swarm of rebels on that flank, was wrecked at Jug Tavern on August 3, thirty miles north of Covington. Stoneman and his captured fellow officers were in Macon by then, locked up with the unfortunates they had set out to liberate, and the enlisted men were in much the same position, though considerably worse off so far as the creature comforts were concerned, sixty miles to the southwest at Andersonville.

"On the whole," Sherman reported to Washington in one of the prize understatements of the war, "the cavalry raid is not deemed a success."

In plain fact, aside from McCook's fortuitous interception of the 800-mule train — the break in the track at Lovejoy's, for example, amounted to nothing worse than a two-day inconvenience, after which the Macon & Western was back in use from end to end — the raid not only failed to achieve its purpose, it was also a good deal harder on the raiders than on the raided. Sherman's true assessment was shown by what he did, on the return of his badly cut up horsemen, rather than by what he wrote in his report. Garrard's division, which had suffered least, was dismounted and used to occupy the intrenchments Schofield vacated when he began his swing around the city in Howard's wake, and the other two were reorganized, after a period of sorely needed rest and refitment, into units roughly half their former size. Not that Sherman expected much from them, offensively speaking, in the critical days ahead. "I now became satisfied," he said later, "that cavalry could not, or would not, make a sufficient lodgment on the railroad below Atlanta, and that nothing would suffice but for us to reach it with the main army."

But that turned out to be about as difficult an undertaking as the one assigned to Stoneman and McCook. For one thing — against all his expectations, which were founded on the belief that Hood by now had shot his wad — he had no sooner begun his counterclockwise wheel, shifting Howard around in rear of Schofield and Thomas to a position west of the city so that his right could be extended to reach the vital railway junction at East Point, than he was confronted with still a third

sortie by his Confederate opponent, quite as savage as the other
two.

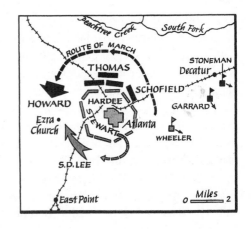

All had gone well on the
first day, July 27; Howard
pulled out undeterred and took
up the march, first north, then
west along the near bank of
Peachtree Creek. Riding south
next morning in rear of Logan,
whose corps was in the lead,
Sherman and the new army commander came under fire from a
masked battery as they approached the Lickskillet Road, which ran due
east into Atlanta, three miles off. Howard did not like the look of things,
and said so. "General Hood will attack me here," he told his companion,
who scoffed at the notion: "I guess not. He will hardly try it again." But
Howard remained persuaded that he was about to be struck, explaining
later that he based his conviction on previous acquaintance with the man
who would do the striking; "I said that I had known Hood at West Point,
and that he was indomitable."

Indomitable. Presented thus with a third chance to destroy an
isolated portion of the enemy host, Hood had designed still another
combined assault, once more after the manner of Lee and Jackson, to
forestall this massive probe around his left. His old corps, now under
Stephen D. Lee — the South Carolinian had been promoted to lieutenant
general and brought from Alabama to take over from Cheatham —
would march out the Lickskillet Road on the morning of July 28 to
occupy a position from which it could block Howard's extension of
the Union right and set him up for a flank attack by Stewart, who
would bring his corps out the Sandtown Road that evening, a mile in
Lee's rear, to circle the head of the stalled blue column and strike from
the southwest at Howard's unguarded outer flank next morning. Hardee,
reduced to three divisions, each of which received a brigade from the
fallen Walker's broken-up division, would hold Atlanta's inner line
against whatever pressure Schofield and Thomas might exert. Lee, who
had assumed command only the day before, moved as ordered, determined to prove his mettle in this first test at his new post — two
months short of his thirty-first birthday, he was six years younger than
anyone else of his rank in the whole Confederacy — but found himself
involved by midday, three miles out the Lickskillet Road, near a rural
chapel known as Ezra Church, in a furious meeting engagement that
left him no time for digging in or even getting set. So instead he took
the offensive with all three of his divisions.

They were not enough: not nearly enough, as the thing developed. Howard, who was only two years older than Lee and no less anxious to prove his mettle, having also assumed command the day before, had foreseen the attack (or anyhow forefelt it, despite Sherman's scoff) and though there was no time for intrenching, once he had called a halt he had his lead corps throw up a rudimentary breastwork of logs and rails; so that when Lee's men charged — "with a terrifying yell," the one-armed commander would recall — they were "met steadily and repulsed." They fell back, then charged again, with the same result. Busily strengthening their improvised works between attacks, Logan's four divisions stood their ground, reinforced in the course of the struggle by others from Dodge and Blair, while Sherman rode back and alerted Thomas to be ready to send more. These last were unneeded, even though Hood by then had abandoned his plan for a double envelopment and instead told Stewart to go at once out the Lickskillet Road to Lee's assistance. Stewart added the weight of one division to the contest before sundown, without appreciable effect. "Each attack was less vigorous and had less chance than the one before it," a Union veteran was to note.

Alarmed by reports coming in all afternoon from west of Atlanta, Hood had Hardee turn his corps over to Cheatham, who had returned to his division, and proceed without delay to Ezra Church to take charge of the other two. Old Reliable arrived to find that the battle had sputtered out, and made no effort to revive it. Lee and Stewart between them had lost some 2500 killed and wounded — about the same number that had fallen along Peachtree Creek eight days ago — as compared to Howard's loss of a scant 700. Nor was that the worst of it, according to Hardee, who afterwards declared: "No action of the campaign probably did so much to demoralize and dishearten the troops engaged in it."

Sherman knew now that he had been wrong, these past five days, in thinking that Hood had shot his wad in the Battle of Atlanta. He would have been considerably closer to the truth, however, if he had reverted to this belief on the night that followed the Battle of Ezra Church. Moreover, there were Confederates in the still smoky woods, out beyond Howard's unbroken lines, who would have agreed with him; almost.

"Say, Johnny," one of Logan's soldiers called across the breast-works, into the outer darkness. "How many of you are there left?"

"Oh, about enough for another killing," some butternut replied.

This attitude on both sides, now that another month drew to a close, was reflected in their respective casualty lists. Including his cavalry subtractions, which were heavy, Sherman had lost in July about 8000 killed, wounded, and missing — roughly the number that fell in June, and better than a thousand fewer than fell in May. The over-all Federal total, from the outset back at Tunnel Hill, came to just under 25,000.

Hood, on the other hand, had suffered 13,000 casualties in the course of his three sorties, which brought the Confederate total, including Johnston's, to 27,500. That was about the number Lee had lost during the same three-month span in Virginia, whereas Sherman had lost considerably fewer than half as many as Meade. Grant could well be proud of his western lieutenant, if and when he got around to comparing the cost, in men per mile, of the campaigns in Georgia and the Old Dominion, West and East.

Still, there was a good deal more to war than mere killing and maiming. "Lee's army will be your objective point," he had instructed Meade before the jump-off, only to have the eastern offensive wind up in a stalemate, a digging contest outside Petersburg. Similarly, he had told Sherman to "move against Johnston's army," and the red-haired Ohioan had done just that — so long as the army was Johnston's. But now that it was Hood's, and had come out swinging, a change set in: particularly after Ezra Church, the third of Hood's three roaring sorties. Lopsided as that victory had been for Sherman, it served warning that, in reaching for the railroad in his adversary's rear, his infantry might do no better than his cavalry had done, and indeed might suffer as severely in the process.

Inching southward all the following week he found rebel intrenchments bristling in his path. On August 5, having brought Schofield around in the wake of Howard, he reinforced him with a corps from Thomas and ordered the drive on the railroad resumed. Schofield tried, the following morning, but was soon involved in the toils of Utoy Creek and suffered a bloody repulse. It was then that the change in Sherman — or, rather, in his definition of his goal — became complete. Formerly the Gate City had been no more than the anvil on which he intended to hammer the insurgent force to pieces. Now it became the end-all objective of his campaign. He would simply pound the anvil.

"I do not deem it prudent to extend any more to the right," he wired Halleck next day, "but will push forward daily by parallels, and make the inside of Atlanta too hot to be endured."

In line with McPherson's proposal at their farewell interview, he sent to Chattanooga for siege guns and began a long-range shelling of the city, firing over the heads of its defenders and into its business and residential districts. "Most of the people are gone; it is now simply a big fort," he informed his wife that week, and while this was by no means true at the time, it became increasingly the case with every passing day of the bombardment. "I can give you no idea of the excitement in Atlanta," a southern correspondent wrote. "Everybody seems to be hurrying off, especially the women. Wagons loaded with household furniture and everything else that can be packed upon them crowd every street, and women old and young and children innumerable are hurrying to and fro. Every train of cars is loaded to its utmost capacity.

The excitement beats everything I ever saw, and I hope I may never witness such again." Presently, though the destruction of property was great and the shelling continued day and night, the citizens learned to take shelter in underground bombproofs, as at Vicksburg the year before, and Hood said later that he never heard "one word from their lips expressive of dissatisfaction or willingness to surrender." Sherman's reaction was to step up the rate of fire. "We can pick out almost any house in town," he boasted to Halleck. He was by nature "too impatient for a siege," he added, but "One thing is certain. Whether we get inside of Atlanta or not, it will be a used-up community when we are done with it."

His troops shared his ebullience, if not his impatience, finding much to admire in this notion of bloodless engagement at long range. "There goes the Atlanta Express!" they cheered as the big shells took off at fifteen-minute intervals over their and the rebel trenches. When one of the outsized guns developed the habit of dropping its projectiles short, they turned and shouted rearward through cupped hands: "Take her away! She slobbers at the mouth." Sherman moved among them, a reporter noted, with "no symptoms of heavy cares — his nose high, thin, and planted with a curve as vehement as the curl of a Malay cutlass — tall, slender, his quick movements denoting good muscle added to absolute leanness, not thinness." Uncle Billy, they called him, with an affection no blue-clad soldiers had shown for a commander, West or East, since Little Mac's departure from the war. What was more, unlike McClellan, he shared their life as well as their rations, though a staffer recorded that he was mostly "too busy to eat much. He ate hardtack, sweet potatoes, bacon, black coffee off a rough table, sitting on a cracker box, wearing a gray flannel shirt, a faded old blue blouse, and trousers he had worn since long before Chattanooga. He talked and smoked cigars incessantly, giving orders, dictating telegrams, bright and chipper."

Partly this was exuberance. Partly it was fret, which he often expressed or covered in such a manner. Either way, it was deadly: as was shown in a message he sent Howard, August 10, amid the roar of long-range guns. "Let us destroy Atlanta," he said, "and make it a desolation."

★ ★ ★

Sherman's ebullience was heightened by news that arrived next day, roundabout from Washington, of a great naval victory scored the week before by Farragut down in Mobile Bay. Long the target of various plans that had come to nothing until now — including Grant's, which went badly awry up the Red that spring with the near destruction of Banks's army and Porter's fleet — this last of the South's major Gulf of Mexico ports, second only to Wilmington as a haven for blockade runners, had been uppermost in Farragut's mind ever since the fall of New Orleans, more than two years ago. He then solicited the Department for permission to steam booming into the bay before its defenses could be strengthened, only to be told that he and his sea-going vessels would continue to prowl the Mississippi until the big river was open from source to mouth. By the time this was accomplished, a year later at Port Hudson, both the admiral and his flagship *Hartford* were sorely in need of rest and repairs. However urgent its priority, the reduction of Mobile would have to await their return, respectively, from Hastings-on-Hudson, the Tennessee-born sailor's adoptive home, and the Brooklyn Navy Yard.

A Christmas visit to New York City was disrupted by an intelligence report that reached him amid the splendors of the Astor House, confirming his worst fears. Not only had Mobile's defenders greatly strengthened the forts guarding the entrance to the harbor; refugees now declared that they also were building a monster ironclad up the Alabama River, more formidable in armament and armor than any warship since the *Merrimac*. Farragut knew, from a study of what the latter had done in Hampton Roads before the *Monitor*'s arrival — as well as from his own experience, near Vicksburg, when the *Arkansas* steamed murderously through the blue flotilla — just what damage one such vessel could do to any number of wooden ships. The answer, he saw, was to get back down there fast and, if possible, go up the river and destroy her before she was ready to engage; or else acquire some ironclads of his own, able to fight her on a give-and-take basis. In any case, after four months of rest and relaxation, he was galvanized into action. He went straight to Brooklyn and served notice that he expected the workmen to have the *Hartford* ready for sea by the evening of January 3. She was, and he dropped anchor at Pensacola two weeks later.

Off Mobile next day, January 18, he learned at first hand, not only that the rebel ironclad existed, as rumored, but also that she was now in the mouth of Dog River, up at the head of the bay. C.S.S. *Tennessee* was her name, and Admiral Franklin Buchanan, former commander of the *Merrimac-Virginia* and ranking man in the Confederate navy, was in charge; "Old Buck," Farragut called him, though at sixty-four Buchanan was only a year his senior and in fact had five years less service, having waited till he was fifteen to become a midshipman, which Farragut had done at the age of nine. Informed of a rumor that the ram was about to come down and attack the nine blockaders on station outside the bay, the Federal admiral braced his captains for the shock, and though he had small personal use for the new-fangled weapons ("If a shell strikes the side of the *Hartford*," he explained, "it goes clean through. Unless somebody happens to be directly in the path, there is no damage excepting a couple of easily plugged holes. But when a shell makes its way into one of those damned tea-kettles, it can't get out again") he submitted an urgent request for at least a pair of monitors. "If I had them," he told Washington, "I should not hesitate to become the assailant instead of awaiting the attack."

Actually, though she had just completed the 150-mile downriver run from Selma, where she was built, there was little danger that the *Tennessee* would steam out into the Gulf. At this point, indeed, there was doubt that she could even make it into the bay, since she drew fourteen feet of water and the depth over Dog River Bar was barely ten. Ingenuity, plus three months of hard labor, solved the problem by installing "camels" — large floats attached to the hull below the water line — which lifted her enough to clear the bar with a good tide. By mid-May she was in Mobile Bay, and Farragut got his first distant glimpse of her from a gunboat cruising Mississippi Sound; "a formidable-looking thing," he pronounced her, though to one of his lieutenants "she looked like a great turtle."

More than 200 feet in length and just under 50 in the beam, she wore six-inch armor, backed by two solid feet of oak and pine, and carried six hard-hitting 6.4- and 7-inch Brooke rifles, one forward and one aft, mounted on pivots to fire through alternative ports, and two in each broadside. Her captain was Commander J. D. Johnston, an Alabama regular who had spent the past two years on duty in the bay, and her skeleton crew was filled out with volunteers from a Tennessee infantry regiment, inexperienced as sailors but proud to serve aboard a vessel named for their native state. Two drawbacks she had, both grave. One was that her engines, salvaged from a river steamboat, gave her a top speed of only six knots, which detracted from her maneuverability and greatly reduced her effectiveness as a ram. The other was that her steering chains led over, rather than under, her armored rear deck, and thus would be exposed to enemy fire. However, she also had one awesome feature new to warfare, described by her designer as "a hot water attachment to her boilers for repelling boarders, throwing one stream forward of the casemate and one abaft." What was more, with Buchanan directing events, there was every likelihood that the device would be brought into play; for he was a proud, determined man, with a fondness for close-quarter fighting and no stomach for avoiding dares.

"Everybody has taken it into their heads that one ship can whip a dozen," he wrote a friend while the ironclad was being readied for action, "and if the trial is not made, we who are in her are damned for life; consequently, the trial must be made. So goes the world."

Mobile's reliance was by no means all on the iron ram, however. In addition to three small paddle-wheel gunboats that completed the gray squadron — *Morgan* and *Gaines*, with six guns each, and *Selma* with four, all unarmored except for strips of plate around their boilers — three dry-land installations guarded the two entrances down at the far end of the thirty-mile-long bay. The first and least of these, Fort Powell, a six-gun earthwork on speck-sized Tower Island, a mile off Cedar Point, covered the approach from Mississippi Sound, off to the west, through Grant's Pass. Another was Fort Gaines, a pentagonal structure on the eastern tip of Dauphin Island, crowned with sixteen guns that commanded the western half of the main entrance, three miles wide, between there and Mobile Point, a long narrow spit of sand at whose extremity — the site of old Fort Bowyer, whose smoothbores had repelled the British fifty years ago — Fort Morgan, the stoutest and most elaborate of the three defensive works, reared its mass of dark red brick. This too was a five-sided structure, double-tiered and mounting no less than forty heavy guns in barbette and casemates, together with seven more in an exterior water battery on the beach in front of its northwest curtain. Both entrances had been narrowed by rebel contrivance, the one from the Sound by driving pilings from Cedar Point to Tower Island and from the northern end of Dauphin Island to within about half a mile of Fort Powell, the one from the Gulf by sinking others southeastward from Fort Gaines to within a mile of Mobile Point, while just in rear of the remaining gap a triple line of mines (called "torpedoes") had been strewn and anchored, barely out of sight below the surface, to within about two hundred yards of the western tip of the spit of land across the way. The eastern limit of this deadly underwater field was marked by a red buoy, fixed there for the guidance of blockade runners whose pilots could avoid sudden destruction by keeping to the right of it and steaming directly under the high-sited guns of Fort Morgan, almost within pistol range of those in the water battery on the beach.

Farragut planned to take that route, mainly because there seemed to be no other. Grant's Pass was too shallow for all but the lightest of his vessels, which would be no match for the iron ram once they entered the bay, and the combination of piles and mines denied him the use of any part of the main Gulf channel except that scant, gun-dominated 200-yard stretch just off the tip of Mobile Point. He was willing to take his chances there, as he had done in similar runs past Forts Jackson and St Philip and the towering bluffs at Vicksburg and Port Hudson, yet he did not enjoy the notion of getting inside the bay with the forts alive in his rear, his wooden ships crippled, and the *Tennessee* likely to pound or butt them into flotsam. Contemplating this, he saw more clearly than ever the need for ironclads of his own, and though four of these had been promised him by now, two from the Atlantic squadron and two from the Mississippi, none had arrived by the time the squat metallic rebel monster steamed down the bay and dropped anchor behind Fort Morgan on May 20, intending either to await the entrance of the Union fleet or else run out and smash it in the Gulf. Farragut stormed at the delay, his patience stretched thin by the nonarrival of the monitors.

"I am tired of watching Buchanan," he wrote home in June, "and

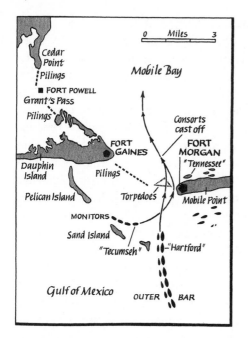

wish from the bottom of my heart that Buck would come out and try his hand upon us. The question has to be settled, iron versus wood, and there never was a better chance. . . . We are today ready to try anything that comes along, be it wood or iron, in reasonable quantities."

His plan was for the monitors to lead the way, holding to the right of the red buoy and providing an iron screen for the wooden ships as the two columns made their parallel runs past Fort Morgan, then going on to engage the ram in an all-out fight inside the bay, with such help as the multi-gunned sloops could provide. He would more or less ignore Fort Gaines while steaming in, not only because it was more than two miles off, but also because he planned to distract the attention of its gunners by having the army make a landing on the other end of Dauphin Island, then move east to invest the work from the landward side; after which Morgan would be served in the same fashion. But here too was a rub. The army, like the monitors, though promised, did not come. First there was Banks's drawn-out involvement up the Red, then a delay while Canby got the survivors back to New Orleans and in shape for the march to Mobile — which finally was cancelled when Grant was obliged to summon all but a handful to Virginia in late June, as replacements for Meade's heavy casualties. Canby visited the fleet in early July and agreed to send Major General Gordon Granger with 2000 men in transports, admittedly a small force but quite as large as he felt he could afford.

Farragut had to be satisfied, and in any case his impatience was mainly with the monitors, which still had not arrived. By way of diversion from the heat and boredom, both of which were oppressive, he rehearsed the run past Fort Morgan, and the fight that was to follow inside the bay, on a wardroom table grooved with the points of the compass, maneuvering little boat-shaped wooden blocks carved for him by the *Hartford*'s carpenter. Meanwhile, Buchanan's inactivity puzzled and irked him more and more. "Now is the time," he declared in mid-July. "The sea is as calm as possible and everything propitious. . . . Still he remains behind the fort, and I suppose it will be the old story over again. If he won't visit me, I will have to visit him. I am all ready as soon as the soldiers arrive to stop up the back door of each fort."

He was not, of course, "all ready," nor would he be so until the monitors were on hand, the *Albemarle* having redemonstrated in April and May, at Plymouth and in the North Carolina Sound from which she took her name, what was likely to happen to his wooden ships if he had no ironclads of his own to stand between them and the *Tennessee.* Then on July 20 the first of the promised four arrived from the Atlantic coast; *Manhattan* she was called, wearing ten inches of armor on her revolving turret, which carried two 15-inch guns. Ten days later the *Chickasaw* put in from New Orleans, double turreted with a pair of 11-inch guns in each, followed next day by her sister ship *Winnebago.* All were on hand by August 1 except the *Tecumseh,* en route from the Atlantic in the wake of her twin *Manhattan.* Farragut found the waiting even harder now that it was about to end; he improved the time by instructing his skippers in their duties, using the tabletop wooden blocks to show just where he expected their ships to be put in all eventualities. Meantime, as he had been doing for the past ten days, he continued to send out nightly boat crews, under cover of darkness and with muffled oars, to grapple for or sink as many as possible of the torpedoes anchored between the end of the line of pilings southeast of Dauphin Island and the red buoy just off Mobile Point. A number were so removed or destroyed, and the admiral was pleased to learn that many were found to be duds, their firing mechanisms having long been exposed to the corrosive effect of salt water.

Granger's 2000 soldiers arrived on August 2. They were taken around into Mississippi Sound the following night for a landing on the west end of Dauphin Island, and from there began working their way through heavy sand toward the back door of Fort Gaines. *Tecumseh* still had not appeared, but Farragut now was committed. "I can lose no more days," he declared. "I must go in day after tomorrow morning at daylight or a little later. It is a bad time, but when you do not take fortune at her offer you must take her as you can find her." Despite a heavy squall that evening, the grapplers went about their work in the mine field, undetected, and early next morning, August 4, the admiral took his fleet captains aboard the tender *Cowslip* for a closer look at the objective, cruising under the lee of Sand Island where the three monitors were anchored, ready to move out. Returning he went to his cabin, took out pen and paper, and composed a provisional farewell. "My dearest Wife: I write and leave this letter for you. I am going into Mobile Bay in the morning, if God is my leader, as I hope He is, and in Him I place my trust. . . . The Army landed last night, and are in full view of us this morning. The *Tecumseh* has not yet arrived."

Just then she did, steaming in from Pensacola to take position at the head of the iron column on the far side of Sand Island. The Union line of battle was complete. Asked at bedtime if he would consent to giving the men a glass of grog to nerve them up for the fight next morning, Farragut replied: "No, sir. I never found that I needed rum to enable me to do my duty. I will order two cups of good coffee to each man at 2 o'clock, and at 8 o'clock I will pipe all hands to breakfast in Mobile Bay."

Fog delayed the forming of the line past daybreak, the prearranged time for the start of the run, but a dawn breeze cleared the mist away by sunup, which came at 5.30 this Friday morning, August 5. As the four monitors began their movement eastward off the lee shore of Sand Island, in preparation for turning north beyond the line of pilings and the mine field — at which point the wooden column of seven heavy ships, each with a gunboat lashed to its port side for reserve power in case its boilers or engines were knocked out, would come up in their left rear for the dash past Mobile Point and the brick pentagon looming huge and black against the sunrise — Farragut was pleased to see that fortune had given him the two things he prayed for: a westerly wind to blow the smoke of battle away from the fleet and toward the fort, and a flood tide that would carry any pair of vessels on into the bay, even if both were disabled. Captain James Alden's 2000-ton 24-gun *Brooklyn* led the way, given the honor because she was equipped with chase guns and an antitorpedo device called a cowcatcher. Then came Flag Captain Percival Drayton's *Hartford* with the admiral aboard, followed by the remaining five, *Richmond, Lackawanna, Monongahela, Ossipee,* and *Oneida,* each with its gunboat consort attached to the flank away from the fort and otherwise readied for action in accordance with instructions issued as far back as mid-July: "Strip your vessels and prepare for the conflict. Send down all superfluous spars and rigging. Trice up or remove the whiskers. Put up the splinter nets on the starboard side, and barricade the wheel and steersmen with sails and hammocks. Lay chains or sandbags on the deck over the machinery to resist a plunging fire. Hang the sheet chains over the side, or make any other arrangements for security that your ingenuity may suggest." As a result, according to a Confederate who studied the uncluttered ships from Mobile Point, "They appeared like prize fighters ready for the ring."

Buchanan, aboard the *Tennessee,* got word that they were coming at 5.45, shortly after they started his way. He hurried on deck in his drawers for a look at the Yankee vessels, iron and wood, and while he dressed passed orders for the ram and its three attendant gunboats to move westward and take up a position athwart the main channel, just in rear of the inner line of torpedoes, for crossing the Union T if the enemy warships — eighteen of them, mounting 199 guns, as compared to his own four with 22 — passed Fort Morgan in an attempt to enter the bay. Balding, clean-shaven like Farragut, with bright blue eyes and a hawk nose, the Marylander assembled the *Tennessee*'s officers and crew on her gun deck and made them a speech that managed to be at once brief and rambling. "Now, men, the enemy is coming, and I want you to do your duty," he began, and ended: "You shall not have it said when you leave this vessel that you were not near enough to the enemy, for I will meet them, and you can fight them alongside of their own ships. And if I fall, lay me on the side and go on with the fight."

Farragut came on deliberately in accordance with his plan, the flagship crossing the outer bar at 6.10 while the iron column up ahead was making its turn north into the channel. Ten minutes later the lead monitor *Tecumseh* fired the opening shot, a 15-inch shell packed with sixty pounds of powder and half a bushel of cylindrical flathead bolts. It burst squarely over the fort, which did not reply until shortly after 7 o'clock, when the range to *Brooklyn*, leading the wooden column, had been closed to about a mile. Morgan's heaviest weapon was a 10-inch Columbiad, throwing a projectile less than half the weight of the one from *Tecumseh*, but the effect was altogether memorable for a young surgeon on the *Lackawanna*, midway down the line of high-masted vessels. "It is a curious sight to catch a single shot from so heavy a piece of ordnance," he later wrote. "First you see the puff of white smoke upon the distant ramparts, and then you see the shot coming, looking exactly as if some gigantic hand has thrown in play a ball toward you. By the time it is half way, you get the boom of the report, and then the howl of the missile, which apparently grows so rapidly in size that every green hand on board who can see it is certain that it will hit him between the eyes. Then, as it goes past with a shriek like a thousand devils, the inclination to do reverence is so strong that it is almost impossible to resist it."

Now the action became general, and by 7.30 the leading sloops, closing fast on the sluggish monitors, had their broadsides bearing fairly on the fort, whose gun crews were distracted by flying masonry, clouds of brickdust, and an avalanche of shells. Then two things happened, one in each of the tandem columns, for which Farragut had not planned while rehearsing the operation on the table in his cabin. Directly ahead of the flagship, *Brooklyn* had to slow to keep from overtaking the rear monitor *Chickasaw*. Presently, to the consternation of all astern, Alden stopped and began making signals: "The monitors are right ahead. We cannot go on without passing them. What shall we do?" While Farragut was testily replying, "Go ahead!" — and the guns of the fort and water battery, less than half a mile away, were stepping up their fire — Commander Tunis Craven of the *Tecumseh*, at the head of the iron column, reacted to a similar crisis in quite a different way, though it too involved a departure from instructions. Approaching the red buoy that marked the eastern limit of the mine field, he saw the breakers off Mobile Point, just off his starboard bow, and said to his pilot, out of fear of running aground: "It is impossible that the admiral means us to go inside that buoy." He ordered a hard turn to port, which carried the *Tecumseh* to the left, not right, of the red marker. But not for long. A

sudden, horrendous explosion against her bottom, square amidships —
whether of one or more torpedoes was later disputed — shook and
stopped the iron vessel, set her lurching from side to side, and sent water
pouring down her turret as she wallowed in the waves.

All aboard her must have known the hurt was mortal, though no
one guessed how short her agony would be. Craven and his pilot, for
example, standing face to face at the foot of the ladder that led to the
only escape hatch, staged a brief, courtly debate.

"Go ahead, Captain."

"After you, Pilot."

So they said; "But there was nothing after me," the pilot later
testified. As he put his foot on the top rung of the ladder, *Tecumseh* and
her captain dropped from under him.

Through a sight slit in the turret of *Manhattan*, next in line, an
engineer watched the lead monitor vanish almost too abruptly for belief.
"Her stern lifted high in the air with the propeller still revolving, and
the ship pitched out of sight like an arrow twanged from the bow."
With her went all but a score of her 114-man crew, including four who
swam to Mobile Point and were taken captive, while the others who
managed to wriggle out before she hit bottom were picked up by a
boat from the *Hartford*'s consort, *Metacomet*.

Farragut sent the boat, though the fact was he had problems
enough on his hands by then, including the apparent likelihood that such
rescue work was about to be required in his own direction. *Brooklyn*'s
untimely halt, practically under Morgan's guns, had thrown the wooden
column into confusion; for when she stopped her bow yawed off to starboard, subtracting her broadside from the pounding the fort was taking,
and what was worse she lay nearly athwart the channel, blocking the
path of the other ships. Nor was that the end of the trouble she and her
captain made. Alarmed by the sudden dive of the *Tecumseh* ("Sunk by
a torpedo! Assassination in its worst form!" he would protest in his
report) Alden spotted, just under his vessel's prow, "a row of suspicious-
looking buoys" which he took to be floats attached to mines. He reacted
by ordering *Brooklyn*'s engines reversed, and this brought her bearing
down, stern foremost, on the *Hartford*. Farragut, who had climbed the
mainmast rigging as far as the futtock shrouds for a view above the
smoke — he was tied there with a rope passed round his body by a
sailor, sent aloft by Drayton, lest a collision or a chance shot bring
him crashing to the deck some twenty feet below — angrily hailed the
approaching sloop, demanding to know the cause for such behavior, and
got the reply: "Torpedoes ahead."

Like the *Brooklyn*, which took 59 hits in the course of the fight,
Hartford was absorbing cruel punishment from the guns on Mobile
Point: particularly from those in the water battery, whose fire was point-
blank and deadly. Men were falling fast, their mangled bodies placed in

a row on one side of the deck, while the wounded were sent below in numbers too great for the surgeons to handle. A rifled solid tore a gunner's head off; another took both legs off a sailor who threw up his arms as he fell, only to have them carried away by still another. Farragut looked back down the line, where the rest of his stalled vessels were being served in much the same fashion, and saw that it would not do. He either had to go forward or turn back. In his extremity, he said later, he called on God: "Shall I go on?" and received the answer from a commanding voice inside his head: "Go on." *Brooklyn* blocked the channel on the right, so he asked the pilot, directly above him in the maintop, whether there was enough water for the *Hartford* to pass her on the left. The pilot said there was, and the admiral, exultant, shouted down to Drayton on the quarterdeck: "I will take the lead!" Signaling "close order" to the ships astern, he had the *Metacomet* back her engines and the flagship go all forward. This turned her westward, clear of *Brooklyn*, which she passed as she moved out. Someone called up a reminder of Alden's warning, but Farragut, lashed to the rigging high above the smoke of battle, with Mobile Bay in full view before him, had no time or mind for caution. "Damn the torpedoes!" he cried. "Full speed ahead!"

Ahead he went, followed by the others, west of where the *Brooklyn* lay until she rejoined the column — and west, too, of the red buoy marking the eastern limit of the mine field. Though Farragut had been encouraged by the work of his nighttime grapplers, who not only had removed a considerable number of mines in the course of the past two weeks, but also reported a high percentage of duds among them, *Tecumseh* had just given an only-too-graphic demonstration of what might await him and all his warships, iron or wood, as a result of this sudden departure from his plan to avoid the doom-infested stretch of water the *Hartford* now was crossing. And sure enough, while she steamed ahead with all the speed her engines could provide, the men on deck — and, even worse, the ones cooped up below — could hear the knock and scrape of torpedo cases against her hull and the snap of primers designed to ignite the charges that would blast her to the bottom. None did, either under the *Hartford* or any of the vessels in her wake, but the passage of Morgan became progressively more difficult as the lead sloops steamed out of range and left the tail of the column, along with the slow-moving monitors, to the less-divided attention of the cannoneers in the fort and on the beach. *Oneida*, which brought up the rear, took a 7-inch shell in the starboard boiler, scalding her firemen with escaping steam, and another that burst in the cabin, cutting both wheel ropes. Powerless and out of control, she too made it past, tugged along by her consort, only to emerge upon a scene of even worse destruction, just inside the bay.

Buchanan had succeeded in his design to cross the Union T; with the result that when Farragut ended his sprint across the mine field he found the *Tennessee* and the three rebel gunboats drawn up to receive him in line ahead, presenting their broadsides to the approaching column, whose return fire was limited to the vessels in the lead, and even these could bring only their bow guns into play. *Hartford*'s was promptly knocked out by a shot from *Selma*, smallest of the three, and this was followed by another that passed through the chain armor on the flagship's starboard bow, killing ten men, wounding five, and hurling bodies, or parts of bodies, aft and onto the decks of the *Metacomet*, lashed alongside. Farragut kept coming, with *Brooklyn* and *Richmond* close astern, and managed to avoid an attempt by Buchanan to ram and sink him, meantime bringing his big Dahlgrens to bear on the gunboats, one of which then retired lamely toward Fort Morgan, taking water through a hole punched in her hull. This was the *Gaines*; she was out of the fight, and presently so were the others, *Morgan* and *Selma*; for *Hartford* and *Richmond* cast off their consorts to engage them and they fled. *Metacomet* led the chase, yawing twice to fire her bow gun, but then stopped firing to concentrate on speed. While *Morgan* made it to safety under the lee of Mobile Point, *Selma* kept running eastward across the shallows beyond the channel, still pursued despite the *Metacomet*'s deeper draft. Out on the bow of the northern vessel, a leadsman was already calling one foot less than the ship drew, but her captain, feeling the soft ooze of the bottom under her keel, refused to abandon the chase. "Call the man in," he told his exec. "He is only intimidating me with his soundings."

Persistence paid. Overtaken, *Selma* lost eight killed and seven wounded before she hauled down her flag. Westward, the *Gaines* burned briskly, set afire by her crew, who escaped in boats as she sank in shallow water. Only *Morgan* survived, anchored under the frown of the fort's guns to wait for nightfall, when she would steal around the margin of the bay to gain the greater safety of Mobile, inside Dog River Bar.

Left to fight alone, Buchanan steamed after the *Hartford* for a time, still hoping to ram and sink her, despite the agility she had shown in avoiding his first attempt, but soon perceived that her speed made the chase a waste of effort; whereupon he turned back and made for the other half-dozen sloops, advancing in closer order. *Tennessee* passed down the line of high-walled wooden men-of-war, mauling and being mauled. Two shots went through and through the *Brooklyn*, increasing her toll of killed and wounded to 54, but another pair flew high to miss the *Richmond*. Both ships delivered point-blank broadsides that had no effect whatever on the armored vessel as she bore down on *Lackawanna*, next in line, and *Monongahela*, which she struck a glancing blow, then swung round to send two shells crashing into the *Ossipee*. That left *Oneida*, whose bad luck now turned good, at least for the moment.

Aboard the ram, defective primers spared the crippled ship a pounding; then one gun fired a delayed shot that cost the northern skipper an arm and the use of his 11-inch after pivot, which was raked. *Tennessee* turned hard aport in time to meet the three surviving monitors, just arriving, and exchanged volleys in passing that did no harm on either side. Then she proceeded to Fort Morgan and pulled up, out of range on the far side of the channel.

Farragut dropped anchor four miles inside the bay, and the rest of the blue flotilla, wood and iron, steamed up to join him, their crews already at work clearing away debris and swabbing the blood from decks, while belowdecks surgeons continued to ply their scalpels and cooks got busy in the galleys. It was 8.35; he was only a bit over half an hour behind schedule on last night's promise to "pipe all hands to breakfast in Mobile Bay" by 8 o'clock. All the same, despite the general elation at having completed another spectacular run past formidable works, rivaling those below New Orleans and at Vicksburg and Port Hudson, there was also a tempering sorrow over the loss of the *Tecumseh* and considerable apprehension, as well, from the fact that the murderous rebel iron ram was still afloat across the way.

Drayton promptly expressed this reservation to the admiral, who by now had come down from the flagship's rigging and stood on the poop. "What we have done has been well done, sir," he told him. "But it all counts for nothing so long as the *Tennessee* is there under the guns of Morgan." Farragut nodded. "I know it," he said, "and as soon as the people have had their breakfasts I am going for her."

As it turned out, there was no need for that, and no time for breakfast. At 8.50, fifteen minutes after *Hartford* anchored, there was a startled cry from aloft. "The ram is coming!" So she was, and presently those on deck saw her steaming directly for the fleet, apparently too impatient to wait for a fight in which she would have the help of the guns ashore. Farragut prepared for battle, remarking as he did so: "I did not think Old Buck was such a fool."

Fool or not, throughout the pause Buchanan had been unwilling to admit the fight was over, whatever the odds and no matter how far he had to go from Fort Morgan to renew it. Instrumental in the founding of the academy at Annapolis, he had served as its first superintendent and thought too highly of naval tradition to accept even tacit defeat while his ship remained in any condition to engage the enemy. "If he won't visit me, I will have to visit him," his adversary had remarked three weeks ago, and Buchanan felt much the same about the matter now as he gazed across three miles of water at the Yankee warships riding at anchor in the bay — *his* bay — quite as if there was no longer any question of their right to be there. Gazing, he drew the corners of his mouth down in a frown of disapproval, then turned to the *Tennessee*'s captain. "Follow them up, Johnston. We can't let them off that way." With that, the ram started forward: one six-gun vessel against a total of seventeen, three of them wearing armor heavier than her own, mounting 157 guns, practically all of them larger than any weapon in her casemate. That Buchanan was in no mood for advice was demonstrated, however, when one of his officers tried to call his attention to the odds. "Now I am in the humor, I will have it out," he said, and that was that. The ram continued on her way.

The monitors having proved unwieldy, Farragut's main reliance was on his wooden sloops, particularly the *Monongahela* and the *Lackawanna*, which were equipped with iron prows for ramming. Their orders were to run the ram down, while the others pitched in to do her whatever damage they could manage with their guns. Accordingly, when the *Tennessee* came within range about 9.20, making hard for the flagship, *Monongahela* moved ahead at full speed and struck her amidships, a heavy blow that had no effect at all on the rebel vessel but cost the sloop her iron beak, torn off along with her cutwater. *Lackawanna* rammed in turn, with the result that an eight-foot section of her stem was crushed above and below the waterline. *Tennessee* lurched but held her course, and the two flagships collided nearly head on. "The port bow of the *Hartford* met the port bow of the ram," an officer aboard the Federal vessel later wrote, "and the ships grated against each other as they passed. The *Hartford* poured her whole port broadside against the ram, but the solid shot merely dented the side and bounded into the air. The ram tried to return the salute, but owing to defective primers only one gun was discharged. This sent a shell through the berth-deck, killing five men and wounding eight. The muzzle of the gun was so close to the *Hartford* that the powder blackened her side."

When the two ships parted Farragut jumped to the port quarter rail and held to the mizzen rigging while he leaned out to assess the damage, which was by no means as great as he had feared. Finding the perch to his liking he remained there, lashed to the rigging by friendly hands for the second time that day, and called for Drayton to give the *Tennessee* another thump as soon as possible. As the *Hartford* came about, however, she was struck on the starboard flank by the *Lackawanna*, which was also trying to get in position, crushing her planking on that side and upsetting one of the Dahlgrens. "Save the admiral! Save the admiral!" the cry went up, for it was thought at first that the flagship was sinking, so great was the confusion on her decks. Farragut untied himself, leaped down, and crossed to the starboard mizzen rigging, where he again leaned out to inspect the damage, which though severe did not extend to within two feet of the water. Again he ordered full speed ahead, only to find the *Lakawanna* once more looming on his starboard quarter. At this, one witness later said, "the admiral became a trifle excited." Forgetting that he had given the offending ship instructions to lead the ram attack, he turned to the communications officer on the bridge.

"Can you say 'For God's sake' by signal?"

"Yes, sir."

"Then say to the *Lackawanna*, 'For God's sake, get out of our way and anchor.' "

By now the ironclad had become the target for every ship that could get in position to give her a shot or a shove, including the double-turreted *Chickasaw*, which "hung close under our stern," the *Tennessee*'s pilot afterwards declared, "firing the two 11-inch guns in her forward turret like pocket pistols." Such punishment began to tell. Her flag-staff went and then her stack, giving the ram what one attacker called "a particularly shorn, stubby look" and greatly reducing the draft to her fires. Her steam went down, and then, as a sort of climax to her disablement, the monitor hard astern succeeded in cutting her rudder chain, exposed on the afterdeck, so that she would no longer mind her helm. Still she kept up the fight, exploiting her one advantage, which was that she could fire in any direction, surrounded as she was, without fear of hitting a friend or missing a foe. Presently, though, this too was reduced by shots that jammed half of her gunport shutters against the shield, thereby removing them from use. When this happened to the stern port, Buchanan sent for a machinist to unjam it, and while the man was at work on the cramped bolt, an 11-inch shell from the *Chickasaw* exploded against the edge of the cover just above him. "His remains had to be taken up with a shovel, placed in a bucket, and thrown overboard," a shipmate would recall. One of the steel splinters that flew inside the casemate struck Buchanan, breaking his left leg below the knee. "Well, Johnston," he said to the *Tennessee*'s captain as he was taken up to be carried down to the berth deck, "they've got me. You'll have to look out for her now. This is your fight, you know."

Johnston did what he could to sustain the contest with the rudderless, nearly steamless vessel, blind in most of her ports and taking heavy-caliber punches from two big sloops on each quarter and the monitor astern. Finally he went below and reported the situation to Buchanan. "Do the best you can, sir," the admiral told him, teeth gritted against the pain from the compound fracture of his leg, "and when all is done, surrender." Returning topside, the Alabamian found the battle going even worse. Unable to maneuver, the ram could not bring a single gun to bear on her tormentors; moreover, Johnston afterwards reported, "Shots were fairly raining upon the after end of the shield, which was now so thoroughly shattered that in a few moments it would have fallen and exposed the gun deck to a raking fire of shell and grape." He lowered the *Tennessee*'s ensign, in token of her capitulation, and when this did not slacken the encircling fire — it had been shot down before, then raised again on the handle of a rammer staff poked through the overhead grille of the smoky casemate — "I then decided, although with an almost bursting heart, to hoist the white flag."

At 10 o'clock the firing stopped, and presently Farragut sent an officer to demand the wounded admiral's sword, which then was handed over. *Tennessee*'s loss of two men killed and nine wounded brought the Confederate total for all four ships to 12 killed and 20 wounded. Union losses were 172 killed, more than half in the *Tecumseh*, and 170 wounded. Their respective totals, 32 and 342, were thus about in ratio of the strength of the two fleets, though in addition 243 rebel sailors were captured aboard *Selma* and the ironclad.

"The Almighty has smiled upon me once more. I am in Mobile Bay," Farragut wrote his wife that night, adding: "It was a hard fight, but Buck met his fate manfully. After we passed the forts, he came up in the ram to attack me. I made at him and ran him down, making all the others do the same. We butted and shot at him until he surrendered."

Westward across the bay, as he wrote, there was a burst of flame and a loud explosion off Cedar Point. The garrison of Fort Powell, taken under bombardment from the rear that afternoon by one of the big-gunned monitors at a range of 400 yards, had evacuated the place under cover of darkness and set a slow match to the magazine. Next morning the fleet dropped down and began shelling the eastern end of Dauphin Island, where Fort Gaines was under pressure from the landward side by Granger and his soldiers. This continued past nightfall, and the fort's commander asked for terms the following day, August 7. Told they were unconditional, he accepted and promptly surrendered his 818 men, together with all guns and stores. That left Fort Morgan; a much tougher proposition, as it turned out.

While the troops were being taken aboard transports for the shift to Mobile Point and a similar rear approach to the fortifications there, Farragut submitted under a flag of truce a note signed by himself and Granger, demanding the unconditional surrender of Fort Morgan "to prevent the unnecessary sacrifice of human life which must follow the opening of our batteries." The reply was brief and negative. "Sirs: I am prepared to sacrifice life, and will only surrender when I have no means of defense. . . . Respectfully, etc. *R. L. Page*, Brigadier General."

Approaching fifty-seven, Richard Page was a Virginian, a forty-year veteran of the Union and Confederate navies, who had transferred to the army five months ago when he assumed command of the outer defenses of Mobile Bay. His beard was white, his manner fiery; "Old Ramrod" and "Bombast Page" were two of his prewar nicknames, and if he bore a resemblance to R. E. Lee (both were born in 1807) it was no wonder. His mother had been Lee's father's sister.

Farragut's run past Morgan had come as a shock to its defenders, who fired close to 500 shots at the slow-moving Yankee column. "I do

not see how I failed to sink the *Hartford*," Page said ruefully, shaking his
head as the smoke cleared; "I do not see how I failed to sink her." Fort
Powell's evacuation and the unresistant capitulation of Fort Gaines,
neither of which had been done with his permission, angered and made
him all the more determined to resist to the utmost the amphibious seige
that got under way on August 9, shortly after he rejected unconditional
surrender. Granger's men had been put ashore that morning on the bay
side of Mobile Point, just over a mile to the east of the fort, and
by nightfall — after they had performed the back-breaking labor of
hauling guns and ammunition through shin-deep sand, which one of
them said was "hot enough during the day for roasting potatoes" —
took the east curtain and ramparts under fire with their batteries, while
the sloops and ironclads, including the captured *Tennessee*, poured in
shells and hotshot from the bay and Gulf. The fort shook under this
combined pounding, but Page was no more of a mind to surrender now
than he had been when he first declined the combined demand at
midday.

For two weeks this continued, and throughout that time the
pressure grew. Daily the troops drew closer on the landward side, increasing the number of weapons they brought to bear until at last there
were 25 guns and 16 heavy mortars, their discharges echoed by those
from the ships beyond and on both sides of the point. The climax came
on August 22, when 3000 rounds were flung at the fort in the course
of a twelve-hour bombardment, under whose cover the blue infantry extended its parallels to within reach of the glacis. All but two of the
fort's guns were silenced and the citadel was burning; sharpshooters
drew beads on anything that showed above the ramparts, and 80,000
pounds of powder had to be removed from the magazine and flooded,
so close were the flames. Practically all that remained by now was
wreckage and scorched debris. At 5 o'clock next morning two last shots
were fired by the defenders, and one hour later the white flag went up.
Farragut sent Drayton to arrange the formal surrender, which took
place that afternoon amid the rubble. He had Buchanan's sword for a
trophy, but he did not get Page's. The general and all his officers, displaying what Farragut called "childish spitefulness," had broken or
thrown away their side arms just before the ceremony.

The admiral did get another 546 prisoners, however, which
brought the total to better than 1700 on land and water — and he did
get Mobile Bay, which after all was what he had come for. Blockade
running might continue on the Atlantic coast, where Wilmington and
Charleston still held out, but it was ended on the Gulf except for the
sealed-off region west of the Mississippi, which in any case lay outside
the constricting Anaconda coils. Mobile itself, thirty miles away at
the head of the bay, was no part of Farragut's objective. Except as a
port, it contributed little to the South's defense, and it was a port no

longer. Moreover, Canby not only lacked the strength to expel the town's defenders; he could not have afforded to garrison it afterwards, so urgent were the calls for replacements for the men who had fallen in Georgia and, above all, in Virginia.

Best of all the immediate gains obtained from the naval battle, though, was the elation that followed, throughout the North, the announcement of the first substantial victory that had been scored, East or West, in the three months since the opening of Grant's spring offensive. Lincoln and his political supporters were pleased above all, perhaps, with the lift it seemed to give his chances for survival in the presidential contest, which by then was less than three months off.

As usual, there was bad news with the good, and in this case the bad was double-barreled, concerning as it did a pair of highly spectacular reverses, one afloat and one ashore. In Washington on August 12, while the celebration of Farragut's week-old triumph over the *Tennessee* was still in progress at the Navy Department — word had come belatedly by wire from Ben Butler, who read of the bay battle in a Richmond paper smuggled through his Bermuda Hundred lines the day before — the telegraph line from coastal New Jersey began to chatter about a mysterious rebel cruiser at work off Sandy Hook. Yesterday she had taken seven prizes, and today she was adding six more to her list, which would reach a total of thirty U.S. merchant vessels within the week. It was as if the *Alabama*, eight weeks in her watery grave outside Cherbourg, had been raised, pumped out, and sped across the Atlantic to lay about her in a manner even more destructive than when she was in her prime. Quickly, all the available Federal warships within reach were ordered out to find and sink her at all costs. But who, or what, was she? Where had she come from? Who was her captain?

She was the *Tallahassee*, a former blockade runner, built up the Thames the year before and purchased that summer by the Confederates, who converted her into a raider by installing three guns and sent her out from Wilmington under Commander John T. Wood, a onetime Annapolis instructor, grandson of Zachary Taylor, aide to Jefferson Davis, and participant in a number of naval exploits, including the *Merrimac-Monitor* fight, New Bern, and the retaking of Plymouth. Setting out on the night of August 6 he showed the blockaders a clean pair of heels; for that was the ship's main virtue, speed. Twin stacked, with a 100-horsepower engine driving each of her two screws, she was 220 feet in length and only 24 in the beam, a combination that gave her a top speed of seventeen knots and had enabled her, on her shakedown cruise, to make the Dover-Calais crossing in seventy-seven minutes. Five mornings later, 500 miles up the Atlantic coast, *Tallahassee* encountered her first prize, the schooner *Sarah Boyce*, and before the day was over she ran down six more Union merchant vessels, ransoming the last to put all prisoners ashore. That was Thursday, August 11; "Pirate off Sandy Hook capturing and burning," the commandant of the Brooklyn Navy Yard wired Washington. Friday, off Long Island, she took six prizes, Saturday two, and Sunday — as if by way of resting on the Sabbath — one. By now she was cruising the New England coast, and on Monday she took six ships, Tuesday five, and Wednesday three, rounding out a week that netted her thirty prizes, all burned or scuttled except seven that were ransomed to clear her crowded decks of captured passengers and crews. On August 18, running low on coal, she put into the neutral port of Halifax to refuel.

Under instructions from the Queen, and over ardent protests from the American consul, the Nova Scotia authorities gave Wood twenty-four hours to fill his bunkers, and when this did not suffice they granted him a twelve-hour extension. *Tallahassee* steamed out the following night in time to avoid half a dozen enemy warships that arrived next day, the vanguard of a fleet of thirteen ordered to Halifax as soon as the consul telegraphed word of the raider's presence in the harbor. She headed straight for Wilmington, taking so little chance on running out of coal that she only paused to seize one prize along the way, and arrived on the night of August 26 to speed and shoot her way through the blockade flotilla and drop anchor up the Cape Fear River, whose entrance was guarded by Fort Fisher. Her twenty-day cruise had cost the enemy 31 merchant vessels and had given Wood's fellow countrymen some welcome news to offset the bad from Mobile Bay, where Fort Morgan had fallen three days ago. They took pride in the fact that "this extemporaneous man-of-war," as Jefferson Davis called the *Tallahassee*, had "lit up the New England coast with her captures," and they could tell themselves, as well, that no matter what misfortunes befell their regular navy, outnumbered as it invariably was in combat, their irregular navy (so to speak) had won them the admiration of the world and was rapidly scouring the seas of Yankee shipping.

That was the first Federal reverse. The second, which occurred simultaneously ashore, was quite as spectacular and, if anything, even more "irregular" — as was often the case in operations involving Bedford Forrest. He had been given a free rein to conduct the defense of North Mississippi by Major General Dabney Maury, who succeeded to command of the Department of Alabama, Mississippi, and East Louisiana in late July, when Stephen Lee left to join Hood at Atlanta. "We must do the best we can with the little we have," Maury wrote from Meridian in early August, "and it is with no small satisfaction I reflect that of all the commanders of the Confederacy you are accustomed to accomplish the very greatest results with small means when left to your own untrammeled judgment. Upon that judgment I now rely."

Forrest took him at his word. "All that can be done shall be done," he replied, adding that since he lacked "the force to risk a general engagement" in resisting the next blue incursion, he would "resort to all other means." Other means, in this case, included a raid on Memphis, the enemy's main base, under occupation for better than two years. Tactically, such a strike would be likely to disrupt the plans of the Federals for extending their conquest deep into Mississippi. Moreover, Forrest himself — a former alderman — would not only derive considerable personal satisfaction from returning to his home town, which no Confederate had entered, except as a spy or prisoner, since its fall in June of 1862; he would also be exacting vengeance for a battle fought the month before, near Tupelo, which was as close to a defeat as he had come so far in his career. Lee had been in command of the field, one week before his departure for Atlanta, but the memory rankled and Forrest was anxious to wipe it out or anyhow counterbalance it.

Hard on the heels of Brice's Crossroads in mid-June, when he received orders from Sherman "to make up a force and go out and follow Forrest to the death, if it costs 10,000 lives and breaks the Treasury," C. C. Washburn, the Memphis commander, assigned the task to A. J. Smith, reinforcing two of his divisions, just returned from their excursion up and down Red River, with Bouton's brigade of Negro infantry and Grierson's cavalry division, both of them recent graduates of the hard-knocks school the Wizard of the Saddle was conducting for his would-be conquerers down in Mississippi. On July 5 this column of 14,200 effectives, mounted and afoot, supported by six batteries of artillery and supplied with twenty days of rations — "a force ample to whip anything this side of Georgia," Washburn declared — set out southward from La Grange, fifty miles east of Memphis. Sherman's orders by then had been expanded; Smith and his gorilla-guerillas, who had polished their hard-handed skills in Louisiana under Banks, were to "pursue Forrest on foot, devastating the land over which he passed or may pass, and make him and the people of Tennessee and Mississippi realize that, although [he is] a bold, daring, and successful leader, he will bring ruin and misery on any country where he may pause or tarry. If we do not punish Forrest and the people now," the red-haired Ohioan wound up, "the whole effect of our past conquests will be lost."

Three days out, and just over fifty miles down the road, Smith showed that he took this admonition to heart by burning much of the town of Ripley, including the courthouse, two churches, the Odd Fellows Hall, and a number of homes. Next day, July 9, still mindful of his instructions to "punish Forrest and the people," he pressed on across the Tallahatchie and through New Albany, trailed by a swath of desolation ten miles wide.

Ahead lay Pontotoc, and beyond it Okolona, where Sooy Smith had come to grief five months before, checked almost as disastrously as Sturgis had been at nearby Brice's Crossroads, a month ago tomorrow. So far, only token opposition to the current march had developed, but at

Pontotoc, which he cleared on July 11, this new Smith began to encounter stiffer resistance. Butternut troopers hung on the flanks of the
column, as if to slow it down before it made contact with whatever
was waiting to receive it up ahead, perhaps at Okolona. Smith would
never know; for at dawn on July 13, well short of any ambush being
laid for him there or south of there, he abruptly changed direction and
struck out instead for Tupelo, fifteen miles to the east on the Mobile &
Ohio, "his column well closed up, his wagon train well protected, and
his flanks covered in an admirable manner."

So Forrest's scouts informed him at Okolona, where he was waiting — it was his forty-third birthday — for both Smith and Stephen
Lee, who was on the way with 2000 troops and had ordered him not to
commit his present force of about 6000 until these reinforcements got
there to reduce the odds. Arriving from the south to find that the blue
column had veered east, Lee took charge of pressing the pursuit. His
urgency was based on reports from Dabney Maury, at Mobile, that
Canby was preparing to march from New Orleans and attack the city
from the landward side; Lee wanted Smith dealt with quickly so that
the men he had brought to reinforce Forrest could be sent to Maury.
"As soon as I fight I can send him 2000, possibly 3000," he explained in
a dispatch to Bragg, though he added that this depended on whether the
Mississippi invaders did or did not "succeed in delaying the battle."
Smith was capable and canny, halting from time to time to beat off
rearward threats while Grierson's horsemen rode on into Tupelo and
began tearing up track above and below the town. All day the Federal
infantry marched, then called a halt soon after nightfall at Harrisburg,
two miles west of Tupelo, which had grown with the railroad and
swallowed the older settlement as a suburb. Forrest came up presently
in the darkness and "discovered the enemy strongly posted and prepared
to give battle the next day."

Smith was at bay, and though his position was a stout one, nearly
two miles long and skillfully laid out — flanks refused, rear well covered
by cavalry, the line itself strengthened with fence rails, logs, timbers
from torn-down houses, and bales of cotton — Forrest counted this a
happy ending to an otherwise disappointing birthday. "One thing is
certain," he told Lee; "the enemy cannot remain long where he is. He
must come out, and when he does, all I ask or wish is to be turned loose
with my command." No matter which way Smith headed when he
emerged fretful and hungry, Forrest said, "I will be on all sides of him,
attacking day and night. He shall not cook a meal or have a night's
sleep, and I will wear his army to a frazzle before he gets out of the
country."

Lee could see the beauty of that; but he had Mobile and Canby
on his mind, together with the promises he had made to Bragg and
Maury, and did not feel that he could afford the time it would take to

deal with the penned-up bluecoats in this manner. There were better that 14,000 of them, veterans to a man, and though he had only about 8000 troops on hand he issued orders for an all-out assault next morning. Forrest would take the right and he the left. Together they would storm the Union works, making up for the disparity in numbers by the suddenness and ardor of their charge.

Ardor there was, and suddenness too, but these turned out to be the qualities that robbed Lee of what little chance he had for success in the first place. July 14 dawned hot and still, and the troops on line were vexed by delays in bringing several late-arriving units into position for the attack. Around 7.30, a Kentucky brigade near the center jumped the gun and started forward ahead of the others, who followed piecemeal, left and right, with the result that what was to have been a single, determined effort, all along the line, broke down from the outset into a series of individual lunges. Smith's veterans, snug behind their improvised breastworks, blasted each rebel unit as it advanced. "It was all gallantry and useless sacrifice," one Confederate was to say. To Smith, the disjointed attack "seemed to be a foot race to see who should reach us first. They were allowed to approach, yelling and howling like Comanches, to within canister range.... They would come forward and fall back, rally and forward again, with the like result. Their determination may be seen from the fact that their dead were found within thirty yards of our batteries." None got any closer, and after two hours of this Lee called a halt. He had lost 1326 killed and wounded and missing, Smith barely half that many, 674.

Skirmishing resumed next morning, but so fitfully and cautiously that it seemed to invite a counterattack. Smith instead clung fast to his position. He did, that is, until midday, when he was informed that much of the food in his train had spoiled in the Mississippi heat, leaving only one day's rations fit to eat, and that his reserve supply of artillery ammunition was down to about a hundred rounds per gun: whereupon he decided to withdraw northward, back in the direction he had set out from ten days ago, even though this meant leaving his more grievously wounded men behind in Tupelo. There followed the curious spectacle of a superior force retreating from a field on which it had inflicted nearly twice as many casualties as it suffered and being harassed on the march by a loser reduced to less than half the strength of the victor it was pursuing. In any case, after setting fire to what was left of Harrisburg, the Federals not only withdrew in good order and made excellent time on the dusty roads; they also succeeded, when they made camp at sunset on Town Creek, five miles north, in beating off a rebel attack and inflicting on Bedford Forrest, whom Lee had put in charge of the pursuit — and whom Smith had been told to "follow to the death" — his third serious gunshot wound of the war. The bullet struck him in the foot (the base of his right big toe, to be explicit) causing him so much pain that he had to relinquish the command, temporarily at least, and retire to a dressing station.

Smith kept going, unaware of this highly fortunate development, back through New Albany and across the Tallahatchie. Midway between there and La Grange he encountered a supply train sent to meet him. He kept going, despite this relief, and returned to his starting point on July 21, after sixteen round-trip days of marching and fighting. "I bring back everything in good order; nothing lost," he informed Washburn, who found the message so welcome a contrast to those received from other generals sent out after Forrest that he passed it along with pride to Sherman.

Far from proud, Sherman was downright critical, especially of the resultant fact that Forrest had been left to his own devices, which might well include a raid into Middle Tennessee and a strike against the blue supply lines running down into North Georgia. Engaged at the time in the Battle of Atlanta, Sherman replied that Smith was "to pursue and continue to follow Forrest. He must keep after him till recalled. . . . It is of vital importance that Forrest does not go to Tennessee." Smith returned to Memphis on July 23, miffed at this unappreciative reaction to his campaign, and began at once to prepare for a second outing, one that he hoped to improve beyond reproach.

This time the invasion column would number 18,000 of all arms, one quarter larger than before, and he would proceed by a different rout — down the Mississippi Central, which he would repair as he advanced, thus solving the problem of supplies whose lack had obliged his recent withdrawal in mid-career. By August 2 the railroad was in running order down to the Tallahatchie, and Washburn notified Sherman that Smith's reorganized command, which he assured him could "whip the combined force of the enemy this side of Georgia and east of the Mississippi," would set out "as soon as possible. . . . Forrest's forces were near Okolona a week since," he added, saving the best news for last; "Chalmers in command. Forrest [has] not been able to resume command by reason of wound in fight with Smith. I have a report today that he died of lockjaw some days ago."

It was true that Chalmers was in nominal command, but not that Forrest was dead, either of lockjaw or of any other ailment, although a look at him was enough to show how the rumor got started. Troubled by a siege of boils even before he was wounded, "sick-looking, thin as a rail, cheekbones that stuck out like they were trying to come through the skin, skin so yellow it looked greenish, eyes blazing" — one witness saw him thus at Tupelo that week — he rode about the camps in a buggy, his injured foot propped on a rack atop the dashboard, waiting impatiently for it to heal enough for him to mount a horse and resume command of his two divisions. They were all that were left him now, about 5000 horsemen, after his casualties at Harrisburg and the departure of Stephen Lee, first for Mobile (where the reinforcements he took with him turned out not to be needed, Grant having ruled out Canby's attack by diverting his troops to Virginia) and then for Atlanta, to join Hood. Partly, too, Forrest's haggard appearance was a result of the recent bloody repulse he had suffered in the assault on Smith. Even though he had advised against the attack, and was thereby absolved from blame for its failure, he was unaccustomed to sharing in a defeat and he burned with resentment over the useless loss of a thousand of his men, just at a time when they seemed likely to be needed most. Smith, he knew, was refitting in Memphis and would soon be returning to North Mississippi, stronger than before and with a better knowledge of the pitfalls. Sure enough, by early August the new blue column of 18,000 effectives had moved out to Grand Junction and begun its advance down the Mississippi Central to Holly Springs, a day's march from the Tallahatchie. "We knew we couldn't fight General Smith's big fine army," a butternut artillery lieutenant would recall, "and we knew that we couldn't get any reinforcements anywhere, and we boys speculated about what Old Bedford was going to do."

Old Bedford wondered too, for a time. At first he thought Smith's movement down the railroad was a feint, designed to "draw my forces west and give him the start toward the prairies." Back in command — and in the saddle, though he only used one stirrup — he sent Chalmers's division over to cover the Mississippi Central, but kept Buford's around Okolona to oppose what he believed would be the main blue effort. He soon learned better. On August 8 Smith moved in strength from Holly Springs and forced a crossing of the Tallahatchie, sending his cavalry ahead next day to occupy Oxford, twelve miles down the line. Forrest wired Chalmers to "contest every inch of ground," and set out at once for Oxford with Buford's division. Grierson fell back when he learned of this on August 10, and Smith remained at the river crossing, constructing a bridge to ensure the rapid delivery of supplies when he continued his march south. It was then, in this driest season of the Mississippi year, that the rain began to fall. It fell and kept falling for a week, marking what became known thereafter in these parts as "the wet August."

Both sides were nearly immobilized by the deepening mud and washouts, but they sparred as best they could, in slow motion, and planned for the time ahead. On August 18, though the weather still was rainy, Smith began inching southward; muddy or not, he had made up his mind to move, however slowly.

So by then had Forrest. At 5 o'clock that afternoon he assembled on the courthouse square at Oxford, after a rigorous "weeding out of sick men and sore-back and lame horses," close to 2000 troopers from two brigades and Morton's four-gun battery. In pelting rain and under a sky already dark with low-hanging clouds, the head of the column took up the march westward; Chalmers, left behind with the remaining 3000, had been told to put up such a show of resistance to the advancing Federals, who outnumbered him six to one, that Smith would not suspect for at least two days that nearly half of Forrest's command had left his front and was moving off to the west — in preparation for turning north around his flank, some were saying up and down the long gray column. "It got abroad in camp that we were going to Memphis," one rider later wrote. "That looked radical, but pleased us."

They knew they were right next morning, after a night march of twenty-five miles across swollen creeks and up and down long slippery hills, when they reached Panola and crossed the Tallahatchie, taking the route of the Mississippi & Tennessee Railroad, which ran north some sixty bee-line miles to Memphis. Four separate invasions they had repulsed in the past six months, three by pitched battle, one by sheer bluff, and now they were out to try their hand at turning back the fifth with a strike at the enemy's main base, close to a hundred miles in his rear. Radical, indeed. But Forrest knew what he would find when he got there; home-town operatives had kept him well informed. Washburn, under repeated urgings from Sherman to strengthen Smith to his utmost, had stripped the city's defense force to a minimum, and Fort Pickering, whose blufftop guns bore on the river and the city, but not on its landward approaches, offered little in the way of deterrent to an operation of this kind; Forrest did not intend to stay there any longer than it took his raiders to spread confusion among the defenders and alarm them into recalling Smith, who by now was skirmishing with Chalmers around Oxford, unaware that the man he was charged with following "to the death" had already rounded his flank and was about to set off an explosion deep in his rear.

Twenty miles the butternut column made that day, north from Panola to Senatobia, lighter by about two hundred troopers whose mounts had broken down before they reached the Tallahatchie and turned back, along with all but two of Morton's guns, whose teams were increased to ten horses each to haul them. The rain had stopped, as if on signal from the Wizard. All day the sun beamed down on roads and fields, but only enough, after eight days of saturation, to change the mud from slippery to sticky.

One mile north of Senatobia, which he cleared at first light, August 20, Forrest came upon Hickahala Creek, swollen to a width of sixty feet between its flooded banks; a formidable obstacle, but one for which he had planned by sending ahead a detachment to select a crossing point and chop down two trees on each bank, properly spaced, the stumps to be used for the support of a pair of cables woven from muscadine vines, which grew to unusual size and in great profusion in the bottoms. By the time the main body came up, the suspension cables had been stretched and were supported in midstream by an abandoned flatboat, which in turn was buoyed up by bundles of poles lashed to its sides. All that remained was for the span to be floored, and this was done with planks the troopers had ripped from gins and cabins on the approach march. In all, the crossing took less than an hour; but six miles north lay the Coldwater River, twice as wide. That took three, the work party having hurried ahead to construct another such grapevine bridge with the skill acquired while improvising the first. The heaviest loads it had to bear were the two guns, which were rolled across by hand, and several wagons loaded with unshucked corn for the horses, which were unloaded, trundled empty over the swaying rig, and then reloaded on the opposite bank. Forrest set the example by carrying the first armload, limping across on his injured foot, much to the admiration and amusement of his soldiers. "I never saw a command more like it was out for a holiday," one later wrote, while the general himself was to say: "I had to continually caution the men to keep quiet. They were making a regular corn shucking out of it."

Many of them, like him, were on their way home for the first time in years, and it was hard to contain the exuberance they were feeling at the prospect. Eight miles beyond the Coldwater by dark, Forrest called a rest halt at Hernando, where he had spent most of his young manhood, twenty-five miles from downtown Memphis. Near midnight the column pushed on, reduced to about 1500 sabers (so called, though for the most part they preferred shotguns and navy sixes) by the breakdown of another 200-odd horses, and stopped at 3 a.m. just short of the city limits, there to receive final instructions for the work ahead — work that was based on detailed information smuggled out by spies. One detachment under the general's brother, Captain William Forrest, would lead the way over Cane Creek Bridge and ride straight for the Gayoso House on Main Street, where Washburn's predecessor Stephen Hurlbut was quartered while awaiting reassignment; two other detachments, one of them under another brother, Lieutenant Colonel Jesse Forrest, would proceed similarly to capture Brigadier General R. P. Buckland, commander of the garrison, and Washburn himself, both of whom were living with their staffs in commandeered private residences. Two major generals and a brigadier would make a splendid haul and Forrest intended to have them, along with much else in the way of spoils assigned to still other detachments. Half an hour before dawn of this foggy Sunday morning, August 21, the head of the column entered the sleeping city whose papers had carried yesterday a special order from the department commander, prohibiting all "crying or selling of newspapers on Sunday between the hours of 9 a.m. and 5 p.m.," the better to preserve the peace and dignity of the Sabbath.

In some ways, the raid — the penetration itself — was anticlimactic. For example, all three Federal generals escaped capture, one because he slept elsewhere that night (just *where* became the subject of much scurrilous conjecture) and the other two because they were alerted in time to make a dash for safety under Fort Pickering's 97 guns, which Forrest had no intention of storming. Buckland woke to a hammering, a spattering of gunfire some blocks off, and leaned out of his upstairs bedroom window to find a sentry knocking at the locked door of the house. He called down, still half asleep, to ask what was the matter.

"General, they are after you."

"Who are after me?"

"The rebels," he was told.

He had time to dress before hurrying to the fort. Not so Washburn, who had to make a run for it in his nightshirt through back alleys; so sudden was the appearance of the raiders at his gate, he barely had time to leave by the rear door as they entered by the front. By way of consolation, Jesse Forrest captured two of his staff officers, along with his dress uniform and accouterments. Bill Forrest got even less when he clattered up Main Street to the Gayoso and, without pausing to dismount, rode his horse through the hotel doorway and into the lobby; Hurlbut, as aforesaid, had slept elsewhere and had only to lie low, wherever he was, to avoid capture. This he did, and survived to deliver himself of the best-remembered comment anyone made on either side in reference to the raid. "They removed me from command because I couldn't keep Forrest out of West Tennessee," he declared afterwards, "and now Washburn can't keep him out of his own bedroom."

By then enough blue units had rallied to bring on a number of vicious little skirmishes and fire-fights, resulting in a total of 35 Confederates and 80 Federals being killed or wounded, in addition to 116 defenders captured — many of them officers, rounded up in their night clothes at the Gayoso and elsewhere — along with some 200 horses. All this time, surprise reunions were in progress around town, despite the fact that recognition was not always easy: as, for example, in the case of a young raider who hailed his mother and sister from the gate of the family home, only to find that they had trouble identifying a tattered mud-spattered veteran as the boy they had kissed goodbye when he left three years ago, neatly turned out in well-pressed clothes for a war that would soon be won. At 9 o'clock, satisfied that he had created enough disturbance to produce the effect he wanted, Forrest had the recall sounded and began the prearranged withdrawal. Beyond Cane Creek he paused to return, under a flag of truce, Washburn's uniform, which his brother Jesse proudly displayed as a trophy of the raid. (Whatever deficiencies he might show in other respects, Washburn knew how to return a courtesy. Some weeks later he sent Forrest, also under a flag of truce, a fine gray uniform made to measure by the cavalryman's own prewar Memphis tailor.) The column then took up the southward march, clearing Hernando that afternoon to ride back across the Tallahatchie and into Panola, late the following day. "If the enemy is falling back, pursue them hard," Forrest instructed Chalmers in a message taken cross-country by a courier who found him just below Oxford, still resisting Smith's advance.

That admonition — "pursue them hard" — was presently translated into action. Smith had entered Oxford that morning, but had no sooner done so than he began to backpedal in response to the news, brought forward under armed escort, that Forrest had raided Memphis the day before. Withdrawing, the Federals set fire to the courthouse, along with other public buildings and a number of private residences. "Where once stood a handsome little country town," an Illinois correspondent wrote, "now only remain the blackened skeletons of houses, and smouldering ruins." Smith's retrograde movement was hastened by a follow-up report next day, August 23, that the raiders were returning to Memphis for a second and heavier strike. The report was false (Forrest was still at Panola, a hard two-day march to the south, resting his troopers from their 150-mile excursion through the Mississippi bottoms) but was almost as disruptive, in its effect, as if it had been true. Alarm bells rang; regulars and militiamen turned out — "eager for the fray," one of the latter said — and Washburn asked the naval commander to have a gunboat steam downriver, below Fort Pickering, to shell the southern approaches to the city. This was done, but with no more than pyrotechnical effect, since the raiders were only there by rumor, not in fact. "The whole town was stampeded," Washburn's inspector general declared, calling the reaction "the most disgraceful affair I have ever seen." This too had its influence. Within another two days no part of A. J. Smith's command remained below the Tallahatchie, and so closely did Chalmers press him, in accordance with Forrest's instructions, that he soon abandoned close to a hundred miles of telegraph wire along the route from the river-crossing, all the way back to the outskirts of Memphis.

Washburn put the best possible interpretation on the outcome of the visit paid him by the raiders. "The whole Expedition was barren of spoils," he wrote his congressman brother Elihu. "They were in so great a hurry to get away that they carried off hardly anything. I lost two fine horses, which is about the biggest loss of anybody." So did Sherman tend to look on the bright side of the event. "If you get the chance," he wired Washburn on August 24, the day after the big stampede, "send word to Forrest that I admire his dash but not his judgment. The oftener he runs his head against Memphis the better."

There was much in that; Forrest's activities, these past four months, had been limited to North Mississippi and the southwest corner of Tennessee, with the result that he had been kept off Sherman's all-important supply line throughout this critical span. But it also rather missed the point that, with Memphis under cower and afflicted with a bad case of the shakes, the Wizard now was free to ride in practically any direction he or his superiors might choose: including Middle Tennessee, a region that nurtured a vital part of that supply line. The question was whether there was time enough, even if he were given his head at last, for Forrest's movement to be of much help to Hood in besieged Atlanta.

★　★　★

Encouraged by Wheeler's recent victories over Stoneman and McCook, which he believed more or less disposed of the blue cavalry as a threat, Hood by then had thrown his own cavalry deep into the Union rear in North Georgia and East Tennessee, hoping, as he explained in a wire requesting the President's approval, that by severing Sherman's life line he would provoke him into rashness or oblige him to retreat. Davis readily concurred, having urged such a strike on Johnston, without success, from the outset to the time of his removal. He replied that he shared Hood's hope that this would "compel the enemy to attack you in position," but added, rather pointedly, and in a tone not unlike Lincoln's when cautioning Grant, down near Richmond the month before, on the heels of repulses even more costly than Hood had just suffered around Atlanta: "The loss consequent upon attacking him in his intrenchments requires you to avoid that if practicable."

Wheeler set out on August 10, taking with him some 4500 effectives from his eight brigades and leaving about the same number behind, including William Jackson's three-brigade division, to patrol and protect Hood's flanks and rear while he was gone. His itinerary for the following week, northward along the Western & Atlantic, resembled a synopsis, in reverse, of the Johnston-Sherman contest back in May. Marietta, Cassville, Calhoun, Resaca: all were hit on a five-day ride that saw the destruction of some thirty miles of track and the rebuilt bridge across the Etowah. On August 14, after detaching one brigade to escort his prisoners and captured livestock back to Atlanta, he began a two-day demonstration against Dalton, then continued north, around and beyond Chattanooga, to Loudon. He intended to cross the Tennessee River there, but found it in flood and had to continue upstream nearly to Knoxville, where he detached two more brigades to wreck the railway bridge at Strawberry Plains, then turned southwest, beyond the Holston and the Clinch, to descend on the Nashville & Chattanooga Railroad, which he broke in several places before he recrossed the Tennessee at Tuscumbia, Alabama, on September 10, his twenty-eighth birthday. At a total cost of 150 casualties on this month-long raid, in the course of which he "averaged 25 miles a day [and] swam or forded 27 rivers," Wheeler reported the seizure of "1000 horses and mules, 200 wagons, 600 prisoners, and 1700 head of beef cattle," and claimed that his command had "captured, killed, or wounded three times the greatest effective strength it has ever been able to carry into action."

As an exploit, even after allowing for the exaggeration common to most cavalry reports, this was much. In other respects, however, it amounted to little more than a prime example of how events could transform a tactical triumph into a strategic cipher. Although Wheeler accomplished practically everything he was sent out to do, and on a grander scale than had been intended, the only real effect of the raid was not on Sherman — whose work gangs were about as quick to repair damage to the railroads as the gray troopers had been to inflict it — but on Hood, who was deprived thereby of half his cavalry during the critical final stage of the contest for Atlanta; which, in point of fact, had ended before Wheeler recrossed the Tennessee. One further result of the raid, also negative, was that Hood at last was convinced, as he said later, "that no sufficiently effective number of cavalry could be assembled in the Confederacy to interrupt the enemy's line of supplies to an extent to compel him to retreat."

Sherman was no more provoked into rashness than he was into retreat, but Wheeler's absence did encourage him, despite the recent failure of such efforts, to venture still another cavalry strike at the Macon & Western, Hood's only remaining rail connection, whose rupture would oblige him to evacuate Atlanta for lack of supplies. Another persuasive factor was Judson Kilpatrick. Back in the saddle after a ten-week convalescence from the wound he had taken at Resaca, he seemed to Sherman just the man to lead the raid. Unlike Garrard — who, in Sherman's words, would flinch if he spotted "a horseman in the distance with a spyglass" — Little Kil had a reputation as a fighter, and though in the present instance he was advised "not to fight but to work," only boldness would assure success. Reinforced by two brigades from Garrard, the bandy-legged New Jerseyite took his division southeast out of Sandtown on the night of August 18, under instructions to "break up the Macon [rail]road about Jonesboro," twenty miles below Atlanta. He got there late the following day, unimpeded, and began at once to carry out Sherman's orders, passed on by Schofield: "Tell Kilpatrick he cannot tear up too much track nor twist too much iron. It may save this army the necessity of making a long, hazardous flank march."

First he set fire to the depot, then turned his attention to the road itself. But before he had ripped up more than a couple of miles of track he was attacked from the rear by a brigade of Texans from Jackson's division. Kilpatrick pressed on south, pursued by this and Jackson's other two brigades, but ran into infantry intrenched near Lovejoy Station and veered east, then north to reënter his own lines at Decatur. That was on August 22, and he proudly reported that he had done enough damage to Hood's life line to remove it from use for the next ten days. Sherman was delighted: but only overnight. Next morning, heavy-laden supply trains came puffing into Atlanta over tracks he had been assured were demolished. Told "not to fight but to work," Kilpatrick apparently had not done much of either, or else the rebel crews were as adept at repairs as their Union counterparts north of the city. In any case, Sherman said later, "I became more than ever convinced that cavalry could not or would not work hard enough to disable a railroad properly, and therefore resolved at once to proceed to the execution of my original plan."

This was the massive counterclockwise slide, the "grand left wheel around Atlanta," which he had designed to bring on the fall of the city by transferring all but one of his seven infantry corps around to the south, astride its only rail connection with the outside world. Interrupted at Ezra Church in late July, the maneuver had been resumed only to stall again in the toils of Utoy Creek in early August. Since then, Sherman had sought by continuous long-range shelling, if not to convert the Gate City into "a desolation," as he had proposed two weeks ago, then in any case to reduce it to "a used-up community," and in this he had succeeded to a considerable extent, though not at a rate that matched his impatience, which was quickened by the spirit-lifting news of Farragut's triumph down in Mobile Bay. Now — Kilpatrick having failed, in Wheeler's absence, to spare him "the necessity of making a long, hazardous flank march" — he was ready to resume his ponderous shift. Leaving Slocum's corps (formerly Hooker's) north of Atlanta, securely intrenched in a position from which to observe the reaction there and also protect the railway bridge across the Chattahoochee, he pulled all three armies rearward out the Sandtown Road

on August 26 and started them south the following day in three wide-sweeping arcs, Howard and Schofield on the left and right, Thomas as usual in the center. Their respective objectives, all on the Macon Railroad, were Rough & Ready Station, four miles below East Point; Jonesboro, ten miles farther down the line; and a point about midway between the two. Thomas and Howard took off first, having longer routes to travel, and reached the inactive West Point Railroad next day at Red Oak and Fairburn, where

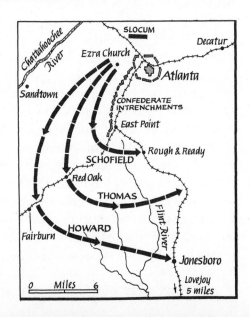

they were to swing east. Then Schofield set out on his march, which was shorter but was presumably much riskier, since he would be a good deal closer to the rebels massed in and around Atlanta. As it turned out, however, he met with no more resistance than Howard and Thomas had done in the course of their wider sweeps; which was practically none at all. Welcome as this nonintervention was, Sherman also found it strange, particularly in contrast to his opponent's previous violent reaction to any attempt to move across his front or round his flank.

Hood's reaction, or nonaction, was stranger than any Federal supposed, being founded on a total misconception of what his adversary was up to. Not that his error had been illogically arrived at; it had not; but the logic, such as it was, was based insubstantially on hope. Suddenly, on August 26, after weeks of intensive shelling, the bombardment of Atlanta stopped as abruptly as a dropped watch, and when patrols went out at midday to investigate this unexpected silence — which somehow was even heavier with tension than the diurnal uproar that preceded it — they found the Union trenches empty and skirmishers posted rear-guard-fashion along and on both sides of the road leading west to Sandtown and the Chattahoochee. Apparently a mass movement was in progress in that direction. Only on the north side of the city, in position to defend the indispensable railroad crossing and forward base, were the old works still occupied in strength. Hood's spirits took a leap at the news; for the brigade detached by Wheeler the week before, up near Calhoun, had returned that morning with its haul of prisoners and cattle and a first-hand account of the extensive damage so far done to the Western & Atlantic, including the burning of the vital span across the Etowah. Wheeler himself, according to a report just in, was beyond Chattanooga with the rest of his command, preparing by now to cross the Tennessee River and descend on the blue supply line below Nashville. All this was bound to have its effect; Sherman must already be hurting for lack of food and ammunition. Indeed, there was testimony on hand that this was so. Six days ago, a woman whose home was inside Schofield's lines had appealed to one of his division commanders for rations, only to be refused. "No," she was told; "I would like to draw, myself. I have been living on short rations for seven days, and now that your people have torn up our railroad and stolen our beef cattle, we must live a damned sight shorter." On such evidence as this, and out of his own sore need for a near miracle, Hood based his conclusion that Sherman, threatened with the specter of starvation by Wheeler's disruption of his life line, was in full retreat across the Chattahoochee with all of his corps but one, left temporarily in position north of the city to cover the withdrawal by rail of what remained of his sorely depleted stockpile of provisions.

Orders went out for Jackson to bring his overworked troopers in from the flanks and take up the pursuit toward Sandtown. Jackson did, beginning next day, but reported that the bluecoats seemed to him to be regrouping, not retreating. Hood rejected this assessment, preferring to believe that his cavalry simply lacked the strength to penetrate the Federal rear guard. So near the end of his military tether that he had nothing to fall back on but delusion, he held his three corps in the Atlanta intrenchments, which had been extended down to East Point, awaiting developments.

They were not long in coming. Sherman had Howard and Thomas spend a day astride the West Point Railroad, "breaking it up thoroughly," as he said, lest the rebels someday try to put it back in commission. His veterans were highly skilled at such work by now, and he later described how they went about it. "The track was heaved up in sections the length of a regiment, then separated rail by rail; bonfires were made of the ties and of fence rails on which the rails were heated, carried to trees or telegraph poles, wrapped around and left to cool." Not content with converting the rails into scrap iron — "Sherman neckties," the twisted loops were called — he then proceeded against the roadbed itself. "To be still more certain, we filled up many deep cuts with trees, brush, and earth, and commingled with them loaded shells, so arranged that they would explode on an attempt to haul out the bushes. The explosion of one such shell would have demoralized a gang of negroes, and thus would have prevented even the attempt to clear the road." Next morning, August 30, he started both armies east toward the headwaters of Flint River, which flowed south between the two converging railroads, the one he had just undone in his rear and the one ahead, whose loss would undo Hood.

Elated at the prospect of achieving this objective, he accompanied Thomas on the march, and as they approached the Flint that afternoon — still without encountering serious opposition, though the Macon road lay only a scant two miles beyond the river — he exulted to the Virginian riding beside him: "I have Atlanta as certainly as if it were in my hand!"

Hood by now had begun to emerge from his wishful three-day dream. Reports that Union infantry had appeared in strength on the West Point road the day before, above and below Fairburn and Red Oak, obliged him to concede that part at least of Sherman's host was headed for something other than the Chattahoochee River, and when follow-up dispatches informed him this morning that the same blue wrecking force was moving eastward, in the direction of the Macon road, he knew he had to act. All surplus goods were ordered packed for shipment out of the nearly beleaguered city, by whatever routes might be available when the time came, and Hardee was told to shift to Rough & Ready, bracing his corps for the defense of the rail supply line, there or farther down, while Lee moved out to take his place at East Point, under instructions to be ready for a march in either direction, southward to reinforce Hardee or back north to assist Stewart in the close-up defense of Atlanta, depending on which turned out to need him worst. Old Straight remained in the works that rimmed the city, not only because of Slocum's hovering menace, but also because Hood had revised — indeed, reversed — his estimate of the enemy's intentions. It seemed to him that Sherman was trying to draw him out of Atlanta with a strike at his supply line, say by half the Federal force, so that when he moved to meet this threat, the other half, concealed till then near the Chattahoochee, could swoop down and take the city. Hood's job, as he assessed it, was to avoid being lured out in such numbers that Atlanta would fall in their absence, its scantly manned intrenchments overrun, and yet at the same time to prevent the seizure or destruction of the Macon Railroad, whose loss would require him to give up the city for lack of subsistence.

Caught thus between the blue devil and the deep blue sea, Hood saw no choice, now that he had been shaken out of the dream that transformed his red-haired opponent from a destroyer into a deliverer, except to try to meet these separate dangers as they developed. All in all, outnumbered as he was, the situation was pretty much as Sherman was describing it to Thomas even now, a dozen-odd miles to the south: "I have Atlanta as certainly as if it were in my hand." What had the earmarks of a frothy boast — of a kind all too common in a war whose multi-thumbed commanders were often in need of reassurance, even if they had to express it themselves — was in fact merely a tactical assessment, somewhat florid but still a good deal more accurate than most.

Or maybe not. When Hood heard from Hardee, around midday, that the blue march seemed to be aimed at both Rough & Ready and Jonesboro, ten miles apart, he saw once more a chance to strike the enemy in detail. And having perceived this he was no less willing to undertake it than he had been three times before, in as many costly sorties. Now as then he improvised a slashing assault designed to subject a major portion of the Union host to destruction. His plan — refined to deal with a later, more specific report that Logan's corps had crossed the Flint that afternoon and gone into camp within cannon range of Jonesboro, supported only by Kilpatrick's horsemen, while the other two corps of the Army of the Tennessee remained on the west bank of the stream — was for Hardee to fall upon this exposed segment early next morning and "drive the enemy, at all hazards, into Flint River, in their rear." Moreover, when the rest of Howard's troops attempted to come to Logan's assistance they could be whipped in detail with help from Lee, whose corps would set out down the railroad from East Point at the same time Hardee's moved from Rough & Ready on a night march that would put them in position for attack at first light, August 31. To make certain that his plan was understood, Hood wired both generals to leave their senior division commanders in charge of the march to Jonesboro and report to him in Atlanta, by rail, for the usual face-to-face instructions, which experience had shown were even more necessary than he had thought when he first took charge of the Army of Tennessee.

In Atlanta that night, at the council of war preceding this Fourth Sortie, Hood expanded his plan to include a follow-up attack September 1. After sharing in tomorrow's assault, which would drive the Federals away from the Macon road and back across the Flint, Lee was to return to Rough & Ready Station, where he would be joined by Stewart for an advance next morning, down the west bank of the river, that would strike the flank of the crippled bluecoats, held in position overnight by Hardee, and thus complete their destruction. This was in some ways less risky and in others riskier than Hood knew, believing as he did that only Howard's army was south of the city, which thus would be scantly protected from an assault by Thomas and Schofield. For that reason, Hood took what he believed was the post of gravest responsibility: Atlanta, whose defenses would be manned, through this critical time, only by Jackson's dismounted troopers and units of the Georgia militia. It was late when the council broke up and Hardee, who was put in charge of the attack, boarded a switch engine for a fast ride to Jonesboro. He arrived before dawn, expecting to find his and Lee's corps being posted for the assault at daybreak. Neither was there; nor could he find anyone who could tell him where they were — Lee's, which that general must have rejoined by now, or his own, which had set out southward from Rough & Ready the night before.

Howard remained all morning in what he called a "saucy position," content to reinforce Logan's corps, intrenched on the east bank of the Flint, with a single division from Dodge, who was away recuperating from being struck on the forehead by a bullet the week before. He expected to be attacked by a rebel force that seemed to be gathering in Jonesboro, less than a mile across the way; that was why he kept most of his troops out of sight on the west side of the river, hoping, now that Logan's men had had plenty of time to strengthen their intrenchments, that the graybacks would come to him, rather than wait for him to storm their works along the railroad. But when nothing had come of this by the time the sun swung past the overhead, he decided he would have to prod them. He told Logan to move out at 3 o'clock. At 2.45, just as Black Jack's veterans were preparing to leave their trenches, long lines of butternut infantry came surging out of Jonesboro in far greater numbers than Howard had expected while trying to provoke them into making an attack.

Hardee was even tardier in launching Hood's Fourth Sortie than he had been in either of the other two committed to his charge, the first having opened two hours behind schedule, the second nearly seven, and this one more than nine. Yet here again the blame was hard to fix. Cleburne, left in corps command when Old Reliable went to Atlanta the night before, had found enemy units blocking his line of march and had had to detour widely around them, which delayed his arrival in Jonesboro until an hour after sunrise; while Lee, whose longer route was even worse obstructed, did not come up till well past noon. As a result, it was 2 o'clock before Hardee could get the two road-worn corps into jump-off positions and issue orders for the attack. These were for Cleburne to turn the enemy's right and for Lee to move against their front as soon as he heard Cleburne's batteries open. Such a signal had often failed in the past, and now it did so here. Mistaking the clatter of skirmishers' rifles for the roar of battle, Lee started forward on his own and thus exposed his corps to the concentrated fire of the whole Union line, with demoralizing results. Cleburne then moved out, driving Kilpatrick's troopers promptly across the Flint, but found Logan's works too stoutly held for him to effect a lodgment without assistance. Hardee urged Lee to renew his stalled advance, only to be told that it was impossible; Howard was bringing reserves across the river to menace the shaken right. In reaction, Hardee called off the attack and ordered both Cleburne and Lee to take up defensive positions, saying later: "I now consider this a fortunate circumstance, for success against such odds could at best have only been partial and bloody, while defeat would have [meant] almost inevitable destruction to the army."

That ended the brief, disjointed Battle of Jonesboro; or half ended it, depending on what Howard would do now. Lee and Cleburne had suffered more than 1700 casualties between them, Logan and Kilpatrick less than a fourth as many, and these were the totals for this last day of August, as it turned out, since Howard did not press the issue. Late that night, in response to Hood's repeated summons, Hardee detached Lee's three divisions for the return march north, tomorrow's scheduled follow-up offensive down the west bank of the Flint having been ruled out by the failure of today's attempt to set up Howard for the kill.

What Hood now wanted Lee for, though, was to help Stewart hold Atlanta against the assault he expected Sherman to make next morning with the other two Federal armies, which he still thought were lurking northwest of the city. He presently learned better. Soon after dark, reports came in that bluecoats were across the Macon road in strength at Rough & Ready, as well as at several other points between there and Jonesboro. Lee not only confirmed this when he reached East Point at daylight, having managed to slip between the enemy columns in the darkness; he also identified them as belonging to Schofield and Thomas. This was a shock, and its meaning was all too clear. Atlanta was doomed. The only remaining question, now that Sherman had the bulk of his command astride the city's last rail supply line, squarely between Hardee and the other two corps, was whether the Army of

Tennessee was doomed as well. Hood and his staff got to work at once on plans for the evacuation of Atlanta and the reunion, if possible, of his divided army, so that it could be saved to fight another day.

Such a reunion was not going to include Hardee's third of that army if Sherman had his way. Primarily he had undertaken this six-corps grand left wheel as a railroad-wrecking expedition, designed to bring on the fall of Atlanta by severing its life line, but now that he saw in Hardee's isolation an opportunity to annihilate him, he extended its scope to achieve just that. Both Schofield and Thomas were told to move on Jonesboro without delay, there to combine their three corps with Howard's three — a total of more than 60,000, excluding cavalry — for an assault on Hardee's 12,500, still licking the wounds they had suffered in their repulse the day before. While this convergence was in progress Howard put the rest of Dodge's corps across the Flint, where Logan confronted the rebels in their works, and sent Blair to cut the railroad south of town and stand in the path of any escape in that direction. Noon came and went, this hot September 1, still with no word from Thomas or Schofield, who were to attack the Confederates on their right while Howard clamped them in position from the front. Sherman fumed at the delay, knowing the graybacks were hard at work improving their intrenchments, and kept fuming right up to 3 o'clock, when the first of Slow Trot Thomas's two corps arrived, formerly John Palmer's but now under Jeff C. Davis, Palmer having departed in a huff after a squabble with Schofield, who he claimed had mishandled his troops in the Utoy Creek fiasco. The other Cumberland corps, David Stanley's, was nowhere in sight, and in fact did not turn up till after sundown, having got lost on its cross-country march, and Schofield moved so slowly from Rough & Ready, tearing up track as he went, that he arrived even later than Stanley. Combined with the detachment of Blair to close the southward escape hatch, the nonappearance of these two corps reduced the size of the attacking force by half. But that still left Sherman with considerably better than twice the number he faced, and he also enjoyed the advantage of having Davis come down unexpectedly on the enemy right, which was bent back across the railroad north of town.

Davis was a driver, a hard-mannered regular who had come up through the ranks, thirty-six years old, with wavy hair and a bushy chin-beard, a long thin nose and the pale, flat eyes of a killer; which he was. Still a brigadier despite his lofty post and a war record dating back to Sumter, he had been denied promotion for the past two years because of the scandal attending his pistol slaying of Bull Nelson in Kentucky, long ago in '62, and he welcomed such assignments as this present one at Jonesboro, seeing in them opportunities to demonstrate a worth beyond the grade at which he had been stopped in his climb up the military ladder. He put his men in line astride the railroad — three divisions, containing as many troops as Hardee had in all — and sent them roaring down against the rebel flank at 4 o'clock. Cleburne's division was posted there, in trenches Lee had occupied the day before. Repulsed, Davis dropped back, regrouped quickly, and then came on again in a mass assault that went up and over the barricade to land in the midst of Brigadier General Dan Govan's veteran Arkansas brigade. Two batteries were overrun and Govan himself captured, along with more than half his men. "They're rolling them up like a sheet of paper!" Sherman cried, watching from an observation post on Howard's front.

But Granbury's Texans were next in line, and there the rolling stopped. Cleburne shored up his redrawn flank, massing fire on the lost salient, and Davis had all he could do to hold what he had won. Unwilling to risk a frontal assault by Howard, Sherman saw that what he needed now was added pressure on the weakened enemy right by Stanley, who was supposed to be coming up in rear of Davis. Angrily he turned to Thomas, demanding to know where Stanley was, and the heavy-set Virginian, who already had sent courier after courier in search of the errant corps, not only rode off in person to join the hunt, but also did so in a manner that later caused his red-haired superior to remark that this was "the only time during the campaign I can recall seeing General Thomas urge his horse into a gallop." Even so, the sun had set by the time Stanley turned up, and night fell before he could put his three divisions in attack formation. Darkness ended this second day of the Battle of Jonesboro, which cost Sherman 1275 casualties, mostly from Davis's corps, and Hardee just under 1000, two thirds of them captured in the assault that cracked his flank.

Disgruntled, Sherman bedded down, hopeful that tomorrow, with Schofield up alongside Stanley, he would complete the fate he planned for Hardee. He had trouble sleeping, he would recall, and soon after midnight, to add to his fret, "there arose toward Atlanta sounds of shells exploding, and other sounds like that of musketry." This was disturbing; Hood might well be doing to Slocum what he himself intended to do to Hardee. Yesterday he had instructed Thomas to have Slocum "feel forward to Atlanta, as boldly as he can," adding: "Assure him that we will fully occupy the attention of the rebel army outside of Atlanta." This last he had failed to do, except in part, and it seemed to him likely, from those rumblings twenty miles to the north, that he had thereby exposed Slocum to destruction by two thirds of Hood's command. Other listeners about the campfire disagreed, interpreting the muffled clatter as something other than battle, and Sherman decided to settle the issue by visiting a nearby farmhouse, where he had seen lights burning earlier in the evening. Shouts brought the farmer out into the yard in his nightshirt. Had he lived here long? He had. Had he heard such rumblings before? Indeed he had. That was the way it sounded when there was heavy fighting up around Atlanta.

The noise faded, then died away; which might have an even more gruesome meaning. Sherman returned to his campfire, still unable to sleep. Then at 4 o'clock it rose again, with the thump and crump and muttering finality of a massive coup de grâce. Again it died, this time for good. Dawn came, and with the dawn a new enigma. Thomas and Schofield moved as ordered, the latter on the left to sweep across the rebel rear — "We want to destroy the enemy," Sherman told them, anxious to be done with the work at hand — but found that Hardee had departed under cover of darkness and the distractive far-off rumblings from the north. Sherman took up the pursuit, southward down the railroad, still wondering what had happened deep in his rear. This was the hundred and twentieth day of the campaign, and while he was at Jonesboro another month had slipped into the past, costing him 7000 casualties and his adversary 7500: a total to date of 31,500 Federals and 35,000 Confederates, rough figures later precisely tabulated at 31,687 and 34,979 respectively. Close to 20,000 of the latter had been suffered by Hood in the nearly seven weeks since he took over from Johnston, while Sherman had lost just under 15,000 in that span.

Presently, as the six blue corps toiled southward down the railroad in search of Hardee's three vanished divisions, Schofield sent word that he took last night's drumfire rumblings from the direction of Atlanta to be the sound of Hood blowing up his unremovable stores, in preparation for evacuation. Two hours later, at 10.25, he followed this with a report that a Negro had just come into his lines declaring that the rebs were departing the city "in great confusion and disorder." Unconvinced, still troubled about "whether General Slocum had felt forward and become engaged in a real battle," Sherman kept up his pursuit of Hardee until he came upon him near Lovejoy Station, six miles down the line, his corps posted in newly dug intrenchments "as well constructed and as strong as if these Confederates had a week to prepare them." Such was his assessment after a tentative 4 o'clock probe was savagely repulsed. "I do not wish to waste lives by an assault," he warned Howard, explaining more fully to Thomas: "Until we hear from Atlanta the exact truth, I do not care about your pushing your men against breastworks." Still fretted by doubts about Slocum, he maintained his position of cautious observation through sunset into darkness. "Nothing positive from Atlanta," he informed Schofield within half an hour of midnight, "and that bothers me."

Finally, between then and sunup, September 3, a courier arrived with a dispatch from Slocum, who was not only safe but was safe inside Atlanta. Alerted by last night's racket, just across the way — it turned out to be the explosion of 81 carloads of ammunition, together with five locomotives, blown up in relays when they were found to be cut off from escape by the loss of the Macon road — he had felt his way forward at daylight to the city limits, where the commander of his lead division encountered a delegation of civilians. "Sir," their leader said with a formal bow. His name, it developed, was James M. Calhoun, and that was strangely fitting, even though no kinship connected him with the South Carolina original, John C. "The fortunes of war have placed the city of Atlanta in your hands. As mayor of the city I ask protection for noncombatants and private property." Slocum telegraphed the news to Washington: "General Sherman has taken Atlanta," and passed the word to his chief, approaching Lovejoy by then, that Hood had begun his withdrawal at 5 p.m. the day before, southward down the Mc-Donough Road and well to the east of the Macon & Western, down which Howard and Thomas and Schofield were marching.

This meant that Hood had crossed their front and flank with Stewart and Lee and the Georgia militia, last night and yesterday, and by now had reunited his army in the intrenchments hard ahead at Love-joy Station. Wise by hindsight, Sherman began to see that he had erred in going for Hardee, snug in his Jonesboro works, when he might have struck for the larger and more vulnerable prize in retreat on the Mc-Donough Road beyond. Moreover, if he had been unable to pound the graybacks to pieces while he had them on the Atlanta anvil, there seemed little chance for success in such an effort now that they were free to maneuver as they chose. Such at last was the price he paid for having redefined his objective, not as the Army of Tennessee — "Break it up," Grant had charged him at the outset, before Dalton — but rather as the city that army had been tied to, until now.

In any case, he had it, and he was ready and anxious to take possession in person. "Atlanta is ours, and fairly won," he wired Halleck. "I shall not push much farther in this raid, but in a day or so will move to Atlanta and give my men some rest."

✗ 3 ✗

Slocum's wire, received in Washington on the night of the day it was sent — "General Sherman has taken Atlanta" — ended a hot-weather span of anxiety even sorer than those that followed the two Bull Runs, back in the first two summers of the war. The prospect of stalemate, at this late stage, brought on a despondency as deep as outright defeat had done in those earlier times, when the national spirit displayed a resilience it had lost in the course of a summer that not only was bloody beyond all past imagining, but also saw Early within plain view of the Capitol dome and Democrats across the land anticipating a November sweep. Farragut's coup, down in Mobile Bay, provided no more than a glimmer of light, perfunctorily discerned before it guttered out in the gloom invoked by Sherman's reproduction, on the outskirts of Atlanta, of Grant's failure to take Richmond when he reached it the month before. Both wound up, apparently stalled, some twenty miles beyond their respective objectives, and by the end of August it had begun to appear that neither of them, having overshot the mark, was going to get back where he had been headed at the outset.

Nowhere, East or West or in between, was the disenchantment so complete as it was on the outskirts of Petersburg by then. Partly this was because of the high price paid to get there (Meade's casualties, exclusive of Butler's, were more than twice as heavy as Sherman's, though the latter had traveled nearly twice as far by his zigzag route) and partly too because, time and again, the public's and the army's expectations had been lifted only to be dashed, more often than not amid charges of incredible blundering, all up and down the weak-linked chain of command. A case in point, supplementing the fiasco that attended the original attack from across the James, was an operation that came to be called "The Crater," which occurred in late July and marked a new high (or low) for mismanagement at or near the top, surpassing even Cold Harbor in that regard, if not in bloodshed.

Early that month, after the failure of his probe for the Weldon Railroad in late June, Grant asked Meade how he felt about undertaking a new offensive against Lee's center or around his flank. Faced as he was with the loss of Wright, whose corps was being detached just then to counter Early's drive on Washington, Meade replied that he was doubtful about the result of either a flank or a frontal effort, citing "the facility with which the enemy can interpose to check an onward movement." However, lest his chief suppose that he was altogether without aggressive instincts or intentions — which, in point of fact, he very nearly was by now — Meade did let fall that he had in progress a work designed to permit a thrust, not through or around, but *under* the Confederate intrenchments. Burnside was digging a mine.

The proposal had come from a regimental commander, Lieutenant Colonel Henry Pleasants, whose 48th Pennsylvania was made up largely of volunteers from the anthracite fields of Schuylkill County, one of whom he happened to hear remark, while peering through a firing slit at a rebel bastion some 150 uphill yards across the way: "We could blow that damned fort out of existence if we could run a mine shaft under it." Formerly a civil engineer engaged in railroad tunneling, Pleasants liked the notion and took a sketch of it to his division commander, Brigadier General Robert Potter, who passed it along to corps. Burnside told Pleasants to start digging, then went himself to Meade for approval and assistance. He got Meade's nod, apparently because the work at least would keep some bored men busy for a time, but not his help, his staff having advised that the project was impractical from the engineering point of view. No such tunnel could exceed 400 feet in length, the experts said, that being the limit at which fresh air could be provided without ventilation shafts, and this one was projected to extend for more than 500 feet from the gallery entrance to the powder chamber at its end.

Pleasants had been hard at work since June 25, the day Burnside told him to start burrowing into the steep west bank of an abandoned railway cut, directly in rear of his picket line and well hidden from enemy lookouts. By assigning his men to shifts so that the digging went forward round the clock, he managed to complete the tunnel within a month — though his miners later claimed they could have done the job in less than half that time, if they had been given the proper tools. Not that Pleasants hadn't done his best in that regard. Denied any issue of special implements, such as picks, he contrived his own with the help of regimental blacksmiths, converted hardtack boxes into barrows for moving dirt, took over a wrecked sawmill to cut timbers and planks for shoring up the gallery walls and roof, and even borrowed a theodolite, all the way from Washington, when Meade's engineers declined to lend him one of theirs. Technical problems he solved in much the same improvisatory fashion, including some which these same close-fisted experts defined as prohibitive; ventilation, for example. Just inside the entrance he installed an airtight canvas door and beneath it ran a square wooden pipe along the floor of the shaft to the diggers at the end, extending it as they progressed. A fireplace near the sealed door sent heated air up its brush-masked chimney, creating a draft that drew the stale air from the far end of the tunnel and pulled in fresh air through the pipe, whose mouth was beyond the door. Working in the comparative comfort of a gallery five feet high, four feet wide at the bottom and two feet at the top — they had sweated and strained and wheezed and shivered through longer hours, with considerably less headroom and under far worse breathing conditions, back home in the Pennsylvania coal fields — the miners completed 511 feet of shaft by July 17.

This put them directly under the rebel outwork, whose defenders they could hear walking about, twenty feet above their heads, apparently unmindful of the malevolent, mole-like activity some half-dozen yards below the ground they stood on. Next day the soldier miners began digging laterally, right and left, to provide a powder chamber, 75 feet long, under the enemy bastion and the trenches on both flanks. By July 23 the pick and shovel work was done. After a four-day rest, Pleasants brought in 320 kegs of black powder, weighing 25 pounds each, and distributed this gritty four-ton mass among eight connected magazines, sandbagged to direct the explosion upward. When his requisition for insulated wire and a galvanic battery did not come through, he got hold of two fifty-foot fuzes, spliced them together, then secured one end to the monster charge and ran the other back down the gallery as far as it would reach; after which he replaced the earth of the final forty feet of tunnel, firmly tamped to provide a certain backstop.

That was on July 28. All that remained was to put a match to the fuze, and get out before the boom.

Next afternoon, with the mine scheduled to be exploded early the following morning, Burnside assembled his division commanders to give them last-minute instructions for the assault that was to be launched through the resultant gap in the rebel works. Of these there were four, though only three of their divisions had done front-line duty so far in the campaign; the fourth, led by Brigadier General Edward Ferrero, was composed of two all-Negro brigades whose service up to now had been confined to guarding trains and rearward installations, largely because of the continuing supposition — despite conflicting evidence, West and East — that black men simply were not up to combat. "Is not a Negro as good as a white man to stop a bullet?" someone asked Sherman about this time, over in Georgia. "Yes; and a sandbag is better," he replied. Like many eastern generals he believed that former slaves had their uses in war, but not as soldiers. Burnside felt otherwise, and what was more he backed up his contention by directing that Ferrero's division, which was not only the freshest but was also by now the largest of the four, would lead tomorrow's predawn charge. By way of preparation, he had had the two brigades spend the past week rehearsing the attack until every member knew just what he was to do, and how; that is, rush promptly forward, as soon as the mine was sprung, and expand the gap so that the other three divisions, coming up behind, could move un-opposed across the Jerusalem Plank Road and onto the high ground immediately in rear of the blasted enemy intrenchments, which would give them a clear shot at Petersburg itself.

He was in high spirits, partly because the digging had gone so well and partly because Meade and Grant, catching a measure of his enthusiasm as the tunnel neared completion, had expanded the operation. Not only were Warren's and Baldy Smith's corps ordered to stand by for a share in exploiting the breakthrough — which was to be given close-up support by no less than 144 field pieces, mortars, and siege guns: more artillery, pound for pound, than had been massed by either side at Gettysburg — but Grant also sent Hancock's corps, along with two of Sheridan's divisions, to create a diversion, and if possible score an accompanying breakthrough, on the far side of the James. Hancock, who had returned to duty the week before, found the Confederates heavily reinforced in front of Richmond: as did Sheridan, who was worsted in a four-hour fight with Hampton on the day the fuze was laid to Pleasants's mine. Still, the feint served its purpose by drawing large numbers of graybacks away from the intended scene of the main effort, about mid-way down the five-mile rebel line below the Appomattox. Intelligence reported that five of Lee's eight infantry divisions were now at Bermuda Hundred or north of the James, leaving Beauregard with only three divisions, some 18,000 men in all, for the defense of the Petersburg rail hub. Moreover, there still was time for Hancock to return tomorrow — the day of Burnside's last-minute council of war — to lend still greater weight to the assault that would accompany the blasting of the under-manned enemy works before daylight next morning.

Burnside was happily passing this latest news along to his lieu-tenants when he was interrupted by a courier from army headquarters, bearing a message that had an effect not unlike the one expected, across the way, when the mine was sprung tomorrow. It contained an order from Meade, approved by Grant, for the assault to be spearheaded not by Ferrero's well-rehearsed Negroes, but by one of the white divisions. This change, which landed like a bomb in the council chamber, was provoked by racism; racism in reverse. "If we put the colored troops in front and [the attack] should prove a failure," Grant would testify at the subsequent investigation, "it would then be said, and very properly, that we were shoving those people ahead to get killed because we did not care anything about them."

Stunned, Burnside tried to get the order rescinded, only to be told that it would stand; Meade was not about to give his Abolitionist critics this chance to bring him down with charges that he had exposed black recruits to slaughter in the forefront of a long-shot operation. By now the scheduled assault was less than twelve hours off, all but four of them hours of darkness, and the ruff-whiskered general, too shaken to decide which of his three unrehearsed white divisions should take the lead, had their commanders draw straws for the assignment. It fell to Brigadier General James H. Ledlie, a former heavy artilleryman, least experienced of the three. Potter and Brigadier General Orlando Willcox would attack in turn, behind Ledlie; Ferrero would bring up the rear.

As they departed to alert their troops, Burnside could find con-solation only in reports that the Confederates — two South Carolina regiments, posted in support of the four-gun battery poised above the sealed-off powder chamber — seemed to have abandoned their former suspicion that they were about to be blown skyward. For a time last week they had tried countermining, without success, and when the underground digging stopped, July 23, so did their attempts at inter-section. Apparently they too had experts who advised them that such a tunnel was impracticable; with the result that when the sound of picks and shovels stopped, down below, they decided that the Yanks had given up, probably after a disastrous cave-in or mounting losses from asphyxiation.

Eventually the troops were brought up in the darkness, groping their way over unfamiliar terrain to take up assigned positions for the jump-off: Ledlie's division out front, just in back of the ridge where the pickets were dug in, Potter's and Willcox's along the slope of the rail-way cut, and Ferrero's along its bottom, aggrieved at having been shunted to the rear. Elsewhere along the Union line the other corps stood by, including Hancock's, which had returned from its demonstration beyond the James. Shortly after 3 o'clock Pleasants entered the tunnel to light the fuze. The guns and mortars were laid, ammunition stacked and cannoneers at the ready, lanyards taut. Burnside had his watch out, observing the creep of its hands toward 3.30, the specified time for the springing of the mine. 3.30 finally came; but not the explosion. Half an hour went by, and still the night was black, unsplit by flame. Another half hour ticked past, bringing the first gray hint of dawn to the rearward sky, and though Pleasants had accepted his mine-boss sergeant's offer to go back into the tunnel and investigate the delay, there still was no blast. Grant, losing patience, considered telling Burnside to forget the explosion and get on with his 15,000-man assault. Daylight grew, much faster now, and the flat eastern rim of earth was tinted rose, anticipating the bulge of the rising sun, by the time the sergeant and a lieutenant who had volunteered to join him — Harry Reese and Jacob Douty were their names — found that the fuze had burned out at the splice. They cut and relit it and scrambled for the tunnel entrance, a long 150 yards away, emerging just before 4.44, when the 8000-pound charge, twenty feet below the rebel works, erupted.

"A slight tremor of the earth for a second, then the rocking as of an earthquake," an awed captain would recall, "and, with a tremendous blast which rent the sleeping hills beyond, a vast column of earth and smoke shoots upward to a great height, its dark sides flashing out sparks of fire, hangs poised for a moment in mid-air, and then, hurtling down with a roaring sound, showers of stones, broken timbers and blackened human limbs, subsides — the gloomy pall of darkening smoke flushing to an angry crimson as it floats away to meet the morning sun." Another watcher of that burgeoning man-made cloud of dust and turmoil, a brigadier with Hancock, left an impression he never suspected would be repeated at the dawn of a far deadlier age of warfare, just over eighty years away: "Without form or shape, full of red flames and carried on a bed of lightning flashes, it mounted toward heaven with a detonation of thunder [and] spread out like an immense mushroom whose stem seemed to be of fire and its head of smoke."

Added to the uproar was the simultaneous crash of many cannon, fired by tense gunners as soon as they saw the ground begin to heave from the overdue explosion. Ledlie's men, caught thus between two shock waves, looked out and saw the rising mass of earth, torn from the hillside hard ahead, mount up and up until it seemed to hover directly above them, its topmost reaches glittering in the full light of the not-yet-risen sun. As the huge cluster started down, they recovered at least in part from their shock and reacted by breaking in panic for the rear. This was not too serious; their officers got them back in line within ten minutes and started them forward before the dust and smoke had cleared.

But what happened next was serious indeed. In his dismay over the last-minute change in orders, Burnside had neglected to have the defensive tangle of obstacles cleared from in front of the parapets, with the result that the attack formation was broken up as soon as the troops set out. Instead of advancing on a broad front, as intended — a brigade in width, with the second brigade coming up in close support — they went forward through a hastily improvised ten-foot passway that not only delayed their start but also confined them to a meager file of wary individuals who advanced a scant one hundred yards, then stopped in awe of what they saw before them. Where the Confederate fort had stood there now was a monstrous crater, sixty feet across and nearly two hundred feet wide, ranging in depth from ten to thirty feet. All was silent down there on its rubbled floor except for the thin cries of the wounded — who, together with the killed, turned out to number 278 — mangled by the blast and buried to various depths by the debris.

As Ledlie's soldiers stood and gazed at this lurid moonscape, strewn with clods that ranged in size up to that of a small house, they not only forgot their instructions to fan out right and left in order to widen the breakthrough for the follow-up attack; they even forgot to keep moving. At last they did move, but not far. For more than a month their fighting had been confined to rifle pits and trenches, and now here at their feet was the biggest rifle pit in all the world. They leaped into it and busied themselves with helping the Carolinian survivors, many of whom, though badly dazed, had interesting things to say when they were uprooted and revived. Ledlie might have gotten his division back in motion by exhortation or example, but he was not available just now. He was immured in a bombproof well behind the lines, swigging away at a bottle of rum he had cadged from a staff surgeon. It later developed that this had been his custom all along, in times of strain. In any case, there he remained throughout what was to have been a fast-moving go-for-broke assault on Petersburg, by way of the gap Henry Pleasants had blown in the rebel line.

That gap was already larger than any Federal knew. When the mine was sprung, the reaction of the graybacks right and left of the hoisted battery was the same as that of the intended attackers across the way. They too bolted rearward, panicked by the fury of the blast, and thus broadened the unmanned portion of their line to about 400 yards. What was more, it remained so for some time. The second and third blue waves rolled forward, paused in turn on the near rim of the crater, much as the first had done, and then, like it, swept down in search of cover amid the rubble at the bottom. By then, most of the bolted Confederates had returned to their posts on the flanks of the excavation, and Beauregard was bringing up reinforcements, along with all the artillery he could lay hands on.

They arrived, men and guns, at about the time Burnside's fourth wave started forward. Loosed at last (but without Ferrero; he had joined Ledlie in the bombproof, nearly a quarter-mile away) the Negro soldiers advanced in good order. "We looks like men a-marching on, We looks like men of war," they sang as they came up in the wake of the other three divisions, which were scarcely to be seen, having vanished quite literally into the earth. Disdaining the crater, they swung around it, in accordance with the maneuver they had rehearsed, and drove for the high ground beyond. However, now that the defenders had rallied and been reinforced, they not only failed to get there; they also lost a solid third of their number in the attempt — 1327 out of just under 4000. "Unsupported, subjected to a galling fire from batteries on the flanks, and from infantry fire in front and partly on the flank," a witness later wrote, "they broke up in disorder and fell back to the crater."

Conditions there were not much better. In some ways they were worse. Presently they were much worse in every way. More than 10,000 men, crowded hip to hip in a steep-walled pen less than a quarter-acre in extent, presented the gray cannoneers with a compact target they did not neglect. Counterbattery work by the massed Union guns was excellent, but the surviving rebel pieces, including hard-to-locate mortars, still delivered what one occupant of the crater termed "as heavy a fire of canister as was ever poured continuously upon a single objective point." The result was bedlam, a Bedlam in flames, and this got worse as the enemy infantry grew bolder, inching closer to the rim of the pit, where marksmanship would be about as superfluous as if the shots were directed into a barrel of paralyzed fish. Anticipating this, some bluecoats chose to run the gauntlet back to their own lines, while others preferred to remain and risk the prospect: which was soon at hand. Around 9.30, with Grant's disgusted approval, Meade had cancelled the follow-up attack and told Burnside to withdraw his corps.

But that was easier said than carried out. Burnside by then had fallen into a state of euphoric despair, much as he had done at Fredericksburg twenty months ago, under similar circumstances, and delayed transmission of the order till after midday, apparently in hope of some miraculous deliverance. Shortly after noon, two brigades from Mahone's division — they had slipped away from Warren's front unseen — gained the lip of the crater, where they added rapid-fire rifle volleys to the horror down below, then followed up with a bayonet charge that shattered what little remained of blue resistance. Hundreds surrendered, thousands fled, more hundreds fell, and the so-called Battle of the Crater was soon over. It had cost Burnside 3828 men, nearly half of them captured or missing, and losses elsewhere along Meade's line raised the Union total above 4000 for the day; Confederate casualties, mostly wounded, came to about one third that number. By nightfall, all that remained as evidence of this latest bizarre attempt to break Lee's line was a raw scar, about midway down its length below the Appomattox, which in time would green over and loose its jagged look, but would never really heal.

Nor would a new bitterness Southerners felt as a result of this affair. Not only had they been blown up while sleeping — "a mean trick," they declared — but for the first time, here in the Old Dominion, black soldiers had been thrown into the thick of a large-scale fight. That was something far worse than a trick; that was infamy, to Lee's men's way of thinking. And for this they cursed their enemy in cold blood. "Eyes gleamed, teeth clenched," a nurse who tended Mahone's wounded would recall, "as they showed me the locks of their muskets, to which blood and hair still clung, when, after firing, without waiting to reload, they had clenched the barrels and fought hand to hand." Privately — like the troopers who stormed Fort Pillow, out in the wilder West — they admitted to having bayoneted men in the act of surrender, and they were by no means ashamed of the act, considering their view of the provocation. It was noted that from this time forward there were no informal truces in the vicinity of the Crater. Sniping was venomous and continuous, dawn to dusk, along that portion of the line.

Ledlie (but not Ferrero, who was somehow overlooked in the caterwaul that followed) presently departed, condemned by a Court of Inquiry for his part in the mismanagement of what Grant pronounced "the saddest affair I have witnessed in this war." Burnside left even sooner, hard on the heels of a violent argument with Meade, an exchange of recriminations which a staff observer said "went far toward confirming one's belief in the wealth and flexibility of the English language as a medium of personal dispute." Meade wanted the ruff-whiskered general court martialed for incompetence, but Grant, preferring a quieter procedure, sent him home on leave. "He will never return whilst *I* am here," Meade fumed.

Nor did he. Resigning from the service, Ambrose Everett Burnside, forty years old, returned to his business pursuits in Rhode Island, where he not only prospered but also recovered the geniality he had lost in the course of a military career that required him to occupy positions he himself had testified he was unqualified to fill. In time he went into politics, serving three terms as governor, and would die well into his second term as a U.S. senator, twenty years after the war began.

Tactically speaking, Lee no doubt regretted Burnside's departure. He would miss him, much as he missed McClellan, now in retirement, and John Pope and Joe Hooker, who had been shunted to outlying regions where their ineptitudes would be less costly to the cause they served. This was not to say that mistakes came cheap from those commanders who remained near the violent center. Meade's losses for July, swollen by the botched attempt to score an explosive breakthrough near its end, totaled 6367, and he had scarcely an inch of ground to show for their subtraction. Yet Lee could take small comfort in the knowledge that his own were barely half that. In contrast to his custom in the old aggressive days, when a battle was generally followed by a Federal retreat, he now not only derived no positive gain for his losses; he was also far less able to replace them, so near was the Confederacy to the bottom of its manpower barrel. "There is the chill of murder about the casualties of this month," one of his brigadiers reported from the Petersburg intrenchments. Even such one-sided triumphs as the Crater were getting beyond his means, and much the same thing could be said of Early's recent foray to the gates of Washington, which, for all its success in frightening the authorities there, had failed to lure the Army of the Potomac into staging another Cold Harbor south of the James.

That was what Lee had wanted, and even expected. "It is so repugnant to Grant's principles and practice to send troops from him," he wrote Davis, "that I had hoped before resorting to it he would have preferred attacking me." Instead, Grant had detached two corps whose partial arrival discouraged Early from storming the capital defenses and obliged him to fall back across the Potomac. After a brief rest at Leesburg, in defiance of the superior blue force charged with pressing his pursuit, Old Jube returned to the lower Shenandoah Valley and continued to maneuver between Winchester and Harpers Ferry, Jackson style, as if about to move on Washington again. Before his adversaries managed to combine against him — they were drawn from four separate departments, with desk-bound Halleck more or less in charge by telegraph — he lashed out at George Crook near Kernstown, July 24, and after inflicting close to 1200 casualties, drove him all the way north across the Potomac. Following this, in specific retaliation for Hunter's burning of the homes of three prominent Virginians, Early sent two brigades of cavalry under John McCausland to Chambersburg, Pennsylvania, to demand of its merchants, under penalty of its destruction, $100,000 in gold or a cool half-million in greenbacks. When they refused, McCausland evacuated the 3000 inhabitants and set fire to the business district. That was on July 30, the day of the Crater, and by midnight two thirds of the town was in ashes, another casualty of a war that was growing harsher by the month.

Lee's acute concern for Early — whose foot-loose corps, though badly outnumbered, not only continued to disrupt the plans of the Union high command by bristling aggressively on both banks of the Potomac just upstream from Washington, but also served through this critical stretch of time as a covering force for the grain-rich Shenandoah region and the Virginia Central Railroad — was increased on August 4, five days after the Crater, by reports that Grant was loading another large detachment of troops aboard transports at City Point. "I fear that this force is intended to operate against General Early," Lee told Davis, "and when added to that already opposed to him, may be more than he can manage. Their object may be to drive him out of the Valley and complete the devastation they [had] commenced when they were ejected from it." In point of fact, next to provoking his adversary into making a headlong assault on his intrenchments, there was nothing Lee wanted more than just such a weakening of the pressure against them. However, there were limits beyond which a precarious balance would be lost; Early's defeat would mean the loss, as well, of the Shenandoah Valley and the Virginia Central, both necessary for the survival of the rest of the army, immobilized at Petersburg and Richmond. Lee conferred next day with the President and reached the conclusion that, whatever the risk to his thinly held works beyond the James, he would have to strengthen Early. Accordingly, on August 6 he ordered Richard Anderson to leave at once, with Kershaw's division of infantry and Fitz Lee's of cavalry, for Culpeper, where he would be in a position either to speed back to Richmond by rail, in case of an emergency there, or else to fall on the flank and rear of the Federals, just beyond the Blue Ridge, in case they advanced up the Valley.

As usual, Lee was right about Grant's intentions, though in this case they were more drastic than he knew. Not only did the Federal commander plan to "complete the destruction" begun by Hunter before Early drove him off; he already had directed that this was to be accomplished by a process of omnivorous consumption. When Early fell back in turn from Washington in mid-July, Grant told Halleck to see to it that he was pursued by "veterans, militiamen, men on horseback, and everything that can be got to follow," with specific instructions to "eat out Virginia clean and clear as far as they go, so that crows flying over it for the balance of this season will have to carry their own provender with them."

Nothing much had come of that, so far. The crows waxed fat on the Valley harvest, deep in Early's rear, while Halleck, convinced that all his doubts about Grant's movements since Cold Harbor had been confirmed by the events of the past month, fumbled his way through a pretense of directing the "pursuit" from his desk in Washington. "*Entre nous*," he wrote Sherman on July 16, "I fear Grant has made a fatal mistake in putting himself south of James River. He cannot now reach Richmond without taking Petersburg, which is strongly fortified, crossing the Appomattox, and recrossing the James. Moreover, by placing his army south of Richmond he opens the capital and the whole North to rebel raids. Lee can at any time detach 30,000 to 40,000 men without our knowing it till we are actually threatened. I hope we may yet have full success, but I find that many of Grant's general officers think the campaign already a failure." Old Brains was determined to play no active role in what he saw as a discredited operation, and Grant soon found there was little he himself could do from an even greater distance. One answer might be for him to go up the Potomac and take charge of the stalled pursuit, but the fact was he had problems enough on his hands at Petersburg just then, including Meade's immovability, Burnside's mine, and the presence of Ben Butler, who by virtue of his rank would assume command of all the forces south of the James if Grant went up the country.

Unable to get Butler transferred (though he tried — only to find that this was no time to risk offending a prominent hard-war Democrat who might retaliate by taking the stump against the Administration) Grant turned on his one-time favorite Baldy Smith, who by now, mainly because of what Rawlins called "his disposition to scatter the seeds of discontent throughout the army," had become as much of a thorn in Grant's side as he had been in his cock-eyed superior's all along. On July 19 he was relieved and Major General Edward Ord, in temporary command at Baltimore, was brought down to take charge of his three divisions. Similarly, when the dust of the Crater settled, Burnside was superseded by his long-time chief of staff, Major General John G. Parke. Both of these new corps commanders — Ord was forty-five, a West Pointer like Parke, who was thirty-six — had fought under Grant at Vicksburg, and he was pleased to have them with him, here in front of Petersburg, to help conduct another siege.

None of this improved conditions northwest of Washington, however, and on the last day of July, with the ashes of Chambersburg still warm in that direction, Grant went down the James to Fortress Monroe for a conference with Lincoln about the situation Early had created up the Potomac.

For weeks he had favored merging the separate departments around the capital under a single field commander, though when he suggested his classmate William Franklin for the post — Franklin was conveniently at hand in Philadelphia, home on leave from Louisiana — he was told that the Pennsylvanian "would not give satisfaction," apparently because of his old association with McClellan, which still rankled in certain congressional minds. Rebuffed, Grant then considered giving Meade the job, with Hancock as his successor in command of the Army of the Potomac, but then thought better of it and decided that David Hunter, with his demonstrated talent for destruction, was perhaps the best man for the assignment after all. By the time he got to Fort Monroe on July 31, however, he had changed his mind again, and with the President's concurrence announced his decision next day in a telegram to Halleck: "I want Sheridan put in command of all the troops in the field, with instructions to put himself south of the enemy and follow him to the death."

Back in Washington, Lincoln saw the order two days later, and though he already had approved the policy announced, he was so taken with the message that he felt called upon to wire its author his congratulations — together with a warning. "This, I think, is exactly right as to how our forces should move," he replied, "but please look over the dispatches you may have received from here, even since you made that order, and discover, if you can, [whether] there is any idea in the head of anyone here of 'putting our army south of the enemy' or of 'following him to the death' in any direction. I repeat to you it will neither be done nor attempted unless you watch it every day and hour and force it."

This last was sound advice, and Grant reacted promptly despite his previous reluctance to leave the scene of his main effort. Delaying only long enough to compose a carefully worded note for Butler — "In my absence remain on the defensive," he told him, adding: "Please communicate with me by telegraph if anything occurs where you may wish my orders" — he was on his way down the James within two hours of reading Lincoln's message. In Washington next morning he visited neither the White House nor the War Department, but went instead to the railway station and caught a train for Monocacy Junction, where Hunter had gathered the better part of the 32,500-man force supposed to be in hot pursuit of Early. Grant arrived on August 5 to find him in a state of shock, brought on by having been harassed for more than a month by the rebels and his superiors, who had confused him with conflicting orders and unstrung his nerves with alarmist and misleading information. In any case, his jangled state facilitated the process of removal. Displaying what Grant later called "a patriotism none too common in the army," Hunter readily agreed not only to stand aside for Sheridan, whom he outranked, but also to step down for Crook, who took over his three divisions when he presently departed for more congenial duty in the capital.

Sheridan arrived on August 6, in time for a brief interview with Grant, who also gave him a letter of instructions. Two of his three cavalry divisions had been ordered up from Petersburg, and these, combined with the troops on hand, the Harpers Ferry garrison, and the rest of Emory's corps en route from Louisiana, would give him a total of just over 48,000 effectives: enough, Grant thought, to enable him to handle Jubal Early and any other problem likely to arise as he pressed south toward a reunion with Meade near Richmond, wrecking as he went. He would have to take preliminary time, of course, to acquaint himself with his new duties in an unfamiliar region, as well as to restore some tone to Hunter's winded, footsore men, now under Crook, and to Wright's disgruntled veterans, who had little patience with the mismanagement they had recently undergone. But Grant made it clear — despite protests from Stanton and Halleck, being registered in Washington even now, that the thirty-three-year-old cavalryman was too young for the command of three full corps of infantry — that he looked forward to hearing great things from this direction before long, when Sheridan began to carry out what was set forth in his instructions. "In pushing up the Shenandoah Valley, as it is expected you will have to do first or last," the letter read, "it is desirable that nothing should be left to invite the enemy to return. Take all provisions, forage, and stock wanted for the use of your command. Such as cannot be consumed, destroy. . . . Bear in mind, the object is to drive the enemy south, and to do this you want to keep him always in sight. Be guided in your course by the course he takes."

The interview was brief because Grant was in a hurry to get back down the coast before Lee reached into his bag of tricks and dangled something disastrously attractive in front of Butler's nose. Returning to Washington, he boarded the dispatch steamer that had brought him up Chesapeake Bay four days ago, and stepped ashore at City Point before sunrise, August 9.

His haste came close to costing him his life before the morning ended. Around noon he was sitting in front of his headquarters tent, which was pitched in the yard of a high-sited mansion overlooking the wharves and warehouses of the ordnance supply depot he had established near the confluence of the James and the Appomattox, when suddenly there was the roar of an explosion louder than anything heard in the region since the springing of Pleasants's mine, ten days back. "Such a rain of shot, shell, bullets, pieces of wood, iron bars and bolts, chains and missiles of every kind was never before witnessed. It was terrible — awful — terrific," a staffer wrote home. Grant agreed. "Every part of the yard used as my headquarters is filled with splinters and fragments of shell," he telegraphed Halleck before the smoke had cleared.

By then it was known that an ammunition barge had exploded, along with an undeterminable number of the 20,000 artillery projectiles on its deck and in its hold, though whether by accident or by sabotage was difficult to say, all aboard having died in the blast, which scattered parts of their bodies over a quarter-mile radius and flung more substantial chunks of wreckage twice that far. A canal boat moored alongside, for example, was loaded with cavalry saddles that went flying in every direction, one startled observer said, "like so many big-winged bats." These were nearly as deadly in their flight as the unexploded shells, and contributed to the loss of 43 dead and 126 injured along the docks, while others, killed or wounded on the periphery — including a head-quarters orderly and three members of Grant's staff — nearly doubled both those figures. "The total number killed will never be known," an investigator admitted, though he guessed at "over 200," and it was not until the war ended that the cause of the disaster was established by the discovery of a report by a rebel agent named John Maxwell.

He had stolen through the Union lines the night before, bringing with him a "horological torpedo," as he called the device, a candle box packed with twelve pounds of black powder, a percussion cap, and a clockwork mechanism to set it off. Reaching City Point at daybreak — about the same time Grant arrived — he went down to the wharves to watch for a chance to plant his bomb. It came when he saw the captain of a low-riding ammunition vessel step ashore, apparently intent on business: whereupon the agent set the timer, sealed the box, and delivered it to a member of the crew, with a request from the skipper to "put it down below" till he returned. "The man took it without question," Maxwell declared, "while I went off a little distance." His luck held; for though, as he said, he was "terribly shocked by the explosion," which soon followed, he not only was uninjured by falling debris, he also made it back in safety to the Confederate lines, having accomplished overnight, with a dozen pounds of powder, more damage, both in lives and property, than the Federals had done ten days ago with four tons of the stuff, after a solid month of digging.

Fearful though the damage was — estimates ran to $2,000,000 and beyond — wrecked equipment could be repaired and lost supplies replaced. More alarming, in a different way, was an intelligence report, just in, that Lee had detached Anderson's entire First Corps three days ago, along with Fitz Lee's cavalry, to reinforce Early out in the Valley. If true (which it was not, except in part; Anderson had been detached, but only with Kershaw's, not all three of his infantry divisions) this would give Early close to 40,000 soldiers, veterans to a man; enough, in short, to enable him to overrun Sheridan's disaffected conglomeration for a second crossing of the Potomac, this time with better than twice the strength of the one that had wound up at the gates of Washington last month. As things stood now, Lincoln might or might not survive the November election, but with 40,000 graybacks on the outskirts of the capital, let alone inside it, there was little doubt which way the votes would go. And as the votes went, so went Grant — a hard-war man, unlikely to survive the inauguration of a soft-war President. Promptly he got off a warning to Little Phil that his adversary was being reinforced to an extent that would "put him nearer on an equality with you in numbers than I want to see." What was called for, under the circumstances, was caution: particularly on the part of a young general less than a week in command, whose total strategy up to now could be summarized in his watchword, "Smash 'em up!"

Caution he recommended; caution he got. Sheridan had begun an advance from Halltown, near Harpers Ferry, and had pressed on through Winchester, almost to Strasburg — just beyond which, after cannily fading back, Early had taken up a strong position at Fisher's Hill, inviting attack — when word came on August 14, via Washington, that Anderson was on the way from Richmond, if indeed he had not come up already, with reinforcements that would enable Early to go over to the offensive with close to twice his estimated present strength of better than 20,000 veterans. Little Phil, experiencing for the first time the loneliness of independent command, reacted with a discretion unsuspected in his makeup until now. "I should like very much to have your advice," he wrote Grant, rather plaintively, as he began a withdrawal that presently saw him back at Halltown, within comforting range of the big guns at Harpers Ferry.

Early too returned to his starting point in the Lower Valley, skirmishing with such enemy units as he could persuade to venture beyond reach of the heavy batteries in their rear, and resumed his harassment of the Baltimore & Ohio, threatening all the while to recross the Potomac for another march on the Yankee capital. He had 16,500 men, including detached cavalry, and when Kershaw and Fitz Lee joined him the total came to 23,000: about half the number his adversary enjoyed while backing away from a confrontation. The result was a scathing contempt which Old Jube did not bother to conceal, remarking then and later that Sheridan was not only "without enterprise" but also "possessed an excessive caution which amounted to timidity." As the stand-off continued, on through August and beyond, Early's confidence grew to overconfident proportions. "If it was his policy to produce the impression that he was too weak to fight me, he did not succeed," he said of Little Phil, "but if it was to convince me that he was not an energetic commander, his strategy was a complete success."

Grant meantime had not been long in finding that only one of Anderson's divisions had left the Richmond-Petersburg front; yet he still thought it best for Sheridan to delay his drive up the Valley until pressure from Meade obliged Lee to recall the reinforcements now with Early. Accordingly, he began at once to exert that pressure, first on one bank of the James, pulling the few Confederate reserves in that direction, then the other. Hancock, with his own and one of Butler's corps, plus the remaining cavalry division, was ordered to repeat the northside maneuver he had attempted on the eve of the Crater. This began on August 14, the day Sheridan started to backtrack, and continued on the morrow, but with heavier casualties than before and even less success. Attacking at Deep Bottom Run with hopes of turning the Chaffin's Bluff defenses, Hancock found veterans, not reserves, in occupation of Richmond's outer works, and suffered a repulse. A renewal of the assault next day, just up the line, brought similar results until he called it off, confessing in his report that his men had not behaved well in the affair. His losses were just under 3000, more than three times Lee's, but Grant had him remain in position to distract his opponent's attention from a second offensive, off at the far end of the line.

Warren had the assignment, which was basically to repeat the late-June effort to get astride the Weldon Railroad a couple of miles southwest of where the present Union left overlapped the Jerusalem Plank Road. This time he succeeded. Moving with four divisions on the morning of August 18 he struck the railroad at Globe Tavern, four miles south of Petersburg, and quickly dispossessed the single brigade of cavalry posted in defense of the place while most of the gray infantry

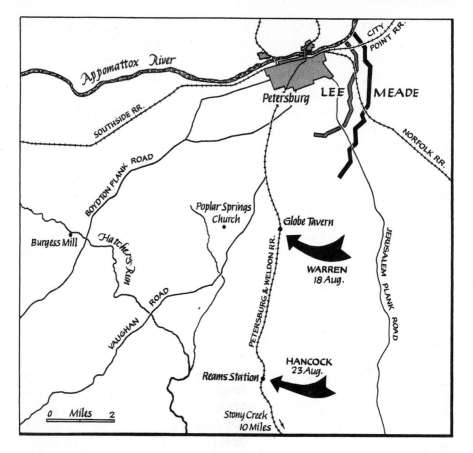

confronted Hancock on the far side of the James. Elated by their success, the attackers pushed north from the tavern, but soon found that holding the road was a good deal harder than breaking it had been. Beauregard counterattacked that afternoon, using such troops as he could scrape together, then more savagely next morning, when A. P. Hill came down with two of his divisions. Warren lost 2700 of his 16,000 men, captured in mass when two brigades were caught off balance in poorly aligned intrenchments, but managed to recover the ground by sundown. That night he fell back to a better position, just over a mile down the line, where he was reinforced for two more days of fighting before the Confederates were willing to admit that they could not dislodge him. His casualties for all four days came to 4500, while the rebel loss was only 1600 — plus of course the Weldon Railroad; or anyhow the final stretch of track. Lee at once put teamsters to work hauling supplies in wagons by a roundabout route from the new terminus at Stony Creek, twenty miles below Petersburg and about half that distance beyond the limits of Federal destruction.

Grant was determined to lengthen this mule-drawn interval, if only to keep up the pressure he hoped would bring Anderson back from the Valley, and when Hancock recrossed the James on August 21 —

the day Lee gave up trying to drive Warren off the railroad — he received orders to proceed south with two of his divisions, plus Gregg's troopers, for a follow-up strike at the vital supply line near Reams Station, about five miles below Globe Tavern and ten above Stony Creek. He reached his objective on August 23, and by the close of the following day had torn up three miles of track beyond it. That night, while resting his wreckers for an extension of their work tomorrow, he learned that A. P. Hill was moving in his direction. Arriving at noon, Little Powell drove in the blue cavalry so fast that the infantry had little time to get set. The main blow fell on three New York regiments, green troops lately assigned to Gibbon's division, some of whom fled, while most surrendered, and to Hancock's further outrage a reserve brigade, ordered into the resultant gap, "could neither be made to go forward nor fire." Before darkness ended the fighting, better than 2000 men here and elsewhere along the Union line chose prison over combat. Two more divisions were on the way as reinforcements, but Hancock decided not to wait for them and instead pulled out that night. He had lost 2750 killed or wounded or missing, along with nine guns, a dozen battle flags, and well over 3000 rifles abandoned on the field. Hill's loss was 720.

This came hard for Hancock — "Hancock the Superb," newsmen had called him ever since the Seven Days; *Hancock,* who had broken Pickett's Charge, stood firm amid the chaos of the Wilderness, and cracked the Bloody Angle at Spotsylvania — as well as for his veteran lieutenants, especially John Gibbon, former commander of the Iron Brigade, whose division had been considered one of the best in the whole army until it was bled down to skeleton proportions and then fleshed out with skulkers finally netted by the draft. Ashamed and angered, Gibbon submitted his resignation, then was persuaded to withdraw it, though he presently left both his division and the corps: the hard-driving II Corps, which had taken more than forty enemy colors before it lost one of its own, and then abandoned or surrendered twelve of these in a single day at Reams Station, August 25. After that, even Grant was obliged to admit that its three divisions were unfit for use on the offensive, now and for some time to come, and Hancock's adjutant later said of his chief's reaction to the blow: "The agony of that day never passed from that proud soldier, who for the first time, in spite of superhuman exertions and reckless exposure on his part, saw his lines broken and his guns taken."

Back at Petersburg next day, Hill was pleased but not correspondingly elated, having done this sort of thing many times before, under happier circumstances. Moreover, it was much the same for Lee, who saw deeper into the matter. A month ago, in a letter to one of his sons, he had said of Grant, with a touch of aspersion: "His talent and strategy consists in accumulating overwhelming numbers." Now he was faced with the product of that blunt, inelegant strategy — that "talent" — which included not only the loss of the final stretch of the Weldon Railroad, but also the necessity for extending his undermanned Petersburg works another two miles westward to match the resultant Federal extension beyond Globe Tavern.

Of the two problems thus posed for him, the first might seem more irksome at the moment, coming as it did at a time when the army's reserve supply of corn was near exhaustion; but the second was potentially the graver. For while there were other railroads to bring grain from coastal Georgia and the Carolinas — the Southside line, on this bank of the Appomattox, and the Richmond & Danville, coming down from beyond the James for an intersection at Burkeville — the accustomed influx of recruits from those and other regions had dwindled to a trickle. Lee could scarcely replace his losses, let alone avoid the thinning of a line already stretched just short of snapping. "Without some increase of our strength," he warned Seddon, even as Hill was moving against Hancock, "I cannot see how we are to escape the natural military consequences of the enemy's numerical superiority." Ten days later he reviewed the situation in a letter to the President, stressing "the importance of immediate and vigorous measures to increase the strength of our armies. . . . The necessity is now great," he said, "and will soon be augmented by the results of the coming draft in the United States. As matters now stand, we have no troops disposable to meet movements of the enemy or to strike where opportunity presents, without taking them from the trenches and exposing some important point. The enemy's position enables him to move his troops to the right or left without our knowledge, until he has reached the point at which he aims, and we are then compelled to hurry our men to meet him, incurring the risk of being too late to check his progress and the additional risk of the advantage he may derive from their absence. This was fully illustrated in the late demonstration north of James River, which called troops from our lines here, who if present might have prevented the occupation of the Weldon Railroad."

Across the way, at City Point, admonitions flowed in the opposite direction. Halleck warned Grant in mid-August that draft riots were likely to occur at any time in New York and Pennsylvania, as well as in Indiana and Kentucky: in which case he would be called upon, as Meade had been last summer, to furnish troops to put them down. Anticipating such troubles between now and the election in November, Old Brains suggested it might be well for the army to avoid commitment to any operation it could not discontinue on short notice. "Are not the appearances such that we ought to take in sail and prepare the ship for a storm?" he asked.

Grant thought not, and said so. Such police work should be left for the various governors to handle with militia, which should be called out now for the purpose. "If we are to draw troops from the field to keep the loyal states in harness," he declared, "it will prove difficult to suppress the rebellion in the disloyal states." Besides, he added, to ease the pressure on Lee at Petersburg and Richmond would be to allow him to reinforce Hood at Atlanta, just as he had reinforced Bragg at Chickamauga a year ago this month, and that "would insure the defeat of Sherman." In short, Grant had no intention of relaxing his effort on either bank of the James, whatever civilian troubles might develop up the country in his rear.

Lincoln read this reply on August 17 and promptly telegraphed approval. "I have seen your dispatch expressing your unwillingness to break your hold where you are. Neither am I willing. Hold on with a bulldog grip, and chew and choke as much as possible."

Scanning the words at his headquarters overlooking City Point, Grant laughed aloud — a thing he seldom did — and when staffers came over to see what had amused him so, passed them the message to read. "The President has more nerve than any of his advisers," he said.

Nerve was one thing, hope another, and Lincoln was fast running out of that: not so much because of the current military situation — though in point of fact this was glum enough, on the face of it, with Meade and Sherman apparently stalled outside Petersburg and Atlanta, Forrest rampant in Memphis, and the *Tallahassee* about to light up the New England coast with burning merchantmen — as in regard to his own political survival, which was seen on all sides as unlikely, especially in view of what had happened this month in his native Kentucky despite some highly irregular efforts to forestall defeat for a party that soon was still worse split by the Wade-Davis Manifesto. Six days after his chew-and-choke message to Grant, and six days before the Democrats were scheduled to convene in Chicago to nominate his November opponent — a time, he would say, "when as yet we had no adversary, and seemed to have no friends" — Lincoln sat in his office reading the morning mail. Thurlow Weed, an expert on such matters, recently had informed him that his reëlection was impossible, the electorate being "wild for peace." Now there came a letter from Henry J. Raymond, editor of the friendly *New York Times* and chairman of the Republican National Executive Committee, who said much the same thing.

"I feel compelled to drop you a line," he wrote, "concerning the political condition of the country as it strikes me. I am in active correspondence with your staunchest friends in every state, and from them all I hear but one report. The tide is setting strongly against us." Oliver Morton, Simon Cameron, and Elihu Washburne had respectively warned the New Yorker that Indiana, Pennsylvania, and Illinois were probably lost by now. Moreover, he told Lincoln, he was convinced that his own state "would go 50,000 against us tomorrow. And so of the rest. Nothing but the most resolute action on the part of the government and its friends can save the country from falling into hostile hands. . . . In some way or other the suspicion is widely diffused that we can have peace with Union if we would. It is idle to reason with this belief — still more idle to denounce it. It can only be expelled by some authoritative act, at once bold enough to fix attention and distinct enough to defy incredulity and challenge respect."

What Raymond had in mind was another peace commission, armed with terms whose rejection by Richmond would "unite the North as nothing since the firing on Fort Sumter has hitherto done." Lincoln knew only too well how little was apt to come of this, having tried it twice in the past month, and was correspondingly depressed. If this was all that could save the election he was whipped already. Sadly he took a sheet of paper from his desk and composed a memorandum.

> Executive Mansion
> Washington, Aug. 23, 1864
>
> This morning, as for some days past, it seems exceedingly probable that this Administration will not be reëlected. Then it will be my duty to so coöperate with the President-elect as to save the Union between the election and the inauguration; as he will have secured his election on such ground that he cannot possibly save it afterwards.
>
> A. LINCOLN

He folded the sheet, glued it shut, and took it with him to the midday cabinet meeting, where, without so much as a hint as to the subject covered, he had each member sign it on the back, in blind attestation to whatever it might contain — a strange procedure but a necessary precaution, since to tell them what was in the memorandum would be to risk increasing the odds against his reëlection by having it spread all over Washington, by sundown, that he himself had predicted his defeat. "In this peculiar fashion," his two secretaries later explained, "he pledged himself and the Administration" (so far, at least, as the pledge was binding: which was mainly on himself, since he alone knew the words behind the seal) "to accept loyally the anticipated verdict of the people against him, and to do their utmost to save the Union in the brief remainder of his term of office."

Not that he did not intend to do all he could, despite the odds, in the eleven weeks between now and the day the issue would be settled. Treading softly where he felt he must, and firmly where he didn't, he attended to such iotas as recommending in advance to field commanders that Indiana soldiers, who were required by law to be present to cast their ballots, be given furloughs in October to go home and offset the pacifist vote in their state election, considered important as a forecast of what to expect across the nation in November and as an influence on those whose main concern was that their choice be a winner. Besides, he foresaw trouble for his opponents once they came out in the open, where he had spent the past four years, a target for whatever mud was flung. The old Democratic rift, which had made him President in the first place, was even wider than it had been four years ago, except that now the burning issue was the war itself, not just slavery, which many said had caused it, and Lincoln expected the rift to widen further when a platform was adopted and a candidate named to stand on it. The front runner was Major General George B. McClellan, who was expected to attract the soldier vote, although numbers of Democrats were saying they would accept no candidate "with the smell of war on his garments." Either way, as Lincoln saw the outcome, platform and man were likely to be mismatched, with the result that half the opposition would be disappointed with one or the other, perhaps to the extent of bolting or abstaining when Election Day came round. "They must nominate a Peace Democrat on a war platform, or a War Democrat on a peace platform," he told a friend who left that weekend for the convention in his home state, "and I personally can't say I care much which they do."

He was right. Convening in Chicago on August 29, in a new pine Wigwam like the one set up for the Republicans in 1860, the Democrats heard New York's Governor Horatio Seymour establish the tone in a keynote speech delivered on taking the gavel as permanent chairman. "The Administration cannot save the Union. We can. Mr Lincoln views many things above the Union. We put the Union first of all. He thinks a proclamation more than peace. We think the blood of our people more precious than edicts of the President." After this, the assembly got down to adopting a platform framed in part by Clement L. Vallandigham, the nation's leading Copperhead and chairman of the Resolutions Committee, who had returned last year from presidential banishment, first beyond the rebel lines, then back by way of Canada, to run unsuccessfully for governor of Ohio. The former congressman's hand was most apparent in the peace plank, which resolved: "That this convention does explicitly declare, as the sense of the American people, that after four years of failure to restore the Union by the experiment of war . . . justice, humanity, liberty, and the public welfare demand that immediate efforts be made for a cessation of hostilities, with a view to an ultimate convention of the States, or other peaceable means, to the end that at the earliest practicable moment peace may be restored on the basis of the Federal Union of the States."

The stress here, as in Seymour's keynote speech, was on achieving peace through restoration of the Union, not "at any price," as was claimed by hostile critics. Vallandigham had emphasized this on the eve of the convention, saying: "Whoever charges that I want to stop this war in order that there may be Southern independence charges that which is false, and lies in his teeth, and lies in his throat!" But presently the nominee himself lent strength to the charge by repudiating the plank in question. It was McClellan, as expected; he was chosen by acclaim on the first ballot, with Congressman George H. Pendleton of Ohio, long an advocate of negotiated peace, as his running mate. Ten days after his nomination — a delay that prompted a Republican wit to remark in the interim that Little Mac was "about as slow in getting up on the platform as he was in taking Richmond" — he tendered the notification committee his letter of acceptance. "I could not look in the face of my gallant comrades of the army and navy who have survived so many bloody battles," he declared, "and tell them that their labors and the sacrifices of so many of our slain and wounded brethren have been in vain, that we had abandoned that Union for which we have so often periled our lives. A vast majority of our people, whether in the army and navy or at home, would, as I would, hail with unbounded joy the permanent restoration of peace, on the basis of the Union under the Constitution, without the effusion of another drop of blood. But no peace can be permanent without Union."

Thus McClellan sought to deal with the dilemma Lincoln had foreseen, and wound up infuriating the faction that admired what he rejected: as Lincoln also had foreseen. But that was not as important by then as it had seemed the week before, when the charge that the "experiment of war" had been a failure, East and West, was one that could perhaps be contested but could scarcely be refuted in the face of evidence from practically every front. Aside from Farragut's coup in Mobile Bay — seen now as rather a one-man show, with the credit all his own — incredible casualties had produced only stalemates or reverses, whether out in North Mississippi, down around Richmond and Atlanta, or up in the Shenandoah Valley. United in their anticipation of victory at the polls in November, whatever internal troubles racked the party, the Democrats adjourned on August 31, having wound up their business in jig time. Then two days later fate intervened, or seemed to. Slocum's wire reached Washington on September 2, followed next day by Sherman's own: "Atlanta is ours, and fairly won."

Church bells rang across the land as they had not rung since the fall of Vicksburg, fourteen months ago. "Sherman and Farragut have knocked the bottom out of the Chicago platform," Seward exulted, and Lincoln promptly tendered "national thanks" to the general and the admiral, issuing at the same time a Proclamation of Thanksgiving and Prayer, to be offered in all churches the following Sunday, for "the glorious achievements" of the army and the navy at Atlanta and in Mobile Bay. Grant too rejoiced, and telegraphed Sherman next day: "In honor of your great victory, I have ordered a salute to be fired with *shotted* guns from every battery bearing upon the enemy." Within earshot of that cannonade, the editor of the Richmond *Examiner* spoke of "disaster at Atlanta in the very nick of time when a victory alone could save the party of Lincoln from irretrievable ruin. . . . It will obscure the prospect of peace, late so bright. It will also diffuse gloom over the South."

Gladdened by congratulations from all sides, including some from political associates who he knew had been about to desert what they had thought was a sinking ship, Lincoln enjoyed the taste of victory so well that it made him hungry for still more. "Sheridan and Early are facing each other at a deadlock," he wired Grant on September 12. "Could we not pick up a regiment here and there, to the number of say ten thousand men, and quietly but suddenly concentrate them at Sheridan's camp and enable him to make a strike? This is but a suggestion." A suggestion was enough. Grant replied next day that he had been intending for a week "to see Sheridan and arrange what was necessary to enable him to start Early out of the Valley. It seems to me it can successfully be done." Content to have Meade in charge while he was gone — Butler was conveniently on leave — he set out the following day on his second trip up the Potomac in six weeks. Once more without stopping in Washington, he reached Sheridan's headquarters near Harpers Ferry on September 16.

"That's Grant," a veteran sergeant told a comrade, pointing him out. "I hate to see that old cuss around. When that old cuss is around there's sure to be a big fight on hand."

This applied even more to the present visit than to most, since Grant had in his pocket a plan for a campaign to drive Early all the way to Richmond, destroying first the Shenandoah Valley and then the Virginia Central Railroad in his wake. However, he was not long in finding that Little Phil had plans of his own which he was anxious to place in execution, having received from a spy in Winchester, just that morning, word that the time was ripe for an advance. A Quaker schoolteacher, Rebecca Wright by name, had smuggled out a note, wrapped in tinfoil and cached in the mouth of a Negro messenger, informing him that Anderson had left the Valley two days ago, with Kershaw's division and three batteries of artillery, recalled by Lee to help meet the stepped-up pressure from Meade on both sides of the James. What was more, Early — encouraged, as Lee had been in withdrawing the reinforcements, by his opponent's apparent quiescence under cover of the guns on Bolivar Heights for the past month — had posted three of his four infantry divisions in scattered positions above Winchester, toward the Potomac, to promote the fear that he was about to take the offensive with many more troops than the 18,000 or so which Sheridan now knew were all he had. Sheridan's plan was to use his field force of 40,000 not merely to drive Early from the Valley but to annihilate him by attacking his lone division at Winchester, then moving over or around it to cut off the escape of the rest up the Valley Turnpike.

Grant heard the ebullient young general out, and finding him "so clear and so positive in his views, and so confident of success," said nothing about the plan that remained in his pocket. Instead — today was Friday — he asked if the whole blue force could be ready to move by Tuesday. Sheridan replied that, subject to Grant's approval, he intended to take up the march before daybreak Monday, September 19. Grant thought this over, then nodded and issued his briefest order of the war: "Go in."

He left next morning, and though he still avoided Washington he managed a side excursion to Burlington, New Jersey, where his wife had taken a house after coming East. That night and part of Sunday he spent with her and the children, then returned to City Point on Monday, hoping for news of the Valley offensive, which had been scheduled to open that morning. Delayed by breakdowns, Sheridan's wire did not arrive till the following day, but when it did it more than justified the buildup of suspense. Headed "Winchester, 7.30 p.m." — itself a confirmation of success — the telegram read: "I have the honor to report that I attacked the forces of General Early on the Berryville pike at the crossing of

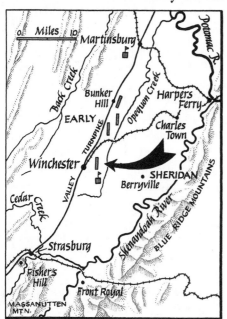

Opequon Creek, and after a most stubborn and sanguinary engagement, which lasted from early in the morning until 5 o'clock in the evening, completely defeated him." There followed a list of their losses, including "2500 prisoners, five pieces of artillery, nine army flags, and most of their wounded," but a companion message, written in greater heat by his chief of staff, better caught the public's fancy, being quoted in all the papers: "We have just sent them whirling through Winchester, and we are after them tomorrow. This army behaved splendidly."

Actually, there had been a good deal more to it than that. For one thing, Sheridan's loss was considerably heavier than Early's — just over 5000 killed, wounded, or missing, as compared to just under 4000 — and for another, despite his achievement of surprise at the outset, he had come close to getting whipped before he got rolling. On the approach march, against orders, Wright brought his corps train along, old-army style, which so clogged the Berryville Pike in his rear that Emory was unable to cross Opequon Creek in time to join the dawn assault on Ramseur's division and Fitz Lee's troopers, posted three miles east of

Winchester. Ramseur alternately held his position and withdrew slowly, in good order, and thus not only gave Early time to call in his other three infantry divisions, six to ten miles north of town, but also enabled him to launch a counterattack by Gordon and Rodes when Emory came up around midmorning, led onto the field by Sheridan himself, who, in a rage at the delay, had ordered Wright's wagons flung into ditches to clear the pike. Here fell Robert Rodes, the tall blond Virginia-born Alabamian who had led Jackson's flank attack at Chancellorsville, thirty-five years old and a veteran of all the army's major battles, from First Manassas on. Shot from his horse while directing the charge into the breach between Emory and Wright, he did not live to see it healed by the latter's reserves when they arrived. Emory, badly shaken — he had finished at West Point in 1831, the year Sheridan was born — had to be reinforced by Crook, whose two divisions had been intended for use in a flanking effort to block the path of a Confederate escape. Still, as the fight continued the weight of numbers told. Early, with some 14,000 men on hand, gave ground steadily all afternoon, under pressure from Sheridan's 38,000, and finally, about 5 o'clock, fell back through the streets of the town and retreated up the Valley Turnpike, which Fitz Lee's horsemen managed to keep open although Fitz himself had had to retire from the conflict, pinked in the thigh by a stray bullet. The battle — called Third Winchester by the defenders and Opequon Creek by the attackers — was over. Early did not stop till he reached Fisher's Hill, beyond Strasburg, twenty miles to the south, where Sheridan had ended his advance the month before, preceding his withdrawal to Harpers Ferry.

Grant's response next day was threefold. Wiring Stanton a recommendation that Sheridan be rewarded with a promotion to regular-army brigadier (which was promptly conferred) he also ordered the firing of a hundred-gun celebration salute in front of Richmond, just as he had done two weeks ago in Sherman's honor, and telegraphed Sheridan his congratulations for "your great victory," adding: "If practicable, push your success and make all you can of it."

Sheridan — whose 5018 casualties, though more than a thousand heavier than Early's 3921, had cost him only an eighth of his command, whereas Early had lost a solid fourth — intended to do just that. Late next day, with a force that was now three times the size of the one he was pursuing, he called a halt near Strasburg, advancing two corps across Cedar Creek and holding the third in reserve while he went forward to study the rebel position, two miles beyond the town. He found it quite as formidable as it had been six weeks ago, when he had declined to test its strength.

Massanutton Mountain, looming dead ahead between the sun-glinted forks of the Shenandoah, divided the Valley into two smaller valleys: Luray on the left, beyond Front Royal, and what remained of the main valley on the right, narrowed at this point to a width of about four miles between the North Fork of the Shenandoah River and Little North Mountain, a spur of the Alleghenies. His flanks anchored east and west on the river and the mountain, Early also enjoyed the advantage of high ground overlooking a boggy stream called Tumbling Run, which the Federals would have to cross, under fire from massed artillery and small arms, if they were to attack him from the front. Down to fewer than 10,000 effectives as a result of his battle losses and the need for detaching two of Fitz Lee's three brigades to hold the midway notch in Massanutton (lest Sheridan send part of his superior force up the Luray Valley for a crossing there to get astride the turnpike at New Market, twenty miles in the Confederate rear) Early had to dismount troops from his other cavalry division, under Lunsford Lomax — most of whom had arrived too late for yesterday's fight, having been involved in railroad wrecking around Martinsburg, some fifty miles to the north — to man the western extension of his four-mile line to the lower slopes of Little North Mountain. Although the Winchester defeat had gone far toward disabusing him of the notion that his opponent "possessed an excessive caution which amounted to timidity," he had confidence in the natural strength of his position on Fisher's Hill, as well as in the veterans who held it, and believed that the bluecoats had little choice except to come at him head-on, in which case they were sure to be repulsed.

He was mistaken: grievously mistaken, as it turned out. Sheridan intended to approach him only in part from the front, using Wright's three and Emory's two divisions to fix him in place while Crook's two, kept hidden in reserve, made a flanking march, under cover of Little North Mountain, for a surprise descent on the Confederate left — where Early, expecting an assault on his right center, had posted his least dependable troops. All next day this misconception was encouraged by the sight of heavy blue columns filing through Strasburg, down toward Tumbling Run. Moreover, here as at Winchester two days ago, Little Phil intended to do more than merely whip or wreck his adversary; he planned to bag him entirely, and with this in mind he detached two of his three cavalry divisions, under Torbert, for a fast ride up Luray Valley and across Massanutton Mountain, through the midway notch in its knife-edge crest, to get control of the Valley Turnpike at New Market and thus prevent the escape of such gray fugitives as managed to slip through the net he would fling over Fisher's Hill tomorrow.

Crook set out before dawn, September 22, marching with flags and guidons trailed to keep them from being spotted by butternut lookouts while he rounded the wooded upper slopes of Little North Mountain, beyond the rebel left. Wright and Emory began their frontal demonstration after sunup, banging away with all their guns and bristling along Tumbling Run, as if about to splash across at any moment. This was a drawn-out business, continuing well past midday, since Crook's West Virginians — so-called because that was where they had done most of their fighting until now, though in fact they were in large part from Ohio, with a sprinkling of Pennsylvanians and New Yorkers thrown in to leaven or "easternize" the lump — had a long hard way to travel, much of it uphill. Finally at 4 o'clock, twelve hours after they set out, they struck.

"Flanked! Outflanked!" the cry went up on Early's left as the dismounted horsemen he had scorned from the outset, calling them buttermilk rangers and worse, fled before the onslaught of Crook, whose two divisions came whooping down the mountainside to strike them flank and rear. Eastward along Fisher's Hill, where the defenders had begun to remark that Sheridan must have lost his nerve and called off the attack he had been threatening all day, the confusion spread when Wright's corps joined the melee, advancing division by division across Tumbling Run as the gray line crumbled unit by unit from the shattered left. Fearful of being trapped in the angle between river and run, they too bolted, leaving the teamless cannoneers to slow the blue advance while they themselves took off, first down the rearward slope, then southward up the turnpike.

"Forward! Forward everything!" Sheridan yelled, coursing the field on his black charger and gesturing with his flat-topped hat for emphasis. "Don't stop! Go on!" he shouted as his infantry overran and captured twelve of the guns on Fisher's Hill.

Anticipating "results still more pregnant," he counted on Averell, whose division he presently launched in pursuit of the rebels fleeing through the twilight, to complete the Cannae he had had in mind when he sent Torbert with two divisions up the Luray Valley for a crossing of Massanutton to cut off Early's retreat at New Market. Alas, both cavalry generals failed him utterly in the crunch. Torbert came upon Fitz Lee's two brigades, posted in defense of a narrow gorge twelve miles beyond Front Royal, and decided there was nothing to be gained from being reckless. He withdrew without attempting a dislodgment. Sheridan was "astonished and chagrined" when he heard of this next morning. But his anger at Torbert was mild compared to what came over him when he learned that Averell had put his troopers into bivouac the night before to spare them the risk of attacking Early's rear guard in the darkness. Enraged, Little Phil fired off a message informing the cavalryman that he expected "resolution and actual fighting, with necessary casualties, before you retire. There must be no more backing and filling," he fumed, and when Averell did no better today, despite this blistering, he relieved him of command and sent him forthwith back to West Virginia, "there to await orders from these headquarters or higher authority."

By that time Early had cleared New Market, and though Sheridan kept up the pursuit beyond Harrisonburg, where the graybacks turned off eastward around the head of Massanutton to find shelter near one of the Blue Ridge passes a dozen miles southeast of Staunton, he had to be content with what he had won at Fisher's Hill and picked up along the turnpike afterwards. This included four additional guns, which brought the total to sixteen, and more than a thousand prisoners. Early's over-all loss, in the battle and on the retreat, was about 1400 killed, wounded, and missing; Sheridan's came to 528.

Gratifying as the comparison was, another was even more so. When Sheridan took over Hunter's frazzled command at Monocacy eight weeks ago, the rebs were bristling along the upper Potomac, as if their descent on Washington the month before had been no more than a rehearsal for a heavier blow. Now they were a hundred miles from that river, and it seemed doubtful they would ever return to its banks, so complete had been his triumph this past week, first near Winchester and then, three days later, at Fisher's Hill. "Better still," Grant replied to his protégé's announcement of the second of these victories, "it wipes out much of the stain upon our arms by previous disasters in that locality. May your good work continue is now the prayer of all loyal men."

Exultation flared among Lincoln supporters, whose number had grown considerably in the course of the three-week September span that opened with news of Atlanta's fall and closed with this pair of Shenandoah victories to balance the tally East and West. The candidate himself was in "a more gleeful humor," friends testified after visits to the White House. "Jordan has been a hard road to travel," he told one caller, "but I feel now that, notwithstanding the enemies I have made and the faults I have committed, I'll be dumped on the right side of that stream."

Abrupt though it was, he had cause for this change in mood from gloom to glee. Within two weeks of his August 23 pledge-prediction, countersigned blindly by the cabinet as a prelude to defeat, the news from Sherman down in Georgia produced a scurry by disaffected Jacobins to get back aboard the bandwagon: especially after the mid-September elections in Maine and Vermont showed the party not only holding its own, contrary to pre-Atlanta expectations, but also registering a slight gain. These straws in the wind grew more substantial with the announcement of Sheridan's triumphal march up the Valley. Salmon Chase paid his respects at the White House, then left to take the stump in Ohio, Vallandigham's stamping ground, while Horace Greeley, privately declaring that he intended to "fight like a savage in this campaign — I hate McClellan," he explained — announced that the *Tribune* would "henceforth fly the banner of Abraham Lincoln for President." Even Ben Wade and Henry Davis, whose early-August manifesto had sought to check what they called his "encroachments," took to the stump, like Chase, in support of the very monster they had spent the past two months attacking, though they maintained a measure of consistency by spending so much of their time excoriating the Democratic nominee that they had little left for praise in the other direction. "To save the nation," Wade told a colleague in explanation of his support for a leader he despised, "I am doing all for *him* that I could possibly do for a better man."

Meantime Lincoln, no doubt as amused as he was gratified by these political somersaults, did not neglect the particulars incident to victory and available to the candidate in office. Patronage and contracts were awarded to those who could do most for the party, and a binding promise went to James Gordon Bennett that he would be appointed Minister to France in exchange for his support in the New York *Herald*. There remained the thorny problem of Frémont, whose continuation in the race threatened to siphon off a critical number of die-hard radical voters. These had long been calling for the removal of Montgomery Blair, whose presence in the cabinet they considered an affront, and though Lincoln, aware that his compliance would be interpreted as an act of desperation, had resisted their demand for the Postmaster General's removal, now that Atlanta had turned the tide he felt willing to be persuaded: provided, that is, he got something commensurate in exchange.

The something in this case was Frémont's withdrawal, and he got it without having to drop the pretense of unwillingness he had kept up all along. "The President was most reluctant to come to terms, *but came*," Zachariah Chandler informed his wife after serving as go-between in the bargain. On September 22 — by coincidence, the day Sheridan hustled Early off Fisher's Hill — Frémont renounced his candidacy. "The union of the Republican Party has become a paramount necessity," he explained in his announcement of withdrawal, but he added, by way of a backhand lick in parting: "In respect to Mr Lincoln I continue to hold exactly the sentiments contained in my letter of acceptance. I consider that his administration has been politically, militarily, and financially a failure, and that its necessary continuance is a cause of regret for the country."

Blair's head rolled next day. "My dear Sir," Lincoln wrote him: "You have generously said to me more than once that whenever your resignation could be a relief to me it was at my disposal. The time has come." There followed compliments and thanks, if not regrets. Blair saw clearly enough that he was in fact "a peace offering to Frémont and his friends." The thought rankled. "The President has, I think, given himself, and me too, an unnecessary mortification in this matter," he wrote his wife before clearing out his desk, "but then I am not the best judge and I am sure he acts from the best motives." A good party man, like all the Blairs, he soon was out wooing voters for the chief who had let him go when bargain time came round.

While this high-level politicking was in progress up the country, Grant tried another pendulum strike at opposite ends of Lee's line, first north then south of the James. Encouraged by news from the Valley, which seemed to show what determination could accomplish, he was also provoked by a mid-September coup the rebel cavalry scored at his expense. On Coggins Point, six miles downriver from his head-quarters, a large herd of cattle awaited slaughter for Meade's army; or so it was thought until a rustling operation, dubbed "Hampton's Cattle Raid," caused the beef to wind up in stomachs unaccustomed to such fare. Hampton set out with three brigades on a wide swing around the Union left, September 14, and reached his objective before dawn two days later. Two brigades fought a holding action, hard in the Federal rear, while the third rounded up the animals on Coggins Point; then all three turned drovers and rode back into their own lines next day with just over 300 prisoners and just under 2500 beeves, at a cost of fewer than 60 casualties. Lee's veterans were feasting on Yankee beef by the time Grant returned from his Harpers Ferry conference with Sheridan to find that in his absence, and to his outrage, the graybacks had foraged profitably half a dozen miles in rear of City Point. Determined to avenge this indignity — and aware, as well, that the year was about to move into the final month before the national election, still without the main eastern army having chalked up a gain to compare with those scored recently in Georgia and the nearby Shenandoah Valley — he told Meade to pro-ceed with another of those sequential right-left strikes, such as he had attempted twice in the past month, designed to throw Lee off balance and overrun at least a portion of his works.

Both times before, the initial attack north of the James had been made by Hancock, but his corps by now was practically *hors de combat* as a result of these and other efforts there and elsewhere. So this time the assignment went to Butler. Presumably refreshed by his recent leave, the Massachusetts general drew up a plan whereby 20,000 men from Kautz's cavalry and the two corps of infantry under Ord and David Birney — successors to the disgruntled and departed Baldy Smith and Quincy Gillmore — crossed the river on the night of September 28 for a double-pronged assault on Forts Harrison and Gilmer, works that were part of Richmond's outer line, down near the James, and covered Lee's critical Chaffin's Bluff defenses. Ord, coming up on schedule through a heavy morning fog, launched an all-out attack which quickly overran the first of these, a mile beyond the river, along with its surprised and meager garrison, though at the cost of a crippling wound that caused him to be carried off the field. Alerted by the racket, just over a mile away, the defenders of Fort Gilmer were ready when Birney struck. Repulsed, he drew back and struck again, with help from Ord, only to find that the place had been reinforced from Richmond, where the tocsin still was sounding. Grant arrived that afternoon to order still a third assault, which was also unsuccessful, and the effort here was abandoned in favor of bracing Fort Harrison against Lee's expected attempt to retake it. This came next day, September 30, when two gray divisions and part of a third, 10,000 men in all, came over from Petersburg under Richard Anderson to make three desperate attacks, all of which failed. Butler's loss for the two days was 3327 of all arms. Lee's was about 2000; plus the fort.

This last was no great deprivation. Lee promptly drew a retrenchment in rear of Fort Harrison, still beyond small-arms range of Chaffin's Bluff, that resulted in a stronger line than the one laid out before. Still, Ben Butler had provided northern journalists with an item fit for crowing over, and best of all — potentially at least — Lee once more had been decoyed into stripping that portion of his defenses where the main blue effort was about to land, off beyond the far end of the long curve of intrenchments south of the James.

Warren and Parke, with two divisions each and Gregg's cavalry in support, set out westward from Globe Tavern while Butler's assault on the forts was in progress. Their mission was to cut, and if possible hold, both the Boydton Plank Road and the Southside Railroad, the two remaining arteries whose severance would bring on the collapse of Petersburg. They were stopped next day along Vaughan Road, less than halfway to the first of these objectives, by Hampton, who skirmished with Warren's column at Poplar Springs Church. Moving west to meet the threat with two divisions from the Petersburg defenses — already weakened by the detachment of Anderson for the attempt to retake Fort Harrison that same day — A. P. Hill encountered Parke at nearby Peebles Farm. Badly shot up, Parke managed to hang on until Warren sent reinforcements to help him hold his ground along Squirrel Level Road, where both corps dug in at nightfall. That was the limit of their lateral advance, and it cost them 2889 casualties, all told, as compared to about 900 for Hill and Hampton. With scarcely a pause for rest, the Federals got busy with picks and shovels, constructing a line of intrenchments from their new position, back east to Globe Tavern, two miles away on the Weldon Railroad. Lee, of course, was obliged to conform, extending once more the length of line his dwindling army had to cover to keep its flank from being turned.

By ordinary standards, Grant's gain in this third of his pendulum strikes at the Richmond-Petersburg defenses — a rather useless rebel earthwork, one mile north of the James, plus a brief stretch of country road, two miles beyond the previous western limit of his line — was incommensurate with his loss of just over 6000 men, a solid half of them captives already on their way to finish out the struggle in Deep

South prison camps, as compared to just under 3000 for Lee, most of them wounded and soon to return to the gray ranks. But with the presidential contest barely five weeks off, this was no ordinary juncture. Ordinary standards did not apply. What did apply was that Lincoln supporters now had something they could point to, down around the Confederate seat of government itself, which seemed to indicate, along with recent developments in Atlanta and the Shenandoah Valley, that the war was by no means the failure it had been pronounced by the opposition in Chicago, five weeks back.

In recognition of this, Democrats lately had shifted their emphasis from the conduct to the nature of the war; "The Constitution as it is, the Union as it was," was now their cry. How effective this would prove was not yet known, for all its satisfying ring. But the evidence from Pennsylvania, Ohio, and Indiana, all of which held their state and congressional elections on October 11, was far from encouraging to those who were out of power and wanted in. With help from Sherman, who at Lincoln's urging not only granted furloughs wholesale to members of the twenty-nine Hoosier regiments in his army down in Georgia, but also sent John A. Logan and Frank Blair with them on electioneering duty, all three states registered gains for the Union ticket, both in Congress and at home.

"There is not, now, the slightest uncertainty about the reëlection of Mr Lincoln. The only question is, by what popular and what electoral majority?" Chase had told a friend in Ohio the week before, and once the ballots were tallied in these three states — all considered spheres of Copperhead influence — *Harper's Weekly* was quick to agree with the former Treasury head's assessment: "The October elections show that unless all human foresight fails, the election of Abraham Lincoln and Andrew Johnson is assured."

Neither of these nominees campaigned openly, any more than McClellan or Pendleton did, but their supporters around the country — men of various and sometimes awesome talents, such as the stout-lunged New Orleans orator, who "when he got fairly warmed up," one listener declared, "spoke so loud it was quite impossible to hear him" — more than made up for this traditional inactivity, which was designed to match the dignity of offices too lofty to be sought. Behind the scenes, other friends were active, too; especially those on the Union executive committee, responsible for funding the campaign. Cabinet members were assessed $250 each for the party coffers, and a levy of five percent was taken from the salaries of underlings in the War, Treasury, and Post Office departments. Gideon Welles alone refused to go along with this, pronouncing the collectors "a set of harpies and adventurers [who] pocket a large portion of the money extorted," and though workers in the Brooklyn Navy Yard "walked the plank in scores" for demonstrating support or sympathy for the opposition, Welles was by no means as active in this regard as Edwin Stanton, who at a swoop fired thirty War Department clerks for the same cause, including one whose sole offense was that he let it be known he had placed a bet on Little Mac. Such methods had produced excellent results in the recent state elections, held four weeks, to the day, before the national finale, scheduled for November 8, when still better returns were not only hoped for but expected, as the result of yet a third Sheridan-Early confrontation, providentially staged within three weeks of that all-important first Tuesday following the first Monday in November.

After Fisher's Hill, Sheridan's progress southward up the Valley — described by a VI Corps veteran as "a grand triumphal pursuit of a routed enemy" — ended at Mount Crawford, beyond the loom of Massanutton, where he gave his three infantry corps some rest while the cavalry raided Staunton and Waynesboro, a day's march ahead on the Virginia Central. Grant wanted the whole force, horse and foot, to move in that direction and down that railroad for a junction with Meade, wrecking Lee's northside supply lines as it went. "Keep on," he wired, "and your good work will cause the fall of Richmond." But Sheridan, with Hunter's unhappy example before him — not to mention that of bluff John Pope, who had tried such a movement two years ago, only to wind up riding herd on Indians out in Minnesota — replied that, even though Early had been eliminated as a deterrent, this was "impracticable with my present means of transportation. . . . I think that the best policy will be to let the burning of the crops in the Valley be the end of this campaign, and let some of this army go elsewhere." Lured by the notion of bringing Wright's hard-hitting corps back down the coast to Petersburg, Grant agreed that Sheridan would do well to make a return march down the Valley, scorching and smashing left and right to ensure that this classic "avenue of invasion" would no longer furnish subsistence even for those who lived there, let alone for Lee's army around Richmond. "Carry off stock of all descriptions, and negroes, so as to prevent further planting," he reminded Little Phil, elaborating on previous instructions. "If this war is to last another year we want the Shenandoah Valley to remain a barren waste."

He knew his man. Beginning the countermarch October 6, Sheridan reported the following night from Woodstock, forty miles away, that he had "destroyed over 2000 barns filled with wheat, hay, and farming implements; over 70 mills filled with flour and wheat; have driven in front of the army over 4000 head of stock, and have killed and issued to the troops not less than 3000 sheep. . . . Tomorrow I will continue the destruction of wheat, forage, &c. down to Fisher's Hill. When this is completed the Valley, from Winchester up to Staunton,

92 miles, will have but little in it for man or beast." Others attested to his proficiency in destruction, which continued round the clock. "The atmosphere, from horizon to horizon, has been black with the smoke of a hundred conflagrations," a correspondent wrote, "and at night a gleam brighter and more lurid than sunset has shot from every verge.... The completeness of the devastation is awful. Hundreds of nearly starving people are going north. Our trains are crowded with them. They line the wayside. Hundreds more are coming." They had little choice, a staff captain noted, having been "left so stripped of food that I cannot imagine how they escaped starvation."

To hurt the people, the land itself was hurt, and the resultant exodus was both heavy and long-lasting. A full year later, an English traveler found the Valley standing empty as a moor.

By now, although Early was being careful to maintain a respectful distance with his twice-defeated, twice-diminished infantry, butternut cavalry was snapping at the heels of the blue column, and Sheridan took this as continuing evidence of the timidity his own cavalry had shown, just over two weeks ago, after Fisher's Hill. Approaching that place from the opposite direction, October 9, he gave Torbert a specific order: "Either whip the enemy or get whipped yourself," then climbed nearby Round Hill for a panoramic view of the result. It was not long in coming. After crossing Tom's Brook, five miles short of Strasburg, Torbert had Merritt and Custer whirl their divisions around and charge the two pressing close in their rear under Lomax and Tom Rosser, who had recently arrived from Richmond with his brigade. Startled, the gray troopers stood for a time, exchanging saber slashes till their flanks gave way, then panicked and fled southward up the pike, pursued by the whooping Federals, who captured eleven of the dozen rebel guns in the course of a ten-mile chase to Woodstock and beyond, along with some 300 graybacks on fagged horses. "The Woodstock Races," the victors dubbed the affair, taking their cue from the Buckland Races, staged at Custer's expense by Jeb Stuart, a year ago this month, on the far side of the Blue Ridge. His temper cooled, his spirits lifted, Sheridan passed through Strasburg and crossed Cedar Creek next morning to put Crook's and Emory's corps in bivouac on the high ground, while Wright prepared his three divisions for an eastward march through Ashby's Gap, as agreed upon beforehand, to rejoin Grant at Petersburg.

They set out two days later, on October 12: only hours, as it developed, before Early reappeared on Fisher's Hill, five miles to the south. He had been reinforced from Richmond, not only by Rosser's cavalry brigade, but also by Kershaw's infantry division, which had been with him last month until it was recalled by Lee on the eve of the Federal strike at Winchester. Aware of these acquisitions, Sheridan was not disturbed, knowing as he did that they barely lifted Early's strength

to half his own. If Old Jubal was in search of a third drubbing, he would
be happy to oblige him when the time came.

All the same, he recalled the three VI Corps divisions from Ashby's
Gap next day, deferring their departure until the situation cleared, and
set about making his Cedar Creek position secure against attack while
he determined his next move. Amid these labors, which included
preparations for a horseback raid to break up the railroad around
Charlottesville, he was summoned to Washington by Halleck for a
strategy conference, October 16. He left that morning to catch a train
at Front Royal, and when he got there he was handed a telegram from
Wright, whom he had left in command on Cedar Creek, quoting a
message just intercepted from a rebel signal station on Massanutton
Mountain: "Be ready to move as soon as my forces join you, and we
will crush Sheridan." The signature was *Longstreet*; which was news in
itself, if the message was valid. Little Phil considered it "a ruse," however, designed to frighten him out of the Valley, and he declined to be
frightened. Besides, he had confidence in Wright, who assured him:
"I shall hold on here until the enemy's movements are developed, and
shall only fear an attack on my right, which I shall make every preparation for guarding against and resisting." Aside from calling off the
Charlottesville raid, Sheridan did not change his plans. Boarding the
train for Washington, he advised Wright: "Look well to your ground
and be well prepared. Get up everything that can be spared," he added,
and promised to return within two days, "if not sooner."

He was right in assuming the intercepted dispatch was a plant,
and right as well about its purpose. But he was altogether wrong if he
thought his twice-whipped adversary did not intend to try something
far more drastic if the invoked ghost of Old Peter failed to frighten
him away. In point of fact, so thoroughly had the bluecoats scorched
the country in his rear, Early believed he had no choice except "to
move back for want of provisions and forage, or attack the enemy
in his position with the hope of driving him from it." Another reason,
despite his usual crusty disregard for the opinions of others in or out
of the army, was that he had a reputation to retrieve; "To General
Sheridan, care of General Early," cynics had chalked on the tubes of
guns sent from Richmond to replace the 21 pieces he had lost in battle
this past month, exclusive of the eleven abandoned by the cavalry last
week in its panicky flight from Tom's Brook to Woodstock. Admittedly, with the blue force nearly twice his size, securely in position
on high ground, its front covered by a boggy creek and one flank
anchored on the Shenandoah, the odds against a successful assault were
long. But his predecessor Jackson, in command of these same troops,
had taught him how far audacity could go toward evening such odds,
and Lee himself, in a letter that followed the sending of reinforcements, had just told him: "I have weakened myself very much to

strengthen you. It was done with the expectation of enabling you to gain such success that you could return the troops if not rejoin me yourself. I know you have endeavored to gain that success, and believe you have done all in your power to assure it. You must not be discouraged, but continue to try. I rely upon your judgment and ability, and the hearty coöperation of your officers and men still to secure it. With your united force it can be accomplished."

Sustained and appealed to thus, Early was "determined to attack." But how, against such odds, could he do so with any real hope of success? Crippled as he was by arthritis, which aged him beyond his not quite forty-eight years and prohibited mountain climbing, he sent John Gordon, his senior division commander since the fall of Rodes, and Major Jedediah Hotchkiss, a staff cartographer inherited from Jackson, atop Massanutton to study the enemy position, which lay spread out below them, facing southwest along Cedar Creek. Crook's two divisions were nearest, on the Federal left, then Emory's two, beyond the turnpike, and finally Wright's three, on the distant right, where most of the blue cavalry was posted, obviously in expectation that if an attack was made it would come from that direction. Hotchkiss had discovered and recommended the route for the movement around Hooker's flank at Chancellorsville, but what he and Gordon saw from their high perch this bright fall morning, October 18, was an opportunity for an end-on strike that might outdo even Stonewall's masterpiece. A night march around the steep north face of Massanutton,

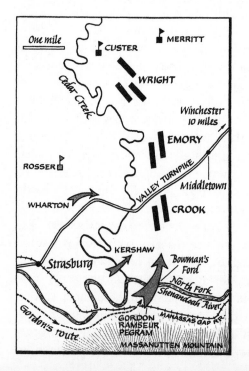

following a crossing of the Shenandoah near Fisher's Hill, would permit a recrossing of the river beyond its confluence with Cedar Creek, and this in turn would place the flanking column in direct confrontation with the unsuspecting Union left, which could be assaulted at first light in preparation for further assaults on Emory and Wright, once Crook's position had been overrun. Gordon, in fact, was so confident of success that when he came down off the mountain to urge the adoption of the plan, he offered to take all responsibility for any failure that occurred.

Early had never been one to avoid responsibility, nor did

he delay approval of the plan. He would march tonight and strike at dawn, he announced at a council of war called that afternoon. Gordon would be in charge of the turning column made up of his own and the divisions of Ramseur and Rodes, the latter now commanded by its senior brigadier John Pegram, recently recovered from the leg wound he had taken in the Wilderness. Kershaw would move through Strasburg, also under cover of darkness, and attack on the right of the Valley pike, crossing lower Cedar Creek to join the flanking effort as soon as he heard Gordon open fire, and Brigadier General Gabriel Wharton — successor to Breckinridge, who had been recalled to eastern Virginia on the eve of Fisher's Hill — would advance along and to the left of the turnpike, accompanied by Rosser's troopers, to menace and fix the Federals in position on the far side of the creek while the massed Second Corps, with Kershaw's help, struck their flank and drove them north across his front. Rosser then would take up the pursuit, as would Lomax, whose horsemen were to come upon the field by a roundabout march through Front Royal in order to cut off the blue retreat this side of Winchester, fifteen miles beyond Middletown, which was close in the Union rear. The plan was elaborate, involving a convergence by three columns, but it seemed pat enough to Early and his lieutenants, who went straight from the meeting to prepare for the various night marches designed to yield revenge for the two defeats they had recently suffered, here in the Valley from which their army took its name. The first of these — Third Winchester — had occurred exactly a month ago tomorrow, and this made them and their butternut veterans all the more eager to get started on the observance of that anniversary.

Aided by the light of a moon only three nights past the full, Gordon's column set out shortly after dark, the men of all three divisions having left their cooking utensils and even their canteens behind to avoid any give-away clink of unnecessary metal, and was in position in the shadows close to Bowman's Ford before daybreak, half a mile beyond the confluence of Cedar Creek and the river, prepared to splash across on signal. Similarly, accompanied by Early and his staff, as well as by most of the army's guns, Kershaw moved undetected around Strasburg to the near bank of the creek, across which he could see low-burnt campfires glowing in the darkness. Wharton followed, turning off to the left of the macadamized pike, preceded by Rosser, whose troopers rode at a walk to muffle the sound of hoofbeats on the stony ground. At 4.30, after an hour's wait on the creekbank, Early told Kershaw to go ahead and cross. He did, and while he was getting his men back into column on the other side, the boom of Rosser's horse artillery came from well upstream, along with the rattling clatter of picket fire nearby on the right, where Gordon was fording the Shenandoah just off the unalerted Union flank. The surprise was complete, if not quite overwhelming at the outset. "As we emerged from a thicket into the open," one of Kershaw's South Carolinians later wrote, "we could see the enemy in great commotion. But soon the works were filled with half-dressed troops, and they opened a galling fire upon us."

Kershaw charged, and as he did so, racing uphill through the spreading dawn, Gordon struck the left rear of the hastily formed blue line, which promptly broke. Elated (for these were Crook's men, the so-called West Virginians who had flanked them unceremoniously off Fisher's Hill four weeks ago) the Confederates surged forward on a broad front across the turnpike, pursuing and taking prisoners by the hundreds. With only a bit more time for getting set, Emory's corps fared little better, its unbraced ranks plowed by shells from rebel batteries massed on a hill beyond the creek. Fugitives from the four routed divisions fled northward through Wright's camps, in rear of which his Potomac veterans were falling in for battle. By now the sun was rising, alternately bright and pale as drifts of smoke blew past it, and the graybacks — joined at this stage by Wharton, who had been left with nothing in his front — came on yelling as they drove Wright's troops northeast across the open fields, first to a second and then to still a third position nearly two miles in rear of Middletown, where Jackson had captured Banks's wagon train in May of '62. This seemed to some a comparable achievement, while others went further afield in search of a parallel triumph. "The sun of Middletown! The sun of Middletown!" Early kept exclaiming, as if to say he had found his Austerlitz.

It was now past 9 o'clock, and he was delighted that within a scant four hours he had driven seven infantry divisions from the field with only five of his own, taking in the process more than 1300 prisoners, 18 guns, and an uncounted number of flags.

He was delighted; but he was also satisfied, it seemed. "Well, Gordon, this is glory enough for one day," he declared on meeting the Georgian near the front soon afterward. They stood looking across the fields at the Yankees reduced to stick men in the distance. "This is the 19th," he went on. "Precisely one month ago today we were going in the opposite direction." Gordon too was happy, but his thoughts were on the immediate future, not the past. "It is very well so far, General," he replied, "but we have one more blow to strike, and then there will not be left an organized company of infantry in Sheridan's army." His chief demurred. "No use in that. They will all go, directly." The Georgian was doubtful, and said so, indicating the bluecoats on the horizon. "This is the VI Corps, General. It will not go unless we drive it from the field." Once more Early shook his head. "Yes, it will go directly," he insisted as he continued to wait for the whipped Federals to withdraw.

Gordon said no more just then, but he later wrote: "My heart went into my boots." He was remembering "that fatal halt on the first day at Gettysburg," as well as Old Jube's daylong refusal, back in May, to let him strike Grant's unguarded flank in the Wilderness, which he believed had cost the Army of Northern Virginia the greatest of all its victories.

His heart might have sunk still deeper if he had known what was happening, across the way, while he and his chief stood talking. Sheridan had just arrived and was reassembling his scattered army for an all-out counterattack. True to his promise to return from the capital in two days, "if not sooner," he had slept last night in Winchester and had heard the guns of Cedar Creek, some fifteen miles away, while still in bed this morning. Dismissing the cannonade as "irregular and fitful" — most likely a reconnaissance-in-force by one of Wright's brigades — he tried to get back to sleep, without success. At breakfast, the guns still were muttering in the distance, faint but insistent, and he ordered his staff and cavalry escort to saddle up without delay. On the way out of town, he noticed "many women at the doors and windows of the houses, who kept shaking their skirts at us and who were otherwise markedly insolent in their demeanor." It occurred to him that they "were in rapture over some good news," mysteriously received, "while I as yet was utterly in ignorance of the actual situation." What was more, the sound of firing seemed to be moving to meet him; an ominous development. But it was not until he crossed Mill Creek, beyond Kernstown, and reached the crest of a low hill on the far side, that he and his staff and escort saw their worst fears confirmed by "the appalling spectacle of a panic-stricken army."

His first notion was to rally what was left of his command, here if not still farther back toward Winchester, for a last-ditch stand against the rebel force, which might or might not include Longstreet and his famed First Corps. With this in mind, Little Phil ordered his staff and escort to form a straggler line along the crest of the hill: all, that is, except two aides and a score of troopers, who would proceed with him toward Cedar Creek to find out what had happened.

In the course of the twelve-mile ride — "Sheridan's Ride," it came to be called — his purpose changed. Partly this was because of his aggressive nature, which reasserted itself, and partly it was the result of encountering groups of men along the roadside boiling coffee. That did not seem to indicate demoralization; nor did the cheers they gave when they saw him coming up the turnpike. "As he galloped on," one of the two aides later wrote, "his features gradually grew set, as though carved in stone, and the same dull red glint I had seen in his piercing black eyes when, on other occasions, the battle was going against us, was there now." Grimness then gave way to animation. He began to lift his little flat-topped hat in jaunty salute, rather as if in congratulation for a victory, despite the contradictory evidence. "The army's whipped!" an unstrung infantry colonel informed him, only to be told: "You are, but the army isn't." He put the spurs to Rienzi — an undersized, bandy-legged man, perched high on the pounding big black horse he had named for the town in Mississippi where he acquired him two years ago — and called out to the retreaters, "About face, boys! We are going back to our camps. We are going to lick them out of their boots!" He kept saying that, shouting the words at the upturned faces along the pike. "We are going to get a twist on those fellows. We are going to lick them out of their boots!"

And did just that: but not with the haste his breakneck manner had implied. Arriving about 10.30 he found Crook's corps disintegrated and Emory's not much better off, though most of it at least was still on hand. Wright's, however, was holding firm in its third position, a couple of miles northwest of Middletown, its line extended southeast across the turnpike by Merritt's and Custer's horsemen. Sheridan got to work at once, concentrating on getting Emory's troops, together with a trickle of retreaters who were returning in response to the exhortations he had shouted as he passed them on the pike, regrouped to support Wright in his resistance to the expected third assault by Early's whooping graybacks. Nor was he unmindful, even at this stage, of the fruits a sudden counterstroke might yield. "Tell General Emory if they attack him again to go after them, and to follow them up, and to sock it to them, and to give them the devil. We'll have all those camps and cannon back again." Emory got the message, and reacted with a sort of fervid resignation. "We might as well whip them today," he said. "If we don't, we shall have to do it tomorrow. Sheridan will get it out of us sometime."

Noon came and went, then 1 o'clock, then 2, and Little Phil continued to withhold his hand: as did Early, across the way.

At 3 o'clock, having at last persuaded his chief to let him undertake a limited attack, Gordon probed the Federal position beyond Middletown, but was easily repulsed. Still Sheridan held back, his numbers growing rapidly as more and more blue fugitives returned from their flight down the turnpike. Finally, after interrogating prisoners to make certain Longstreet was not there, he gave orders for a general advance at 4 o'clock. At first, though their ranks were thinned by looters prowling the Yankee camps in search of food and booty, the graybacks refused to budge. But then one of Emory's brigades found a weak spot in the rebel line, and before it could be reinforced Custer struck with his whole division, launching an all-out mounted charge that sundered the Confederate force and sent the two parts reeling back on Cedar Creek. "Run! Go after them!" Sheridan cried. "We've got the God-damnedest twist on them you ever saw!"

Early did what he could; which, at that stage, wasn't much. For the past four hours — hearing nothing from Lomax, whose roundabout march with half the cavalry later turned out to have been blocked near Front Royal by Torbert's third division — he had watched the steady buildup across the way, aware that this, combined with the rearward leakage from his idle ranks, restored the odds to about what they had been at daybreak, when he enjoyed the lost advantage of surprise. Increasingly apprehensive, he withdrew his captured guns beyond Cedar Creek for quick removal in a crisis, and started his nearly two thousand prisoners on their long trek south to Staunton. All this time, the vaunted "sun of Middletown" was declining, and the nearer it drew to the peaks of the Alleghenies the clearer he saw that the Federals not only had no intention of quitting their third position, in which they had little trouble fending off a belated feeling-out by Gordon, but were in fact preparing to launch a massive counterstroke. When it came, as it did at straight-up 4 o'clock, Early managed to withstand the pressure, left and center, until Emory drove a wedge between two of Gordon's brigades, opening a gap into which Custer flung his rapid-firing troopers; whereupon the Georgian's veterans, foreseeing disaster, began a scurry for the crossings in their rear. Rapidly the panic spread to the divisions of Kershaw and Ramseur, next in line. Dodson Ramseur — a major general at twenty-seven, the youngest West Point graduate to attain that rank in the Confederate army — tried his best to stay the rout, appealing from horseback to his men, but took a bullet through both lungs and was left to die in enemy hands next day, near Sheridan's reclaimed Belle Grove headquarters, where he fell.

By then there would be no uncaptured rebels within twenty miles; Sheridan, having spared his hand until he felt that victory was clearly within reach, exploited the break for all he was worth. "It took less time to drive the enemy from the field than it had for them to take it," according to Merritt, whose division clashed with Rosser's and overran the Confederate far left. Early pulled in Wharton and Pegram to brace the center, under assault from the VI Corps, but only succeeded in delaying Wright's advance. Rearward, meantime, a flying column of Union cavalry wrecked the bridge at Spangler's Mill, just west of Strasburg, with the result that the three miles of turnpike between there and the crossing at Cedar Creek were crowded with artillery and vehicles of all kinds, trapped and at the mercy of the pursuers. Little Phil thus recovered all the guns lost that morning, together with 25 of his adversary's, which enabled him to report that he had taken no less than 43 pieces at one swoop, though he neglected to mention that 18 of them were his own, recaptured in the confusion of the gray retreat.

Early fell back to Fisher's Hill in the twilight, intending to make a stand there in the morning, but soon saw that it would not do. Though his casualties were only a bit over half as heavy as Sheridan's this day —

2910, as compared to 5665 — his army, routed for the third time in thirty days, was in no condition for further resistance to an enemy twice its size. He took up the march for New Market before daylight, fighting off Custer's and Merritt's horsemen, who snapped at his heels all the way. Summing it up afterwards, Old Jube remarked sadly: "The Yankees got whipped. We got scared."

No explanation could shield him now, however, from the blame about to be heaped upon his head by his own people; blame that outweighed the praise that had come his way, three months ago, when he hovered defiantly on the outskirts of the northern capital. Indeed, the brightness of that midsummer exploit only served to deepen, by contrast, the shadows that gathered in this dark autumn of the Confederacy, which some were already saying would be its last. In the past thirty days Early had fought three full-scale battles, and all three had turned out to be full-scale routs. It mattered little to his critics that he had obliged Grant to lessen the pressure on Lee by detaching a veteran corps from Meade and rerouting another, on its way by sea to reinforce him, in order to meet Jubal's threat, first on the far and then on the near side of the Potomac. Nor did it matter that in the course of his follow-up campaign in the Valley, where he was outnumbered roughly three-to-one from start to finish, he inflicted a total of 16,592 casualties on his adversary — the equivalent of still another blue corps, by Sheridan's own count, and about as many combat troops as he himself had been able to scrape together for any one of those several confrontations — at a cost of less than 10,000 of his own. What mattered in the public's estimation was that, here on the field of Stonewall Jackson's glory, Early had been whipped three times running, each time more soundly than before. Tart of tongue, intolerant of the shortcomings of others since the outset of the war, the former Commonwealth's Attorney of Franklin County now found himself accused of ineptness, inefficiency, incompetence, even drunkenness and cowardice, in the journals and in public and private talk, here in his native Virginia as well as elsewhere in the South.

It was otherwise for Sheridan, whose praises now were being sung throughout the North. "With great pleasure," Lincoln wrote him, three days after Cedar Creek, "I tender to you and your brave army the thanks of the nation and my own personal admiration and gratitude for the month's operations in the Shenandoah Valley, and especially for the splendid work of October 19." The following evening, shortly before midnight, he was awakened by Assistant Secretary of War Charles A. Dana, who had just arrived from Washington to present him with the most prized of all rewards: his commission as a major general in the regular army, together with a commendation from the Adjutant General's office citing him "for the personal gallantry, military skill, and just confidence in the courage and patriotism of his troops . . .

whereby, under the blessing of Providence, his routed army was re-organized, a great national disaster averted, and a brilliant victory achieved." Riding through the camps with Little Phil next morning, October 25, Dana thought he had never seen a general so popular with all ranks: not even Sherman or Pap Thomas — maybe not even Mc-Clellan in his heyday.

Grant by then was ready to try still another of his pendulum swings at Lee. After ordering a second hundred-gun salute fired with shotted guns in honor of his protégé's third victory in the Valley, he wrote his wife: "I hope we will have one here before a great while to celebrate," and put his staff to work at once on plans for the heaviest strike, so far, at the Richmond-Petersburg defenses. Butler would feint north of the James, with the same number as before, but this time the lunge around the enemy right would be made by no less than 43,000 troops from Hancock, Warren, and Parke, on the theory that what two corps had failed to achieve, just under a month ago, might be accomplished now by three.

On October 27, with Butler already over the river, demonstrating for all he was worth at Fair Oaks, the companion blow was launched. As a further diversion, Parke was to hit the western end of the gray line, just east of Hatcher's Run, while Hancock and Warren swung wide around that stream to cross the Boydton Plank Road and then press north to get astride the Southside Railroad. Alas, no part of this flanking effort went well, and most parts went very badly indeed. Parke encountered stiff resistance and was stalled, and though Hancock made it to his initial objective on schedule, he had to stop and wait for Warren, who was delayed by difficult terrain. While Hancock waited Hill and Hampton struck him flank and front, attacking with about half of the 23,000 effectives Lee had kept south of the river, and forced him to withdraw that night, nearly out of ammunition and altogether out of patience. Meantime Warren turned east, under orders from Grant to help Parke envelop the Hatcher's Run defenses, but was unable to cross the creek; so he too withdrew. None of the three corps in this direction, Parke's or Hancock's or Warren's, had carried out its part of a plan whose only tangible result was the loss of 1758 men — plus the confirmation of Hancock's resolution to seek duty elsewhere; which he would do the following month, suffering as much from recent damage to his pride as from the continuing discomfort of his Gettysburg wound. North of the James, where Lee was not deceived by his gyrations around Fair Oaks, Butler lost 1103 killed, wounded, and missing, as compared to a Confederate loss of 451 there and perhaps twice that number in the opposite direction, along the Boydton Road and Hatcher's Run.

All lines remained the same, north and south of the river, as both armies prepared to go into winter quarters. No more discouraged by this latest failure than he had been by those others outside Petersburg and Richmond, Grant maintained what Lincoln called his "bulldog grip," prepared to "chew and choke" as long as need be. He could fail practically any number of times, and only needed to succeed but once. "I will work this thing out all right yet," he told his wife in a home letter.

In any case, this late-October affair down around Richmond went practically unnoticed by a public still absorbed in the recent Shenandoah drama, finding it restorative of the romantic, picture-book aspect so long missing from the war. "The nation rings with praises of Phil Sheridan," the Chicago *Tribune* noted, three days after the famous ride that saved the day at Cedar Creek and prompted black Rienzi's master to change his name to Winchester in commemoration of the exploit. Various poets tried their hand at the subject, including Herman Melville, but the one who caught the public's fancy best was T. Buchanan Read in a ballad titled "Sheridan's Ride."

> *Hurrah! Hurrah for Sher-i-dan!*
> *Hurrah! Hurrah for horse and man!*

its refrain went. Availing himself of a poetic license which the general he praised sometimes employed in his reports, Read doubled the distance of the gallop, eliminated all stops along the way, and had Rienzi himself announce the nick-of-time arrival to the troops:

> *"I have brought you Sheridan, all the way*
> *From Winchester, down to save the day."*

Widely read and recited, the piece made a fine recruiting and electioneering appeal, especially when delivered by professionals such as James E. Murdoch, a retired actor and celebrated "reader," whose declamation of the poem at a theater in Cincinnati on November 1, just one week before the presidential contest was to be settled at the polls, threw the crowd into a frenzy of approval for the war and for the men who fought and ran it.

✗ 4 ✗

Elsewhere — not only in the embattled heartland of the South, but also in places as far afield as Kansas, Vermont, and Brazil — both sides undertook desperate measures, throughout the critical two-month span that opened with the fall of Atlanta, in attempts to influence militarily the early-November political decision that perhaps would begin to end the war itself, come Inauguration Day. For example:

Aside from an abortive Union gunboat probe down White River in late June, which was turned back at Clarendon before the flotilla could enter the Arkansas to help patrol that line of Federal occupation, there had been no significant clash of arms in the Transmississippi since Frederick Steele retired from Camden in late April and Banks and Porter abandoned in May their effort to ascend the Red. Since then, Kirby Smith had seemed content to rest on his laurels, clinging precariously to what was left of Texas, Louisiana, Arkansas, and the Indian Territory — "Kirby-Smithdom," this vast but empty stretch of the continent was called — and resisted all efforts by Richmond and homesick subordinates to persuade him to go over to the offensive, either toward New Orleans or Saint Louis. Discontent to have so many good troops standing idle, even against such odds as here obtained, the authorities instructed him in mid-July to prepare Richard Taylor's corps, along with "such other infantry as can be spared," for a prompt movement across the Mississippi to assist in the defense of Atlanta and Mobile. Smith passed the order to Taylor, who had been sulking in Natchitoches for the past six weeks, his hurt feelings, if not his animosity toward his chief, somewhat relieved by a promotion to lieutenant general as a reward for his repulse of Banks. Eager to shake the dust of Kirby-Smithdom from his feet, Taylor looked into the possibility of a crossing, either by ferries or by the employment of what would have been the longest pontoon bridge in history, but replied in the end that it couldn't be done, since the Federals, getting wind of the project, had stationed ironclads at twelve-mile intervals all the way from Vicksburg past the mouth of the Red, with gunboats on constant patrol between them, day and night. "A bird, if dressed in Confederate gray, would find it difficult to fly across the river," a reconnoitering cavalryman declared.

Regretfully, for he was as anxious to get rid of Taylor as Taylor was to be quits with him, Smith informed his superiors in Virginia that the shift could not be made. By then the year had moved into August, and Richmond's answer solved at least a part of his problem by dusting the gadfly Taylor off his back. Stephen Lee having been sent to Georgia to head a corps under Hood, the Kentucky-born Louisianian (and presidential brother-in-law) was ordered to replace him in command of the Department of Alabama, Mississippi, and Eastern Louisiana, temporarily under Maury at Mobile. On a moonless night, within a week of receiving the order on August 22, Taylor crossed the river in a dugout canoe, swimming his mare alongside, and set out eastward for his new headquarters in Meridian. Before he reached it, Smith — or, more specifically, Sterling Price — had placed an alternate plan in execution, back in the Transmississipi, by launching 12,000 horsemen northward into Missouri.

Originally designed to draw attention away from the downriver crossing, the operation was now to be undertaken for its own sake: first against St Louis, where government warehouses bulged with the

goods of war, then westward along the near bank of the Missouri
River to the capital, Jefferson City — whose occupation, however brief,
would refurbish the somewhat tarnished star representing the state on
the Confederate battle flag — then finally back south "through Kansas
and the Indian Territory, sweeping that country of its mules, horses,
cattle, and military supplies." So Price was told by Smith in his instructions for the raid, which was also to serve the double-barreled purpose
of discouraging the departure of still more bluecoats to lengthen the
odds against Hood and Lee, east of the Mississippi, and of attracting
recruits to the gray column as it swept through regions whose
voters were about to get their chance, as the case was being put to them
in the campaign already under way, to "throw off the yoke of oppres-
sion." Mounted on Bucephalus, a warhorse as gray as its rider and
stockily built to withstand his two hundred and ninety dead-weight
pounds, Old Pap left Camden on August 28 and was joined next day at
Princeton by the divisions of Marmaduke and Fagan, who rode with
him across the Arkansas River at Dardanelle on September 2, midway
between Little Rock and Fort Smith, neither of whose blue garrisons
ventured out to challenge the invaders. At Pocahontas on the 13th, up
near the Missouri line, Jo Shelby added his division to the column, now
12,000 strong, with fourteen guns, though only about two thirds of the
troopers were adequately armed — a deficiency Price intended to repair
when he encountered opposition. On September 19, the day before his
fifty-fifth birthday, he crossed into his home state, headed for Ironton,
eighty miles to the north, terminus of the railroad running south out of
St Louis, another eighty miles away. At nearby Pilot Knob there was a
Union fort, Fort Davidson, with a garrison of about one thousand men
and seven guns, and he had chosen this as his first prize of the campaign, to be followed by those other, larger prizes, north and west.

Assembling his three divisions at Fredericktown on the 25th —
a day's ride east of Pilot Knob, which he intended to move against
tomorrow — he received news from St Louis that was both good and bad,
from different points of view. Department Commander William Rosecrans, on learning in early September that the graybacks had crossed the
Arkansas in strength, wired Halleck a request that A. J. Smith's two veteran divisions, then aboard transports at Cairo on their way to rejoin Sherman after service up the Red and in North Mississippi, be sent instead
to help defend Missouri against this new incursion. Old Brains complied
by ordering Smith upriver at once to "operate against Price & Co."
This meant that one purpose of the raid had been achieved before the
first blow landed; Price not only had discouraged the sending of more
troops east across the Mississippi, he had even provoked a drain in the
opposite direction, though at the cost of lengthening the odds against
fulfilling his other objectives, including the strike at goods-rich St Louis,
whose defenses now were manned by Smith's 8000 gorilla-guerillas, in

addition to its regular complement. In any case, after sending a brigade to rip up track on the railroad above Ironton and thus prevent the sudden arrival of reinforcements, he completed his plans for the reduction of Fort Davidson, twenty miles west of Fredericktown, and had it invested by nightfall the following day. He badly wanted its thousand-man garrison and their arms: especially those seven guns, whose addition would increase by half the firepower of the artillery he had brought along for blasting a path through his beloved Missouri.

Brigadier General Thomas Ewing, commander of the District of St Louis — Sherman's brother-in-law and author, too, of last year's infamous Order 11, which emptied Missouri's western counties of civilians in an attempt to ferret out guerillas whose bloody work grew bloodier in reaction to the hardships thus imposed on their women and children — had come down to the fort on an inspection trip, only to have the railroad cut in his rear, and decided not to abandon the place under threat from ten times the number he had for its defense. Accordingly, when a rebel delegation came forward under a flag of truce that night, demanding surrender, he sent it back with a defiant challenge, and when the demand was repeated a few hours later he did the same thing, adding that he would fire on the next white flag that approached his works. These were extremely stout, heptagonal in shape, with earthen walls nine feet tall and ten feet thick, surrounded by a dry moat as deep as the walls were high. Next day, September 27, they were tested in a furious six-hour fight that cost the attackers 1500 casualties, half again more than the total number of defenders, who lost 200. Falling back at dark, Old Pap's troopers began the construction of scaling ladders to use when they renewed the assault at dawn, and Ewing, knowing the fort could not hold out past then — and that he himself, as the author of Order 11, was unlikely to survive capture — assembled a council of war to decide whether to surrender or risk attempting a getaway. The vote was for the latter; which succeeded. Under cover of darkness the blue garrison built a drawbridge, draped it with canvas to muffle the sound of boots and hoofs, and withdrew undetected through a gap in the gray lines, leaving behind a slow fuze laid to the powder magazine. Slogging along in a column of twos, Ewing and his 800 survivors were well out the road to Rolla, seventy miles northwest, when the magazine blew with a great eruption of flame that gave the investors their first hint the fort was empty.

Marmaduke and Shelby, furious over their losses and fairly itching to fit Ewing for a noose, wanted to take out after him at once, but their fellow Missourian Price, already regretting a fruitless three-day interlude which had deprived him of more than a tenth of his command and netted him nothing but rubble and spiked guns, was unwilling to use up still more time on a project that he suspected had already cost him whatever chance there had been for surprising Rosecrans in St Louis.

Sure enough, after following the Iron Mountain Railroad to within thirty miles of the city, he found its garrison reinforced to a strength reportedly greater than his own. So he turned west, as planned — though he had not intended to do so empty-handed — up the south bank of the Missouri, wrecking bridges and culverts along the Pacific Railroad as he proceeded, first across the Gasconade River and then the Osage, which he cleared on October 6 to put his raiders within easy reach of Jefferson City.

But this too was untakable, he decided upon learning that its defenses were manned by bluecoats drawn from beyond the river despite a flurry of apprehension caused there the week before by a ruthless attack on Centralia, fifty miles north of the capital, by a force of about 200 butternut guerillas under William Anderson, who bore and lived up to the nickname "Bloody Bill." A former lieutenant in William C. Quantrill's gang, of Lawrence and Fort Baxter fame, he had quarreled with his chief in Texas and returned to his old stomping ground, near the Missouri-Kansas border, along with other disaffected members of the band, including George Todd and David Pool, as well as Frank James and his seventeen-year-old brother Jesse. Clattering into Centralia at midday, September 27 — the day of the Fort Davidson assault, one hundred and fifty miles southeast at Pilot Knob — they held up a stagecoach and an arriving train, killed two dozen unarmed soldiers aboard on furlough, along with two civilians who tried to hide valuables in their boots, and left hurriedly, with $3000 in greenbacks from the express car, when three troops of Union cavalry unexpectedly appeared and gave chase. Three miles out of town, the guerillas turned on their pursuers, who numbered 147, and shot dead or cut the throats of all but 23 who managed to escape on fast horses. "From this time forward I ask no quarter and give none," Anderson had announced on the square in Centralia, and then proceeded to prove he meant it, first in town and then out on the prairie.

Price's decision to forgo a strike at Jefferson City, the main political objective of his raid, was based on more than information that the capital had been reinforced, not only from beyond the Missouri, but also from scattered posts on this side of the river, including Springfield and Rolla. He learned too, while skirmishing on the outskirts after crossing the Moreau, that Rosecrans, supposedly left holding the bag in St. Louis, had sent Smith's 8000 infantry westward in his wake, along with 7000 troopers under Major General Alfred Pleasonton, who had served the better part of a year as cavalry commander in the Army of the Potomac until Grant replaced him with Sheridan, back in March, and sent him west to share Old Rosy's exile. Price was aware that any prolonged attempt to break through the capital defenses was likely to be interrupted by the arrival of Pleasonton and Smith, now toiling along the demolished Pacific Railroad with a combined strength greater than his own. Moreover, scouts coming in from the Kansas border, a hundred and forty miles in the opposite direction, reported that more than 20,000 regulars and militia were being assembled there for his reception by the department commander, Major General Samuel R. Curtis, his old Pea Ridge adversary. The thing to do, he reasoned, was get there fast, before Curtis got organized or Smith and Pleasonton came up in his rear to make the fight for Kansas City a two-front affair. Accordingly, he turned his back on the state capitol, plainly visible on its hill beyond the treetops, and continued his march another forty miles upriver to Boonville, which he reached October 9. Riding due west for Lexington, sixty-odd miles away — the scene of his one unassisted victory, back in the first September of the war, hard on the heels of the triumph he had shared with Ben McCulloch at Wilson's

Creek — he put Marmaduke's division in the lead and had Shelby strike out left and right at Sedalia and Glasgow, both of which were taken on the 15th, together with their garrisons, while Fagan covered the rear, on the lookout for Pleasonton's horsemen, who were known to have reached Jefferson City four days ago. Four days later at Waverly, his home town on the south bank of the Missouri, twenty miles short of Lexington, Shelby encountered a force of Coloradans and Kansans under Major General James Blunt, brought in from the plains by Curtis and sent forward to delay the approach of the raiders. Here were fired the opening shots of what turned out to be a week-long running skirmish, covering more than a hundred miles of the border region, with several pauses for full-scale engagements along the way.

Shelby drove Blunt back through Lexington, October 20, and on across the Little Blue next day, fighting house-to-house through Independence to the Big Blue, just beyond. Curtis had established a line of works along the opposite bank, manned by 4000 regulars and an equal number of Kansas militia, some 16,000 of whom had come forward in the current emergency, though only about one fourth of them were willing to cross into Missouri, the remainder having called a halt at the state line, half a dozen miles to the west. His plan was to hang on there, securely intrenched, till Pleasonton came up in Price's rear, then go over to the offensive, east and west, against the graybacks trapped between the Big and Little Blues. It did not work out quite that way: partly because of the timid militia, skulking rearward on home ground, but mainly because of black-plumed Jo Shelby. While Marmaduke and Fagan took the bluecoats under fire from across the river on the morning of the 22d, Shelby splashed his three brigades across an upstream ford to flank the defenders out of their works and throw them into retreat on Westport, immediately south of Kansas City and within two miles of the state line. As a result, when Pleasonton arrived that night he found Curtis's intrenchments bristling in his path, occupied by the butternut invaders he had been trailing ever since he left St Louis, three weeks back.

Confronted east and west by forces that totaled three times his own, Old Pap took stock and pondered his next move. Staffers advised that this be south without delay, while the long road home lay open for a withdrawal in good order. But he was urged by Shelby, whose blood was up, to take advantage of a position which, though not without obvious dangers, fairly glittered with Napoleonic possibilities. Using one division to hold Pleasonton in check on the far side of the Big Blue, he could move with the other two against Curtis at nearby Westport, then turn, having disposed of the Kansan and his green militia, to crush Pleasonton and thus cap the raid with a stunning double victory; after which, according to Shelby, he could proceed at his leisure, rounding up Federal garrisons and Confederate recruits, as intended from the

outset, on the final leg of his march back across the Arkansas. Price
liked the notion, partly for its own glittering sake, partly because of
the chance it gave him to put a gainful end to a campaign that so far
had profited his country and his reputation next to nothing. Accordingly, after lodging Marmaduke's two brigades in the Union intrenchments overlooking the Big Blue, he ordered Fagan and Shelby to prepare
their six for the attack on Curtis, whose troops were deployed along
Brush Creek below Westport, at daybreak tomorrow, October 23.

Pleasonton, having posted his four brigades for a dawn assault on
the former Union works across the river west of town, spent the night in
Independence. A graduate of West Point and the hard-knocks school
of combat in the East — including Brandy Station, where he had taken
Jeb Stuart's measure on the eve of Gettysburg — he intended to do to
Price tomorrow what Price had done to Curtis today; that is, dispossess
him of those works. Even though no blue infantry was at hand (A. J.
Smith's two divisions had turned south at Lexington, under orders from
Rosecrans to head off a rebel swerve in that direction, and thus were
removed from all possible contact with the raiders, now or later) the
forty-year-old cavalryman was satisfied he could do the job on his
own, and with this in mind had his cannoneers keep heaving shells
across the Blue to discourage the intrenched defenders from getting
much sleep till after midnight, a scant five hours before he planned to
strike them.

By that time Curtis was planning to strike them too, despite his
mistrust of the balky militia that comprised about four fifths of his
command. Persuaded by Blunt — as Price had been by Shelby —
that a victory was within his reach if he would only grasp it, the fifty-
nine-year-old department head reversed his previous decision to fall
back on Fort Leavenworth, twenty-five miles north on the Missouri,
and agreed instead, under pressure from Blunt and others at a council
of war in the Gillis House that night in Kansas City, to go over to the
offensive in the morning. Down along Brush Creek all this while, his
green recruits were kept awake by the boom of Pleasonton's guns on
the far side of the river and by the nerve-jarring crump of shells on the
near bank, close in their rear. "I'd rather hear the baby cry," one married
volunteer remarked. Presently the guns left off, but he continued to
fret, confiding in a friend that he expected to be killed in tomorrow's
contest, and found small comfort in assurances that the future life was
superior to this one. "Well, I don't know about that," he said, still
worried.

His chances for survival were better than he knew. Next day's
battle, though numerically the largest ever fought in the Transmississippi — out of 40,000 Federals and Confederates on the field, close to
30,000 were engaged, as compared to just under 27,000 at Pea Ridge,
the next largest, and only about half that many at Wilson's Creek —

was neither as hotly contested nor as bloody as both sides had expected when they lay down to sleep the night before. Fagan and Shelby went forward as ordered, shortly after daybreak, and threw Curtis's greenhorns into skittery retreat, much as Shelby had predicted and Curtis, who watched the action through a spyglass from the roof of a convenient farmhouse, had feared. But not for long. Thrown back on Westport and the Kansas line, the militiamen and regulars, outnumbering the attackers better than two to one, not only rallied and held their own against renewed assaults by the yelling graybacks, but even, in response to a horseback appeal from their commander, who came down off his roof to ride among them, began massing for a counterattack to recover the lost ground along the creek. Whereupon, in this moment of crisis — it was now about midmorning — Price was informed that Pleasonton had broken Marmaduke's line on the near bank of the Big Blue and was approaching his right rear, threatening to come between the raiders and their train, parked southward on the road he had been persuaded not to take the night before.

Enraged to find the dawn attack deferred to await his arrival from Independence, Pleasonton had begun his day with on-the-spot dismissals of two brigade commanders — "You're an ambulance soldier and belong in the rear," he told one of the brigadiers, shaking a cowhide whip in his face quite as if he meant to use it — and peremptory orders for their successors to throw everything they had against Byram's Ford, a strongly defended crossing on the rebel right. He did this on the theory that the enemy would least expect a major effort there, and the result was all he hoped for. When the dismounted horsemen splashed across the ford, through the abatis on the opposite bank, then up and over the intrenchments on the ridge beyond, he followed with a third brigade to deepen and widen the breakthrough, while the fourth came on behind. Marmaduke's rattled defenders, turned suddenly out of their works by twice their number, fled rearward across the prairie that stretched to the Kansas line, unobstructed except by the trees along Brush Creek, where Price's effort against Curtis was in crisis.

Pleasonton reined in his horse to watch them flee, and as he did he stabbed the air with one hand, pointing at the sticklike figures, running or wavering, near and far. "Rebels! Rebels! Rebels!" he shouted at his troopers, who had stopped, much as he himself had done, to watch this flight across the rolling tableland. "Fire! Fire, you damned asses!" he kept shouting.

There was not much time for that, however. Faced with the threat of annihilation on the open prairie, Price disengaged Fagan, pulled him back alongside Marmaduke's reassembled fugitives, and used them both to cover the withdrawal of his train, southward down the road on which it had been parked for ready accessibility or a sudden getaway. Shelby — as was only fair, since he was the one who had talked his chief into this predicament in the first place — was charged with stalling the blue pursuit, at least until the wagons and guns and the other two divisions, remounted to make the best possible time, escaped the closing jaws of the trap and got a decent head start down the road to Little Santa Fe, a dozen miles below on the Kansas border. Hemmed in as he was on three sides (and grievously outnumbered; Curtis and Pleasonton had just over 20,000 infantry and cavalry engaged from first to last — less than three quarters of their total force — while Price had only about 9000 — all that he had arms for) this was no easy task; but Shelby managed it in style, cutting his way out with a mounted charge in the final stage, near sunset, to join the gray column grinding its way south in the darkness. Too ponderous for even heavy-hocked Bucephalus to bear his weight for long, Price rode in a carriage on the retreat, depressed by the knowledge that Westport — sometimes disproportionately referred to as "the Gettysburg of the Transmississippi," though in point of fact it was fought for no real purpose and settled nothing — had merely added another repulse to his long list of reverses, east and west of the Mississippi River. Fortunately it was not a costly one, however. Neither commander filed a casualty report, but their losses seem not to have reached a thousand men on either side.

A heavier defeat, with heavier losses, came two days later, fifty miles beyond Little Santa Fe, soon after the raiders crossed the Marais des Cygnes, which flowed eastward into Missouri and the Osage. They had made good time, marching day and night through wet and blustery weather, but Pleasonton and Curtis dogged their heels, eager to close in for the kill. Swinging west to take advantage of better roads leading south beyond the Kansas line, Price halted Marmaduke on the far bank of the tributary river — mostly referred to hereabouts as the Mary Dayson — in hope of delaying his pursuers at that point. This the Missouri West Pointer did, briefly at least, and then fell back to a similar position on Mine Creek, three miles below, where Fagan had been deployed to support the rear-guard effort with ten of the column's fourteen pieces of artillery. Here on that same morning, October 25, occurred the first and last full-scale engagement between regulars, Federal and Confederate, to be fought on Kansas soil. The first Price knew of its outcome was when he saw troops from both divisions come stumbling toward him in disorder, pursued by whooping bluecoats, mounted and afoot. All ten guns were lost in the rout, along with close to a thousand prisoners, including Marmaduke himself, Brigadier General William Cabell — Old Pap's only other West Pointer, in charge of one of Fagan's Arkansas brigades — and four colonels. Hit in the arm and thrown from his horse, Marmaduke was taken single-handedly by James Dunlavy, an Iowa private, who marched his muddy, dejected captive directly to army headquarters. "How much longer have you to serve?" the department commander asked. Told, "Eight months, sir," Curtis turned to his adjutant: "Give Private Dunlavy a furlough for eight months." The Iowa soldier left for home next day, taking with him the long-haired rebel general's saber for a souvenir of the war that was now behind him, and Marmaduke and Cabell were soon on their way to northern prison camps, the war behind them too.

Once more Price called Shelby back to contest a further advance by the exultant Federals, who were delayed in following up their victory by an argument that broke out between Curtis and Pleasonton as to whether the latter's prisoners were to be sent to Leavenworth or St Louis and thus be credited to Curtis or to Rosecrans. While Shelby fought successive rear-guard actions on the Little Osage and the Marmiton, Price reassembled the other two divisions and pressed on south with the train. Beyond the Little Osage the road forked, one branch leading to Fort Scott, six miles south across the Marmiton, the other back southeast into Missouri. Formerly the fort had been on Old Pap's list of trophies to be picked up on this final leg of the raid, but now he had neither the time nor the strength to move against it. After pausing to lighten the train by burning some 400 wagons, together with the excess artillery ammunition — excess because only one four-gun battery remained — he took the left-hand fork and set out on a forced march of just over sixty miles to Carthage, down near the southwest corner of his home state. Although most of the blue pursuers stopped for food and a night's sleep at Fort Scott, and though Shelby managed to keep the rest from overtaking the train and its escort, still the night-long day-long night-long trek, ending at Carthage on the morning of the 27th, was an experience not soon forgotten by those who made it. "I don't know that a longer march graces history; a fatal day for horse flesh," one weary raider noted in his journal at its close.

Price rewarded their efforts with a full day's rest, then resumed the march next morning, hoping to reach and cross the Arkansas River, still more than a hundred miles away, without having to stop for another time- and man-killing fight for survival. His hope was not fulfilled. At Newtonia that afternoon, twenty-odd miles beyond Carthage, the Federals came up in his rear and obliged him to turn and form ranks for a battle no one knew was to be the last ever fought between regular forces west of the Mississippi. Back at Fort Scott two days ago, the Kansas militia and two of the Missouri cavalry brigades had retired from the chase — as had Pleasonton himself, after falling sick — but Curtis, with his regulars and Blunt's plainsmen still on hand, as well as Pleasonton's other two brigades, was determined to overtake the still-outnumbered raiders before they escaped. Here at Newtonia he got his chance; along with cause to regret it. Spotting dust clouds south of town, Blunt thought Price was attempting a getaway and galloped hard around his flank to cut him off, only to be cut off himself by Shelby, who handled him roughly until other blue units broke through to cover his with-

drawal. The fighting sputtered out at sundown, with little or no advantage on either side, and Price took up his march southward, un-
pursued, while Curtis waited for Blunt to lick his wounds. "I must
be permitted to say that I consider him the best cavalry officer I ever
saw," Old Pap wrote gratefully of Shelby in his report of the campaign:
an opinion echoed and enlarged upon by Pleasonton years later, when
he said flatly that the Missourian was "the best cavalry general of the
South."

Curtis rested briefly, then proceeded, no longer in direct pursuit
of Price, who veered southwest beyond Newtonia, but rather by a
shorter route, due south across the Arkansas line, in hope of intercepting
the raiders when they swung back east to recross the Arkansas River between Fort Smith and Little Rock; probably at Dardanelle, he figured,
where they had crossed on their way north eight weeks ago. Hurrying
from Pea Ridge to the relief of Fayetteville, which was reported under
attack by a detachment from the rebel main body at Cane Hill, just
under twenty miles southwest, the Kansan supposed that his cut-off
tactics had succeeded. When he reached Fayetteville on November 4,
however, he not only found the attackers gone, he also learned that
his adversary was moving en masse in the opposite direction, away from
the trap contrived for his destruction. Reduced by casualties and desertions, badly worn by a thousand miles of marching, and even lower in
spirits than he was on food and ammunition — which was low indeed
— Price was in no condition to risk another heavy engagement, and to
avoid one he had decided not to attempt a march east of Fort Smith,
whose garrison would be added to the force that would surely intercept
him before he made it across the river in that direction. Instead, he would
move on west, toward Tahlequah in the Indian Territory, for an upstream crossing of the Arkansas twenty-odd miles beyond the border.
Curtis followed as far as a north-bank settlement called Webber's Falls,
November 8, only to find that the raiders, assisted by friendly Choctaws,
had destroyed all the available boats on reaching the south bank the day
before. So he pronounced the campaign at an end, fired a 24-gun salute
in celebration, the booms reverberating hollowly across the empty plains,
and turned back toward Kansas, glad to be done with an opponent who,
as he declared in closing his report, had "entered Missouri feasting and
furnishing his troops on the rich products and abundant spoils of the
Missouri Valley, but crossed the Arkansas destitute, disarmed, disorganized, and avoiding starvation by eating raw corn and slippery-elm
bark."

Worse things were said of Price by his own soldiers in the course
of their detour through the wintry territorial wilds. "God damn Old
Pap!" was among the milder exclamations on the march, and afterwards
there was to be a formal inquiry into charges of "glaring mismanagement
and distressing mental and physical military incapacity." One trooper

wrote that his unit subsisted for four days on parched acorns, while another told how he and his comrades butchered and devoured a fat pony along the way. A cold wind cut through their rags, freezing the water in their canteens, and coyotes laughed from the darkness beyond their campfires, a terrifying sound to men too weak from hunger or dysentery to keep up with the column. Even so, hundreds fell out in the course of this last long stage of the raid, south through Indian country, down across the Red into Texas, and finally back east to Laynesport, Arkansas, which they reached on December 2, still a hundred miles west of Camden, which Price had left just over three months ago. Though he put the case as best he could in his report — "I marched 1434 miles; fought 43 battles and skirmishes; captured and paroled over 3000 Federal officers and men . . . [and] do not think I go beyond the truth when I state that I destroyed in the late expedition to Missouri property to the amount of $10,000,000 in value" — his claim that his own losses totaled fewer than a thousand men, in and out of combat, scarcely tallied with the fact that he returned with only 6000, including recruits, or barely half the number who had ridden northward with him in September.

Whatever the true figures were, in men or money, and however great the disruption had been along the Missouri River and the Kansas border, this last campaign in the Transmississippi had no more effect on the outcome of the national conflict than did a much smaller, briefer effort made at the same time, up near the Canadian border, against St Albans, a Vermont town of about 5000 souls. This too was a raid designed to bring home to voters remote from the cockpit of war — Westport and St Albans were both just under a thousand miles from Charleston — some first-hand notion of the hardships involved in a struggle they were about to decide whether to continue or conclude: with the difference that the New England blow was struck primarily at what was reputed to be a New Englander's tenderest spot, his wallet.

First Lieutenant Bennett Young, a twenty-one-year-old Kentuckian who had ridden with Morgan, reconnoitered St Albans on a visit from Canada, fifteen miles away, and returned on the evening of October 18 with twenty followers, most of them escaped or exchanged prisoners like himself. Arriving in twos and threes to avoid suspicion, they checked into various hotels and boarding houses, then assembled at 3 o'clock the following afternoon in the town square, where they removed their overcoats to reveal that each wore a gray uniform and a pair of navy sixes. At first, when Young announced that the place was under formal occupation and ordered all inhabitants to gather in the square, the townspeople thought they were being treated to some kind of joke or masquerade, but when the raiders began discharging pistols in the direction of those who were slow to obey the lieutenant's order, they knew better. Meantime, three-man details proceeded to the three banks and gathered up all the cash on hand, though not before outraged citizens began to shoot at them from second-story windows. In the skirmish that ensued, one townsman was killed, three invaders were wounded, and several buildings around the square were set aflame with four-ounce bottles of Greek fire, brought along to be flung as incendiary grenades.

Back in Canada not long after nightfall, once more in civilian dress, Young and his men counted the take from this farthest north of all Confederate army operations. It came to just over $200,000; none of which ever found its way to Richmond, as originally intended, being used instead to finance other disruptions in other Federal regions that had not felt the hand of war till now.

★ ★ ★

Afloat as ashore, throughout this critical span of politics and war, there were desperate acts by desperate men intent on winning a reputation before it was too late. Commander Napoleon Collins, for example, a fifty-year-old Pennsylvanian with thirty years of arduous but undistinguished service, learned while coaling at Santa Cruz de Tenerife in mid-September that the rebel cruiser *Florida* had been there for the same purpose the month before; reports attending her departure, August 4, were that her next intended port of call was Bahia, just around the eastern hump of South America, some 1500 nautical miles away. His orders, as captain of the U.S.S. *Wachusett* — a sister ship of the *Kearsarge* — were to intercept and sink her, much as Winslow had sunk the *Alabama* three months ago off Cherbourg, and he wasted no time in clearing the Canaries for Brazil. Arriving in early October he did not find the prize he sought in Bahia harbor; nor, despite her six-week head start and her reputed greater speed, had she been there. Apparently the Santa Cruz report was false, or else she had been terribly busy on the way. Then two days later, shortly after dark, October 4, a trim, low-lying sloop of war put into All Saints Bay, and when Collins dispatched a longboat to look her over he found to his delight that the report had been true after all. The twin-stacked handsome vessel, riding at anchor no more than a long stone's throw off his starboard flank, was indeed the *Florida*, one of the first and now the last of the famed Confederate raiders that had practically driven Federal shipping from the Atlantic.

Since her escape from Mobile Bay in January of the previous year, *Florida* had burned or ransomed 37 prizes, and to these could be added 23 more, taken by merchantmen she had captured and converted into privateers, thereby raising her total to within half a dozen of the *Alabama*'s record 66. Most of the time she had been in Commander John Maffitt's charge, but since the beginning of the current year, Maffitt having fallen ill, she had been under her present skipper, Lieutenant

Charles M. Morris. Her most recent prize was taken a week ago, and Collins had it very much in mind to see that she took no more. Employing Winslow's tactics, he sent Morris next day, through the U.S. consul at Bahia, a formal invitation to a duel outside the three-mile limit. But Morris not only declined the challenge, he even declined to receive the message, addressed as it was to "the sloop *Florida*," quite as if he and his ship were nationless. He would leave when he saw fit, he said, having been granted an extension of the two-day layover allowed by international law, and would be pleased to engage the *Wachusett* if he chanced to meet her on the open sea. Collins absorbed the failure of this appeal to "honor," which had worked so well for Winslow against Semmes, then fell back on a secondary plan, rasher than the first and having nothing whatever to do with honor. Tomorrow night would be the *Florida*'s third in Bahia harbor, and he was determined, regardless of the security guaranteed by her presence in a neutral port, that it would be her last.

Suspecting nothing, Morris coöperated fully in the execution of the plan now being laid for his undoing. He had had the shot withdrawn from his guns, as required by law before entering the harbor, and assured the port authorities — who seemed disturbed by the thought of what he (not Collins, with whose government their own had long-standing diplomatic relations) might do in the present edgy situation — that he would commit no hostile act, in violation of their neutrality, against the enemy vessel anchored off his flank. This done, he let his steam go down, hauled his fires, and gave the port and starboard watches turnabout shore leave while off duty. On the night of October 6 he went ashore himself, with several of his officers, to attend the opera and get a good night's sleep in a hotel, leaving his first lieutenant aboard in charge of half the crew. Long before dawn next morning he was awakened by the concierge, who informed him that his ship was under attack by the *Wachusett* in the harbor down below.

Collins had planned carefully and with all the boldness his given name implied. Slipping his cables in the deadest hour of night, he backed quietly to give himself space in which to pick up speed for a ram that would send the raider to the bottom, then paused to build up a full head of steam before starting his run on the stroke of 3 o'clock. His intention was to bear straight down on the sitting vessel and thus inflict a wound that would leave her smashed beyond repair; but *Wachusett* went a bit off course and struck instead a glancing blow that crushed the bulwarks along the rebel's starboard quarter and carried away her mizzenmast and main yard. Convinced that he had inflicted mortal damage, Collins was backing out to let his adversary sink, when there was a spatter of small arms fire from the wreckage on her deck. He replied in kind and added the boom of two big Dahlgrens for emphasis, later saying:

"The *Florida* fired first." As he withdrew, however, he saw that the raider was by no means as badly hurt as he had thought. Accordingly, he changed his plan in mid-career and decided to take her alive. Guns reloaded, he stopped engines at a range of one hundred yards and called out a demand for the sloop's immediate surrender before he blew her out of the water.

Aboard the crippled *Florida*, with no steam in her boilers, no shot in her guns, and only a leave-blown skeleton crew on hand, the lieutenant left in charge had little choice except to yield, though he did so under protest at this hostile action in a neutral port. Collins promptly attached a hawser to the captive vessel and proceeded to tow her out to sea, fired on ineffectively by the guns of a harbor fort and pursued by a Brazilian corvette which he soon outdistanced. Morris arrived from the hotel in time to see the two sloops leave the bay in this tandem fashion, *Wachusett* in front and his own battered *Florida* in ignominious tow, and though he too protested this "barbarous and piratical act," they were by then beyond recall on the high seas, bound for Norfolk.

After a stopover in the West Indies, Napoleon Collins brought the two warships into Hampton Roads on November 12, both under their own power. There he received a welcome as enthusiastic as the one that had greeted his former squadron commander, Captain Charles Wilkes — also at one time skipper of the *Wachusett* — following his removal, three years ago, of Mason and Slidell from the British steamer *Trent*. Seward, on learning of what had happened in Bahia harbor, was only too aware that the two cases were uncomfortably similar, except that this was an even more flagrant violation of international law. Like the two Confederate envoys, the *Florida* was likely to prove an elephant on the State Department's hands, and he began to regret that Collins had not sunk her outright instead of bringing her in, since there could be little doubt that the courts would order her returned intact to the neutral port where he had seized her. "I wish she was at the bottom of the sea," the Secretary was afterwards reported to have remarked in discussing the affair with David Porter, recently transferred from duty on the Mississippi to command the North Atlantic Blockading Squadron. "Do you mean it?" Porter asked, and Seward replied: "I do, from my soul." The admiral returned to his headquarters in Hampton Roads and ordered the captive sloop moved to Newport News and anchored, as an act of poetic justice, near the spot where the *Merrimac* had sunk the *Cumberland*. In the course of the shift, the raider collided with a transport, losing her jibboom and figurehead and being severely raked along one side. She began leaking rather badly, and though her pumps were put to work, suddenly and mysteriously in the early-morning hours of November 28 she foundered and went to the bottom, nine fathoms down. Or maybe not so mysteriously after all; Porter subsequently confided that he had put an engineer aboard with orders to "open her sea cock before midnight, and do not leave that engine room until the water is up to your chin."

This might or might not account for her loss (for with Porter as an unsupported witness, no set of facts was ever certain) but in any case Seward's task in responding to the formal Brazilian protest, which arrived next month, was greatly simplified. "You have justly expected that the President would disavow and regret the proceedings at Bahia," he replied, adding that the captain of the *Wachusett* would be suspended from duty and court-martialed. As for the rebel sloop, there could be no question of returning her, due to "an unforeseen accident which casts no responsibility upon the United States." All the same, a U.S. gunboat was to put into All Saints Bay on the Emperor's birthday, two years later, and fire a 21-gun salute as the *amende honorable* for this offense against the peace and dignity of Brazil. Collins himself was tried within six months, as Seward promised, and despite his plea that "the capture of the *Florida* was for the public good," was sentenced to be dismissed from the service. Gideon Welles, much pleased with the commander's response to a situation that had worked out well in the end, promptly set the verdict aside, restored the Pennsylvanian to duty, and afterwards promoted him to captain. Like Charles Wilkes, he would be a rear admiral before he died, a decade later.

Welles's pleasure was considerably diminished, however, by reports that followed hard on the heels of Collins's exploit, indicating that this was by no means the end of rebel depredations against Federal shipping on the sea lanes of the world. By coincidence, on October 8 — the day after the *Florida* was taken under tow in Bahia harbor — the Clyde-built steamer *Sea King*, a fast sailer with a lifting screw, an iron frame, and six-inch planking of East India teak, left London bound for Madeira, which she reached ten days later to rendezvous with a Liverpool-based tender bearing guns and ammunition and James I. Waddell, a forty-year-old former U.S. Navy lieutenant who had gone over to the Confederacy, with equal rank in its infant navy, when his native North Carolina left the Union. He took over at once as captain of the *Sea King*, supervised the transfer and installation of her armament, formally commissioned her as the C.S.S. *Shenandoah*, and set out two days later, October 20, on a cruise designed to continue the *Alabama-Florida* tradition. In point of fact, his mission was to extend that tradition into regions where his country's flag had never flown. Like the raid on St Albans, staged the day before he left Madeira, and the recent 31-prize sortie by the *Tallahassee*, to Halifax and back, *Shenandoah's* maiden effort was designed as a blow at the pocketbooks of New England, although Waddell had no intention of sailing her anywhere near that rocky shore. "The enemy's distant whaling grounds have not been visited by us," Secretary Mallory had noted in an August letter of instructions. "This commerce constitutes one of his reliable sources of national wealth no less than one of his best schools for seamen, and we must strike it, if possible."

Nothing in the new captain's orders precluded the taking of prizes en route to the field of his prime endeavor. He took six — two brigs, two barks, a schooner, and a clipper — between the day he left Madeira and November 12, the day the captive *Florida* steamed into Hampton Roads. Three more he took — another schooner and two barks, bringing the total to nine in as many weeks — in the course of a stormy year-end voyage around the Cape of Good Hope to Hobson's Bay, Australia, where the *Shenandoah* stopped to refit before setting out again, northward through the Sea of Japan and into the North Pacific, to take up a position for intercepting Yankee whaling fleets bound for Oahu with the product of their labors in the Arctic Ocean and the Bering Sea. A whaler filled with sperm oil, Waddell had been told, would give a lovely light when set afire.

Cruisers were and would remain a high-seas problem, mainly viewed through a murk of inaccurate reports. But there were other problems the Union navy considered far more pressing, especially through this critical season of decision, because they were closer to home and the November voters. One was blockade-runners; or, more strictly speaking, the discontent they fostered. Although by now only three out of four were getting through the cordon off the Carolina coast, as compared to twice that ratio two years back, there was general agreement that they could never really be stopped until their remaining ports were sealed from the landward side. Meantime, sleek and sneaky, they kept weary captains and their crews on station in all weathers, remote from combat and promotion and contributing for the most part nothing but their boredom to a war they felt could be quickly won if only they were free to bring their guns to bear where they would count. Another problem was rebel ironclads, built and building, which threatened not only to upset plans for future amphibious gains, but also to undo gains already made.

A prime example of this last, now that the *Merrimac-Virginia*, the *Arkansas*, and the *Tennessee* had been disposed of, was the achievement of the *Albemarle* in reclaiming the region around the Sound whose name she bore. Since mid-April, when she retook Plymouth and blocked ascent of the Roanoke toward Petersburg and Richmond, a stalemate advantageous to the Confederacy had obtained there, and though the commander of the half-dozen Federal vessels lying off the mouth of the river had devised a number of highly imaginative plans for her discomfort — including one that involved the use of stretchers for lugging hundred-pound torpedoes across the intervening swamps, to be planted and exploded alongside the Plymouth dock where she was moored —

none had worked, so vigilant were the graybacks in protecting this one weapon whose loss would mean the loss of everything within range of her hard-hitting rifles, all up and down the river she patrolled. Not since early May, when she tried it and came uncomfortably close to being sunk or captured for her pains, had the ironclad ventured out to engage the fleet, but neither could the Union ships invite destruction by steaming up to engage her at close quarters within the confines of that narrow stream. It was clear, however, that something had to be done about her before long: for there were reports that two more rams were under construction up the river, one of them in the very cornfield where she herself had taken shape. One *Albemarle* was fearful enough to contemplate, even from a respectful distance. A flotilla of three, churning down into the Sound, was quite unthinkable.

The answer came from Lieutenant William B. Cushing, who presented two plans for getting rid of the iron menace. One involved the use of India-rubber boats, to be packed across the swamps to within easy reach of the objective, then inflated for use by a hundred-man assault force that would board the ram under cover of darkness, overpower her crew, and take her down to join the fleet at the mouth of the river, eight miles off. Plan Two, also a night operation, called for the boarding party to move all the way by water in a pair of light-draft steamers, each armed with a bow howitzer and a long spar tipped with a torpedo, to be used to sink the rebel warship if the attempt to seize her failed. He submitted his proposal in July, and when the Hampton Roads authorities chose the second plan and passed it on to Washington — where Welles approved it too, though with misgivings, since it seemed likely to cost the service one of its most promising young officers, not to mention the volunteers he proposed to take along — he left at once for New York, his home state, to purchase "suitable vessels" for the undertaking up the Roanoke.

No one who knew or knew of Cushing, and he was well known by now on both sides of the line, would have been surprised, once they learned that he was the author of the plan, at the amount of risk and verve its execution would require. Wisconsin-born, the son of a widowed schoolteacher, and not yet twenty-two — the age at which his brother Alonzo had died on Cemetery Ridge the year before, a West Pointer commanding one of the badly shot-up batteries that helped turn Pickett's Charge — he already had won four official commendations for similar exploits he had devised and carried out in the course of the past three years. Perhaps this was compensatory daring; he had been at Annapolis until midway through his senior year in 1861, when he was permitted to resign and thus avoid dismissal for unruly conduct and a lack of what the authorities called "aptitude for the naval service." He volunteered as an acting master's mate, in reaction to Sumter, and was restored to the rank of midshipman within six months. "Where there is danger in the battle, there will I be," he informed a kinsman at the time, "for I will gain a name in this war." By now he had done so, and had won promotion to lieutenant, first junior, then senior grade, as well as those four commendations signed by Welles. None of this was enough; he wanted more; nothing less, indeed, than the highest of all military honors. "Cousin George," he wrote as he left New York in mid-October to keep his appointment with the *Albemarle* near Plymouth, "I am going to have a vote of thanks from Congress, or six feet of pine box by the next time you hear from me."

He had secured two open launches originally built for picket duty, screw-propelled vessels thirty feet long and narrow in the beam, of shallow draft and with low-pressure engines for quiet running, his notion being that one could stand by to provide covering fire and to pick up survivors if the other was sunk in the assault. As it turned out, this duplication was useful much sooner than he had expected; for one was lost in a Chesapeake storm on the way down, and he decided to go ahead with a single boat rather than wait for a replacement. Steaming in through Hatteras Inlet — whose bar no Union monitor could cross to ascend the Roanoke and engage the homemade iron ram — he joined the fleet riding at anchor fifty miles up Albemarle Sound. Two days he spent reconnoitering and drilling his volunteer crew, including fourteen men in the launch with him and another twelve in a towed cutter, the latter group to be used to silence rebel lookouts posted aboard the wreck of the *Southfield*, sunk in April a mile downstream from the dock where the *Albemarle* was moored. Soon after moonset, October 26, Cushing began his eight-mile run, the cutter in tow, only to be challenged just beyond the mouth of the river by Federal pickets who nearly opened fire when they heard the launch approaching. He turned back, warned by this apparent mishap that the expedition would have failed, and next day had a carpenter box-in the engine to muffle its sound, then set out again the following night, having added a tarpaulin to reduce the noise still more.

This time all went well on the run upriver. A rainstorm afforded such good additional cover that the launch chugged past the grounded *Southfield* undetected, thus enabling Cushing to keep the cutter with him in hope of using its dozen occupants to help overpower the crew of the ram when he went aboard. But that was not to be. Challenged by a sentry as he drew within hailing distance of the wharf, he changed his plan in mid-career; "Ahead fast!" he called out, and cast the cutter loose with orders to return downriver and deal with the pickets on the *Southfield*. As he approached the ram, a signal fire blazed up ashore and he saw by its light that the ironclad was surrounded by a pen of logs chained in position to shield her from just such an attack as he was about to make. Hailed by a sailor on her deck, he replied with a shot from his howitzer and ran within pistol range for a better look at the problem. The logs were placed too far out for him to reach the ram with the torpedo attached to the tip of its fourteen-foot spar, although closer inspection showed that they perhaps were slimy enough for the launch to slide onto or even over them if it struck hard, at a direct angle. (Getting off or out was of course another matter, but that was no part of the plan as he had revised it.) He came about, under heavy fire from the enemy ship and shore, and picked up speed for the attempt. The launch struck and mounted and slithered across the encircling pen of logs, and Cushing found himself looking into the muzzle of one of the big rifles on the *Albemarle*, which he later described as looming before him like a "dark mountain of iron."

Then came the hardest part. To control and produce the explosion he had three lines tied to his wrists: one to raise or lower the long spar goose-necked to the bow of the launch, another to arm the torpedo by dropping it into a vertical position, and a third to activate the firing mechanism. All three required the coolness and precision of a surgeon performing a delicate operation, since too sudden a pull on any one of the lines would result in a malfunction. In this case, moreover, the surgeon was grievously distracted, having lost the tail of his coat to a blast of buckshot and the sole of one shoe to a bullet. Working as calmly under fire as he had done while rehearsing the performance in the quiet of his quarters, Cushing maneuvered the spar and swung the torpedo under the overhang of the ram's iron deck to probe for a vital spot before he released the firing pin. As he did so, the big rifle boomed, ten feet ahead, and hurled its charge of grape across the bow and into the stern of the stranded launch, which then was swamped by the descent of a mass of water raised by the explosion, nearly strangling all aboard. "Abandon ship!" the lieutenant cried, removing his shoes and shucking off his coat to go over the side.

The river was cold, its surface lashed by fire from the shore and the now rapidly sinking ram, whose captain would later testify that the hole blown in her hull was "big enough to drive a wagon through." Cushing struck out for the opposite bank, intent on escape, and as he did, heard one of his crew, close behind him, give "a great gurgling yell" as he went down. Ceasing fire, the Confederates came out in boats to look for survivors; Cushing heard them call his name, but continued to go with the current, paddling hard to keep afloat until he made it to shallow water, half a mile below. Exhausted, he lay in the mud till daylight, then crept ashore to take cover in the swamp. Later he found an unguarded bateau, and at nightfall began a stealthy trip downstream.

"Ship ahoy! Send a boat!" the crew of a Union patrol ship heard someone call from the darkness of the mouth of the river before dawn. An armed detail sent to investigate presently returned with Cushing and the news that he had sunk the *Albemarle*. Cheers went up, as did rockets, fired to inform the other ships of the triumph scored two nights ago, and before long the weary lieutenant, who had been reported lost with all his crew, was sipping brandy in the captain's cabin. A few days later he was with Porter at Hampton Roads. "I have the honor to report, sir, that the rebel ironclad is at the bottom of the Roanoke River."

By then Plymouth, untenable without the protection of the ram, was back in Federal hands, having been evacuated after its works were taken under bombardment by the fleet on October 31. Upriver, the two unfinished ironclads were burned in their stocks when the whole region passed from rebel occupation. Cushing was promptly rewarded with a promotion to lieutenant commander, along with the thanks of Congress, upon Lincoln's recommendation, for having displayed what Porter called "heroic enterprise seldom equaled and never excelled." Much was expected of him in his future career, and he gave every sign of fulfilling those expectations. Before he was thirty, six years after the conflict ended, he would become the youngest full commander in the U.S. Navy. But that was as far as he went. He died at the age of thirty-two in a government asylum for the insane, thereby provoking much discussion as to whether heroism and madness, like genius and tuberculosis, were related — and, if so, had insanity been at the root of his exploits? or had the strain of performing them, or even of having performed them, been more than a sane man could bear? In any case Farragut himself, in a subsequent conversation with Welles, stated flatly that "young Cushing was the hero of the war."

★ ★ ★

Westward to the Mississippi and north to the Ohio, Confederates did what they could to offset the loss of Atlanta by harassing the supply lines that sustained its Federal occupation. John Morgan was not one of these, for two sufficient reasons. One was that his command had by no means recovered from its unauthorized early-summer excursion into Kentucky, which had cost him half of his "terrible men," along with at least as great a portion of what remained of a reputation already diminished by the collapse of his Ohio raid the year before. The other was that he was dead — shot down in a less-than-minor skirmish on September 4, two days after Atlanta fell and nine months short of his fortieth birthday.

Informed that a blue column had set out from Knoxville for a strike at Saltville and the Southwest Virginia lead mines, he left Abingdon on September 1 and two days later reached Greeneville, Tennessee, where he prepared to confront the raiders when they emerged from Bull's Gap tomorrow or the next day. Down to about 2000 men, he deployed them fanwise to the west, covering three of the four roads in that direction, and retired for the night in the finest house in town, which as usual meant that its owner had Confederate sympathies. Greeneville, like many such places in East Tennessee, was a town with divided loyalties; Longstreet had wintered here, awaiting orders to rejoin Lee, and Andrew Johnson had been its mayor in the course of his rise from tailor to Lincoln's running mate in the campaign now in progress. Around sunup, after a rainy night, Morgan was wakened this Sunday morning by rifle fire, spattering in the streets below his bedroom window, and by a staff captain who brought word that the Union advance guard had arrived by the untended road. He pulled on his trousers and boots and went out by a rear door in an attempt to reach the stable and his horse, but was cut off and had to turn back, taking shelter in a scuppernong arbor that screened the walkway from the house.

"That's him! That's Morgan, over there among the grape vines!" a woman called from across the street to the soldiers pressing their search for the raider.

"Don't shoot; I surrender," Morgan cried.

"Surrender and be God damned — I know you," a blue trooper replied as he raised and fired his carbine at a range of twenty feet.

"Oh God," Morgan groaned, shot through the breast, and collapsed among the rain-wet vines, too soon dead to hear what followed.

"I've killed the damned horse thief!" the trooper shouted, and he and his friends tore down an intervening fence in their haste to get at Morgan's body, which they threw across a horse for a jubilant parade around the town before they flung it, stripped to a pair of drawers, into a muddy roadside ditch. Two captured members of the general's staff were allowed to wash and dress the corpse in the house where he had slept the night before, and others, returning after the enemy withdrew, reclaimed the body and sent it back to Abingdon, where his widow — the former Mattie Ready, pregnant with the daughter he would never see — had it removed to a vault in Richmond, to await the time when it could be returned in peace to the Bluegrass region he had loved and raided. That was the end of John Hunt Morgan.

It was otherwise with Forrest. Not only was he still very much alive, he now also had a department commander who would use him for something more than repelling Memphis-based raids into North Mississippi; would use him, indeed, on raids of his own against Sherman's life line up in Middle Tennessee. One of Richard Taylor's first acts, on assuming command at Meridian in early September, was to notify his presidential brother-in-law of this intention, while summoning the cavalryman to headquarters for instructions. Davis approved, and Forrest arrived by rail on September 5, "a tall, stalwart man, with grayish hair, mild countenance, and slow and homely of speech."

Taylor saw him thus for the first time, two weeks after his Memphis strike — three days after Atlanta fell and the day after Morgan died — though he knew him, of course, by reputation: nothing in which had prepared him for the Wizard's initial reaction to the news that he was to be sent at last "to worry Sherman's communications north of the

Tennessee River." Forrest responded more with caution than with elation, inquiring about the route prescribed, the problem of subsistence, his
possible lines of retreat in case of a check, and much else of that nature.
"I began to think he had no stomach for the work," Taylor later wrote.
But this was in fact his introduction to the Forrest method; for presently,
he noted, "having isolated the chances of success from causes of failure
with the care of a chemist experimenting in his laboratory," the Tennessean rose and brought the conference to an end with an abrupt transformation of manner. "In a dozen sharp sentences he told his wants, said
he would leave a staff officer to bring up his supplies, asked for an engine
to take him back north to meet his troops, informed me he would march
with the dawn, and hoped to give an account of himself in Tennessee."

That was how Taylor would recall the parting, but here again he
misconstrued the method. Far from marching "with the dawn," Forrest
took ten days to get ready before he set out from below Tupelo with
everything in order, plans all laid and instructions clearly understood by
subordinates charged with carrying them out. Chief among these was
Abraham Buford, in command of his own two brigades and one from
Chalmers, who would remain behind to patrol the region around Memphis. Eight guns rolled with the column, which left on September 16
with just over 3500 effectives, anticipating a meeting near the Tennessee
River with nearly a thousand Alabama troopers under William Johnson,
who had shown his mettle at Brice's Crossroads back in June. At Tuscumbia on the 20th Forrest also met someone he had not expected: Joe
Wheeler. The diminutive Georgian was recrossing the river to wind up
his long raid through East and Middle Tennessee, begun on August 10.
Although the destruction he had wrought was about as extensive as he
claimed to Hood, he neglected to add that Sherman's road gangs had
repaired the damage about as fast as it was inflicted, often appearing on
the scene before the twisted rails were cool. Moreover, there was something else the young West Pointer did not include in his report, and this
was the condition of his command. Grievously diminished (for he
tallied only his combat losses, which were barely a twentieth of the
total suffered in the course of his six-week ride from Atlanta, up to
Strawberry Plains near Knoxville, then back into North Alabama) the
survivors were scarecrow examples of what could happen to troopers
off on their own behind enemy lines. Originally 4500 strong — the
number Forrest would have when Johnson joined tomorrow — they
now counted fewer than 2000. A good many of the missing were stragglers whose mounts had broken down, and Forrest wrote Taylor that
night, amid preparations for crossing the river next day: "I hope to be
instrumental in gathering them up."

Fording his horsemen and floating his guns and wagons across on
flatboats, he camped the following night on the north bank of the river,
five miles west of Florence, which he passed through next morning,

September 22, on the way to his main objective, the Tennessee & Alabama Railroad, just over forty miles to the east. One of Sherman's two main supply lines, running from Nashville through Columbia and Pulaski to Decatur, where it joined the Memphis & Charleston to connect with Chattanooga and Atlanta, its nearest point was Athens, and that was where Forrest was headed. He got there after sunset on the 23d to begin his investment of the town and its adjoining fort, a ditched and palisaded work a quarter-mile in circumference, occupied by a force of 600 infantry and considered impregnable to assault: as indeed perhaps it was, although no one would ever know. Soon after daybreak John Morton opened fire with his eight guns, "casting almost every shell inside the works," according to the garrison commander. Before long, Forrest halted fire to send in a white-flag note demanding "immediate and unconditional surrender." The Federal declined, but then unwisely consented to a parley, in the course of which Forrest pulled his customary trick of exposing troops and guns in triplicate, thereby convincing his adversary that he was besieged by a host of 15,000 of all arms, with no less than two dozen cannon. Capitulation came in time for the graybacks to give their full attention to a relief column that arrived from Decatur to take part in a brief skirmish before joining the surrender. Reduction of two nearby railway blockhouses raised the day's bag to 1300 prisoners, two pieces of artillery, 300 horses, and a mountain of supplies and equipment, including two locomotives captured with their cars in Athens. Forrest put the torch to the stores and installations, issued the horses to those of his men who needed them, smashed the rolling stock, and sent the prisoners back through Florence for removal south. Then he took up the march northward along the railroad, wrecking as he went.

Halfway to the Tennessee line next morning, September 25, he came upon the Sulphur Branch railway trestle, 72 feet high and 300 long, guarded by a double-casemated blockhouse at each end and a large fortress-stockade with a garrison of about one thousand men. Surrender declined, Morton opened fire and kept it up for two cruel hours, slamming in 800 rounds that left the fort's interior "perforated with shell, and the dead lying thick along the works." So Forrest would report, adding that a repeated demand for surrender was promptly accepted. This time the yield was 973 bluecoats, two more guns, another 300 horses, and a quantity of stores. Again he sent his prisoners rearward, together with the captured guns and four of his own, so greatly had the bombardment reduced his supply of artillery ammunition, and after setting fire to the two blockhouses, the buildings in the fort, and the long trestle they had been designed to shield, rode on north to the Elk River, which he reached next day, about midway between Athens and Pulaski. Here too there was a blockhouse at each end of a bridge even longer than the trestle at Sulphur Branch; but they were unmanned, abandoned by a commander who had heard from below how little protection they afforded, either to the installations they overlooked or to the garrisons they contained. Forrest burned them, along with the Elk River span, and pushed on to Richland Creek, seven miles beyond the Tennessee line and the same distance from Pulaski. Here there was a 200-foot-long truss bridge, stoutly built to take the weight of heavy-laden supply trains. The raiders crossed and sent it up in flames.

Now the character of the expedition changed. "Enemy concentrating heavily against me," Forrest notified Taylor the following night, September 27, from the vicinity of Pulaski. Touched where he was tender, Sherman had reacted hard and fast, sending George Thomas himself from Atlanta with two divisions to take charge in Middle Tennessee, with instructions for "the whole resources" of the region, including Kentucky and North Alabama, to be "turned against Forrest ... until he is disposed of." Other divisions were on the way by rail and river from Memphis and Chattanooga, and Rosecrans had been urged to return A. J. Smith's gorillas from Missouri. As a result, fully 30,000 reinforcements were converging by now from all directions upon Pulaski, where Lovell Rousseau, arriving from Nashville to meet the threat, already had more men in its fortifications than were in the gray column on its outskirts. "Press Forrest to the death," Thomas wired ahead, "keeping your troops well in hand and holding them to the work. I do not think that we shall ever have a better chance than this."

The chance was not as good as the blue Virginian thought: not yet at any rate. Though he kept his Pulaski defenders "well in hand," Rousseau found the raiders gone from his front next morning. Forrest had built up his campfires the night before, and leaving them burning had pulled out. Having done what he could, at least for the present, to cripple the Tennessee & Alabama, he now was moving toward that other, more vital supply line, the Nashville & Chattanooga, fifty miles to the east. He was obliged, however, to do it no more than superficial damage, learning from scouts when he got beyond Fayetteville on the 29th that the Chattanooga road was heavily protected by reinforcements hurried up it from Georgia and down it from Kentucky. He contented himself with detaching a fifty-man detail to tear up wires and track around Tullahoma, then confused the regathering Federals still more by splitting his force in two. Buford turned south with his division and Morton's four remaining guns, under orders to return to the Tennessee River by way of Huntsville, which he was to capture if possible, and tear up track on the Memphis & Charleston, between there and Decatur, before recrossing. Forrest himself, with the other two brigades, turned northwest through Lewisburg, then north across Duck River, passing near his Chapel Hill birthplace on the last day of September to descend once more, at high noon of the following day, on the already hard-hit Tennessee & Alabama near Spring Hill, ten miles north of Columbia and about

four times that distance above Pulaski, which he had left four days ago.

He turned south, ripping up track, capturing three more blockhouses — mainly by bluff, since Buford had the guns — firing bridges, and smashing culverts all the way to Columbia, which he bypassed on October 2 to avoid the delay of a gunless fight with the bluecoats in its works. The time had come to get out, and Forrest, as one of his troopers said, was "pretty good on a git." Taking off southwest away from what remained of the Tennessee & Alabama, he moved by country roads through Lawrenceburg, where he camped on the night of the 3d, and crossed the Alabama line the next day to return to Florence on October 5, one day less than two weeks after he left it. Buford was there ahead of him, having found Huntsville too stoutly garrisoned to be taken, and though the Tennessee was swollen past fording he had managed to get his men and guns across in relays on three rickety ferries, swimming the horses alongside. Now it was Forrest's turn.

A slow and risky business, with the enemy reported close astern, the piecemeal crossing took two full days, and was only accomplished, a veteran would recall, with "considerable disregard of the third commandment." Fretted and tired, the general was in the last boat to leave. While helping to pole against the swift-running current he noticed a lieutenant standing in the bow and taking no part in the work. "Why don't you take hold of an oar or pole and help get this boat across?" The lieutenant replied that, as an officer, he did not feel "called on to do that kind of work" while private soldiers were available to perform it. Astounded by this implied reproach — for he himself was as hard at work as anyone aboard — Forrest slapped the young man sprawling into the river, then held out the long pole and hauled him back over the gunwale, saying: "Now, damn you, get hold of the oars and go to work! If I knock you out of the boat again I'll let you drown." Another passenger observed that the douched lieutenant "made an excellent hand for the balance of the trip."

In the two weeks spent south of Nashville, within the great bend of the Tennessee, Forrest had captured 2360 of the enemy and killed or wounded an estimated thousand more, at a cost to himself of 340 casualties, only 47 of whom were killed. He had destroyed eleven blockhouses, together with the extensive trestles and bridges they were meant

to guard, and had taken seven U.S. guns, 800 horses, and more than
2000 rifles, all of which he brought out with him, in addition to fifty
captured wagons loaded with spoils too valuable for burning. Best of
all, he had wrecked the Tennessee & Alabama so thoroughly that even
the skilled blue work crews would need six full weeks to put it back
in operation. Indeed, Taylor was so encouraged by this Middle Tennessee expedition that he promptly authorized another, to be aimed this
time at Johnsonville, terminus of the newly extended Nashville & North-
western Railroad, by which supplies, unloaded from steamboats and
barges on the Tennessee, were sent to Sherman by way of Nashville,
seventy-five miles due east. A blow at this riverport depot, whose yards
and warehouses were crowded with stores awaiting transfer, would go
far toward increasing the Union supply problem down in Georgia, and
Forrest spent only a week resting and refitting his weary troopers,
summoning Chalmers to join him en route, and adding a pair of long-
range Parrotts to Morton's two batteries, before he took off again for
Johnsonville, a hundred miles north of Corinth, to which he had returned
on October 9.

Much was expected of this follow-up strike, even though the
first — successful as it had been, within its geographic limitations —
had failed to achieve its major purpose, which was to make Sherman turn
loose of Atlanta for lack of subsistence for his army of occupation. Not
only did the red-haired Ohioan by then have ample stockpiles of supplies,
he also had the scarcely interrupted use of the Nashville & Chattanooga
line, having repaired within twelve hours the limited damage inflicted
near Tullahoma by the fifty-man detail Forrest had detached when he
turned north beyond Fayetteville. If the raid had been made a month
or six weeks earlier, while the Federals were fighting outside Atlanta,
opposed by an aggressive foe and with both overworked railroads barely
able to meet their daily subsistence needs, the result might have been
different. Even so, Forrest with only 4500 troopers had managed to
disrupt Sherman's supply arrangements, as well as the troop dispositions
in his rear, and had brought him to the exasperated conclusion, expressed
to Grant on October 9, that it would be "a physical impossibility to protect the roads, now that Hood, Forrest, Wheeler, and the whole batch
of devils are turned loose without home or habitation."

✗ 5 ✗

First there had been the fret of verbal contention. Drawing back from
Jonesboro, as he said, "to enjoy a short period of rest and to think well
over the next step required in the progress of events," Sherman announced on September 8 that "the city of Atlanta, being exclusively required for warlike purposes, will at once be evacuated by all except the

armies of the United States." He foresaw charges of inhumanity, perhaps from friends as well as foes, but he was determined neither to feed the citizens nor to "see them starve under our eyes. . . . If the people raise a howl against my barbarity or cruelty," he told Halleck, "I will answer that war is war and not popularity-seeking."

Sure enough, when Mayor Calhoun protested that the suffering of the sick and aged, turned out homeless with winter coming on, would be "appalling and heart-rending," Sherman replied that while he gave "full credit to your statement of the distress that will be occasioned," he would not revoke his orders for immediate resettlement. "They were not designed to meet the humanities of the case, but to prepare for the future struggle. . . . You cannot qualify war in harsher terms than I will. War is cruelty, and you cannot refine it. . . . You might as well appeal against the thunder storm as against these terrible hardships of war. . . . Now you must go," he said in closing, "and take with you your old and feeble, feed and nurse them, and build for them, in more quiet places, proper habitations to shield them against the weather until the mad passions of men cool down and allow the Union and peace once more to settle over your old homes at Atlanta. Yours in haste."

Hood attacked as usual, head down and full tilt, in response to a suggestion for a truce to permit the removal southward, through the lines, of the unhappy remnant of the city's population. He had, he said, no choice except to accede, but he added: "Permit me to say that the unprecedented measure you propose transcends, in studied and ingenious cruelty, all acts ever brought to my attention in the dark history of war. In the name of God and humanity, I protest."

"In the name of common sense," Sherman fired back, "I ask you not to appeal to a just God in such a sacrilegious manner. You who, in the midst of peace and prosperity, have plunged a nation into war — dark and cruel war — who dared and badgered us to battle, insulted our flag, seized our arsenals and forts." There followed an arm-long list of Confederate outrages, ending: "Talk thus to the marines, but not to me, who have seen these things. . . . If we must be enemies, let us be men and fight it out as we propose to do, and not deal in such hypocritical appeals to God and humanity. God will judge us in due time, and he will pronounce whether it be more humane to fight with a town full of women and the families of a brave people at our backs, or to remove them to places of safety among their own friends."

For two more days, though both agreed that "this discussion by two soldiers is out of place and profitless," the exchange continued, breathy but bloodless, before a ten-day truce was agreed on and the exodus began. Union troops escorted the refugees, with such clothes and bedding as they could carry, as far as Rough & Ready, where Hood's men took them in charge and saw them south across the fifteen-mile railroad gap to Lovejoy Station, within the rebel lines. Sherman was glad to see them go, and truth to tell had rather enjoyed the preceding altercation, which he saw as a sort of literary exercise, beneficial to his spleen, and in which he was convinced he had once more gotten the best of his opponent. But in other respects, having little or nothing to do with verbal fencing, he was far less satisfied, and a good deal more perturbed.

On September 8, the day he ordered Calhoun and his people to depart, he also issued a congratulatory order proclaiming to his soldiers that their capture of Atlanta "completed the grand task which has been assigned us by our Government." This was untrue. Welcome as the fall of the city was at this critical time — he was convinced, for one thing, that it assured Lincoln's reëlection, and for another he could present it, quite literally, to his troops as a crowning reward for four solid months of combat — his real objective, agreed on beforehand and identified by Grant in specific instructions, was the Army of Tennessee; he had been told to "break it up," and Atlanta had been intended merely to serve as the anvil upon which the rebel force was to be fixed and pounded till it shattered. That had been, and was, his true "grand task." Not only was Hood's army still in existence, it was relatively intact, containing close to 35,000 effectives, even with Wheeler gone for the past month; whereas Sherman's own, though twice as strong as Hood's at the time of occupation, started dwindling from the wholesale loss of veterans whose three-year enlistments ran out about the time the truce began. Subtractions from the top were even heavier in proportion. Schofield had to return for a time to Knoxville to attend to neglected administrative matters in his department, and Dodge, wounded soon after he received a promotion to major general, took off on sick leave, never to return; his corps was broken up to help fill the gaps in Howard's other two, whose commanders, Logan and Blair — "political soldiers," Sherman scornfully styled them — had been given leaves of absence to stump for Lincoln in their critical home states. Presently even George Thomas was gone, along with two of his nine infantry divisions, sent back to Tennessee when the news came down that Forrest was on the rampage there, scooping up rear-guard detachments and providing the rail repair gangs with more work than they could handle in a hurry.

Various possibilities obtained, even so, including a march on Macon, Selma, or Mobile; but what the army needed most just now was rest and refitment, a brief period in which to digest its gains and shake its diminished self together, while its leader pondered in tranquillity his next move. Fortified Atlanta seemed an excellent place for this, although the situation afforded little room for error. "I've got my wedge pretty deep," Sherman remarked in this connection, "and must look out I don't get my fingers pinched." One drawback was that the interlude surrendered the initiative to Hood, who had shown in the past that he would be quick to grasp it, however stunned his troops might be as a result of their recent failures, including the loss of the city in their charge. Wheeler's damage to the supply line running back to Chattanooga had long since been repaired, but it seemed likely that his chief would strike there again, this time in heavier force; perhaps, indeed, with all he had.

This was in fact what Hood intended, if only because he felt he had no other choice. Determined to do *some*thing, yet lacking the strength to mount a siege or risk another large-scale confrontation on the outskirts of Atlanta, he had begun to prepare for a rearward strike while exchanging verbal shafts with his opponent inside the city. First he asked Richmond for reinforcements, and was told: "Every effort [has been] made to bring forward reserves, militia, and detailed men for the purpose.... No other resource remains." This denial had been expected, but it was promptly followed by another that had not. By gubernatorial proclamation on September 10, one week after Atlanta's fall, Joe Brown withdrew the Georgia militia beyond Confederate reach, granting blanket furloughs for his "pets," as they were called, "to return to their homes and look for a time after other important interests," by which he meant the tending of their farms. Discouraged but not dissuaded by this lengthening of the numerical odds, Hood held to his plan for a move northward, requesting of the government that the 30,000 Andersonville inmates, ninety miles in his rear, be transferred beyond reach of the Federals in his front and thus permit him to shift his base from Lovejoy Station, on the Macon & Western, to Palmetto on the Atlanta & West Point; that is, from south of the city to southwest. This, he explained in outlining his proposed campaign, would open the way for him to recross the Chattahoochee, west of Marietta, for a descent on the blue supply line north of the river. Sherman most likely would follow to protect his communications, leaving a strong garrison to hold Atlanta; in which event Hood would be able to fight him with a far better chance of winning than if he tried to engage him hereabouts, with the odds at two-to-one. If, on the other hand, Sherman responded to the shift by moving against Augusta, Mobile, or some other point to the east or south, Hood would return and attack his rear. In any case, whatever risk was involved in his proposal, he was convinced that this was the time to act, since "Sherman is weaker now than he will be in the future, and I as strong as I can expect to be."

Richmond, approving this conditional raid-in-force, ordered the transfer of all able-bodied prisoners from Andersonville, near Americus, to stockades down in Florida. This began on September 21, by which time Hood had completed his twenty-mile shift due west to Palmetto, about the same distance southwest of Atlanta, and had his subordinates hard at work on preparations for the march north around Sherman's flank. They were still at it, four days later — September 25, a rainy Sunday that turned the red dust of their camps to mire — when Jefferson Davis arrived for a council of war.

He came for other purposes as well, including the need — even direr now than at the time of his other western trips, in early winter and late fall of the past two years, when Bragg had been the general in trouble — "to arouse all classes to united and desperate resistance." Outwardly at least, Davis himself never quailed or wavered under adversity, Stephen Mallory would testify after working close to him throughout the war. "He could listen to the announcement of defeat while expecting victory, or to a foreign dispatch destructive to hopes widely cherished, or to whispers that old friends were becoming cold or hostile, without exhibiting the slightest evidence of feeling beyond a change of color. Under such circumstances, his language temperate and bland, his voice calm and gentle, and his whole person at rest, he presented rather the appearance of a man, wearied and worn by care and labor, listening to something he knew all about, than of one receiving ruinous disclosures." But this reaction was by no means characteristic of the high-strung people, in or out of uniform, to and for whom he was responsible as Commander in Chief and Chief Executive: and it was especially uncharacteristic now that the Federal penetration of the heartland had regional leaders of the caliber of Brown and Aleck Stephens crying havoc and talking of calling the dogs of war to kennel. Leaving Richmond five days ago, the day after Early's defeat at Winchester provided a companion setback in the eastern theater, Davis remarked to a friend: "The first effect of disaster is always to spread a deeper gloom than is due to the occasion." Then he set out for Georgia, as he had done twice before, in an attempt to dispel or at any rate lighten the gloom that had gathered and deepened there since the fall of Atlanta, three weeks back.

Army morale was a linked concern. Addressing himself to this on the day of his arrival at Palmetto, he attempted to lift the spirits of the troops with a speech delivered extemporaneously to Cheatham's Tennesseans, who flocked to meet him at the station. "Be of good cheer," he told them, "for within a short while your faces will be turned homeward and your feet pressing the soil of Tennessee."

Shouts of approval greeted this extension of the plan Hood had proposed; but other responses had a different tone. "Johnston! Give us Johnston!" Davis heard men cry or mutter from the ranks, and though he made no reply to this, it pointed up another problem he had come west to examine at first hand — the question of possible changes in the structure of command. Hardee, for example, had recently repeated his request for a transfer that would free him from further service under Hood, who blamed him for the collapse of two of his three Atlanta sorties, as well as for his failure to whip the enemy at Jonesboro, which had brought on the fall of the city. So Hood said, at any rate, wiring Richmond: "It is of the utmost importance that Hardee should be relieved at once. He commands the best troops in this army. I must have another commander." One or the other clearly had to go. Now at Palmetto, in tandem interviews, Davis heard the two generals out, recriminations abounding, and arrived at a decision that pleased them both: Hood by replacing Hardee with Cheatham, his senior division commander, and Hardee by ordering him to proceed at once to Charleston, where he would head the Department of South Carolina, Georgia, and Florida.

That was Beauregard's old bailiwick, and he was there even now, conducting a rather superfluous inspection of the coastal defenses. But there would be no overlapping of duties when Hardee arrived, since Davis planned for the Creole to be gone by then, summoned west as the solution to another command problem in the Army of Tennessee, this one at the very top. In mid-September, just before he left Richmond, he had received from Samuel French, who led a division in Stewart's corps, a private communication reminiscent of the famous round-robin letter that reached him after Chickamauga. This one was signed only by French, though it was written, he said, at the request of several high-ranking friends "in regard to a feeling of depression more or less apparent in parts of this army." His suggestion — or theirs, for the tone of the letter was strangely indirect — was that the President "send one or two intelligent officers here to visit the different divisions and brigades to ascertain if that spirit of confidence so necessary for success has or has not been impaired within the past month or two." Hood was not mentioned by name or position, as Bragg had been in the earlier document, but he was clearly responsible for conditions in a command which he had assumed "within the past month or two" and from which, the letter implied, he ought to be removed. This, combined with the public outcry over the loss of Atlanta, was part of what prompted the President's visit, and even before he set out he had arrived at a tentative solution to the problem by inviting Beauregard to go along. Old Bory was down in Charleston at the time, and Davis could not wait for him. He did, however, ask R. E. Lee to find out whether the Louisianian would be willing to return to duty in the West. Frustrated by subservience to Lee for the three months since Petersburg came under formal siege, Beauregard replied that he would "obey with alacrity" any such order for a transfer, and Davis wired from Palmetto for the Creole to meet him in Augusta on his way back in early October.

Beauregard, receiving the summons, assumed that he was about to return, as Hood's successor, to command of the army that had been taken from him more than two years ago, after Shiloh and the evacuation of Corinth. In this he was mistaken: though not entirely. Davis had it in mind to put him in charge not only of Hood's but also of Taylor's department, the whole to be known as the Military Division of the West, containing all of Alabama and Mississippi, together with major parts of Georgia and Louisiana and most of Tennessee. Assigned primarily in an advisory capacity, he would exercise direct control of troops only when he was actually with them — and only then, in Davis's words, "whenever in your judgment the interests of your command render it expedient." This was the position in which Johnston had fretted so fearfully last year; "a political device," a later observer was to term its creation, "designed to silence the critics of Hood, satisfy the friends of Beauregard, and save face for the Administration." That was accurate enough, as far as it went, but for Davis the arrangement had two other pragmatic virtues. One was that Hood's accustomed rashness might be tempered, if not controlled, by the presence of an experienced superior close at hand, and the other was that there was no room left for Joe Johnston, whose return Davis was convinced would result in a retreat down the length of the Florida peninsula. In any case, Beauregard was highly acceptable to the generals Davis talked with at Palmetto, including Hood, and he was determined to offer him the post when they met in Augusta the following week.

Mainly, though, the presidential visit was concerned with the strategy Hood had evolved for drawing the blue army north by striking at its supply line beyond the Chattahoochee, where he would take up a strong defensive position inviting a disadvantageous attack. Now in discussion this was expanded and improved. If Sherman appeared too strong even then, or if Hood, as Davis put it, "should not find the spirit of his army such as to justify him in offering battle" at that point, he was to fall back down the Coosa River and through the mountains to Gadsden, Alabama, where he would establish a new base, supplied by the railroad from Selma to Blue Mountain, and there "fight a conclusive battle" on terrain even more advantageous to the defender; Sherman, drawn far from his own base back in Georgia, might then be annihilated. If, on the other hand, the Ohioan declined battle on those terms and returned to Atlanta, Hood would follow, and when Sherman, his supply line cut, moved from there, Hood would still pursue: either northward, across the Tennessee — which would undo the Federal gains of the past four months and open the way for a Confederate march on Nashville — or south or east, through Selma or Montgomery to the Gulf or through Macon or Augusta to the Atlantic, in which case the Union rear could be assaulted. That was the expanded plan, designed to cover all contingencies, as Hood and the Commander in Chief developed it over the course of the three-day visit. Then on the evening of September 27 Davis took his leave.

In Macon next morning, at a benefit for the impoverished Atlanta refugees, he took up the spirit-lifting task he had begun at Palmetto when he told the Tennessee soldiers their faces would soon turn homeward. "What though misfortune has befallen our arms from Decatur to Jonesboro," he declared, "our cause is not lost. Sherman cannot keep up his long line of communications; retreat sooner or later he must. And when that day comes, the fate that befell the army of the French Empire in its retreat from Moscow will be re-enacted. Our cavalry and our people will harass and destroy his army, as did the Cossacks that of Napoleon, and the Yankee general, like him, will escape with only a bodyguard....

"Let no one despond," he said in closing, and repeated the words the following day in Montgomery, speaking at the Capitol where he had been inaugurated forty-three months ago. "There be some men," he told the Alabamians, in support of his advice against despondence, "who when they look at the sun can only see a speck upon it. I am of a more sanguine temperament perhaps, but I have striven to behold our affairs with a cool and candid temperance of heart, and, applying to them the most rigid test, am more confident the longer I behold the progress of the war.... We should marvel and thank God for the great achievements which have crowned our efforts."

Closeted that night with Richard Taylor, who had transferred his headquarters from Meridian to Selma, he was glad to learn the particulars of Forrest's current raid into Middle Tennessee, but disappointed to be told that any hopes he retained for securing reinforcements from beyond the Mississippi were quite groundless, not only because the situation there would not permit it, but also because of the gunboats Taylor had had to dodge, even at night in a small boat, when he returned. Davis was able to counter this with news that Hood had begun today a crossing of the Chattahoochee near Campbelltown, twenty miles southwest of Atlanta, for his strike at the Federal life line. Taylor was pleased to hear it, remarking that the maneuver would no doubt "cripple [Sherman] for a time and delay his projected movements." Whatever enthusiasm surged up in him on hearing of this new offensive was certainly well contained. Moreover: "At the same time," he later wrote of the exchange, "I did not disguise my conviction that the best we could hope for was to protract the struggle until spring. It was for statesmen, not soldiers, to deal with the future."

This was chilling in its implications, coming as it did from a friend and kinsman whose opinion he respected and whose experience covered all three major theaters of the war, but Davis refused to be daunted; like Nelson off Copenhagen, putting the telescope to his blind eye, he declined to see these specks upon the Confederate sun. The two men parted to meet no more in the course of a conflict Taylor believed was drawing to a close, and Davis resumed his journey eastward from Montgomery next day, joined en route by Hardee for the scheduled meeting with Beauregard in Augusta on October 2, the President's second Sunday away from Richmond. Old Bory's spirits took a drop when he learned that he was to occupy an advisory rather than a fighting post, but they soon revived at the prospect of conferring with Hood on plans for reversing the western tide of battle. In the end, he was as pleased as

Hardee was with his new assignment, and both generals sat on the rostrum with their chief the following day at a patriotic rally. "We must beat Sherman; we must march into Tennessee," Davis told the Augustans. "There we will draw from 20,000 to 30,000 to our standard, and, so strengthened, we must push the enemy back to the banks of the Ohio and thus give the peace party of the North an accretion no puny editorial can give." Such was the high point of his last speech in Georgia, and having made it he presented the two generals to the crowd. Beauregard, who had fired the first gun of the war, was cheered for saying that he "hoped to live to fire the last," and Hardee, a native son, drew loud applause when he reported that Hood had recently told him "he intended to lay his claws upon the state road in rear of Sherman, and, having once fixed them there, it was not his intention to let them loose their hold."

Next day, October 4 — by which time the three speakers had reached or were moving toward their separate destinations: Beauregard west, Hardee east, and Davis north to the South Carolina capital — Hood had carried out at least the first part of this program. Completing his crossing of the Chattahoochee before September ended, he struck the Western & Atlantic at Big Shanty and Acworth, capturing their garrisons, and now was on the march for Allatoona, the principal Union supply base near the Etowah. Best of all, Sherman had taken the bait and was hurrying northward from Atlanta with most of his army, apparently eager for the showdown battle this gray maneuver had been fashioned to provoke. While the opening stage of the raid was in progress, and even as Hood's troops were tearing up some nine miles of track around Big Shanty, Davis delivered in Columbia the last in his current series of addresses designed to lift the spirits of a citizenry depressed by the events of the past two months.

"South Carolina has struggled nobly in the war, and suffered many sacrifices," he declared, beginning as usual with praise for the people of the state in which he spoke. "But if there be any who feel that our cause is in danger, that final success may not crown our efforts, that we are not stronger today than when we began this struggle, that we are not able to continue the supplies to our armies and our people, let all such read a contradiction in the smiling face of our land and in the teeming evidences of plenty which everywhere greet the eye. Let them go to those places where brave men are standing in front of the foe, and there receive the assurance that we shall have final success and that every man who does not live to see his country free will see a freeman's grave." He himself was on his way back from such a visit, and he had been reassured by what he saw. "I have just returned from that army from which we have had the saddest accounts — the Army of Tennessee — and I am able to bear you words of good cheer. That army has increased in strength since the fall of Atlanta. It has risen in tone; its march is onward, its face looking to the front. So far as I am able to judge, General Hood's strategy has been good and his conduct has been gallant. His eye is now fixed upon a point far beyond that where he was assailed by the enemy. He hopes soon to have his hand upon Sherman's line of communications, and to fix it where he can hold it. And if but a half — nay, one fourth — of the men to whom the service has a right will give him their strength, I see no chance for Sherman to escape from a defeat or a disgraceful retreat. I therefore hope, in view of all the contingencies of the war, that within thirty days that army which has so boastfully taken up its winter quarters in the heart of the Confederacy will be in search of a crossing of the Tennessee River." Having claimed as much, he pressed on and claimed more. "I believe it is in the power of the men of the Confederacy to plant our banners on the banks of the Ohio, where we shall say to the Yankee: 'Be quiet, or we shall teach you another lesson.' "

So he said, bowing low to the applause that followed, and after a day's rest — badly needed, since two weeks of travel on the buckled strap-iron of a variety of railroads amounted to a form of torture rivaling the rack — ended his fifteen-day absence from Richmond on the morning of October 6. The warm bright pleasant weather of Virginia's early fall belied the strain its capital was under; Fort Harrison had toppled just one week ago, creating a dent in the city's defenses north of the James, and the fight next day at Peebles Farm, though tactically a victory, had obliged Lee to extend his already thin-stretched Petersburg lines another two miles west. For Davis, however, any day that brought him back to his family was an occasion for rejoicing. And rejoice he did: especially over its newest member, three-month-old Varina Anne. Born in late June, while the guns were roaring on Kennesaw and Jubal Early was heading north from Lynchburg, she would in time be referred to as the "Daughter of the Confederacy," but to her father she was "Winnie," already his pet name for her mother, or "Pie-Cake," which her sister and brothers presently shortened to "Pie." He was glad to be back with her and the others, Maggie, Little Jeff, Billy, and his wife, who was pleased, despite her distress at the wear he showed, to hear how well the trip had gone in regard to his efforts to lift the flagging morale of the people with predictions of great success for Hood — whose troops were moving northward even now — and "defeat or a disgraceful retreat" for Sherman.

Grant, for one, disagreed with this assessment of the situation in North Georgia. Informed of Davis's late-September prediction that the fate that crumpled Napoleon in Russia now awaited Sherman outside Atlanta, he thought it over briefly, then inquired: "Who is to furnish the snow for this Moscow retreat?"

Afterwards, Sherman took this one step further, professing to have been delighted that the rebel leader's "vainglorious boasts" had in effect presented "the full key to his future designs" to those whom they were intended to undo; "To be forewarned was to be forearmed," he explained. But that was written later, when he seemed to have taken what he called "full advantage of the occasion." Davis in fact had said very little more in his recent impromptu speeches, including his proposal "to plant our banners on the banks of the Ohio," than he (and, indeed, many other Confederate spokesmen) had expressed on previous tours undertaken to lift spirits that had sagged under the burden of defeat. As for Hood's reported promise to "lay his claws" on the railroad north of Atlanta, they were already fixed there by the time Sherman heard from his spies or read in the papers of what Davis or Hardee was supposed to have said — days after Hood's whole army was across the Chattahoochee in his rear. Besides, the red-haired Ohioan was far too busy by then, attempting to deal with this newly developed threat to his life line, to conjecture much about what Hood might or might not have in mind as a next step.

Leaving Slocum's corps to hold Atlanta, he began recrossing the Chattahoochee with the other five — some 65,000 of all arms, exclusive of the two divisions sent back to Tennessee with Thomas the week before — when he discovered on October 3 that Hood, after crossing in force near Campbelltown, was moving north through Powder Springs, apparently with the intention of getting astride the Western & Atlantic somewhere around or beyond Marietta. Sherman rushed a division from Howard north by rail, under Brigadier General John M. Corse, to cover Rome in case the graybacks veered in that direction, but by the time he got the last of his men over the river next day he learned that the rebs had taken Big Shanty and Acworth, along with their garrisons, and had torn up nine miles of track on their way to seize his main supply base at Allatoona, which they would reach tomorrow. He got a message through for Corse to shift his troops by rail from Rome to Allatoona, reinforcing its defenders, and to hang on there till the rest of the army joined him.

Corse complied, but only by the hardest. When Sherman climbed Kennesaw next morning, October 5, he could see the Confederate main body encamped to the west around Lost Mountain, his own men at work repairing the railroad past Big Shanty, just ahead, and gunsmoke lazing up from Allatoona Pass, a dozen air-line miles to the north, where Corse was making his fight. Hood had detached Stewart's corps for the Acworth strike, and Stewart, before heading back to rejoin Hood last night, had in turn detached French's division to extend the destruction to the Etowah. "General Sherman says hold fast; we are coming," the Kennesaw signal station wigwagged Allatoona over the heads of the attackers. Corse — a twenty-nine-year-old Iowan who had spent two years at West Point before returning home to study law and run for public office, only to lose the election and enter the army, as was said, "to relieve the pain of political defeat" — had arrived, although with less than half of his division, in time to receive a white-flag note in which French allowed him five minutes "to avoid a needless effusion of blood" by surrendering unconditionally. He declined, replying: "We are prepared for the 'needless effusion of blood' whenever it is agreeable to you." The engagement that followed was as savage as might have been expected from this exchange. Corse had just under 2000 men, French just over 3000, and their respective losses were 706 and 799 killed, wounded, or captured. After two of the three redoubts had fallen, Corse withdrew his survivors to the third, near the head of the pass, and kept up the resistance, despite a painful face wound and the loss of more than a third of his command. By 4 o'clock, having intercepted wigwag messages that help was on the way from the 60,000 Federals in his rear, French decided to pull out before darkness and Sherman overtook him. Corse was exultant: so much so that when Sherman, still on Kennesaw, inquired by flag as to his condition the following day, he signaled back: "I am short a cheekbone and an ear, but am able to whip all hell yet."

Such was the stuff of which legends were made, including this one of the so-called Battle of Allatoona Pass. "Hold the fort, for I am coming," journalists quoted Sherman as having wigwagged from the top of Kennesaw, and that became the title of P. P. Bliss's revival hymn, inspired by the resolute valor Corse and his chief had shown in defending a position of such great natural strength that the latter had chosen not to risk an attack when he found it looming across his southward path in May. French, moreover, got clean away, long before any blue relief arrived, and when Sherman encountered the high-strung young Iowa brigadier a few days later he was surprised to find on his cheek only a small bandage, removal of which revealed no more than a scratch where the bullet had nicked him in passing, and no apparent damage to the ear he had claimed was lost. Sherman laughed. "Corse, they came damned near missing you, didn't they?" he said.

He laughed, yet the fact was he found small occasion for humor in the present situation. Hood withdrew his reunited army westward beyond Lost Mountain to New Hope Church and Dallas. There he stopped, or anyhow paused. Sherman, however, had no intention of reentering that tangled wasteland, even though this meant leaving the initiative to an adversary who had just shown that he would use it to full advantage and now seemed about to do as much again. Sure enough, when the sun came up on October 7 the graybacks had disappeared. Wiring Slocum that they had "gone off south," Sherman warned that they might be doubling back for a surprise attack on Atlanta, and when he discovered later in the day that they were actually headed north, he charged that Hood was an eccentric: "I cannot guess his movements as

I could those of Johnston, who was a sensible man and only did sensible things."

Delayed by an all-day rain next day, he did not reach Allatoona until October 9, when he heard from scouts that the butternut column was on the march for Rome. But that was not true either, it turned out. Crossing the Coosa River west of Rome, then moving fast up the right bank of the Oostanaula, Hood struck Resaca on October 12 and wrecked a dozen miles of railroad between there and Dalton, where he captured the thousand-man garrison next day and then ripped up another five miles of track on his way to Tunnel Hill, where the contest for North Georgia had begun five months ago. When Sherman moved against him from Rome and Kingston, he fell back through Snake Creek Gap to a position near LaFayette, some twenty miles south of where Bragg and Rosecrans had clashed about this time last year at Chickamauga, and there took up a defensive stance, both flanks stoutly anchored and a clear field of fire to his front. Sherman came on after him from Resaca, reaching LaFayette on October 17. By the time he got his troops arrayed for battle, however, Hood was gone again — vanished westward, across the Alabama line, into even more rugged terrain where Sherman would be obliged to risk defeat a long way from his base. Exasperated, the red-head complained bitterly that everything his adversary had done for the past three weeks was "inexplicable by any common-sense theory." Recalling Jefferson Davis's boast of Hood's intentions: "Damn him," he said testily of the latter. "If he will go to the Ohio River I will give him rations. . . . Let him go north. My business is down South."

Whether this last was to be the case or not was strictly up to the general-in-chief, and that was the main cause of Sherman's irritability through this difficult and uncertain time, even more than the loss of much of the railroad in his rear. The railroad could be rebuilt — would in fact be back in use within ten days — but Hood's evident ability to smash it, more or less at will, might have an adverse influence on the decision Grant had been pondering for the past month, ever since Sherman first made it clear what he meant when he said that his business was "down South."

Back in early May, at the start of his campaign to "knock Jos. Johnston," a staffer had asked what he planned to do at its end; "Salt water," he replied, flicking the ash from his cigar. Mobile and the Gulf had been what he meant, but thanks to Farragut there was not much left in that direction worth the march. He now had a different body of water in mind, rimming a different coast. In brief, his proposal — first made on September 20, while the refugee truce was still in effect below Atlanta — was that the navy secure and provision a base for him on the Atlantic seaboard — probably Savannah, since that was the closest port — and his army would "sweep the whole state of Georgia" on its way there. Such a march, he told Grant, would be "more than fatal to the possibility of Southern independence. They may stand the fall of Richmond, but not of all Georgia," he declared, and added a jocular, upbeat flourish to close his plea: "If you can whip Lee and I can march to the Atlantic, I think Uncle Abe will give us a twenty days' leave of absence to see the young folks."

Grant had doubts. With its attention fixed on Wilmington, the last major port still open to blockade runners, the navy would not willingly divert its strength to a secondary target more than two hundred miles down the coast; besides which, the mounting of such an effort would take months, and previous attempts against Charleston had shown there was little assurance of success, even if every ironclad in the fleet was employed in the attack. His main objection, however, was the continued existence of Hood's army. Speaking in Georgia, Alabama, and South Carolina, hard on the heels of Sherman's proposal, Jefferson Davis announced plans for a northward campaign that might well succeed if Sherman marched eastward and thus removed from Hood's path the one force that could stop him. Grant said as much, opposing the expedition on both counts, but Sherman replied that he did not really need for the navy to take Savannah before he got there; all he wanted was for supply ships to be standing by, ready to steam in after he reduced the city from the landward side. As for Hood, Thomas was on the way to Nashville even now with two divisions which he would combine with troops already there and others on the way; "Why will it not do to leave Tennessee to the forces which Thomas has, and the reserves soon to come to Nashville, and for me to destroy Atlanta and march across Georgia to Savannah or Charleston, breaking roads and doing irreparable damage? We cannot remain on the defensive."

That was written October 1. By the time the message reached City Point, Forrest had rampaged through Middle Tennessee, smashing installations within thirty miles of Nashville, and Hood was across the Chattahoochee, ripping up track on the Western & Atlantic thirty miles north of Atlanta. Grant saw these strikes as confirmation of his objection to Sherman's departure, but Sherman took them as proof of his contention that he was wasting time by remaining where he was; that it was, in fact, as he insisted on October 9, "a physical impossibility to protect the roads, now that Hood, Forrest, Wheeler, and the whole batch of devils are turned loose.... By attempting to hold the roads, we will lose a thousand men each month and will gain no result." Having said as much, he returned to his plea that he himself be "turned loose" to make for the coast. This time, noting that he had some 8000 head of cattle on hand, as well as 3,000,000 rations of bread, and expected to find "plenty of forage in the interior of the state," he went into logistical details of the expedition. "I propose that we break up the railroad from Chattanooga forward, and that we strike out with our wagons for Milledgeville, Millen, and Savannah. Until we can repopulate Georgia, it is useless for us to occupy it; but the utter destruction of its roads, houses, and people will cripple their military resources. . . . I can make this march, and make Georgia howl!"

Hood by then had retired westward, but soon he was on the go again, about to throw another punch at the railroad forty miles farther north. Even before it landed, Sherman predicted that it would be successful and renewed his appeal to be spared the patchwork soldiering that would follow, urging Grant to let him "send back all my wounded and unserviceable men, and with my effective army move through Georgia, smashing things to the sea. Hood may turn into Tennessee and Kentucky," he admitted, "but I believe he will be forced to follow me." In any case, Thomas could handle him, he said, and best of all, "instead of being on the defensive, I will be on the offensive. Instead of my guessing at what he means to do, he will have to guess at my plans. The difference in war would be fully 25 percent. . . . Answer quick, as I know we will not have the telegraph long."

Grant's reply next day, October 12 — the day Hood landed astride the railroad at Resaca — was encouraging. "On reflection I think better of your proposition," he wired back. "It will be much better to go south than to be forced to come north." He suggested that the move be made with "every wagon, horse, mule, and hoof of stock, as well as the Negroes," and that plenty of spare weapons be taken along to "put them in the hands of Negro men," who could serve as otherwise unobtainable reinforcements on the march. All the same, his approval was only tentative, not final, and Sherman continued to fume, irked in front by Hood and from the rear by Grant.

The former got away westward again, through Snake Creek and Ship's gaps, to a position just below LaFayette, which he abandoned at the approach of the blue army, and fell back down the valley of the Chattooga River, across the Alabama line. "It was clear to me that he had no intention to meet us in open battle," Sherman later wrote, "and the lightness and celerity of his army convinced me that I could not possibly catch him on a stern-chase." Angry at being drawn in the direction he least wanted to go — and resentful, above all, at the mounting proof of his error in having turned back to Atlanta, when the city fell to Slocum in his rear, instead of pressing after Hood to achieve the true purpose of his campaign — the red-head called a halt at Gaylesville, thirty miles short of Gadsden, and there continued to fret and fume as October wore away, still with no definite go-ahead from the general-in-chief. Evidence of his snappishness appeared in a telegram he sent a cavalry brigadier, posted at Calhoun on rear-guard duty, when he heard that a sniper had taken pot shots at cars along the newly repaired Western & Atlantic: "Cannot you send over about Fairmont and Adairsville, burn ten or twelve houses of known secessionists, kill a few at random, and let them know that it will be repeated every time a train is fired on from Resaca to Kingston?"

Across the way at Gadsden, while Sherman thus was breathing fire and threatening random slaughter, Hood's troubles were not so much with his superior, Beauregard, as they were with his subordinates, who he felt had let him down. Drawn up for combat near LaFayette the week before, he had "expected that a forward movement of one hundred miles would reinspirit the officers and men to a degree to impart to them confidence, enthusiasm, and hope of victory," but when he took a vote at a council of war, assembled on the eve of what he intended as an all-out effort to whip Sherman, "the opinion was unanimous that although the army was much improved in spirit, it was not in a condition to risk battle against the numbers reported." Disappointed, he withdrew down the Chattooga Valley and the Coosa River to Gadsden for a meeting on October 21 with Beauregard, who had formally assumed command of the new Military Division of the West only four days ago. To the Creole's great surprise, Hood presented for his approval a broad-scale plan, conceived en route, for "marching into Tennessee, with a hope to establish our line eventually in Kentucky."

'Broad-scale' was perhaps not word enough; spread-eagle was more like it. But knowing as he did that time was on the side of the Union — that delay would enable Thomas to complete his buildup in Tennessee and combine with Sherman to corner and crush the fugitive gray army, wherever it might turn — Hood was determined to extend and enlarge the flea-bite offensive by which he had managed, ever since he left Palmetto three weeks back, to keep his adversaries edgy and off-balance. A northward march, into or past the mouth of the Federal lion, was admittedly a risky undertaking, but he was of the Lee-Jackson school, whose primary tenet was that the smaller force must take the longest chances, and moreover he had before him the example of Bragg, who by just such a maneuver after the fall of Corinth, two years ago, had reversed the gloomy situation in this same theater by dispersing the superior enemy combinations then being assembled to bring on his destruction.

His plan, he said, was to cross the Tennessee River at Guntersville, which would place him within reach of Sherman's single-strand rail supply line in the delicate Stevenson-Bridgeport area, and move promptly on Nashville, smashing Thomas's scattered detachments on the way. Possessed of the Tennessee capital, he would resupply his army from its stores, thicken his ranks with volunteers drawn to his banner, and move on through Kentucky to the Ohio, where he would be in a position to threaten Cincinnati and receive still more recruits from the Bluegrass. If Sherman followed, as expected, Hood would then be strong enough

to whip him; after which he would either send reinforcements to beleaguered Richmond or else take his whole command across the Cumberlands to come up in rear of the blue host outside Petersburg. Or if
Sherman did not follow, but instead took off southward for the Gulf
or eastward for the Atlantic, Hood explained that he would move by
the interior lines for an attack on Grant "at least two weeks before he,
Sherman, could render him assistance." Such a shift, he said, winding
up in a blaze of glory, "would defeat Grant and allow General Lee, in
command of our combined armies, to march upon Washington or turn
upon and annihilate Sherman."

Old Bory was amazed, partly by the bold sweep of the plan, which
seemed to him as practicable as it was entrancing, and partly by the
shock of recognition, occasioned by its resemblance to the half-dozen
or so which he himself had submitted to friends and superiors over the
course of the past three years, invariably without their being adopted.
One difference was that he had always insisted on heavy reinforcement at the outset, whereas Hood proposed to strike with what he had.
If this seemed rash, Beauregard could see that it might well be a virtue
in the present crisis, not only because no reinforcements were available,
but also because it would save time, and time was of the essence in a
situation depending largely on how rapidly the invaders moved —
especially against Thomas, who must not be given a chance to pull his
scattered forces together for the protection of the capital in his care. In
any case, approval was little more than a formality; Hood had informed
the government two days ago that he intended to cross the Tennessee,
and only yesterday had wired ahead to Richard Taylor, whose department he had entered for the crossing: "I will move tomorrow for
Guntersville." Beauregard did not withhold his blessing, though after
much discussion he insisted that Wheeler's cavalry, which had rejoined
the army near Rome ten days ago, be left behind to operate against
Sherman's communications and attack his rear if he set out south or
east, through otherwise undefended regions between Atlanta and the
Gulf or the Atlantic. Hood readily agreed to this subtraction when the
Creole added that Forrest would join him on the march, replacing
Wheeler, as soon as he and his troopers returned from their current
raid on Johnsonville; which, incidentally, would add to the Federal
confusion Hood hoped to provoke when he moved on Nashville.

Word went out to the camps that the shift northward would begin at daylight, and their commander later recalled that the news was
greeted with "that genuine Confederate shout so familiar to every
Southern soldier." By this he meant the rebel yell, the loudest of
which no doubt came from the bivouacs of the Tennesseans. Davis had
told them four weeks ago that their feet would soon be pressing native
soil, and now they whooped with delight at finding the promise about to
be kept.

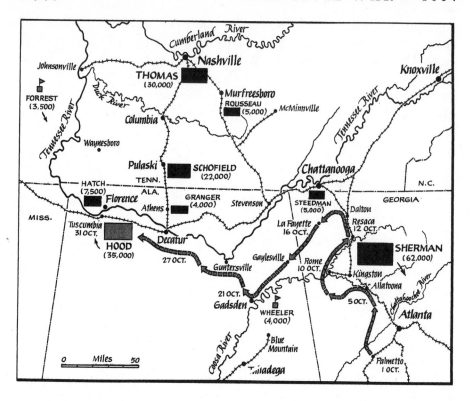

It was kept, although by no means as promptly as they and Beauregard expected when they parted at Gadsden next morning. Guntersville, thirty-odd miles northwest, turned out to be crowded with bluecoats, and Hood decided to veer west for a crossing at Decatur, just over forty miles downriver. However, when he drew close to there on October 26, after four days on the march, he found that it, like Guntersville, was too stoutly garrisoned to be stormed without heavier losses than he felt he could afford; so he pressed on for Courtland, twenty miles beyond Decatur, which he bypassed the following day. It was not until then that Beauregard, who had been off making supply arrangements and was miffed at not having been informed of the change in route, caught up with the column some fifty miles west of its original objective. He was aggrieved not only because the detour had ruled out the disruptive strike at Stevenson, now clearly beyond range of the butternut marchers, but also because of the loss of time, which Sherman and Thomas would surely use to their advantage. He had said from the start that celerity was Hood's best hope for success in this long-odds undertaking; yet five whole days had already been spent in search of a crossing that still had not been reached. Nor was that the worst of it. Informed by his engineers that they did not have enough pontoons to bridge the rain-swollen Tennessee at Courtland, Hood decided to push on and use the partly demolished railway span at Tuscumbia, another twenty-five miles downstream and well over eighty from Guntersville, where he had intended to ford the river a week ago. At Tuscumbia on the last day of October, he further alarmed his superior by announcing that he lacked sufficient provisions for the march that would follow the crossing, as well as shoes for his men and the horses in Jackson's two slim brigades, which were all the cavalry he would have until Forrest returned from Johnsonville, more than a hundred miles downriver to the north.

Taylor had unwelcome news for them in that regard as well. Unmindful of the need for haste, he had waited till Hood drew near Decatur on the 26th to send a courier summoning Forrest, who had left five days ago, and even then had told him to complete his mission before heading back. Hood took this, then and later, as evidence that he had done well to shift his infantry westward in search of a crossing, since this reduced the gap between it and the cavalry he was obliged to wait for anyhow. Moreover, while he marked time at Tuscumbia, doing what he could to repair his supply deficiencies and giving his men some well-earned rest through the first fine days of November, word came back that the delay had perhaps been worth the vexation after all, adding as it did a highly colorful chapter to the legend surrounding the Wizard of the Saddle.

After reaching the Tennessee River near the Kentucky line· on October 28, thirty miles north of Johnsonville, Forrest converted a portion of his 3500 troopers into literal horse marines and put them aboard two Union vessels, the gunboat *Undine* and the transport *Venus*, which he captured by posting batteries at both ends of a five-mile stretch of river to prevent their escape when he took them under fire with other guns along the bank. For three days, November 1–3, while this improvised two-boat navy molested traffic and drew attention northward, he led his horsemen south, up the west bank of the swollen Tennessee, to carry out the devastation that was the purpose of his raid. Well before midday November 4, after losing the *Venus* in an engagement with two gunboats and burning the eight-gun *Undine* to prevent her recapture, the two divisions were directly opposite Johnsonville, masked from view by trees and brush. While Morton was sneaking his guns into position, under orders to open fire at 2 o'clock, Forrest examined with his binoculars the unsuspecting target on the far side of the half-mile-wide river. Three gunboats, eleven transports, and eighteen barges were moored at the wharves, aswarm with workers unloading stores, and beyond them, spread out around a stockade fortress on high ground, warehouses bulged with supplies and acres of open storage were piled ten feet high with goods of every description, covered with tarpaulins to protect them from the weather. Two freight trains were being made up for the run to Nashville, just under eighty miles away, and neither the soldiers at work nor the officers scattered among them seemed aware that they were in any more danger now than they had been at any time since the base — named for the military governor who was Lincoln's running mate in the election only four days off — was put in operation, six months back.

Promptly at 2 o'clock they found out better. Morton having synchronized the watches of his chiefs of section, all ten pieces went off with an enormous bang that seemed to come from a single heavy cannon. For nearly an hour, after this introductory clap of thunder out of a cloudless sky, their fire was concentrated on the gunboats, the most dangerous enemy weapon, and when these were abandoned by their crews, who left them to burn and sink with the transports and barges they had been ordered to protect, the rebel artillerists shifted their attention to the landward installations, including the hilltop fortress whose unpracticed cannoneers replied wildly, blinded by smoke from riverside sheds and warehouses that had been set afire by sparks from the burning wharves and exploding vessels down below. Soon all those acres of high-piled stores were a mass of flames, and the exultant rebel gunners chose individual targets of opportunity, neglected until now. Perhaps the most spectacular of these was a warehouse on high ground, which, when struck and set afire, turned out to be stocked with several hundred barrels of whiskey that burst from the heat and sent a crackling blue-flame river of bourbon pouring down the hillside. Tantalized by the combined aroma of burnt liquor, roasting coffee beans, and frizzled bacon, wafted to them through a reek of gunsmoke, Morton's hungry veterans howled with delight and regret as they kept heaving shells into the holocaust they had created across the way. Forrest himself took a hand in the fun, directing the fire of one piece. "Elevate the breech of that gun a little lower!" he shouted, and the crew had little trouble understanding this unorthodox correction of the range. Within two hours all of Johnsonville was ablaze, resulting in a scene that "beggared description," according to one Federal who confined himself to the comment that it was "awfully sublime."

It was also awfully expensive. The base commander later put his loss at $2,200,000, taking the burned-out steamers and barges into account, but not the three sunken gunboats — four, including the *Undine*, subtracted during the naval phase of the raid, along with three more transports and three barges, mounting a total of 32 guns. Forrest's estimate of $6,700,000 included all of these, and probably came closer to the truth. His own loss, over-all, was two men killed and nine wounded, plus two guns lost when the *Venus* was recaptured. Retiring southward by the glare of flames still visible when he made camp six miles away, he encountered in the course of the next few days a series of couriers from Beauregard, all bearing orders for him to report at once to Hood, who was waiting at Tuscumbia for the outriders he would need on his march north. Forrest did what he could to hurry, but the going was slow through the muddy Tennessee bottoms, especially for the artillery. Even with sixteen horses to each piece, spelled by oxen impressed from farms adjoining the worst stretches along the way, he could see that he would need more than a week to reach Hood in Northwest Alabama.

Beauregard's distress at this development was matched by opposite reactions up the Coosa and beyond the Tennessee. Not only did the delay give Thomas added time to prepare for the blow Hood's drawn-out march had warned him was about to land; it also prompted Sherman to send still more reinforcements to Nashville, even while putting the final touches to his plan for making Georgia howl by slogging rough-shod across it to the sea.

Grant by now had assented unconditionally to the expedition, though not until he recovered from a last-minute fit of qualms brought on by the news that Hood was headed north. Sherman at Gaylesville had not known that the gray army had left Gadsden, thirty miles away, until it turned up near Decatur, ninety miles to the west, on October 26. His reaction, once Hood's departure had ruled out a confrontation near the Alabama-Georgia line, was to send Stanley's corps to strengthen Thomas, and when he learned that Hood was still in motion westward, apparently intending to force a crossing at Tuscumbia, he also detached Schofield's one-corps Army of the Ohio and directed that A. J. Smith's divisions return at once from Missouri to join in the defense of Middle Tennessee. Between them, Stanley, Schofield, and Smith had close to 40,000 men, and these, added to those already on hand — including more than half of Sherman's cavalry, sent back earlier; sizeable garrisons at Murfreesboro, Chattanooga, Athens, and Florence; and recruits coming down from Kentucky and Ohio, in response to Forrest's early-October penetration of the region below Nashville — would give Thomas about twice as many troops as Hood could bring against him. Surely that was ample, even though most of them were badly scattered, others were green, and some had not arrived. Best of all, however, from Sherman's point of view, this new arrangement provided a massive antidote for dealing with Grant's reawakened fears as to what might happen if Old Pap was left to face the invasion threat alone. "Do you not think it advisable, now that Hood has gone so far north, to entirely ruin him before starting on your proposed campaign?" Grant inquired on November 1, and added, rather more firmly: "If you see a chance of destroying Hood's army, attend to that first, and make your other move secondary."

This, of all things, was the one Sherman wanted least to hear, and in his reply he marshaled his previous arguments in redoubled opposition. "No single army can catch Hood," he declared, "and I am convinced that the best results will follow from our defeating Jeff. Davis's cherished plan of making me leave Georgia by maneuvering." Edgy and appre-hensive, fearing a negative reaction, he followed this with a second, more emphatic plea, before there was time for an answer to the first. "If I turn back, the whole effect of my campaign will be lost. By my movements I have thrown Beauregard (Hood) well to the west, and Thomas will have ample time and sufficient troops to hold him. . . . I am clearly of opinion that the best results will follow my contemplated movement through Georgia."

To his great relief, Grant wired back on November 2 that he was finally persuaded that Thomas would "be able to take care of Hood and destroy him." Moreover, he added, echoing his lieutenant's words in closing, "I really do not see that you can withdraw from where you are to follow Hood without giving up all we have gained in territory. I say, then, go as you propose."

Here at last was the go-ahead Sherman had been seeking all along, and now that he had it he moved fast, as if in fear that it might be revoked. Trains that had been shuttling between Chattanooga and Atlanta for the past two months, heavy-laden coming down and empty going back, now made their runs the other way around, returning all but the supplies he would take along in wagons when he set out for the sea with his four remaining corps, two from what was left of the Army of the Cumberland, under Slocum, and two from his old Army of the Tennessee, under Howard. They numbered better than 60,000 of all arms, including a single division of cavalry under Kilpatrick. He saw this mainly as an infantry operation, much like the one against Meridian last year, and had ordered the rest of his troopers back to Nashville for reorganization under James Wilson, who had recently been promoted to major general and sent by Grant to see what he could do about the poor showing western horsemen had been making ever since the start of the campaign. Sherman might have taken him along, a welcome addition on a march into the unknown, except that Thomas would most likely need him worse. Besides, he said, "I know that Kilpatrick is a hell of a damned fool, but I want just that sort of a man to command my cavalry on this expedition."

In "high feather," as he nearly always was when he was busy, he reëstablished headquarters at Kingston, the main-line railroad junction on the Etowah east of Rome, and there, with trains grinding north and rattling south at all hours of the day and night, supervised the final runs before the Western & Atlantic was closed down and its several depot garrisons withdrawn to become part of Major General J. B. Steedman's command at Chattanooga, on call for service under Thomas against Hood. His own army seemed to Sherman in splendid condition, fattened by veterans returning from thirty-day reënlistment furloughs, yet trimmed for hard use by evacuating all who were judged by surgeons not to be in shape for the 300-mile cross-Georgia march. On Sunday, November 6, he took time out to compose a farewell letter to Grant, a general statement of his intention, as he put it, "to act in such a manner against the material resources of the South as utterly to negative Davis' boasted threat." While he wrote, paymasters were active in all the camps, seeing to it that the soldiers would be in an appreciative frame of mind to support the Administration in the election two days off. "If we can march a well-appointed army right through his territory, it is a demonstration to the world, foreign and domestic, that we have a power which Davis cannot resist. This may not be war, but rather statesmanship. Nevertheless it is overwhelming to my mind that there are thousands of people abroad and in the South who reason thus: If the North can march an army right through the South, it is proof positive that the North can prevail."

He would set out, he told his chief, hard on the heels of Lincoln's reëlection — "which is assured" — and would thereby have the advantage of the confusion, not to say consternation, that event would provoke in the breasts of secessionists whose heartland he would be despoiling. What he would do after he reached Savannah he would decide when he got there and got back in touch with City Point. Meantime, he said, "I will not attempt to send couriers back, but trust to the Richmond papers to keep you well advised."

Grant — observing with hard-won equanimity the unusual spectacle of the two main western armies, blue and gray, already more than two hundred miles apart, about to take off in opposite directions — replied next day: "Great good luck go with you. I believe you will be eminently successful, and at worst can only make a march less fruitful than is hoped for."

★　★　★

In Richmond that same day, November 7 — election eve beyond the Potomac — Congress was welcomed back into session by a message from the Chief Executive, who had continued in Virginia the efforts made on his Georgia trip to lift spirits depressed by the outcome of the Hood-Sherman contest for Atlanta. Indeed, Davis went further here today in his denial that the South could be defeated, no matter what calamities attended her resistance to the force that would deny her independence.

After speaking of "the delusion fondly cherished [by the enemy] that the capture of Atlanta and Richmond would, if effected, end the war by the overthrow of our government and the submission of our people," he said flatly: "If the campaign against Richmond had resulted in success instead of failure, if the valor of [Lee's] army, under the leadership of its accomplished commander, had resisted in vain the overwhelming masses which were, on the contrary, decisively repulsed — if we had been compelled to evacuate Richmond as well as Atlanta — the Confederacy would have remained as erect and defiant as ever. Nothing could have been changed in the purpose of its government, in the indomitable valor of its troops, or in the unquenchable spirit of its people. The baffled and disappointed foe would in vain have scanned the reports of your proceedings, at some new legislative seat, for any indication that progress had been made in his gigantic task of conquering a free people." And having said as much he said still more in that regard. "There are no vital points on the preservation of which the continued existence of the Confederacy depends. There is no military success of the enemy which can accomplish its destruction. Not the fall of Richmond, nor Wilmington, nor Charleston, nor Savannah, nor Mobile, nor of all combined, can save the enemy from the constant and exhaustive drain of blood and treasure which must continue until he shall discover that no peace is attainable unless based on the recognition of our indefeasible rights."

He spoke at length of other matters, including foreign relations and finances — neither of them a pleasant subject for any Confederate — and referred, near the end, to the unlikelihood of being able to treat for peace with enemy leaders "until the delusion of their ability to conquer us is dispelled." Only then did he expect to encounter "that willingness to negotiate which is now confined to our side." Meantime, he told the assembled representatives, the South's one recourse lay in self-reliance. "Let us, then, resolutely continue to devote our united and unimpaired energies to the defense of our homes, our lives, and our liberties. This is the true path to peace. Let us tread it with confidence in the assured result."

Nowhere in the course of the long message did he mention tomorrow's election in the North, although the outcome was no less vital in the South — where still more battles would be fought if the hard-war Union party won — than it was throughout the region where the ballots would be cast. For one thing, any favorable reference to McClellan by Jefferson Davis would cost the Pennsylvanian votes he could ill afford now that Atlanta's fall and Frémont's withdrawal had transformed him, practically overnight, from odds-on favorite to underdog in the presidential race. In point of fact, much of the suspense had gone out of the contest, it being generally conceded by all but the most partisan of Democrats, caught up in the hypnotic fury of the campaign, that Little Mac had only the slimmest of chances.

Lincoln himself seemed gravely doubtful the following evening, however, when he crossed the White House grounds, soggy from a day-long wintry rain, to a side door of the War Department and climbed the stairs to the telegraph office, where returns were beginning to come in from around the country. These showed him leading in Massachusetts and Indiana, as well as in Baltimore and Philadelphia, and the trend continued despite some other dispatches that had McClellan ahead in Delaware and New Jersey. By midnight, though the storm delayed results from distant states, it was fairly clear that the turbulent campagin would end in Lincoln's reëlection.

Earlier he had said, "It is strange that I, who am not a vindictive man, should always, except once, have been before the people in canvasses marked by great bitterness. When I came to Congress it was a quiet time, but always, except that, the contests in which I have been prominent have been marked with great rancor." Now he lapsed into a darkly reminiscent mood, telling of that other election night, four years ago in Springfield, and a strange experience he had when he came home, utterly worn out, to rest for a time on a horsehair sofa in the parlor before going up to bed. Across the room, he saw himself reflected in a mirror hung on the wall above a bureau, almost at full length, murky, and with two faces, one nearly superimposed upon the other. Perplexed, somewhat alarmed, he got up to study the illusion at close range, only to have it vanish. When he lay down again it reappeared, plainer than before, and he could see that one face was paler than the other. Again he rose; again the double image disappeared. Later he told his wife about the phenomenon, and almost at once had cause — for both their sakes — to wish he hadn't. She took it as a sign, she said, that he would be reëlected four years later, but that the pallor of the second face indicated that he would not live through the second term.

The gloom this cast was presently dispelled by further reports that put all of New England and most of the Middle West firmly in his column. Around 2 o'clock, word came that serenaders, complete with a band, had assembled on the White House lawn to celebrate a victory whose incidentals would not be known for days. These would show that, out of some four million votes cast this Tuesday, Lincoln received 2,203,831 — just over 55 percent — as compared to his opponent's 1,797,019. Including those of Nevada, whose admission to the Union had been hurried through, eight days ago, so that its three votes could tip the scales if needed, he would receive 212 electoral votes and McClellan only the 21 from Delaware, New Jersey, and Kentucky. Yet the contest had been a good deal closer than these figures indicated. Connecticut, for example, was carried by a mere 2000 votes and New York by fewer than 7000, both as a result of military ballots, which went overwhelmingly for Lincoln, here as elsewhere. Without these two states, plus four others whose soldier voters swung the balance — Pennsylvania, Illinois, Maryland, and Indiana — he would have lost the election. Moreover, even in victory there were disappointments. New York City and Detroit went Democratic by majorities that ran close to three to one, and McClellan not only won the President's native state, Kentucky, he also carried Sangamon County, Illinois, and all the counties on its border. Lincoln could say to his serenaders before turning in that night, "I give thanks to the Almighty for this evidence of the people's resolution to stand by free government and the rights of humanity," but there was also the sobering realization, which would come with the full returns, that only five percent less than half the voters in the nation had opposed with their ballots his continuance as their leader.

Still, regardless of its outcome, he found consolation in two aspects of the bitter political struggle through which the country had just passed, and he mentioned both, two nights later, in responding to another group of serenaders. One was that the contest, for all "its incidental and undesirable strife," had demonstrated to the world "that a people's government can sustain a national election in the midst of a great civil war." This was much, but the other aspect was more complex, involving as it did the providence of an example distant generations could look back on when they came to be tested in their turn. "The strife of the election is but human nature practically applied to the facts of the case," he told the upturned faces on the lawn below the window from which he spoke. "What has occurred in this case must ever recur in similar cases. Human nature will not change. In any future great national trial, compared with the men of this, we shall have as weak and as strong, as silly and as wise, as bad and as good. Let us therefore study the incidents of this, as philosophy to learn wisdom from, and none of them as wrongs to be revenged."

Even so, a cruel paradox obtained. McClellan the loser was soon off on a European tour, a vacation that would keep him out of the country for six months, whereas Lincoln now more than ever, despite the stimulus of victory at the polls, could repeat what he had said two years before, in another time of trial: "I am like the starling in Sterne's story. 'I can't get out.'"

He had this to live with, as well as the memory of that double-image reflection in the mirror back in Springfield: both of which no doubt contributed, along with much else, to the nighttime restlessness a member of the White House guard observed as he walked the long second-story corridor, to and fro, past the door of the bedroom where the President lay sleeping. "I could hear his deep breathing," the sentry would recall. "Sometimes, after a day of unusual anxiety, I have heard him moan in his sleep. It gave me a curious sensation. While the expression of Mr Lincoln's face was always sad when he was quiet, it gave one the assurance of calm. He never seemed to doubt the wisdom of an action when he had once decided on it. And so when he was in a way defenseless in his sleep, it made me feel the pity that would almost have been an impertinence when he was awake. I would stand there and listen until a sort of panic stole over me. If he felt the weight of things so heavily, how much worse the situation of the country must be than any of us realized! At last I would walk softly away, feeling as if I had been listening at a keyhole."

You Cannot Refine It

★ ✗ ☆

INDIAN SUMMER HAD COME TO VIRGINIA while Northerners were going to the polls, muting with its smoky haze the vivid yellow vivid scarlet flare of maples and dogwoods on the Peninsula and down along the sunlit reaches of the James, where close to a hundred thousand blue-clad soldiers, in camps and trenches curving past the mouth of the Appomattox, celebrated or shook their heads at the news that they and more than half the men back home had voted to sustain a war that lacked only a winter of being four years old. Across the way, in the rebel works, the reaction was less mixed — and less intense. Partly this was because of distractions, including hunger and the likelihood of being hoisted by a mine or overrun; partly it proceeded from a sense of contrast between the present molelike state of existence and the old free-swinging foot cavalry days when the Army of Northern Virginia ranged the region from which it took its name but now would range no more.

"We thought we had before seen men with the marks of hard service upon them," an artillery major was to write, recalling his impression of the scarecrow infantry his battalion had been ordered to support on arriving from beyond the river back in June, "but the appearance of this division made us realize for the first time what our comrades in the hottest Petersburg lines were undergoing. We were shocked at the condition, the complexion, the expression of the men ... even the field officers. Indeed, we could scarcely realize that the unwashed, uncombed, unfed, and almost unclad creatures were officers of rank and reputation in the army." Thus he had reacted and reflected in early summer. Now in November he knew that he too looked like that, if not more so, with an added five hard months of wear and tear.

Richmond and Petersburg, semi-beleaguered at opposite ends of the line, were barely twenty crow-flight miles apart, but the intrenchments covering and connecting them had stretched by now to nearly twice that length. From White Oak Swamp on the far left, due east of the capital, these outer works (as distinguished from the 'inner' works, two miles in their rear) ran nine miles south, in a shielding curve, to Chaffin's Bluff on the James; there they crossed and continued for four gun-studded miles along the river's dominant right bank to a westward loop where the Howlett Line — Beauregard's cork in Butler's bottle — began its five-mile run across Bermuda Neck to the Appomattox, then jogged another four miles south, up the left bank of that stream, to connect with the trenches covering Petersburg at such close range that its citizens had grown adept at dodging Yankee shells. The first four miles of these trans-Appomattox installations — disfigured about midway by the red yawn of the Crater — defined the limits of the original blue assault as far south as the Jerusalem Plank Road, where both sides had thrown up imposing and opposing fortifications. Officially dubbed Forts Sedgwick and Mahone, but known respectively by their occupants as Fort Hell and Fort Damnation, these were designed to serve as south-flank anchors, back in June, for the two systems winding northward out of sight. Since that time, however, as a result of Grant's

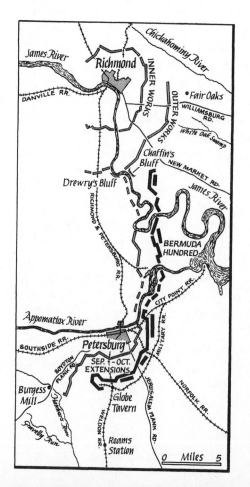

four all-out pendulum strikes (staged one a month, July through October, and costing him some 25,000 casualties, all told, as compared to Lee's 10,000) the gray line had been extended nine miles to the west and southwest, covering the Boydton Plank Road down to Hatcher's Run. All these segments brought the Confederate total to thirty-five miles of earthworks, not including cavalry extensions reaching up to the Chickahominy on the left and down past Burgess Mill to Gravelly Run on the right. Lee's basic problem, with only about half as many troops as he opposed, was that his line was not only longer, it was also more continuous than Grant's, who, having no national capital or indispensable railroad junction close in his rear, had less to fear from a breakthrough at any given point.

Another problem was food; or rather the lack of it. Badly as Lee needed men — and the need was so stringent he could not give his Jewish soldiers a day out of the trenches for Rosh Hashana or Yom Kippur — he saw no way of feeding substantial reinforcements even if they had been available, which they were not. As it was, he barely managed to sustain the troops on hand by reducing their daily ration to a pint of cornmeal, baked into pones when there was time, and an ounce or two of bacon. Moreover, with the Shenandoah Valley put to the torch and only two rail lines open to Georgia and the Carolinas — the Southside out of Petersburg, the Danville out of Richmond — there was little hope that the fare could be improved, despite the fact that the trench-bound men were losing weight and strength at an alarming rate. They looked fit enough, to a casual eye, but would "pant and grow faint" at the slightest exertion, a staffer noted. "General, I'm hongry," some would reply when Lee rode out and asked them how they were. All through this grim time, a veteran would say, "I thanked God I had a backbone for my stomach to lean up against."

Others remarked that the quality of such food as they received was even lower than its quantity; which was low indeed. The meal was unbolted, generally with much of the cob ground in, and alive with weevils. But the bacon remained longest in their memories and nightmares. Nassau bacon, it was called, though one memorialist was to testify that "Nausea with a capital would have been better. It came through the blockade, and we believed it was made from the hog of the tropics and cured in the brine of the ocean. More likely it was discarded ship's pork, or 'salt junk.'... It was a peculiarly scaly color, spotted like a half-well case of smallpox, full of rancid odor, and utterly devoid of grease. When hung up it would double its length. It could not be eaten raw, and imparted a stinking smell when boiled. It had one redeeming quality: elasticity. You could put a piece in your mouth and chew it for a long time, and the longer you chewed it the bigger it got. Then, by a desperate effort, you would gulp it down. Out of sight, out of mind."

Nor was the outer man, in his butternut rags, any better served than the inner. Shoes, for example, had always been a scarce requisition item, and now that the once bounteous yield of well-shod Union corpses had diminished as a dividend of battle, the shortage was acute. Even so, and with cold weather coming on, many soldiers preferred going barefoot to wearing the "pitiable specimens" of footgear issued by the government as a substitute for shoes. "Generally made of green, or at best half-cured leather," one who suffered from them later wrote, "they soon took to roaming. After a week's wear, the heel would be on one side, at an angle to the foot, and the vamp in turn would try to do duty as a sole.... While hot and dry, they would shrink like parchment, and when wet they just slopped all over your feet."

Crippling as this was, other shortages cramped the army's style still more. Chief among these, despite the sacrifice of most of the South's stills, was the scarcity of copper, indispensable in the manufacture of percussion caps, without which not a shot could be fired. Riflemen in the critical outer pits were limited to eighteen caps a day, while their Federal counterparts across the way complained of bruised shoulders from being required to expend no less than a hundred rounds in the same span. Other metals not only were less rare, they also could be salvaged from incoming projectiles, much as boots and overcoats had been scavenged from incoming infantry, back in the days of mobile warfare. "As an inducement to collecting scrap iron for our cannon foundries," a line officer would recall, "furloughs were offered, a day for so many pounds collected. Thus, gathering fragments of shells became an active industry among the troops. So keen was their quest that sometimes they would start toward the point where a mortar shell fell, even before it exploded." Similarly, the loose dirt of the parapets was periodically sifted for spent lead, but only under cover of darkness, when snipers were inactive. Twice each day, an hour before dawn and half an hour before dusk, every regiment mounted the fire step along its portion of the trenches and remained there, on the alert, until full daylight spread or night came down. Between times, round the clock, half the men kept watch, while the other half slept or rested on their arms, ready to assist in repelling an attack whenever their on-duty comrades sounded the alarm.

Outnumbered and outgunned, ill-clad, ill-shod, and invariably hungry, running after fragments of shell as they once had run after rabbits — except that now they were not in direct pursuit of food, for there was none at the scene of the chase, but rather of the chance to win a day out of the trenches, on the roam where a few mouthfuls could be scrounged from roadside gardens ("They stole more from us than the Yankees did; poor things," a farmwife was to say long afterwards) — Lee's veterans fought less by now for a cause than they did for a tradition. And if, in the past six months, this had become a tradition not so much of victory as of undefeat, it had nonetheless been strengthened by the recent overland campaign and now was being sustained by the current stalemate, which was all that Grant's hundred thousand casualties had earned him in this latest On-to-Richmond effort, launched in May. Mainly, though, Lee's veterans fought for Lee, or at any rate for the pride they felt when they watched him ride among them. He had "a fearless look of self-possession, without a trace of arrogance," a Tarheel captain noted, and though a fellow Virginian observed that "he had aged somewhat in appearance," it was also evident that he "had rather gained than lost in physical vigor, from the severe life he had led. His hair had grown gray, but his face had the ruddy hue of health and his eyes were as clear and bright as ever."

Partly this appearance of well-being derived from the extended spell of golden weather, which continued through November into December; Lee had always been responsive to climatic fluctuations, good and bad, even before the onset of what doctors called his rheumatism. A staff cavalryman, however, looking back on this hale, autumnal time — when the general, as he said, "seldom, if ever, exhibited the least trace of anxiety, but was firm, hopeful, and encouraged those around him in the belief that he was still confident of success" — believed he saw deeper into the matter. "It must have been the sense of having done his whole duty, and expended upon the cause every energy of his being, which enabled him to meet the approaching catastrophe with a calmness which seemed to those around him almost sublime."

Perceptive as this was by hindsight, there were other, more evident causes for the confidence he displayed. One was the return of Longstreet in mid-October, on the day of Early's defeat at Cedar Creek. His right arm partly paralyzed by the effects of his Wilderness wound, Old Peter had learned to write with his left hand, and he gladly accepted full responsibility for the defense of that part of the line above the James, where he soon demonstrated that he had lost none of his cool, hard-handed skill in conducting a battle. Lee's wisdom in leaving the fighting there to his "old war horse" was confirmed within eight days of the Georgian's return to duty; no northside drive on Richmond was ever so easily shattered, at such low cost to the defenders, as the one that made up part of Grant's fourth and final pendulum strike, October 27. What was more, the confidence this inspired was enlarged by Hill's and Hampton's canny resistance along Hatcher's Run, where three Federal corps were turned back in confusion the following day, after suffering even heavier losses than had been inflicted on the other two corps, at the far end of the line.

Small wonder, then, that Lee gave an impression of vigor and well-being as he rode north or south, through the flare and haze of Indian Summer, to inspect his nearly forty miles of unbroken line from the Chickahominy down past Burgess Mill. Even Grant, who was slow to learn negative lessons, had apparently been convinced by this latest failure that he would never take the Confederate capital by storm, and this estimate was strengthened in mid-November by the recall of Kershaw's division from Early to join Longstreet, whose reunited First Corps now occupied all the defenses north of the Appomattox, including those across Bermuda Neck. A. P. Hill's Third Corps held the Petersburg intrenchments, supported by Hampton's cavalry on the right, and a new Fourth Corps was improvised by combining the divisions of Hoke and Bushrod Johnson (but only on paper; Hoke remained north and Johnson south of the James) to provide a command for Richard Anderson, commensurate with his rank, after Old Peter's return. With Dick Ewell in charge of the reserves in Richmond, on call for manning the city's inner works, Lee felt that his army was not only back under his immediate control — aside, that is, from Early's three Second Corps divisions, still licking their wounds out on the near rim of the Shenandoah Valley — but also, in the light of its performance against four all-out assaults in as many months by twice its numbers, that it had recovered a considerable measure of the responsive, agile quality that made it like a rapier in his hand.

Still, for all its delicate balance and true temper, the rapier had become an exclusively defensive weapon, swift in parry and effective in occasional riposte, but not employed for months now to deliver a bold, original thrust or slash, as in the days when Lee's aggressive use of it, whether to pink or maim, had dazzled admirers all over the world. Moreover, he knew that in time, without proper care or refurbishment, the fine-honed instrument would wear out (or the fencer would, which came to the same thing) under the constant hammering of the Union broadsword, any one of whose strokes would end the duel if his arm wearied and let it past. "Without some increase of strength," he had warned Seddon more than two months ago, "I cannot see how we can escape the natural military consequences of the enemy's numerical superiority." Nothing much had come of this, nor of a follow-up protest to Bragg one month later: "I get no additions. The men coming in do not supply the vacancies caused by sickness, desertions, and other casualties." Now in November he appealed to the President himself. "Grant will get every man he can. . . . Unless we obtain a reasonable approximation to his force I fear a great calamity will befall us."

Nothing came of that either; Davis could only reply, as he had done to similar pleas from Hood, "No other resource remains." And now that Lincoln's reëlection had dashed Confederate hopes for an early end to the war by negotiation, Lee saw clearly enough that all his skilled resistance had really gained him, north and south of the James, was time — time with which, lacking substantial reinforcements, he could do little except continue to resist; until time ran out, as it finally must, and broke the vicious, tightening circle. His belief that Grant was at last convinced of the folly involved in prolonging a series of bungled attempts to overrun him was encouraged, if not confirmed, when November drew to a close without a major assault having been launched against any part of his works from start to finish, the first such month since the siege began. But he also knew this did not mean there would be a let-up in Grant's efforts to accomplish by attrition what he had failed to achieve by overwhelming force. Expecting renewed strikes at his overworked supply lines, west and south of Petersburg and Richmond, Lee told Davis in early December: "All we want to resist them is men."

Subsequently, looking back on his close association as the general's aide, a staff colonel declared that the two- or three-week span from late November into December was "the most anxious period of Grant's entire military career." Although Horace Porter, who made the statement, had not shared his chief's times of trial out West — after Donelson, when Halleck tried to sack him: after Shiloh, when Sherman persuaded him not to quit the service in dejection: after Vicksburg, when he spent a fretful month watching his army be dismembered, while he hobbled about on crutches from his New Orleans horseback fall — the young West Pointer had practical as well as psychological grounds for his contention that this latest tribulation was the hardest. Those previous afflictions of the spirit had followed significant battlefield successes, two of them even resulting in rebel surrenders, whereas this one came at a time when the best Grant could claim, at any rate for the army under his hand, was a stalemate achieved at a cost in casualties roughly twice as great as the number he inflicted. Victory was a future, not a present thing, as in two of those other three cases, and its nearness — within his reach, as he believed, but not within his grasp, as Lee had shown — was one source of his frustration. Another, which raised this reaction to the pitch of true anxiety, was a growing apprehension that things might go dreadfully awry in Tennessee (or, what was worse, Kentucky) on the very eve of triumph in Virginia. He had never been one to take counsel of his fears, but there were plenty of veteran officers around — including Porter, who had served on McClellan's staff — to remind him that Little Mac once had stood about where he was standing now, close enough to hear the tocsin clang in Richmond, and yet had wound up confronting a Maryland invasion fifty miles northwest of his own capital, which lay more than a hundred miles in rear of Harrison's Landing, just across the way from City Point.

First there was the unavoidable admission that the headlong approach, which by now had cost Meade and Butler some 36,000 casualties between them — 11,000 in the initial June assault, plus 25,000 since — provided no quick solution to the Petersburg dilemma. That came hard for Grant, who seldom acknowledged failure, especially in large-scale undertakings, and in fact declined to do so now; except tacitly, by desisting. Hancock did it for him, though, in a ceremony staged at his headquarters on November 26, when he bid farewell to the once-proud II Corps. Ostensibly, he was returning to Washington under War Department orders to recruit and organize a new I Corps of reënlisted veterans for service in the spring. Nothing was to come of that, however. Nor was there much validity in the claim that he was leaving because of his unhealed Gettysburg wound. The real damage was to his soldier's pride, which had suffered cruelly in the series of dispiriting reverses he and his troops had undergone in the course of the past five months, north of the James and south of the Appomattox. His departure was a measure of the extent to which Grant's breakthrough concept had broken down in the fire of Lee's resistance, and it was clear that the men of the three divisions Hancock left behind would need a great deal of rest and recuperation before they were fit for any such use by his successor, Major General A. A. Humphreys, a fellow Pennsylvanian and West Pointer, who had served as Meade's chief of staff for the past year and was fifty-four years old.

Sharpest of the stings involved in the stalling of Grant's offensive was the fact that he could almost never get his orders carried out as he intended; Baldy Smith had been the first, after the passage of the James, but he was by no means the last offender in this regard. "Three different times has Richmond or Petersburg been virutally in his hands," a military visitor wrote home about this time, "and by some inexcusable neglect or slowness each time his plans were ruined and the opportunity lost. How Grant stands it I do not see." Moreover, there seemed to be no cure for this condition: not even the removal of Baldy and Burnside, along with such lesser lights as Ledlie and Ferrero. These, after all, were only four among the many — including Butler, who could not be dealt with in that fashion, though he was at times, because of his lofty rank and large command, a greater trial than all the rest combined.

Just now, for example, he was at work on a plan for cracking Wilmington's seaward defenses, obviously a top-priority assignment, not only because it would close the South's last major port and thus increase Lee's problem of subsistence, but also because it would divert attention, as well as possible rebel reinforcements, away from Sherman's destination on the Georgia coast, 250 miles below. Yet Butler kept delaying the start of the movement, which he was to make with two of his divisions and the support of David Porter's fleet, by thinking up ways to ensure that the amphibious assault would be brief and successful, without too great a cost in ships and men. His latest notion was to pack an expendable ocean-going steamer with 350 tons of powder and run it under the walls of Fort Fisher, which would be reduced to rubble by the timed explosion, leaving the attackers little to do but move in and take over when the smoke cleared. Grant liked the plan and approved it, though he did not like or approve of the delays. He kept prodding the cock-eyed general, urging him to be off before the Carolinians got word of what was in store for them; but Butler, still "as visionary as an opium eater in council," refused to be hurried, insisting that a close attention to details provided the only guarantee of success. Then on November 27 — the day after Hancock's farewell ceremony — an enemy agent came close to solving Grant's problem by removing the former Bay State politician not only from his command but from the earth.

Butler and Porter were conferring aboard the former's headquarters steamer *Greyhound*, a short distance up the James from Bermuda Landing, "when suddenly an explosion forward startled us, and in a moment large volumes of smoke poured out of the engine room." So Porter later described the mishap, which fortunately was no worse because the explosion set off no others and the flames were soon extinguished, but he marveled at an ingenuity rivaling his companion's in such matters. What was thought at first to have been a boiler accident turned out to have been caused by a "coal torpedo," a blackened piece of cast iron, machined to resemble a lump of coal and loaded with ten pounds of powder, which the rebel agent had somehow placed in the steamer's bunker and a stoker had shoveled into the furnace. "In devices for blowing up vessels the Confederates were far ahead of us, putting Yankee ingenuity to shame," the admiral declared.

Three days later, on the last day of November, Grant learned that part of the Wilmington garrison was being withdrawn to intercept Sherman at Augusta, Georgia, on the theory that he would pass that way en route to Charleston. Not only was this no immediate threat to Sherman, whose true destination was almost a hundred miles farther down the coast, it also simplified Butler's task by reducing, at least for the present, the resistance he would encounter when he struck Wilmington's defenses. Informed of this, the Massachusetts general replied that he was delighted; he would proceed as soon as his floating bomb was ready for use, a further delay having been required by his notion of altering the steamer's lines to make her resemble a blockade runner, which he figured would cause the rebel cannoneers to cheer her, rather than shoot at her, right up to the moment she blew. Grant could see the humor in this, but he was losing patience. Aware that the Confederates would soon have the choice of returning to Wilmington or ganging up on Sherman, he told Butler on December 4 to start for North Carolina at once, "with or without your powder boat." But that did not work either. For ten more days the squint-eyed Butler, unruffled by his superior's apprehensions or his own near brush with death aboard the *Greyhound*, continued to balk and tinker before he got his two divisions onto transports at Hampton Roads and headed down the coast.

Grant's concern for Sherman's welfare, even his survival, off on his own and due to pop up any day now, more than four hundred miles down the seaboard — a ready target for whatever combination of forces the rebels were able to throw in that direction — was real enough, but it was by no means as grievous a source of anxiety as were several others, over which — at least in theory, since he was in direct communication with the subordinates in charge — he could exercise some measure of control. For one thing, as he had told Stanton at the outset, seeking to reassure the Secretary as to the degree of risk involved in cutting loose from Atlanta for the march through Georgia to the coast, "Such an army as Sherman has (and with such a commander) is hard to corner or capture." For another, his over-all design for the

Confederacy's defeat by strangulation did not hinge on the outcome of the current maneuver by his red-haired friend, whose success could shorten but whose defeat would not lengthen the war by so much as a day. Besides, his reliance on Sherman and Sherman's army — once his own — was unmatched by any such feeling of confidence in George Thomas and the scratch collection of recruits, dismounted cavalrymen, and culled veterans Old Tom had been attempting to put together in Middle Tennessee ever since Sherman set out for the sea, leaving Hood and Hood's hard-hitting army alive in his rear, poised for a strike at the critical Union center.

There was the rub. The Rock of Chickamauga was superb on the defensive, and at Chattanooga he had shown what he could do in an assault on a fixed position. But how would Old Slow Trot perform in a fluid situation requiring him to deal with an enemy in motion around his flank? So far the signs were unpromising, and that was the chief source of Grant's anxiety: that Hood would bypass Nashville, where Thomas was intrenched, and cross the Cumberland River unmolested, perhaps on a march all the way to the Ohio. If that happened, all Grant's well-laid plans might come undone in a sudden reversal of the tide of war. Even the siege of Richmond might have to be lifted, in order to furnish troops for the protection of Kentucky, and Sherman's march through Georgia might as well have occurred in a vacuum, ending as it would in nothing more than a long ride north aboard transports, then west by rail to resume the contest with his old adversary in a region two hundred miles in rear of the one through which he had fought his way in May and June.

Lincoln saw it, too, and abandoned for the time, at least by proxy, his hands-off policy with regard to military operations. "The President feels solicitous about the disposition of General Thomas to lay in fortifications for an indefinite period," Stanton wired on December 2. "This looks like the McClellan and Rosecrans strategy of do nothing and let the rebels raid the country. The President wishes you to consider the matter."

Grant did consider the matter and stepped up the pressure, warning Thomas that he would "suffer incalculable injury . . . if Hood is not speedily disposed of. Put forth therefore every possible exertion to gain this end," he told him, but with no more success than he was having at the same time in getting Butler on the go for Wilmington. Stanton returned to the charge, protesting that the Virginian seemed "unwilling to attack because it is hazardous — as if war was anything but hazardous," he sneered — which drew from Grant the admission that, for all of Thomas's reputed bulldog qualities, "I fear he is too cautious to take the initiative." All the same, he tried again, this time with a direct order: "Attack Hood at once and wait no longer. . . . There is great danger of delay resulting in a campaign back to the Ohio River."

This was clear enough, but it only caused the Tennessee commander to shift his ground under prodding from the rear. He had been on the verge of launching an all-out attack, he replied, but "a terrible storm of freezing rain has come on today, which will make it impossible for our men to fight to any advantage."

Thwarted thus at every turn in his efforts to get Butler and Thomas moving, stalled on the outskirts of Richmond by a resistance so discouraging that it had just cost Meade the best of his corps commanders, deprived of any reliable information as to Sherman's progress or misfortune in the Georgia hinterland, and harried as he was beginning to be by superiors who had been altogether forbearing up till now, Grant was determined to do what he personally could at City Point, through this "most anxious period," if only by way of relieving the strain that came with finding how much there was that he could not do elsewhere. One thing he could do, despite his recent abandonment of headlong tactics against Petersburg's intrenchments, was keep up the pressure on its overtaxed supply lines. That would not only add to Lee's subsistence problem, in direct ratio to the degree of success achieved; it would also prevent the old fox from sending reinforcements to Tennessee or Georgia, as he had done the year before, in the absence of such pressure. Accordingly, Grant planned another strike at the Weldon Railroad, this time down near the Carolina line, its purpose being to lengthen the twenty-mile wagon haul the rebels now were obliged to make from Stony Creek, the terminus of the road since August, when Hancock wrecked it that far south. The assignment went to Warren, whose three divisions would be reinforced by one from Humphreys, and Gregg's troopers would go along to screen the march.

First, though, Grant decided to lengthen the numerical odds against his adversary by returning Wright's long-absent corps from the Shenandoah Valley, where all it had been doing for the past six weeks was assist Sheridan in the destruction being visited on that much-fought-over region, once the classic avenue for invasions that played on northern fears, but now not even a source of grain or cattle, practically all of which had been put to the torch or gone under the Union knife. Wright's leading elements began unloading from transports at City Point on December 4; three days later Warren set out on his march to strike the Petersburg & Weldon at the crossing of the Meherrin River, twenty miles beyond Stony Creek.

When Lee discovered that Wright was en route from the Valley to rejoin Meade, he countered by ordering Early to send back two of his divisions, Gordon's and Ramseur's, the latter now under its senior brigadier, John Pegram. Neither arrived in time to help fend off Warren's threat to the railroad, which began on December 7, but the southern commander, gambling on his belief that Grant would attempt no more frontal assaults this year, risked pulling most of Hill's corps out of the Petersburg works to undertake, along with Hampton's cavalry, an interception of what he thought was a drive on Weldon. Next day, however, the weather turned intensely cold. Pelted by sleet, the butternut marchers shivered in their rags, and many fell out of the slow-moving column after slogging barefoot over miles of frozen ground. When those who managed to keep going reached the railroad below Stony Creek, December 9, they found sixteen miles of track ripped up, piles of ties still smoking, heat-twisted rails warm to the touch, and the Federals gone, turned back by home-guard batteries at Hicksford, firing at them from just beyond the Meherrin, as well as by the miserable weather and the near exhaustion of their three-day rations. Hampton overtook and slashed at the flanks of the blue column trudging north, but only managed to kill or capture about a hundred stragglers; the rest got away into their own lines the following day. If there was some criticism of Hill for not having engaged the marauders before they escaped, there was also a feeling of relief that they had not inflicted heavier damage on the already crippled supply line, whose railhead now was forty miles south of Petersburg's hungry defenders.

Winter came with mid-December vengeance, and though the advantage had to be weighed against the suffering of his thinly clad men in the trenches astride the James, Lee knew that the Federals too, for all their sturdy boots, snug overcoats, and rations that warmed them inside as well as out, would be restricted by ice and mud and frozen rain if they continued their efforts to move around his flanks. Moreover, the rough weather afforded him one last chance — however slight, in comparison with what Wright's return brought Grant — to increase the number of troops he could post along his thirty-odd miles of line between White Oak Swamp and Hatcher's Run. When he got word that a six-inch snow had clogged the roads in the upper Valley, he told Early to send the third of his divisions to Richmond in the wake of the other two (which had just arrived) but to remain out there himself, as district commander, with a force reduced to Wharton's undersized infantry division and Rosser's two slim cavalry brigades, in necessarily long-range observation of Sheridan's continuing depredations. Presently the old Second Corps, down to a skeleton strength of fewer than 9000 effectives — the result of its six-month excursion down and up the Valley and its brief side trip to the outskirts of Washington and back — was again an integral, on-hand part of the Army of Northern Virginia.

Lee named Gordon acting corps commander, the first nonprofessional to occupy so high a post. This was an indication of what inroads attrition had made at the upper levels, as was the fact that two of the three divisions were similarly led by their senior brigadiers. Clement Evans, a former Georgia lawyer like his chief, succeeded Gordon, and Bryan Grimes, once a North Carolina planter, had taken over from the fallen Rodes. Only Pegram, a Virginia-born West Pointer, had seen military service before the war. And of the four, including the major general in charge of all three divisions, only Grimes had reached his middle thirties. He was thirty-six; Gordon and Pegram were thirty-two, and Evans was thirty-one.

Glad as Lee was at the reassembling of his army, however shrunken it might be at all its levels, he was also saddened by the knowledge that this had been accomplished at the price of abandoning hope of going over to the offensive. Not since Chancellorsville and the death of Jackson, close to twenty months ago, had he won the kind of brilliant, large-scale victory that brought him and his lean, caterwauling veterans the admiration of the world, and now that the Valley was irretrievably lost, along with Stonewall, his recall of the Second Corps to join the others huddled in the trenches around Petersburg and Richmond set the seal on his admission, however tacit, that the war, however much or little of it was left to fight, was for him and them no longer a pursuit of glory on the road to national independence, but rather a grim struggle for survival, which would take them down a quite different road to the same goal — if they could reach its end. Yet here was where a paradox came in. While Grant reacted to the prospect of ultimate victory by growing jumpy at the thought of having the prize snatched from him just as it seemed about to come within his grasp, Lee faced the ultimate prospect of defeat with "a fearless look of self-possession" and "a calmness which seemed to those around him almost sublime."

Or perhaps there was no paradox in that. Perhaps the two reactions were quite natural, considering the two quite different kinds of strain imposed on these two quite different kinds of men. In some ways, since nothing worse could happen to him than what seemed foreordained, Lee's was the easier role to play. Expectation braced him for the shocks: even the loss, before the month was out, of more than a tenth of the force he had been at such pains to assemble for Richmond's protection in mid-December. Warned that Wilmington was about to be hit, three hundred miles down the coast, he was obliged to send Hoke's division to its defense — a detachment that cost him the equivalent of a solid two thirds of all he had gained by the return of Early's survivors from the Valley. His year-end strength, including 5358 reservists under Ewell, came to 57,134. Across the way, Meade had 83,846 and Butler 40,452: a total of 124,278 for Grant.

Outnumbered two to one, the gaps in their ranks only partly chinked with conscripts, the defenders saw clearly enough that time, which they were being told was on their side, could only lengthen the odds against survival. Good men had fallen and were falling every day, picked off by snipers or dropped by mortars in a roughly man-for-man exchange that worked to the considerable disadvantage of the smaller force, not only because its proportionate loss was twice as heavy on that basis, but also because the replacements being scraped from the bottom of the Confederate barrel did not "supply the vacancies," as Lee had complained to Bragg three months before. Moreover, some who fell could scarcely have been replaced in the best of times: Rodes and Ramseur, for example, or John Gregg and Archibald Gracie, both of whom had won distinction at Chickamauga. Gregg was cut down at the head of his Texas brigade, in a skirmish east of Richmond in October, and Gracie was killed in early December by a shell that burst over a normally quiet stretch of Petersburg intrenchments while he was training a telescope on the works across the way. Such losses, suffered without the compensating stimulus of victory, came hard for the survivors, whose spirits drooped as their numbers dwindled. "Living cannot be called a fever here," a butternut artillerist declared, "but rather a long catalepsy." Desertions rose with the rising proportion of conscripts, many of them netted after years of avoiding the draft, and even the stalwarts who stood by their banners looked forward to furling them — whatever arrangements might have to be made to bring that end about.

"As we lay there watching the bright stars," one veteran lieutenant was to say, "many a soldier asked himself the question: What is this all about? Why is it that 200,000 men of one blood and one tongue, believing as one man in the fatherhood of God and the universal brotherhood of man, should in the nineteenth century of the Christian era be thus armed with all the improved appliances of modern warfare and seeking one another's lives? We could settle our differences by compromising, and all be at home in ten days."

✻　2　✻

Early morning, November 16; Sherman sat his horse on Bald Hill, where the worst of the fighting had raged in July, and looked down on the copse where McPherson had fallen, shot through the back while opposing the second of Hood's three all-out sorties. "Behind us lay Atlanta, smouldering and in ruins," he would recall, "the black smoke rising high in air and hanging like a pall over the ruined city. Away off in the distance, on the McDonough Road, was the rear of Howard's column, the gun barrels glistening in the sun, the white-topped wagons stretching away to the south, and right before us the XIV Corps [of Slocum's column] marching steadily and rapidly, with a cheery look and swinging pace that made light of the thousand miles that lay between us and Richmond."

Leading elements of both columns having stepped off the day before, east and southeast down the railroads, Atlanta had been set afire last night, partly by rear-guard arsonists, who stole away from, then rejoined their units passing through, and partly by design, in accordance

with orders that nothing be left intact that might be of use to the rebs
when they returned. In any case, the results were spectacular. "All the
pictures and verbal descriptions of hell I have ever seen never gave me
half so vivid an idea of it as did this flame-wrapped city tonight," a staff
major wrote in his journal after dodging sparks and debris from explosions as he picked his way through the streets. Dawn showed more than
a third of the town in ashes, with smoke still rising thick and slow from
the longer-lasting fires. While Sherman watched from his hilltop, a mile
beyond the eastward bend of Hood's abandoned fortifications, a band
in the blue column below struck up the John Brown song, and presently
the marchers joined in, roaring the words as they slogged along. "Never
before or since have I heard the chorus of 'Glory, glory, hallelujah!'
done with more spirit or in better harmony of time and place," their red-
haired commander was to say.

He twitched his horse's head to the east and came down off the
hill, trailed by his staff. "Uncle Billy," a weathered veteran hailed him
near the bottom, "I guess Grant is waiting for us at Richmond!" Sherman grinned and rode on, doubling the column. "Atlanta was soon lost
behind the screen of trees, and became a thing of the past. Around it
clings many a thought of desperate battle, of hope and fear, that now
seem like the memory of a dream. . . . I have never seen the place since."

Orders governing the expedition had been issued the week before,
to afford all ranks plenty of time for study before moving out. They
made no mention of route or destination, being mainly concerned with
logistics and rules of conduct for the 62,000 participants, just over 5000
of whom were cavalry, under Kilpatrick, and just under 2000 were
artillery, with 64 guns. Each of the four infantry corps — two in each of
two "wings," both of which were equipped with 900-foot collapsible
pontoon bridges transported in special trains — would move by a separate road, where practicable, and be independent for supplies. "The
army will forage liberally on the country during the march," Sherman
directed, though he specified that the foraging was to be done only by
authorized personnel; "Soldiers must not enter the dwellings of inhabitants or commit any trespass." He hoped to keep nonmilitary damage
to a minimum, but he made it clear that if guerillas or other civilians attempted to interfere with his progress, say by damaging bridges or ob-
structing roads, "then army commanders should order and enforce a
devastation more or less relentless, according to the measure of such
hostility." Privately, he expanded this admonition and directed that
word of it be spread wherever the army went, in hopes that it would
be carried ahead by the rebel grapevine, if not by the rebel papers. "If
the enemy burn forage and corn in our route," he said, "houses, barns,
and cotton gins must also be burned to keep them company."

Every man carried forty rounds of small-arms ammunition on his
person, and another 200 followed in the wagons, along with a twenty-

day supply of hardtack and coffee. Only a five-day reserve of grain went along for the horses, but he figured that was enough to get them clear of the clean-picked region around Atlanta; "I knew that within that time we would reach a country well stocked with corn, which had been gathered and stored in cribs, seemingly for our use, by Governor Brown's militia." The same went for foodstuffs for the men. Pigs and turkeys squealed and gobbled in farmyards all along the 300 miles of unspoiled hinterland his veterans would traverse, and sweet potatoes were waiting to be roasted in the ashes of a thousand campfires every night of the three or four weeks he expected it would take him to reach Savannah, where the navy would be standing by with supply ships.

That the march was made in two divergent columns, each about 30,000 strong and with half the guns, served a triple purpose: first, to avoid the crowding and delays that would result from trying to move all four corps along a single route: second, to broaden not only the foraging area but also the swath of destruction, which thus would be twice as horrendous: and third, to confuse and mislead the enemy as to Sherman's objective or objectives, on the Atlantic and on the way there. Howard's right wing, made up of his two-corps Army of the Tennessee — Blair was back from his electioneering duties, but Major General Peter Osterhaus, Logan's senior division commander, had charge of the XV Corps in the continued absence of his chief, who remained North after stumping for Lincoln — tramped south down the Macon & Western, as if bound for Macon, while Slocum's left wing, containing the corps under Davis and Williams — formerly part of Thomas's Army of the Cumberland, now styled the Army of Georgia — followed the line of the

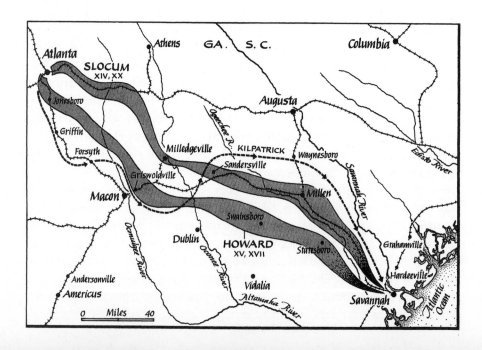

Georgia Railroad, which ran due east to Augusta. By now, most likely, the Confederates must be rushing all available reserves to the defense of both population centers. At any rate that was what Sherman hoped they would do; for he intended to move through neither, but rather through Milledgeville, the state capital, which lay between them.

This began to be fairly obvious to the right-wing marchers on their second day out of Atlanta, when Howard veered southeast from Jonesboro, leaving Kilpatrick to keep up the feint down the railroad nearly to Forsyth, twenty miles short of Macon, where he too turned off to rejoin the infantry column beyond the bypassed town. Slocum continued eastward from Atlanta for three days, ripping up track as he went, and then on the fourth — by which time the two wings were close to fifty miles apart — turned south along the near bank of the Oconee River toward Milledgeville, some forty miles downstream. "God has put a ring in Sherman's nose and is leading him to destruction," a Richmond clergyman had remarked when the widespread march began. But now, as a result of conflicting reports by his adversaries, which in turn were the result of careful planning on his part, scarcely anyone but God and the farmers whose crops he was consuming as he progressed knew where he was.

If the march had its rigors, mainly proceeding from the great distance to be covered and the occasional hard work of bridging creeks and corduroying roads, it also had its attendant compensations derived from the fatness of the land and the skylark attitude of the men fanned out across it in two columns, foraging along a front that varied from thirty to sixty miles in width. "This is probably the most gigantic pleasure excursion ever planned," one of Howard's veterans declared after swinging eastward on the second day out of Atlanta. "It already beats everything I ever saw soldiering, and promises to prove much richer yet." Expectations were as high, and as amply rewarded, in the column to the north. Riding with Slocum past Stone Mountain that same day, Sherman pulled off on the side of the road to review the passing troops and found them unneglectful of such opportunities as had come their way. One marcher who drew his attention had a ham slung from his rifle, a jug of molasses cradled under one arm, and a big piece of honeycomb clutched in the other hand, from which he was eating as he slogged along. Catching the general's eye, he quoted him *sotto voce* to a comrade as they swung past: "Forage liberally on the country."

Sherman afterwards told how he "reproved the man, explaining that foraging must be limited to the regular parties properly detailed," but he was not long in showing that despoilment had a place in his calculations, quite as much as it did in theirs. Four days later, after turning south toward Milledgeville just short of the Oconee, he came upon a well-stocked plantation which he happened to learn belonged to Major General Howell Cobb. A leading secessionist and one-time speaker of the U.S. House and Treasury Secretary under Buchanan, Cobb had been appointed by Joe Brown to command the state reserves in the present crisis; in which capacity — though it turned out there were no "reserves" for him to command — he had been exhorting his fellow Georgians to resist the blue invasion by the destruction of everything edible in its path. "Of course, we confiscated his property," Sherman would recall, "and found it rich in corn, beans, peanuts, and sorghum molasses.... I sent back word to General Davis to explain whose plantation it was, and instructed him to spare nothing. That night huge bonfires consumed the fence rails, kept our soldiers warm, and the teamsters and men, as well as the slaves, carried off an immense quantity of corn and provisions of all sorts."

His aim, he said, in thus enforcing "a devastation more or less relentless," was to convince the planters roundabout "that it is in their interest not to impede our movements." Simultaneously, however, this conclusion was discouraged by the activities of his foragers — "bummers," they were called, and called themselves, although the term had been one of opprobrium at the start — who worked along the fringes of the march, sometimes as "regular parties properly detailed," sometimes not. Isolated plantation owners, mostly wives and mothers whose sons and husbands were with Hood or Lee in Tennessee or Virginia, buried their silver and jewels on hearing of Sherman's approach, and the search for these provided fun, as well as the possibility of profit, for the blue-clad visitors. Out would come the ramrods for a vigorous probing of lawns and flowerbeds. "It was comical to see a group of these red-bearded, barefooted, ragged veterans punching the unoffending earth in an apparently idiotic but certainly most energetic way," an officer who observed them was to write. "A woman standing upon the porch of a house, watching their proceedings, instantly became an object of suspicion, and she was watched until some movement betrayed a place of concealment. Fresh earth thrown up, a bed of flowers just set out, the slightest indication of a change in appearance or position, all attracted the gaze of these military agriculturists. If they 'struck a vein' a spade was instantly put in requisition and the coveted wealth was speedily unearthed. It was all fair spoil of war, and the search made one of the excitements of the march." Other diversions included the shooting of bloodhounds, hated for their use in tracking runaway slaves and convicts through the swamps. Sometimes, by way of a joke, the definition was expanded to cover less offensive breeds. For example, when a poodle's mistress appealed for her lap dog to be spared, the soldier who had caught up the pet and was bearing it off to execution replied: "Madam, our orders are to kill every bloodhound." "But this is not a bloodhound!" she protested, only to be told: "Well, madam, we cannot tell what it will grow into if we leave it behind."

If there was a core of cruelty to such humor, it was precisely in such cruelty that the humor had its source. In time Sherman would concede that "many acts of pillage, robbery, and violence were committed by these parties of foragers." He had also "heard of jewelry taken from women and the plunder of articles that never reached our commissary," though he insisted that such depredations were "exceptional and incidental." In any case, whatever factors contributed to the total, he would report at the end of the march across Georgia that the damage inflicted came to no less than $100,000,000: "at least twenty millions of which has inured to our advantage, and the remainder is simple waste and destruction. This may seem a hard species of warfare," he declared, "but it brings the sad realities of war home to those who have been directly or indirectly instrumental in involving us in its attendant calamities." Such, after all, was one of the main purposes of the expedition, and if, in its course, southern women had been subjected to certain discourtesies in their homes, there was a measure of justice in that as well, since they were among the fieriest proponents of a war that might have ended by now except for their insistence that it be fought to the last ditch. Many of the soldiers believed as much, at any rate. "You urge young men to the battlefield where men are being killed by the thousands, while you stay home and sing *The Bonnie Blue Flag*," an Ohio colonel heard one of his troopers lecture a resentful housewife, "but you set up a howl when you see the Yankees down here getting your chickens. Many of your young men have told us they are tired of war, and would quit, but you women would shame them and drive them back." This applied only to white women, of course. Black ones were far more sympathetic to the invaders, especially on visits to their roadside bivouacs at night. "And they didn't charge us a cent," one grateful infantryman recorded.

So far, except for skittery detachments of butternut cavalry, not so much opposing as observing Kilpatrick's movement down the Macon & Western, neither Union column had encountered any organized resistance. One reason for this, in addition to their confusion as to Sherman's whereabouts or goal, was that the Confederates had little or nothing with which to confront him except Wheeler's 3500 scattered horsemen and an overload of brass. Within a week of his departure from Atlanta, both Hardee and Richard Taylor were at Macon, ordered there from Charleston and Selma by Beauregard — who himself was on the way from North Alabama — to confer with the Governor and his two chief military advisers, Howell Cobb and Major General G. W. Smith. Of these four high-ranking commanders, only the last brought any troops along, and all he had was 3000 Georgia militia summoned back into service by Brown to help meet the impending crisis. Learning that the blue infantry had left the railroad at Jonesboro, Hardee decided that Milledgeville, not Macon, was Howard's intermediary objective on a march that would continue southeast, through Millen to Savannah, and that Slocum would most likely push on eastward, through Augusta, to reach Charleston. He therefore advised that the militia be shifted northward to stand in Slocum's path, while he himself returned by rail to Savannah to prepare for its defense. Brown approving, the four makeshift brigades — so called, though none was much larger than a standard regiment — were ordered to set out at once, commanded by a militia brigadier named P. J. Phillips; Smith remained behind to make arrangements for supplies. That was on November 22, the day Sherman had one of Slocum's divisions clean out Cobb's plantation, ten miles north of Milledgeville, and that was how it came about that a brigade from one of Howard's divisions, ten miles east of Macon, fought that afternoon the only sizeable infantry action of the campaign between Atlanta and the Atlantic.

Aside from the high rate of casualties on one side, in contrast to the low rate on the other, there was little to distinguish the engagement from other such exercises in futility, staged for the most part in the early, picture-book days of the war, when blue and gray were green alike. Howard had bypassed Macon the day before, quarter-circling it clockwise from the north, and today, while Brown and the four generals were conferring, had posted a rear guard beyond Griswoldville, nine miles out the Central Georgia Railroad, which he crossed at that point on his way toward the Oconee for a crossing about midway between Milledgeville and Dublin. This rear guard, a single brigade from the tail division of Osterhaus's corps, had taken position along the crest of a hill one mile east of the station, its flanks protected by swampy ground and with open fields in front. So far, there had been no threat except from rebel troopers, who were easily kept off, but late that afternoon the 1500 defenders saw a heavy column of infantry moving toward them through the town. To their surprise, the marchers formed for attack and came straight at them across the stubble of the fields, displaying what one Federal called "more courage than discretion." With accustomed ease, the XV Corps veterans leveled their rifles and blasted the attackers back, only to see them reassemble and come on again, in much the same style and with similar results. Three times they charged uphill in close formation, and three times they were blown rearward by heavy volleys from the breastworks on the crest; until at last they gave it up and limped away, back through Griswoldville, toward Macon. Whooping, the victors moved out into the field to gather up the booty. Soon, however, the cheers froze in their throats at the sight of what lay before them in the stubble. They saw for the first time, to their horror, that they had been fighting mostly old men and young boys, who lay about in attitudes of death and agony — more than 600 of them in all, as compared to their own loss of 62.

"I was never so affected at the sight of dead and wounded before," an Illinois infantryman afterwards wrote home. "I hope we will never have to shoot at such men again. They knew nothing at all about fighting and I think their officers knew as little." A comrade, reacting not only to this but also to the pillage he had seen and shared in, put his thoughts in stronger words. "There is no God in war," he fumed. "It is merciless, cruel, vindictive, un-Christian, savage, relentless. It is all that devils could wish for."

Slocum's lead corps entered Milledgeville that same afternoon, twenty miles northeast of this scene of innocent valor, and the other arrived the following morning, accompanied by Sherman, who slept that night in the mansion vacated two days ago by Joe Brown, the fifth Confederate governor to be routed from his bed or desk by the approach of blue invaders. Unlike Nashville, Baton Rouge, Jackson, and Little Rock, all firmly in the Federal grip, the Georgia capital underwent only a temporary occupation; Slocum crossed the Oconee next morning, November 24, slogging eastward along the Central Georgia through Sandersville, toward Millen, while Howard took up a parallel route, some twenty miles to the south, toward Swainsboro. Brief as it was, the Milledgeville layover had been welcome, not only as a chance to get some rest after hiking the hundred miles from Atlanta, but also as a diversion from the workaday grind of converting more than sixty miles of railroad into a trail of twisted iron. Ebullient young officers, under the influence of what Sherman called "the spirit of mischief," assembled in the abandoned Hall of Representatives, and there, after a rousing debate, repealed the ordinance of secession and appointed committees to call forthwith on Governor Brown and President Davis for the purpose of landing official kicks on their official rumps. While this parliamentary business was in progress, soldiers ransacked the State House and amused themselves by heaving out of its windows all the books and papers they could find. A New Englander on Osterhaus's staff took private exception to such conduct, which seemed to him to go beyond a line that could not be crossed without a loss, if not of honor, then anyhow of due propriety. "I don't object to stealing horses, mules, niggers, and all such little things," he recorded in his journal, "but I will not engage in plundering and destroying public libraries."

Sherman, wearing low-quarter shoes and only one spur — "a general without boots," an admirer marveled — rode with Slocum, as before, except that Kilpatrick had been shifted from the right wing to provide cover for the flank that would be threatened if Richmond sent reinforcements from Virginia or the Carolinas. Apparently there were none of these; but there was something far more shocking, the red-haired Ohioan discovered when he came upon a division toiling across muddy fields because a young lieutenant had just had a foot blown off by an eight-inch shell that had been fuzed with matches and planted in the road. "This was not war, but murder," Sherman later wrote, "and it made me very angry. I immediately ordered a lot of rebel prisoners to be brought from the provost guard, armed with picks and spades, and made them march in close order along the road, so as to explode their own torpedoes or to discover and dig them up. They begged hard, but I reiterated the order, and could hardly help laughing at their stepping so gingerly along the road, where it was supposed sunken torpedoes might explode at each step."

There was no more trouble with torpedoes on the march after that; nor, indeed, from any other source. "No enemy opposed us," Sherman noted, "and we could only occasionally hear the faint reverberation of a gun to our left rear, where we knew that Kilpatrick was skirmishing with Wheeler's cavalry." In point of fact, though the scheduled rate of march had been reduced from fifteen to ten miles a day, thus assuring an unhurried and therefore thorough job of destruction across a front that varied in width from thirty to fifty miles, there was so little for Howard's wing to do that Blair's corps was summoned north to get in on the demolition of the Central Georgia. Up ahead was Millen, an important railroad junction on the far side of the Ogeechee, where a branch line ran north to Augusta to connect in turn with Wilmington and Richmond; Sherman sent word for Kilpatrick to take the lead and try his hand at effecting a "most complete and perfect break" in the installations there. "Let it be more devilish than can be dreamed of," he told the man he had called "a hell of a damned fool." Meantime both infantry wings kept slogging eastward unmolested, twisting iron and burning as they went. He was pleased to see that his "general orders of devastation" were being heeded by the Georgians in his path. Evidently the grapevine was in operation; "The people did not destroy food, for they saw clearly that it would be ruin to themselves."

At Millen, a hundred miles beyond Milledgeville and Macon, he paused for another one-day rest, two thirds of the way to his goal. Then he was off again, with his two now unequal wings on opposite banks of the Ogeechee, on the final lap of his march to the sea. It was early December now, and here on the left, beyond the river, marchers observed a change in the manner of the citizens whose crops they were despoiling; a change not so much in their attitude toward the invaders, as toward their neighbors across the Savannah River and toward the war itself. "All I ask is that when you get to South Carolina you will treat them the same way," one farmer said, and was echoed by another: "Why don't you go over to South Carolina and serve them this way? They started it." Sherman was encouraged by such talk. At the outset he had retained the option of switching his objective — including a tangential sprint for Pensacola, down on the Gulf — in case he encountered serious resistance. But no such shift was even considered, since there had been no resistance worth the name, either from regulars or guerillas. "Pierce the shell of the Confederacy and it's all hollow inside!" he exulted as he set out from Millen for Savannah, less than a hundred miles to the southeast.

One trouble there was, of increasing concern, despite his efforts to guard against it from the start. In the course of the march now approaching its end, an estimated 25,000 blacks of both sexes and all ages joined the various infantry columns at one time or another, and though at least three fourths of these turned back, either from weariness or homesickness, a considerable number managed to tag along, a growing encumbrance. Sherman tried to discourage this by explaining to their spokesmen — gray-haired preachers, for the most part — that he "wanted the slaves to remain where they were, and not load us down with useless mouths which would eat up the food needed for our fighting men." They nodded agreement, but continued to throng in the wake of each blue column, preferring instant liberty to the promise of eventual freedom, once the war was over. Beyond the Ogeechee the problem became acute, or seemed about to, not only because the land was less fruitful toward the seaboard, but also because of reports that Bragg had reached Augusta with reinforcements; Sherman decided to rid himself, in one way or another, of what might prove a military embarrassment in the event of a clash on that congested flank. He had not followed Grant's suggestion that he recruit able-bodied slaves as reinforcements, in part because he lacked missionary zeal and in part because he considered this a practice that would lead to future ills, both for the army and the country. "The South deserves all she has got from her injustice to the Negro," he would presently tell Halleck, "but that is no reason why we should go to the other extreme." In any case, he was determined to do what he could to disencumber his threatened left of these "useless mouths."

At Ebenezer Creek, which lay between the Ogeechee and the Savannah, about two thirds of the way from Millen to the coast, he found his chance — or, more strictly speaking, had it found for him, and acted upon, by one of his chief lieutenants. Davis's corps brought up the rear of Slocum's wing, and as soon as the last of his infantry cleared the unfordable stream he had his engineers hurriedly take up the pontoon bridge, leaving the refugees who were tailing the column stranded on the opposite bank. Whatever glee Davis and his soldiers felt at the success of this stratagem, which accomplished in short order all that weeks of exhortation and admonition had failed to achieve, was changed to sudden dismay when they saw what followed, first across the way and then in Ebenezer Creek itself. Wailing to find their march toward freedom halted thus in midstride and themselves abandoned to the mercy of Confederate horsemen, who soon would be upon them, the Negroes hesitated briefly, impacted by the surge of pressure from the rear, then stampeded with a rush into the icy water, old and young alike, men and women and children, swimmers and nonswimmers, determined not to be left behind by the deliverers they supposed had come to lead them out of bondage. Many drowned, despite the efforts of the engineers, who, horrified by the sight of the disaster their action had brought on, waded into the muddy creek to rescue as many of the unfortunates as they could reach. "As soon as the character of the unthinking rush and panic was seen," a Federal observer wrote, "all was done that could be done to save them from the water; but the loss of life was still great enough to prove that there were many ignorant, simple souls to whom it was literally preferable to die freemen rather than to live slaves."

In far-off City Point and Washington, all this time, nothing was known except at second hand — and rebel hand, at that — of what had occurred between the western army's high-spirited departure from Atlanta, three weeks back, and the tragic crossing of Ebenezer Creek, within thirty miles of Savannah. Mindful of its commander's plan to alter his route if serious opposition loomed, Grant drew an analogy that was apt: "Sherman's army is now somewhat in the condition of a ground-mole when he disappears under a lawn. You can here and there trace his track, but you are not quite certain where he will come out until you see his head." The President used much the same metaphor when John Sherman came to the White House to ask if there was any news of his brother down in Georgia. Lincoln replied that there was no word of the general's whereabouts or even his destination. "I know the hole he went in at, but I can't tell you the hole he will come out of."

In his December message that week he told Congress, "The most remarkable feature of the military operations of the year is General Sherman's attempted march of three hundred miles directly through the insurgent region. It tends to show a great increase of our relative strength that our General-in-Chief should feel able to confront and hold in check every active force of the enemy, and yet to detach a well-appointed large army to move on such an expedition." In the original draft, a sentence followed: "We must conclude that he feels our cause could, if need be, survive the loss of the whole detached force, while by the risk he takes a chance for the great advantages which would follow success." But this was dropped from the delivered text, on the grounds that it might be thought to show a lack of concern for the lives of 60,000 soldiers being risked on a long-odds gamble, hundreds of miles from the possibility of assistance. No one who was near Lincoln during this critical period would have made that error: least of all a friend who attended a reception at which the Chief Executive stood shaking hands with guests as they arrived. He seemed preoccupied, strangely perfunctory in his greetings, and the friend, refusing to be shuttled along like the others, stood his ground until the tall, sad-faced man emerged from his abstracted mood with a smile of recognition. "How do you do? How do you do?" he said warmly. "Excuse me for not noting you. I was thinking of a man down South."

Understandable as this was at that remove, events were soon to show that such concern had been unwarranted. By now Lincoln's "man down South" was approaching the goal of his trans-Georgia expedition, and those who were with him exulted in the damage they had inflicted and avoided. From first to last, barely two percent of their number, including the wounded, were judged unfit for duty in the course of a nearly four-week march that saw more than two hundred miles of railroad "utterly abolished" and the Confederacy riven. "The destruction could hardly have been worse," a veteran declared, "if Atlanta had been a volcano in eruption and the molten lava had flowed in a stream sixty miles wide and five times as long." Mostly they were young men, even those of highest rank; the twenty commanders of armies, corps, and divisions averaged forty years of age, while the volunteers from civilian life outnumbered the West Pointers, twelve to eight. Close to half their 218 regiments were from Ohio and Illinois, and all but 33 of the rest were from other western states. Their exuberance undiminished by strain or combat — aside, that is, from some momentary sadness after Griswoldville — the marchers treated the whole campaign, one soldier commentator said, as "a vast holiday frolic" and livened their nights, when they might have been sleeping, with occasional sham battles in which the principal weapon was lighted pine knots, flung whirling through the darkness with an effect as gaudy as anything seen in contests whose losses ran into the thousands. Cheering, they closed down upon Savannah's outer defenses on December 9 and 10.

Chief among these was Fort McAllister, a dozen miles to the south, on the right bank of the Ogeechee just above Ossabaw Sound. Sherman decided to reduce it first, thus clearing the way for the navy to steam upriver — if in fact the ships were waiting off the coast, as prearranged — before he moved against the city proper.

The navy was there all right, he discovered when he climbed to the roof of a rice mill, December 13, for a view of the fort and, beyond it, the blue waters of the sound; Howard had set up a signal station atop the mill to study the terrain and report on the progress of the attack by Brigadier General William Hazen's division. This had been Sherman's old Shiloh outfit, and concern for the survivors of those days — when Hazen, a thirty-year-old West Pointer, commanded an Ohio regiment — increased his impatience at finding the assault delayed far into the afternoon. However, while he waited and chafed, a lookout peering eastward spotted what Sherman later described as "a faint cloud of smoke and an object gliding, as it were, along the horizon above the tops of the sedge toward the sea, which little by little grew till it was pronounced to be the smokestack of a steamer." Soon, as the ship drew closer, the watchers identified the U.S. flag at her peak and a signalman asking in wigwag from her deck: "Who are you?" "General Sherman," the answer went back, and when this was followed by another question: "Is Fort McAllister taken?" Sherman replied: "Not yet, but it will be in a minute."

And it was, very nearly within that span. Hazen's division swarmed out of the woods, across flats that had been thickly sown with torpedoes, through the abatis, over the palisade, and into the fort itself, where, as Sherman watched from his distant perch on the rice mill roof, "the smoke cleared away and the parapets were blue with our men, who fired their muskets in the air and shouted so that we actually heard them, or felt that we did." The attack had lasted barely fifteen minutes; Hazen lost 134 killed and wounded, many of them victims of exploding torpedoes, and inflicted 48 casualties on the 250-man garrison, the rest of whom were captured along with fifteen guns. "It's my old division; I knew they'd do it!" Sherman crowed, and had an aide get off a message to Slocum at the far end of the line. "Dear General. Take a good big drink, a long breath, and then yell like the devil. The fort was carried at 4.30 p.m."

That night the ship steamed in through Ossabaw Sound and up the Ogeechee River unopposed. Others followed, next day and the next, bringing 600,000 rations and, best of all – – for, as Sherman said, "This prompt receipt of letters had an excellent effect, making us feel that home was near" — the mail that had been piling up for the troops ever since they left Atlanta, four weeks, to the day, before the fall of Fort McAllister.

There was also news, both good and bad, of recent developments in Virginia and Tennessee, as well as of an effort, less than thirty miles from Savannah, to break the railroad between there and Charleston. That had been two weeks ago, on the last day of November, and practically everything about the operation was unsatisfactory from the Union point of view. From his headquarters up the South Carolina coast at Hilton Head, Major General John G. Foster, successor to Quincy Gillmore as commander of the Department of the South, sent a 5500-man force inland to get astride the railroad near Grahamville Station and thus prevent the Confederates from opposing Sherman with reinforcements sent by rail, in advance of his arrival, from points along the seaboard between there and Richmond. As luck would have it — rebel luck, that is — G. W. Smith reached Savannah that same day with the Georgia militia; Joe Brown's Pets had come roundabout through Albany and Thomasville after their savage treatment, eight days ago, by Howard's rear guard east of Macon. Down to about 1400 effectives as a result of that and other mishaps, they were sent by Hardee to meet Foster's threat to the Charleston & Savannah. Meet it they did, and with such élan, although the odds were as heavy against them here as they had been in their favor back at Griswoldville, that they not only wiped out the stain of that encounter, they also reversed the ratio of casualties suffered. Encountering the invaders at Honey Hill, three miles south of Grahamville, they took up a position confronting a swamp-bound causeway, flung them back, frustrated a flank attack by setting fire to a field of broomsedge, and finally drove them out of range of the railroad, much as had been done two years ago at nearby Pocotaligo, where a similar blue force attempted the same maneuver with no better luck. Smith's loss was 8 killed, 42 wounded. The Federals lost 755, including 88 killed, 623 wounded, and 44 missing.

The newly arrived Westerners professed no great surprise at this defeat, having come to expect such ineptness from their allies in the paper-collar East, even against militia they themselves had trounced so roundly such a short time before. Besides, for all his success in keeping the railroad open northward, Hardee still had fewer than 15,000 inexperienced troops for the defense of Savannah against four times that number of hardened veterans. As for Sherman, he was far more interested in developments back in Middle Tennessee, where part of Thomas's scratch command had already fought one battle, more or less against his wishes, and seemed about to have to fight another, despite his apparent reluctance to do anything but sit tight. In a two-week-old letter, delivered to his red-haired friend at Fort McAllister by the navy, Grant sounded rather put out by the Tennessee situation and the way Old Pap was meeting it, but he expressed no discontent with his own lack of progress around Petersburg and Richmond. In fact, he was looking forward to a shipboard holiday. "After all becomes quiet, and the roads become so bad up here that there is likely to be a week or two when nothing can be done, I will run down the coast to see you," he wrote, adding the happy afterthought: "If you desire it, I will ask Mrs. Sherman to go with me."

Perhaps in part because even those who had wives back home could expect no such reunion by special delivery, most of this had little interest for soldiers who had just completed what was being hailed as one of the great marches of all time. By and large, their feeling was that now that they had reached the East the war would soon be over; but even this they were willing to leave to Uncle Billy, knowing that he would use them to that end when the time was right. They were more concerned with their own letters, reading and rereading them while improving their investment of Savannah and waiting for the siege guns their commander had requisitioned to reduce not only the city's defenses but also their own losses when the hour came for launching the assault. Except for coffee, which ran low at last, not even the delivery of those 600,000 rations provided much of a diversion. The fact was they had never eaten better than they had done for the past month, and Sherman even now was informing Grant that, after setting out from Atlanta with a herd of 5000 cattle and feeding beef to all who wanted it along the way, he had wound up on the coast with twice as many cows as when he started. For some time now a steady diet of sweet potatoes, corn, and pork had palled on northern palates. What they mainly looked forward to, throughout the final week of the march, was oysters, and now that they had reached salt water they had all of them they wanted. Just outside Savannah, over toward Ossabaw Sound, one soldier recorded a sample menu in a letter home: "Oyster soup, oysters on the half shell, roast goose, fried oysters, rice, raisins, and roast oysters."

★　★　★

Hood at last issued orders for the march north from the Tennessee River on November 16, the day Sherman drew rein on Bald Hill, two hundred air-line miles to the southeast, for a farewell look at smouldering Atlanta. Now as before, however — although Forrest, the ostensible cause of the army's marking time ever since it reached the northwest corner of Alabama in late October, had returned from his Johnsonville raid two days ago — there were further delays, occasioned by last-minute supply arrangements and a fierce storm that grew still worse throughout the next four days, converting the rain to sleet and the roads to hub-deep troughs of icy mud. But Hood would wait no longer. Just last week, in a message so characteristic that it was practically superfluous, he had told Jefferson Davis: "You may rely upon my striking the enemy whenever a suitable opportunity presents itself, and that I will spare no effort to make that opportunity." On November 20, a Sunday, he set out, and by the following morning — three weeks, to the day, since his arrival in Tuscumbia, just across the river — the last of his troops filed out of Florence, bound for Nashville and, it might be, the Ohio.

Preceded by Forrest, whose 6000 horsemen swept the front and covered the right flank, the march was in three columns, a three-division corps of just over 10,000 men in each: Stewart by way of Lawrenceburg, Cheatham by way of Waynesboro, thirty miles to the west, and Lee by way of country roads between. All three would converge on Mount Pleasant, seventy miles away by the nearest route, and move together — 38,000 strong, including the three cavalry divisions and the artillery with 108 guns — to Columbia, twelve miles northeast on Duck River, whose crossings at that point were the objective in this first stage of the advance through Middle Tennessee. Hood's purpose was to interpose his army between Thomas, who had been gathering troops at Nashville for the past month, and Schofield, posted eighty miles south at Pulaski with his own and Stanley's corps, detached by Sherman before he set out from Atlanta. Schofield had roughly 30,000 of all arms, Thomas about the same number, and if Hood got between them, in control of the Duck crossings with a force superior to either, he could deal with them individually, in whatever order he chose, and thus score a crowning double victory that would give him the Ten-

nessee capital, together with all
its stores, and clear the way for
his drive to the Ohio; which in
turn — or so ran the dream un-
folded for Beauregard, now departed — would provoke the recall of Sherman, at the end of
his race through the Georgia
vacuum to the sea, and perhaps
free Hood to work the deliverance of Richmond by crossing
the Cumberlands into Virginia
to rejoin his beleaguered hero,
R. E. Lee.

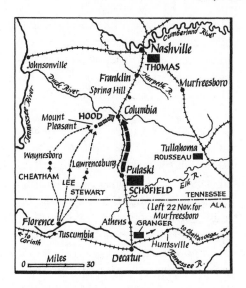

Despite the unseasonably
bitter weather, which alternately
froze the roads iron hard, with ankle-twisting ruts, or thawed them into
quagmires that made every step a wrenching effort, the butternut veterans
clocked good time on their march beyond the Tennessee line. Indeed, so
successful was Forrest in driving Brigadier General Edward Hatch's reinforced cavalry division "from one position to another," thereby preventing any penetration of the screen, that Stewart's corps reached
Lawrenceburg, more than halfway to Columbia, before Schofield,
twenty miles due east at Pulaski, even knew that Hood was not only
on the way around his flank but was also not much farther by now
than he himself was from Duck River, which he would have to cross
if he was to avoid being cut off from Nashville and the other half of
the army Thomas had spent the past month assembling for the defense
of Middle Tennessee. That was on the night of November 22; Schofield began his withdrawal at first light next morning, prodding his five
divisions, 62 guns, and 800 wagons northward up the turnpike. He
knew he was involved in a race whose stakes were life or death, and
thanks to a faster, somewhat shorter track he won it handily by getting
his lead division to Columbia on the 24th, in time to keep the fast-riding
rebel troopers from seizing either of the two bridges across the Duck.
Moreover, he had his entire force dug in along the outskirts of the
south-bank town, guns emplaced, when Hood's infantry arrived from
Mount Pleasant on the 26th and took up a position, that day and the
next, confronting the newly erected breastworks anchored right and
left on the river above and below.

Hood was not discouraged by this loss of a long-odds race in
which some of his troops covered more than a hundred miles on inferior
roads while Schofield's did less than thirty-five on the turnpike. Nor
was he provoked into launching a headlong assault, which in fact was
no longer practicable — let alone judicious — by the morning of No-

vember 28, when he discovered that his one-time West Point room-mate and mathematics coach had withdrawn in the night to the north bank, destroying the two bridges over the river now in his front. What Hood had in mind instead, his lieutenants found when they reported as ordered to his headquarters beside the Pulaski pike that afternoon, was a flanking movement similar to the one he had just attempted, except that this time the odds were by no means long and he once more enjoyed the confidence that came with employing the tactics he had so much admired in Virginia, back in the days when he had both of his legs and the vigorous use of both his arms. As he saw it, later describing the frame of mind that led to the formulation of his plan, "The situation presented an occasion for one of those interesting and beautiful moves upon the chessboard of war, to perform which I had often desired an opportunity.... I had beheld with admiration the noble deeds and grand results achieved by the immortal Jackson in similar maneuvers; I had seen his corps made equal to ten times its number by a sudden attack on the enemy's rear, and I hoped in this instance to be able to profit by the teachings of my illustrious countryman."

The plan itself was as simple as it was bold. James Wilson having joined Schofield beyond the Duck with another 4000 horsemen, Forrest would cross the river today, ten miles upstream at Huey's Mill, and drive the blue cavalry northward, away from possible interference with Hood's infantry, which would cross at dawn at Davis Ford, three miles above the town. Cheatham would lead, his corps being posted on the right, and Stewart would follow, reinforced by one of Lee's divisions. Each would take along a single battery, for emergencies, and leave the rest of the guns behind — an even hundred, as it turned out — for use by Lee, who would demonstrate with them and his two remaining divisions in order to fix the Federals in position on the opposite bank of the river, while the bulk of the superior gray army moved around their left and into their rear at Spring Hill, a dozen miles up the turn-pike from Columbia and about the same distance from Franklin, whose seizure would give the flankers control of the Harpeth River cross-ings, less than twenty miles from Nashville. In other words, another race would start at dawn, and this one too would be a matter of life or death for Schofield, though Hood did not intend for him to know — any more than he had known before — that a contest was in progress until it was at least half over; by which time, in contrast to the previous maneuver, there would be little he could do except look for a round-about avenue of escape. At that point Hood would be free either to turn on his former roommate or, having eliminated him as a factor by holding the rail and turnpike bridges across the Harpeth, plunge straight ahead for the Tennessee capital without delay. He seemed to favor the latter course just now, for he spoke that night, soon after the council of war broke up and the participants went out into the falling snow to alert

their commands for tomorrow's
march, of "calling for volunteers
to storm the key of the works
about the city." Next morning, while Cheatham's men were
moving through the predawn
darkness toward the pontoons
thrown for them at Davis Ford
the night before, he made this
even more emphatic. "The enemy must give me a fight," he
told a friend — Chaplain-Doc-
tor, later Bishop, Charles Quin-
tard — "or I'll be in Nashville
before tomorrow night."

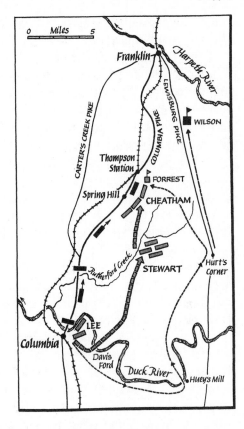

Mindful of the failure of a
similar maneuver four months
ago, which brought on the lost
Battle of Atlanta, he went along
this time in person, as he had not
done before, riding with Cheatham near the head of the flanking column to see for himself
that his Jacksonian plan was
carried out as he intended. The result, throughout the opening phase,
was all he could have hoped for. Both the crossing and the march
north beyond the river, parallel to the turnpike three miles west,
were unimpeded, thanks to Schofield's apparent lack of vigilance and to
Forrest, whose three divisions clashed with Wilson's two at Hurt's
Corner around midday, six miles out, and drove them headlong up
the Lewisburg Pike toward Franklin; Forrest detached a brigade to
keep up the pressure on the fleeing bluecoats and turned northwest with
the rest of his troopers, as ordered, for a strike at Spring Hill in advance
of the infantry. Moving up, Hood halted Stewart's reinforced corps
at Rutherford Creek — presumably to protect his rear in case Schofield
took alarm and moved against him from Columbia, though the steady
booming of Lee's one hundred guns beyond the Duck gave assurance that the two Union corps were still in position on the north
bank, unmindful of the fact that Hood had all his cavalry and all but
two of his nine infantry divisions on their flank or in their rear. Elated,
he told Cheatham, as he rode with him beyond the creek to within
three miles of Spring Hill, to commit his lead division without delay,
alongside Forrest's horsemen, and follow with the other two as soon as
they came up. Meantime, Hood himself rode back to check on Stewart,

whose four divisions could also be committed if they were needed; which seemed unlikely.

By then it was just after 3 o'clock. Behind him, over toward the turnpike in the direction of Spring Hill, a spatter of gunfire presumably announced that Forrest even now was overriding such resistance as the blue garrison could offer, surprised as its few members must be, midway between Columbia and Franklin, to find a host of graybacks bearing down on the little country town a dozen miles in Schofield's rear.

But that was by no means the case: mainly due to the vigilance of James Wilson. Though he lacked the time needed to whip Thomas's defeat-prone horsemen into any shape for standing up even briefly to a superior force of veterans under the Wizard of the Saddle, the young Illinois-born West Pointer had not forgotten the primary cavalry assignment of furnishing his chief with information. In fact he had sent a warning the night before, when, impressed by Forrest's aggressiveness, he notified headquarters that a heavy Confederate movement seemed to be in progress across the Duck, ten miles upstream. Schofield telegraphed word of this to Nashville, and Thomas promptly ordered a further withdrawal to Franklin. Accordingly, while Hood's infantry was passing unobserved over Davis Ford, Schofield started his 800 wagons and most of his guns up the turnpike with a train guard of two divisions under David Stanley, who was told to drop one of them off at Rutherford Creek, to secure the crossing there, and proceed with the other to Spring Hill, which he would cover for the rest of the army, soon to follow. By midmorning Stanley had cleared the creek, about one third of the distance between Columbia and Spring Hill, and learning as he drew near the latter place that rebel troopers were approaching in strength — it was by now past 2 o'clock — he double-timed Brigadier General George Wagner's division into position, just east of the town and the pike, in time to help the two-regiment garrison ward off an all-out mounted attack.

It was a near thing, and a bloody one as well, according to a Wisconsin infantryman who watched the charge get broken up, for the most part by artillery. "You could see a rebel's head falling off his horse on one side and his body on the other, and the horse running and nickering and looking for its rider. Others you could see fall off with their feet caught in the stirrup, and the horse dragging and trampling them, dead or alive. Others, the horse would get shot and the rider tumble head over heels, or maybe get caught by the horse falling on him."

Having repulsed the rebel troopers, who returned piecemeal to probe warily at his defenses, Stanley — Howard's successor as IV Corps commander, thirty-six years old, an Ohio-born West Pointer and peacetime Indian fighter, chief of cavalry under Rosecrans during the last campaign in this region, back in the summer of '63 — proceeded to align his force of just over 5000 for the protection of Spring Hill. Resolute as he was in making his preparations for defense, he was fortunate not to have his resolution strained by awareness that this might have to be attempted against twice that number of gray infantry now crossing Rutherford Creek with Cheatham, less than three miles southeast across the fields, and an even larger number close in their rear with Stewart. In any case, he parked the train between the turnpike and the railroad, west of town, and unlimbered his 34 guns in close support of Wagner's three brigades, disposed along a convex line to the east, both flanks withdrawn to touch the pike above and below. Here, under cover of breastworks hastily improvised by dismantling snake-rail fences, they settled down to their task of keeping Schofield's escape route open in their rear. Around 4 o'clock, half an hour before sundown, the first concerted assault struck their right, driving the flank brigade from its fence-rail works and back on its support, three batteries massed on the southern outskirts of the town for just such an emergency as was now upon them. These eighteen pieces roared and plowed the ranks of the attackers, who stumbled rearward in confusion, having no guns of their own. In the red light of the setting sun, when Stanley saw that their regimental flags bore the full-moon device of Cleburne's division — by common consent, Federal and Confederate, the hardest-hitting in Hood's army — he warned Wagner to brace his men for their return, probably with substantial reinforcements.

They did return, their number doubled by the arrival of another gray division; but little or nothing came of this menace in the end. After milling about in the twilight, apparently with the intention of launching a swamping assault, they paused for a time, as if bemused, and then — incredibly, for they presently were joined by still a third division — went into bivouac, more or less where they were, their cookfires twinkling in the frosty outer darkness, just beyond easy musket range of Spring Hill and the turnpike close in rear of the makeshift breastworks Stanley had feared were about to be rushed and overrun. Meantime Schofield put two more divisions in motion north, leaving one at Columbia to discourage Lee from crossing the Duck, and another at Rutherford Creek, where it had been posted that morning. By midnight the first two had cleared Spring Hill, subjected to nothing worse along the way than sporadic fire from the roadside and the loss of a few stragglers, although there was a clash with some late-roaming butternut troopers at Thompson Station, three miles up the pike. These were soon brushed aside, and the two divisions that followed close behind, from Rutherford Creek and Columbia, encountered even less trouble. As a result, Wagner's division, which formerly had led the march but now brought up the rear, was able to follow the unmolested train and guns out of Spring Hill before dawn. By that time the lead division was at Franklin and had secured the crossings of the Harpeth, within twenty miles of heavily-fortified Nashville.

Just what had happened, out in the cookfire-twinkling darkness beyond the now abandoned Union breastworks east of Spring Hill and the turnpike, was not too hard to establish from such reports as were later made, both on and off the record. *Why* it happened was far more difficult to determine, though many tried in the course of the heated controversy that followed down the years. Still, whatever their persuasion as to a rightful distribution of the guilt — of which, in all conscience, there was enough to go around — a Texas lieutenant in Cleburne's division, after noting that Hood, Cheatham, "and others in high places have said a good deal in trying to fix the blame for this disgraceful failure," arrived at an assessment with which few could disagree: "The most charitable explanation is that the gods of war injected confusion into the heads of our leaders."

After Cleburne's 18-gun repulse he was joined by Bate, who came up on his left. Just as they were about to go forward together, shortly after sunset — Forrest had pulled back for lack of ammunition, the supply train having been left with Lee to disencumber the flanking column — an order came from Cheatham for the attack to be delayed until the third division arrived under Major General John C. Brown, who would give the signal to advance as soon as he got in position on Cleburne's right. Brown came up about 5.30, but finding his own right overlapped by the blue defenders, informed Cheatham that any advance by him "must meet with inevitable disaster." While he waited, obliging Cleburne and Bate to wait as well, Cheatham reported the problem to Hood, who authorized a suspension of the gunless night attack until Stewart arrived from Rutherford Creek. Stewart did not get there at all, however, having been misguided up a country road that paralleled the turnpike. Only his fourth division, detached from Stephen Lee, under Edward Johnson — Old Clubby, captured six months ago in the Spotsylvania Mule Shoe, had recently been exchanged and transferred West — was stopped in time to move into position on the left of Bate, adjoining the turnpike south of town. Stewart by then had received permission to put his other three divisions into bivouac where they were, two miles to the north and well back from the pike. By that time, practically everyone else — Cleburne and Bate and Brown and all their men, stalled on the verge of their twilight assault — had begun to bed down, too: including Hood, who had spent a long day strapped in the saddle, with considerable irritation to the stump of the leg he had lost at Chickamauga. He was close to exhaustion, and there still had been no report that Schofield had begun a rearward movement. In fact, Lee's guns were still growling beyond Duck River, strong evidence that the Federals were still on its north bank, when Hood retired for

the night. Before he did so, he told Cheatham (as Cheatham later testified) that he "had concluded to wait until the morning, and directed me
to hold my command in readiness to attack at daylight."

Not quite everyone was sleeping, he discovered when a barefoot
private came to his farmhouse headquarters some time after midnight
to report that he had seen Union infantry in motion on the turnpike
in large numbers. Hood roused himself and told his adjutant to send
Cheatham orders "to advance a line of skirmishers and confuse the
enemy by firing into his columns." Cheatham passed the word to Johnson, whose division was nearby, but when the Virginian reconnoitered
westward, two miles south of Spring Hill, he found the road lying
empty in the moonlight, with nothing moving on it in either direction.
Most likely he had encountered a gap between segments of the blue
army on the march; in any case, like Hood and Cheatham before him,
he too returned to the warmth of his blankets while Schofield's troops
continued to slog north along the turnpike, just beyond earshot of the
rebels sleeping eastward in the fields. Not all the marchers made it. "We
were actually so close to the pike," a butternut lieutenant later wrote,
"that many Federal soldiers came out to our fires to light their pipes
and were captured." Not even all of these were gathered up, however.
For example, two Confederates were munching cornbread beside a low
fire when a man strolled up; "What troops are you?" he asked, and on
being told, "Cleburne's division," turned and walked off in the darkness.
"Say, wasn't that a Yank? Let's go get him," one grayback said, only
to have his companion reply: "Ah, let him go. If you're looking for
Yankees go down the pike and get all you want."

Amid all this confusion, high and low, one thing at least was clear
with the dawn of the last day in November. Schofield had gotten clean
away, undeterred after darkness fell, except for a brief clash at Thompson Station with one of Forrest's divisions which had managed to capture
a meager supply of ammunition. If Hood was saddened by this Spring
Hill fiasco — "The best move in my career as a soldier," he said later,
"I was thus destined to behold come to naught" — he was also furious,
mainly with Cheatham, but also with almost everyone in sight, including the ragged, barefoot men themselves. In his anger he renewed the
charge that Joe Johnston had spoiled them for use in the offensive. "The
discovery that the army, after a forward march of 180 miles, was still,
seemingly, unwilling to accept battle unless under the protection of
breastworks, caused me to experience grave concern. In my inmost
heart I questioned whether or not I would ever succeed in eradicating
this evil."

This he would say long afterward, not stopping then, any more
than now, to consider what he asked of them in designing still another
of those swift Jacksonian movements that had worked so well two
years ago in Virginia; whereas the fact was, not even Lee's army was

"Lee's army" any longer; let alone Hood's. All the same, he believed
he saw a corrective for the fault. If a flanking maneuver was beyond
the army's capacity, perhaps a headlong assault was not only within
its means but might also provide a cure for its lamentable habit of
flinching at Yankee breastworks and depending so much on its own.
In any case he was determined now to give the thing a disciplinary try
— and he said as much, years later, looking back. "I hereupon decided,
before the enemy would be able to reach his stronghold at Nashville,
to make that same afternoon another and final effort to overtake and
rout him, and drive him into the Harpeth River at Franklin."

✗ 3 ✗

So he said, anticipating vengeance. But when the Army of Tennessee
set out from its camps around Spring Hill that morning — three fourths
of it, at any rate; Stephen Lee was marching from Columbia, a dozen
miles to the south, with his other two divisions and the artillery and
trains — its commander, nearly beside himself with rage at last night's
bungling, seemed "wrathy as a rattlesnake" to one of his subordinates,
who were themselves engaged in a hot-tempered flurry of charges and
countercharges as a result of Schofield's escape from the trap so carefully laid for his destruction. Down in the ranks, where mutual recrimin-
ation afforded less relief, the soldiers "felt chagrined and mortified," one
afterwards remarked, "at the occurrence of the preceding day."
    Yet this soon passed, at least as the dominant reaction, partly
because of the weather, which had faired. "The weather was clear and
beautiful," another infantryman wrote; "the cool air was warmed by
the bright sunshine, and our forces were in fine condition." By way of
added encouragement, the band from a Louisiana brigade, reported to be
the army's best, fell out beside the turnpike and cut loose with a few
rollicking numbers to cheer the marchers tramping past. "Each man
felt a pride in wiping out the stain," the first soldier would recall, while
the second added: "Their spirits were animated by encouraging orders
from General Hood, who held out to them the prospect that at any
moment he might call on them to deal the enemy a decisive blow."
    This was as he had done before, on the march north from Florence,
and the spirit now was much as it had been then, when the promise
was that the Federals were about to be outflanked. For the Tennesseans
the campaign was literally a homecoming, but for all the army's veterans it was a glad return to fields of anticipated glory, when they and
the war were young and hopes were high. Once more patriot-volunteers
of a Second American Revolution, many of them barefoot in the snow,
as their forebears had been at Valley Forge, they were hailed along the
way as returned deliverers, fulfillers of the faded dream that victory

waited on the banks of the Ohio, which was once again their goal. Gladdest of all these scenes of welcome had been the march from Mount Pleasant to Columbia, a region of old families whose mansions lined the pike and whose place of worship — tiny, high-roofed St John's Church, ivy-clad and Gothic, where Bishop-General Polk had preached and his Episcopal kinsmen had their graves amid flowers and shrubbery fresh and green in bleak November — had so impressed Pat Cleburne, for one, that he checked his horse in passing and remarked that it was "almost worth dying for, to be buried in such a beautiful spot." Impromptu receptions and serenades greeted the returning heroes, and prayers of thanksgiving were offered in this and other churches along the way, especially in Pulaski and Columbia, where the Yankees had been thrown into retreat by the gray army's passage round their flank. Spring Hill too had been delivered, though at a heavy cost in Confederate mortification, which soon was transmuted into determination that the bluecoats, having escaped their pursuers twice, would not manage it still a third time unscathed. Accordingly, the seven gray divisions stepped out smartly up the Franklin Turnpike, preceded by Forrest's troopers. Hood was pleased, he later said, to find his army "metamorphosed, as it were, in one night.... The feeling existed which sometimes induces men who have long been wedded to but one policy to look beyond the sphere of their own convictions, and, at least, be willing to make trial of another course of action." In other words, they now seemed ready to charge breastworks, if need be, and he was prepared to take them up on that.

Stewart led the march today, having overshot the mark the night before, and Cheatham followed, accompanied by Johnson's division from Lee's corps, which was three hours in the rear. A dozen miles to the north by 2 o'clock, the vanguard approached Winstead Hill, three miles short of Franklin. On its crest, astride the turnpike, a Union brigade was posted with a battery, apparently under instructions to delay the gray pursuit; but Hood, unwilling to waste time on a preliminary skirmish — perhaps designed by Schofield to give the rest of his army a chance to get away unharmed — swung Stewart's three divisions to the right, along Henpeck Lane, and kept the other four marching straight on up the pike. To avoid being outflanked, the bluecoats limbered their guns and fell back out of sight beyond the rim of the slope up which the head of Cheatham's column now was toiling. When the Tennesseans topped the rise they gave a roaring cheer at the sight of the Harpeth Valley spread before them, with the town of Franklin nestled in a northeastward bend of the river and the Federals intrenched in a bulging curve along its southern and western outskirts. Beyond the crest, on the forward slope of Winstead Hill, Hood turned off to the left of the road, and while his staff got busy setting up a command post, the one-legged general dismounted — painfully, as always, with the help of an orderly who passed him his crutches once he was afoot — and there, in the shade of an isolated linn tree, removed his binoculars from their case for a careful study of the position his adversary had chosen for making a stand.

Schofield had been there since dawn, nine hours ago, and by now had completed the organization of an all-round defense of his Franklin bridgehead, on the off chance that the Confederates would attempt to interfere with the crossing or the follow-up sprint for the Tennessee capital, eighteen miles away. He would have been well on his way there already, safely over the river and hard on the march up the Nashville Pike, except that when he arrived with his two lead divisions, under Jacob Cox and Brigadier General Thomas Ruger, he found that the turnpike bridge had been wrecked by the rising Harpeth and Thomas had failed to send the pontoons he had so urgently requested, two days ago at Columbia, after burning his own for lack of transportation. Placing Cox in charge, he told him to have the two XXIII Corps divisions dig in astride the Columbia Pike, his own on the left and Ruger's on the right, half a mile south of the town in their rear, while awaiting the arrival of the three IV Corps divisions, still on the march from Rutherford Creek and Spring Hill. By the time Stanley got there with Thomas Wood's and Brigadier General Nathan Kimball's divisions, around midmorning, the engineers had floored the railroad bridge with planks ripped from nearby houses and the wagon train had started crossing. Schofield ordered Kimball to dig in on a line to the right of Ruger, extending the works northward so that they touched the river below as well as above the town, and passed Wood's division, along with most of Stanley's artillery, across the clattering, newly-planked railway span to take position on the high far bank of the Harpeth, overlooking Franklin and the fields lying south of the long curve of intrenchments thrown up by the other three divisions. That way, Wood could move fast to assist Wilson's horsemen in dealing with rebel flankers on that side of the river, upstream or down, and Cox was braced for confronting a headlong assault, if that was what developed.

This last seemed highly unlikely, however, since Hood — with two of his nine divisions far in the rear, together with all but eight of his guns — had fewer than 30,000 troops on hand, including cavalry, while Schofield had well above that number — 34,000 of all arms — stoutly intrenched for the most part and supported by 60-odd guns, nearly all of them able to pound anything that tried to cross the two-mile-deep plain that lay between the bristling outskirts of Franklin and the foot of Winstead Hill. Moreover, that deadly stretch of ground was not only about as level as a tabletop, it was also unobstructed. Originally there had been a small grove of locusts in front of Ruger's part of the line, but these had been felled for use as headlogs and abatis. Similarly, on the left, a thick-set hedge of Osage orange had been thinned to clear a field of fire for Cox, leaving only enough of the growth to provide a thorny palisade. There was one obstacle out front: two brigades from Wagner's division, intrenched in an advance position, half a mile down and astride the Columbia Pike, with instructions to remain in observation there unless Hood, when he came up, "showed a disposition to advance in force," in which case they were to retire within the lines and serve as a reserve for the three divisions now in their rear. Otherwise, one defender said, there was "not so much as a mullein stalk" to obstruct the aim of the infantry in the trenches or the cannoneers in emplacements they had selected and dug at their leisure, not yet knowing there could be little or no counterbattery fire, even if the rebels were so foolish as to provoke battle on a field so disadvantageous to them.

Wagner had arrived at noon with the last of the five divisions, weary from yesterday's Spring Hill fight, the all-night vigil behind his fence-rail breastworks, and this morning's hurried march as rear guard of the army. Leaving one brigade on Winstead Hill to serve as a lookout force, he put the other two in position as instructed, half a mile in front of the main line, and set them digging. While they dug, the rest of the troops, snug in their completed works, did what they could to make up for their loss of sleep on last night's march. From across the river, at high-sited Fort Granger — a bastioned earthwork, constructed more than a year ago for the protection of the two critical bridges over the Harpeth — Schofield looked south, beyond the bulge of his semicircular line, and saw the brigade Wagner had left on lookout withdraw in good order down the hill and up the turnpike. He knew from this that the rebels must be close behind, for the brigade commander was Colonel Emerson Opdycke, a thirty-four-year-old Ohioan with a fiery reputation earned in most of the theater's major battles, from Shiloh, where he had been a captain, to Resaca, where he had been badly wounded, back in May, but recovered in time to lead the charge up Kennesaw six weeks later. Sure enough, soon after Opdycke's displacement, the first graybacks appeared on Winstead Hill. They gathered faster and began to flow, rather like lava, in heavy columns down the forward slope and around the east flank of the hill. Schofield watched with mounting excitement. It was now about 3 o'clock; all but the last of his 700 wagons had clattered across the railroad bridge and he had just issued orders for the rest of his men and guns to follow at 6 o'clock, shortly after dark, unless Hood attacked before sunset; which Schofield did not believe he would do, once he had seen what lay before him there along the northern margin of that naked plain.

He was mistaken. Three miles away, under the linn tree on the hillside to the south, Hood completed his study of the Federal dispositions, lowered his glasses, and announced to the subordinates who by now had clustered round him: "We will make the fight."

When he explained what he meant by "make the fight" — an all-out frontal assault, within the hour — consternation followed hard upon doubt by his lieutenants that they had heard aright. They too had looked out over the proposed arena, and could scarcely believe their ears. Attack? here? headlong and practically gunless, against a foe not only superior in numbers but also intrenched on chosen ground and backed by the frown of more than sixty pieces of artillery? ... For a time, only too aware of their commander's repeated scornful charge that they invariably flinched at Yankee breastworks, they held their tongues. Then Ben Cheatham broke the silence. "I do not like the looks of this fight," he said. "The enemy has an excellent position and is well fortified." Leaning on his crutches, his blond beard glinting in the sunlight, Hood replied that he preferred to strike the Federals here, where they had had only a short time to organize their defenses, rather than at Nashville, "where they have been strengthening themselves for three years."

Cheatham protested no more, having been reproached quite enough for one day. But Bedford Forrest — who was familiar with the region, including the location of usable fords over the Harpeth well this side of the enemy position, and who moreover had Hood's respect for his aggressive instincts — spoke out in support of his fellow Tennessean's assessment of the situation, though with a different application. He favored an attack, yet not a frontal one. "Give me one strong division of infantry with my cavalry," he urged, "and within two hours I can flank the Federals from their works." Hood afterwards reported that "the nature of the position was such as to render it inexpedient to attempt any further flanking movement." Just now, however, he expressed doubt that, for all their apparent confidence, the bluecoats would "stand strong pressure from the front. The show of force they are making is a feint in order to hold me back from a more vigorous pursuit."

This put an end to such unasked-for opposition as had been voiced. Hood's fame had begun when he broke Fitz-John Porter's center at Gaines Mill, back in Virginia thirty months ago, and he intended to do the same to Schofield here today. His final order, dismissing the informal council of war, was explicit as to how this was to be accomplished: "Drive the enemy from his position into the river at all hazards."

Stewart, who had rounded Winstead Hill on the approach march, would attack on the right, up the railroad and the Lewisburg Pike, which ran northwest along the near bank of the Harpeth; Loring's division was on that flank of the corps front, French's on the other, over toward the Columbia Pike, and Major General Edward Walthall's was posted astride the railroad in the center. Cleburne and Brown, of Cheatham's corps, would advance due north up both sides of the Columbia Pike, Cleburne on the right, adjoining French, with Bate on Brown's left, extending the line westward to the Carter's Creek Pike, which ran northeast. All three turnpikes converged on the outskirts of Franklin, half a mile in rear of the southward bulge of the Union works; Hood assumed that this configuration would serve to compact the mass, like a hand clenched gradually into a fist, by the time the attackers reached and struck the main blue line. Johnson's division remained in reserve behind the center, for rapid exploitation of any breakthrough right or left, and Forrest's horsemen would go forward on the flanks, near the river in both directions. At 3.45, one hour before sundown, Stewart and Cheatham sent word that their lines were formed and they were ready.

Hood could see them in panorama from his command post, the two corps in an attack formation well over a mile in width, their star-crossed flags hanging limp in the windless air of this last day in November, which was also to be the last in the lives of many who were about to follow those tattered symbols across the fields now in their front: six divisions, twenty brigades, just over one hundred regiments, containing in all some 18,000 infantry, with another 3500 in the four reserve brigades. Promptly Hood's order came down from Winstead Hill for them to go forward, and they did, stepping out as smartly as if they were passing in review; "a grand sight, such as would make a lifelong impression on the mind of any man who could see such a resistless, well-conducted charge," a Federal officer discerned from his post near the blue center, just under two miles across the way. "For the moment we were spellbound with admiration, although we knew that in a few brief moments, as soon as they reached firing distance, all that orderly grandeur would be changed to bleeding, writhing confusion."

It did not work out quite that way just yet. Opdycke, when he retired from the crest of Winstead Hill, had not stopped alongside the other two brigades of Wagner's division, intrenched half a mile in front of the main works, but continued his withdrawal up the turnpike to the designated reserve position in rear of a one-story brick residence owned by a family named Carter, less than a hundred yards inside the lines. Wagner had set up headquarters in a grove of trees beside the pike and just beyond the house, anticipating the arrival of the rest of his troops as soon as the gray host, now gathering two miles to the south, showed what his orders termed "a disposition to advance." Apparently he doubted that Hood would do so at all, after studying the field, or else he believed the preparations would take a lot more time than they actually did. In any case, the mass advance was well under way before the Ohio-born former Hoosier politician, whose view in that direction was blocked by the house and trees, even knew that it had begun. As a result, the two colonels left in charge out front not only delayed their withdrawal, they also chose to stand fast in their shallow works long enough to get off a couple of short-range volleys before retiring. This was to cost Wagner his command within the week, but it cost the men of those two brigades a great deal more today.

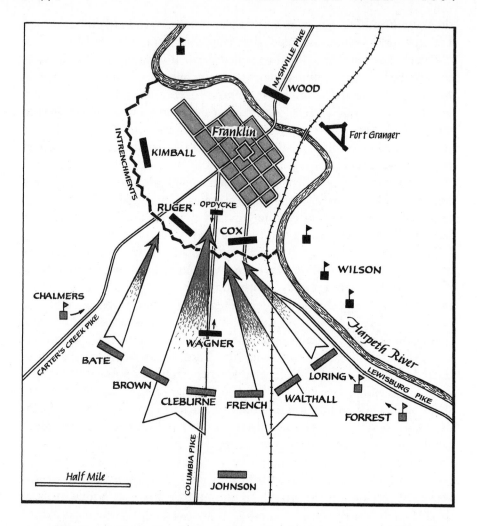

The gray line advanced steadily, preceded by scampering rabbits and whirring coveys of quail, flushed from the brush by the approach of close to 20,000 pairs of tramping feet. When they got within range, the outpost Federals gave them a rattling fusillade that served to check them for a moment; but not for long. Absorbing the shock, the men under Cleburne and Brown — old rivals, from the days when the latter's division was under Cheatham — came on with a rush and a yell, directly against the front and around the flanks of the two unfortunate brigades, both of which gave way in a sudden bolt for the security of the intrenchments half a mile in their rear. Too late; "Let's go into the works with them!" the attackers cried, and pressed the pursuit up the turnpike, clubbing and shooting the terrified bluecoats as they fled. "It seemed bullets never before hissed with such diabolical venom," a Union captain was to say, recalling too that the cries of the wounded, left to the mercy of the screaming graybacks when they fell, "had a pathetic note of despair I had never heard before." More than 700 were captured, hurt or unhurt, and the main-line defenders, dead ahead, were kept from firing at the pursuers by fear of hitting their comrades in the lead. A staff colonel observed, however, that there was little time for thought at this critical juncture. "The triumphant Confederates, now more like a wild, howling mob than an organized army, swept on to the very works, with hardly a check from any quarter. So fierce was the rush that a number of the fleeing soldiers — officers and men — dropped exhausted into the ditch, and lay there while the terrific contest raged over their heads." Of these, the captain who had outrun the hissing bullets noted, "some were found [afterwards] with their thumbs chewed to a pulp. Their agony had been so great that they had stuck their thumbs in their mouths and bit on them to keep from bleating like calves."

That was the kind of battle it was, first for one side, then the other, combining the grisliest features of Pickett's Charge and Spotsylvania's Bloody Angle. Because they had sprinted the last half mile, and had a shorter distance to cover in reaching the southward bulge of the enemy line, Cleburne's and Brown's divisions struck and penetrated the Federal works before the units on their left or right came up to add weight to the effort. In close pursuit of the two fugitive brigades, they not only broke through along the turnpike, they also widened the gap by knocking a regiment loose from the intrenchments on each side and seized four guns still loaded with canister, which they turned on the enemy but could not fire because the battery horses had bolted with the primers in the ammunition chests. Suddenly then it was too late; the blue reserves were upon them, advancing through the smoke with bayonets flashing, and they were too blown from their race up the pike, too confused by their abrupt success, to stand long under the pounding of most of the two dozen guns Cox and Ruger had posted along this part of the line. They yielded sullenly, under savage attack from Opdycke, who had brought his brigade on the run from north of the Carter house, and fell back to find cover in front of the works they had crossed when they broke through. There they stayed, exchanging point-blank fire with the bluecoats on the other side of the ditch.

Stewart by then had come up on the right, where French made contact with Cleburne, but the other two divisions were roughly handled in their attempt to get to grips with the Union left. Approaching a deep railroad cut near the northward bend of the Harpeth, they found it under plunging fire from the guns massed in Fort Granger, and when they changed front to move around this trap they were struck on the flank by other batteries masked on the east bank of the river. Forrest drove these last away by sending Jackson's division across a nearby ford, but Wilson met this threat to Schofield's rear by throwing the rebel troopers back on the crossing and holding them there, under pressure from three times their number. Walthall and Loring meantime had rounded the railway cut and clawed their way through the Osage hedge, only to find themselves confronting an intrenched brigade equipped with repeating rifles that seemed to one observer "to blaze out a continuous sheet of destruction." Here the attackers had all they could do to hang on where they were, though some among them continued to try for a breakthrough: Brigadier General John Adams, for example, who was killed while attempting a mounted leap over the enemy works and whose body was found next morning alongside his horse, dead too, with its forefeet over the Federal palisade. Another of Loring's three brigade commanders, Brigadier General T. M. Scott, was gravely wounded, as was Brigadier General William Quarles of Walthall's division; both were out of the war for good, and in Quarles's brigade, so heavy was the toll of successive commanders, there presently was no surviving officer above the rank of captain. French's division, fighting near the center, also lost two of its three brigade leaders — Colonel William Witherspoon, killed outright, and Brigadier General Francis Cockrell, severely wounded — bringing Stewart's loss to five of the nine brigade commanders in his corps, along with more than half of the colonels and majors who began the attack at the head of his nearly fifty regiments.

Cheatham's losses were heavier still, though they were comparatively light in Bate's division, which only had one of its three brigades engaged when it struck the enemy trenches at an angle; the other two drifted northward to mingle with Chalmers' horsemen beyond the Carter's Creek Pike, where they remained in observation, dodging long-range shots from guns on the Union right. Cleburne and Brown, however, still holding the works astride the Columbia Turnpike in the center, more than made up for any shortage of bloodshed on the Confederate left. The sun by now was behind the rim of Winstead Hill, and in point of fact, so far as its outcome was concerned, the battle was over: had been over, at least in that respect, ever since Opdycke's furious counter-assault stopped and shattered the initial penetration. All that remained was additional killing and maiming, which continued well into the night. "I never saw the dead lay near so thick. I saw them upon each other, dead and ghastly in the powder-dimmed starlight," Opdycke would report. Brown himself was out of the action, badly crippled by a shell, and so were all four of his brigadiers, beginning with G. W. Gordon, who had been captured in the side yard of the Carter house just as the breakthrough was turned back. John C. Carter, who succeeded Brown in command of the division, was mortally wounded shortly afterwards (he would die within ten days) and States Rights Gist and Otho Strahl were killed in the close-quarters struggle that ensued. "Boys, this will be short but desperate," Strahl had told his Tennesseans as they prepared to charge; which was half right. After the repulse he stood in the Federal ditch, passing loaded rifles up to the men on top, and when one of them asked if it might not be wise to withdraw, he replied: "Keep on firing." Then he fell.

The resultant desperation, unrelieved by the saving grace of brevity, was quite as bad as he had predicted for Brown's division, but the strain was even worse for the Arkansans, Mississippians, Alabamians, and Texans next in line, heightened as it was by dread uncertainty as to the fate of their commander. "I never saw men put in such a terrible position as Cleburne's division was," an opposing bluecoat was to say. "The wonder is that any of them escaped death or capture." All too many of them did not; Hiram Granbury had been killed at the head of his Texas brigade in the first assault, and fourteen of the twenty regimental commanders were to fall before the conflict slacked and died away. Meantime a disheartening rumor spread through the ranks that Cleburne was missing — Irish Pat Cleburne, of whom it was said: "Men seemed to be afraid to *be* afraid where he was." He had last been seen going forward in the attack, dismounted because two horses had been shot from under him in the course of the advance. "If we are to die, let us die like men," he told a subordinate, speaking with the brogue that came on him at such times and thickened as the excitement rose. When his second horse was killed by a shot from a cannon, he went ahead on foot through the smoke and din, waving his cap. The hope of his veterans, who idolized him, was that he had been wounded for the third time in the war, or even captured; but this hope collapsed next morning, when his body was found beside the Columbia Pike just short of the enemy works. A single bullet had gone through his heart. His boots had been stolen, along with his sword and watch and everything else of value on him. He was buried first near Franklin, then in St John's churchyard, whose beauty he had admired on the march to his last fight, and finally, years later, back in Arkansas on a ridge overlooking Helena, his home town. His epitaph, as well as that of his division, was pronounced by his old corps commander, William Hardee, who wrote when he learned of his death: "Where this division defended, no odds broke its line; where it attacked, no numbers resisted its onslaught, save only once; and there is the grave of Cleburne."

High on his hillside two miles to the south, Hood knew even less about the progress of the battle than did the troops involved in the moiling, flame-stabbed confusion down below; which was little indeed. He had seen Cleburne and Brown go storming into the Union center, hard on the heels of Wagner's unfortunates, but what happened next was blanketed in smoke that hung heavy in the windless air and thickened as the firing mounted to a sustained crescendo. At 7 o'clock, an hour after full darkness cloaked the field, he committed his reserve division, and though Old Clubby's men attacked with desperation, stumbling over Cheatham's dead and wounded in the gloom, they only succeeded in adding Brigadier General Arthur Manigault's name to the list of a dozen brigade and division commanders who had fallen in the past three hours, as well as nine more regimental commanders, bringing the total to fifty-four; roughly half the number present. Of the twelve generals lost to the army here today, six were dead or dying, one was captured, and three of the remaining five were out of the war for good, while the other two, Brown and Cockrell, would not return for months. Down in the ranks, moreover, this dreadful ratio was approximated; 6252 Confederate veterans were casualties, including 1750 killed in action — as many as had died on either side in the two days of Shiloh or under McClellan throughout the Seven Days: more than had died under Rosecrans at Stones River, under Burnside at Fredericksburg, or under Hood himself in any of his three Atlanta sorties: almost as many, indeed, as Grant had had killed outright when he assaulted at Cold Harbor with three times as many men. Hood had wrecked his army, top to bottom, and the army knew it; or soon would. In the judgment of a Tennessee private who survived the wrecking, he had done so in the manner of a clumsy blacksmith, thinking "he would strike while the iron was hot, and while it could be hammered into shape.... But he was like the fellow who took a piece of iron to the shop, intending to make him an ax. After working for some time, and failing, he concluded he would make him a wedge, and, failing in this, said: 'I'll make a skeow.' So he heats the iron red-hot and drops it in the slack tub, and it went s-k-e-o-w, bubble, bubble, s-k-e-o-w, bust."

Hood did not know this yet, however — and would not have been likely to admit it if he had; Howard's word 'indomitable' still fit. He watched unseeing while the battle continued to rage with the same fury, even though all the combatants had to aim at now was the flash of each other's weapons. "Time after time they came up to the very works," a Union colonel afterwards said of the attackers, "but they never crossed them except as prisoners." Around 9 o'clock the uproar slacked. "Don't shoot, Yanks; for God Amighty's sake, don't shoot!" defenders heard pinned-down rebels implore from the smoky darkness just beyond their parapets. Within two more hours the contest sputtered into silence. Stephen Lee was up by then with his other two divisions and the army's guns, and Hood ordered the attack renewed at daybreak, preceded this time by a hundred-round bombardment. The batteries opened at first light, as directed, then ceased fire when word came back that there was nothing in the works ahead but Federal dead and wounded. Schofield had departed in the night.

That was really all the northern commander had wanted from the outset: a chance to get away, if Hood would only let him. Soon after his arrival the previous morning, on finding the turnpike bridge washed out and no pontoons on hand, he wired Nashville for instructions, and was told to defend the Harpeth crossing unless such an effort would require him "to risk too much." He responded: "I am satisfied that I have heretofore run too much risk in trying to hold Hood in check. . . . Possibly I may be able to hold him here, but do not expect to be able to do so long." Thomas, busy gathering troops to man the capital defenses, then put a limit to his request, in hope that this would serve to stiffen his lieutenant's resistance to the scarcely deterred advance of the rebel column up through Middle Tennessee. "Do you think you can hold Hood at Franklin for three days longer? Answer, giving your views," he wired, and Schofield replied: "I do not believe I can." In point of fact, both question and answer by then were academic. He had already ordered a nighttime withdrawal and Hood had just appeared on Winstead Hill. "I think he can effect a crossing tomorrow, in spite of all my efforts," Schofield added, "and probably tonight, if he attempts it. A worse position than this for an inferior force can hardly be found. . . . I have no doubt Forrest will be in my rear tomorrow, or doing some greater mischief. It appears to me that I ought to take position at Brentwood at once."

Nevertheless — having no choice — he stayed and fought, and won. His casualties totaled 2326, about one third the number he inflicted, and of these more than half were from Wagner's division: just under a thousand killed or captured in the two-brigade rearward sprint up the pike and just over two hundred killed and wounded in the other brigade, when Opdycke saved the day with a counterassault that cost him five of his seven regimental commanders but netted him 394 prisoners and nine Confederate flags. Except for David Stanley, who took a bullet through the nape of his neck and had to be lugged off the field at the height of the melee, no Federal above the rank of colonel was on the list of casualties when Schofield evacuated Franklin between 11 o'clock and midnight, leaving his dead and his nonwalking wounded behind as he crossed the river and set fire to the planked-over bridge in his rear. The blue column reached Brentwood by daylight, halfway to Nashville, and by noon all five divisions were safe in the capital works, alongside the others Thomas had been assembling all this time.

Hood sent Forrest to snap at the heels of the retreating victors, but deferred pursuit by his infantry now in occupation of the field. "Today spent in burying the dead, caring for the wounded, and reorganizing the remains of our corps," a diarist on Cheatham's staff recorded. Never before had even these veterans looked on horror so compacted. In places, hard against the abandoned works, the slain lay in windrows, seven deep; so thick, indeed, that often there was no room for those on top to touch the ground. One of Strahl's four successors was so tightly wedged by corpses, it was noted, that "when he at last received the fatal shot, he did not wholly fall, but was found stiffened in death and partly upright, seeming still to command the ghastly line of his comrades lying beneath the parapet." Blue and gray, in a ratio of about one to five, the wounded soon filled all the houses in the town, as well as every room in the courthouse, schools, and churches. Meantime the burial details were at work, digging long shallow ditches into which the perforated ragdoll shapes were tossed and covered over with the spoil. Federals and Confederates were lodged in separate trenches, and the even greater disparity in their numbers — roughly one to eight — imparted a hollow sound to Hood's congratulatory order, read at the head of what was left of each regiment that afternoon. "While we lament the fall of many gallant officers and brave men," its final sentence ran, "we have shown to our countrymen that we can carry any position occupied by our enemy."

Perhaps the battle did show that; perhaps it also settled in Hood's mind, at last, the question of whether the Army of Tennessee would charge breastworks. But, if so, the demonstration had been made at so high a cost that, when it was over, the army was in no condition, either in body or in spirit, to repeat it. Paradoxically, in refuting the disparagement, the troops who fell confirmed it for the future. Nor was the horror limited to those who had been actively involved; Franklin's citizens now knew, almost as well as did the few survivors among the men they had sent away three years ago, the suffering that ensued once the issue swung to war. This was especially true of the Carter family, an old man and his two daughters who took shelter in their cellar, just in rear of the initial breakthrough point, while the fighting raged outside and overhead. Emerging next morning from their night of terror, they found the body of their son and brother, Captain Tod Carter of Brown's division, Cheatham's corps, lying almost on the doorstep he had come home to when he died.

Nothing daunted — though his 7500 casualties over the past week, including more than 6000 the day before, had reduced his infantry strength to a scant 22,000 — Hood took up the march north that afternoon. Lee's corps was in the lead, only one of its three divisions having been exposed to the Franklin holocaust, and Stewart and Cheatham followed in that order, so severely bled down at all levels that Brown's division, for example, was under a colonel who had never commanded anything larger than a regiment, while several brigades in both these corps were led by officers with even less experience. Hood might have turned back and taken up a defensive position along Duck River, as Bragg had done two years ago under similar circumstances, or even along the Tennessee, which he had left ten days before. That would doubtless have been the most prudent course to follow, especially since one main purpose of the campaign — to provoke a countermarch by Sherman down in Georgia — had clearly failed already; the Ohioan was more than halfway to the Atlantic Ocean by now, and apparently had not given so much as a backward glance at the threat to Thomas, far in his rear. But it was not in the Kentucky-born Texan's nature to take counsel of his fears, if indeed he felt them in the first place, and prudence was by no means an integral part of his makeup. His concern was with quite different factors. One was time, which was running out, and the other was honor. "In truth," he said afterwards, "our army was in that condition which rendered it more judicious the men should face a decisive issue rather than retreat — in other words, rather than renounce the honor of their cause without having made a last and manful effort to lift up the sinking fortunes of the Confederacy. I therefore determined to move upon Nashville."

Moving upon it was no great task; Forrest's troopers by now had called a halt in sight of the Capitol tower and within plain view of the long curve of earthworks behind which Schofield had already taken shelter by the time the gray infantry forded the Harpeth. What Hood would do once he got there was a different matter, however, involving a choice between two highly unpromising alternatives. The first, to launch an immediate all-out assault, was rejected out of hand. No one wanted another Franklin, not even John Bell Hood, and Nashville — similarly cradled in the northward bend of a still wider river, with far stouter intrenchments ready-dug across its face — was Franklin magnified. Besides, after yesterday's grim Confederate subtractions, Schofield alone had more troops than Hood could bring against the place, and Thomas most likely had as many more gathered inside it, raising the numerical odds against the attacker to two, maybe three, to one. Assault was out. Yet so, Hood saw, was the alternative of crossing the Cumberland above or below, as originally envisioned, for a march to the Ohio. This would land him in Thomas's rear, true enough, but so would it put Thomas in Hood's own rear, undiminished and able to summon reinforcements from all over the North, while Hood himself, under the circumstances which now obtained, would scarcely be able to add a single recruit to the rolls of his Franklin-ravaged command. "In the absence of the prestige of complete victory," he later explained in answer to those who had urged the adoption of such a course, "I felt convinced that the Tennesseans and Kentuckians would not join our forces, since we had failed in the first instance to defeat the Federal army and capture Nashville."

Having rejected the notion of retiring southward as an admission of defeat, and having decided to forgo his previous intention of assaulting or bypassing Nashville, which he saw now as an invitation to disaster, he then — either in ignorance or defiance of Napoleon's definition of the passive defensive as "a form of deferred suicide" — settled on a plan that combined, simultaneously or in sequence, the worst features of all three of these dismissed or postponed alternatives. He would march to the outskirts of the Tennessee capital, intrench his army in direct confrontation with the outsized garrison lodged there, and await the inevitable attack, "which, if handsomely repulsed, might afford us an opportunity to follow up our advantage on the spot and enter the city on the heels of our enemy." So he said, apparently remembering the ease with which his troops had followed Wagner's into the Franklin works, but apparently not considering what had happened to them as soon as they achieved the penetration. In any case that was his plan, as he evolved it after the long march north and the frustrations he had encountered, first at Tuscumbia and Florence, where he waited three weeks before setting out, and then at Columbia, Spring Hill, and Franklin, where he not only failed to destroy a sizeable part of his opponent's army, but also came close to destroying his own. Still the old dream held for Hood: perhaps because he had no other to fall back on. "Should [Thomas] attack me in position," he subsequently reported, "I felt that I could defeat him and thus gain possession of Nashville with abundant supplies.... Having possession of the state, we should have gained largely in recruits and could at an early date have moved forward to the Ohio, which would have frustrated the plans of the enemy, as developed in his campaign toward the Atlantic coast." There was that, and there was still the pressure of knowing that this might well be the last chance, either for him or for the Confederacy itself. What better way was there to go down, or out, than in a blaze of glory? He seemed to ask that, later adding: "The troops would, I believed, return better satisfied even after defeat if, in grasping at the last straw, they felt that a brave and vigorous effort had been made to save the country from disaster."

So he went on, making camp that night at Brentwood, and pulled up in front of Nashville the following day, December 2. Lee took position astride the Franklin Pike, with Stewart and Cheatham respectively on his left and right, directly confronting the Union works, which extended northeast and northwest, as far as the eye could follow, from the bend of the river below to the bend above. Disposed along high ground in a ten-mile arc, some three miles from the marble Capitol in plain view on its hill in the heart of town, these required no more than a cursory look to confirm the claim that Nashville, along with Washington and Richmond, was among the three most heavily fortified cities in the land.

That was one part of Hood's problem, and almost at once another became apparent. "The entire line of the army will curve forward from General Lee's center," he directed on arrival, "so that General Cheatham's right may come as near the Cumberland as possible above Nashville, and General Stewart's left as near the Cumberland as possible below Nashville. Each position will be strengthened as soon as taken, and extended as fast as strengthened." But when the three corps settled in, plying spades and picks, it developed that the widest front they could cover with any measure of security was four miles — a good deal less than half the distance required if the line was to stretch to the near bank of the Cumberland in both directions; whereas in fact it did not reach the river in either direction, but left a vacancy of two miles beyond

Cheatham's outer flank and four beyond Stewart's. Of the eight turn-pikes converging spokelike on the capital hub to cross by the single bridge in its rear, four were covered and four remained uncovered, two on the left and two on the right, except by cavalry patrols. Both Confederate flanks thus were exposed to possible turning movements by the greatly superior force in the works ahead.

Hood had little fear of such a threat, however; at least for now. Familiar with his adversary's ponderous manner and lethargic nature, not only over the past six months of confrontation, stalemate, and maneuver, but also from old army days before the war — one had been a lieutenant, the other a major in Sidney Johnston's Texas-based 2d Cavalry — he counted on having as much time as he needed to prepare and improve his position in front of the Tennessee capital. Indeed, so confident was he of this, despite the long numerical odds, that he risked a further re-duction of force, as great as the one he had suffered at Franklin, for the sake of a sideline operation which seemed to offer a chance to make up for the prize he had failed to grasp at Spring Hill, where a sizeable part of the blue host now confronting him slipped through his fingers. Now another isolated segment, though only about one fourth as large, had come within his reach — provided, that is, he was willing to do a little stretching; which he was. When Hood set out from Florence to outflank Schofield at Pulaski, ten days back, Thomas had pulled Granger's 4000 troops out of the region below Athens, directly across the Tennessee River from Decatur, and combined them with Rousseau's 5000 at Murfreesboro, thirty-odd miles down the Chattanooga & Nash-ville from his capital headquarters, in case the gray invasion column veered west to approach or bypass him from that direction. These 9000 bluecoats were still there, and Hood had a mind to gather them up, or at any rate smash the railroad between there and Nashville, before Thomas called them in. Accordingly, while still on the approach march, he detached Bate, whose division had suffered least of the seven en-gaged at Franklin, and sent him crosscountry, reinforced by a brigade from each of the other two corps, for a strike at Murfreesboro and its garrison. Forrest meantime, on Hood's arrival at Nashville, would move down the Chattanooga Railroad with two of his divisions, breaking it up as he went, for a combined attack which he would direct by virtue of his rank.

Although the maneuver served its purpose of keeping Rousseau and Granger from reinforcing Thomas, it failed to achieve the larger design for bagging them entirely. Forrest left with Buford's and Jackson's divisions as soon as Hood came up, and after three days of reducing blockhouses, burning bridges, and wrecking several miles of track, combined with Bate on December 5, some ten miles north of the ob-jective. Next day's reconnaissance disclosed that Murfreesboro was almost as stoutly fortified as Nashville; Fortress Rosecrans, mounting

57 guns and enclosing 200 acres of the field where Bragg had come to grief two years ago this month, was practically unassailable; especially with 9000 defenders on hand to resist the 6500 graybacks moving against it, mounted and afoot. Forrest called a halt and decided instead to lure the garrison out for a fight in the open. In this he was partly successful the following day, December 7, when a 3500-man Union column staged a sally. He posted his infantry in the path of the attackers, with orders to stand firm while he brought his cavalry down on their flank. Everything went as planned, up to the critical moment when Bate's division — spooked no doubt by remembrance of Franklin, where its performance had been less than standard, eight days back — gave way in a panic, unspringing the trap. Forrest rode among the rattled soldiers, appealing to them to stand and fight, then cursing them for refusing to do so. He stood in the stirrups, eyes blazing, face gone red with rage, and began to lay about him with the flat of his saber, whacking the backs of the fleeing troops; to small avail. Ignoring the Wizard as best they could, the retreaters scuttled rearward beyond his grasp, even when he seized a color-bearer's flag, whose staff afforded a longer reach, and swung it bludgeonlike until at last, perceiving that this was equally ineffective, he flung it from him in disgust. "Right comical, if it hadn't been so serious," one veteran was to say.

Fortunately, the Federals did not press the issue, having just been recalled by Rousseau, and Bate was summoned back to Nashville two days later by Hood, who sent another brigade from Cheatham's corps to replace the three that left. Down to about 4500 of all arms — half the number inside the works — Forrest had to be content with bristling to discourage sorties that might have swamped him. This he did with such success that within another two days he felt justified in sending Buford to Andrew Jackson's Hermitage, ten miles northeast of Nashville, with instructions to picket a nearby stretch of the Cumberland and thereby prevent the arrival of reinforcements by that route. Next day, December 12, with the enemy still tightly buttoned up in Fortress Rosecrans, he had the infantry begin completing the destruction of the railroad back to La Vergne, just under twenty miles away. Thus, by the employment of barely half as many troops, Hood was able to prevent an additional 9000 effectives from joining the Nashville garrison: though whether this was wise or not, under the circumstances, was quite another matter. For one thing, even longer odds obtained in the vicinity of the Tennessee capital, where he remained in confrontation with Thomas, and for another, in the showdown battle which now was imminent, it seemed likely to cost him the use of two sorely-needed cavalry divisions, together with the help of their commander, whose talents would be missed.

Reduced as he was, by casualties and detachments, to a strength of less than 24,000 of all arms, it was no wonder one apprehensive infantryman remarked that the Confederate main line of resistance, which stretched and crooked for four miles under the frown of long-range Union guns in permanent fortifications, looked "more like the skirmish line of an investing army than of that army itself." To make matters worse, there had not been time for the completion of such outlying installations as had been planned to strengthen the flanks of the position: particularly on the left, where three redoubts were under construction beyond the Hillsboro Pike, the western limit of Hood's line, to blunt the force of an attack from that direction, whether end-on or oblique. Work on these began, but on the night of December 8, after a spell of deceptively mild weather, the mercury dropped to nearly twenty degrees below freezing and a cold rain quickly turned to sleet and fine-grained snow. By morning, all the trees wore glittering cut-glass armor, each twig sheathed in ice, and the earth was frozen iron hard, unpierceable even with a knife, let alone a shovel. Work stopped, perforce, and the soldiers huddled in unfinished trenches, shivering in their rags. For four days this continued. Then on the fifth — December 13, the winter solstice; Sherman had reached Savannah by now, completing his march across Georgia's midriff, and would capture Fort McAllister before sundown — a thaw set in, relieving the rigid misery in which the besiegers had been locked, but bringing with it troubles of a different kind. The army floundered in Napoleon's "fifth element," unable to move forward, back, or sideways in a Sargasso Sea of mud; all transportation stalled, guns and wagons bellied axle deep, even on main-traveled roads, and no supplies arrived to relieve shortages that had developed during the four-day storm.

It was midway through this doleful immobilized span, with his men and horses frozen or stuck in their tracks by alternate ice and mud, that Hood apparently first became aware, in the fullest sense, of the peril to which he had exposed his troops when he took up his present position in point-blank confrontation with Thomas, whose army was not only superbly equipped and entrenched, but was also better than twice the size of his own. Earlier, when Forrest departed for Murfreesboro with the other two cavalry divisions, Chalmers had been obliged to send one of his two brigades to patrol the region between Cheatham's right and the river, and when he reported that this reduced his strength too much for him to be able to perform that duty adequately on the left, where the distance was twice as great, Hood detached a brigade of infantry from Stewart and posted it beyond the Harding Pike, about midway between his western flank and the river below Nashville. This was not much help, really, for the unit chosen — Brigadier General Matthew Ector's brigade of French's division, now under its senior colonel while Ector recovered from the loss of a leg at Atlanta — was down to fewer than 700 effectives as a result of its heavy casualties at Franklin. Clearly enough, Chalmers' horsemen had more than they could handle in both directions, especially the left, and Hood's alarm was intensified when the ice storm halted work on the outlying redoubts he had ordered installed to provide at least a measure of security for that vulnerable flank.

On December 8, the day the freeze set in, he issued a circular order calling for "regular and frequent roll calls . . . as a preventive of straggling." He used the term as a euphemism for desertion, which had become a growing problem. Of 296 dismounted troopers reassigned to the infantry, all but 42 protested the indignity by departing without leave: a loss that far outweighed the total of 164 recruits who had joined Hood since he entered Tennessee. All too conscious of the odds he faced, the crippled leader of a crippled army implored Beauregard to forward any stray units he could lay hands on, and even appealed to the War Department to order Kirby Smith to send "two or more divisions" from the Transmississippi. This was a forlorn hope if ever there was one, and Seddon was prompt to tell him so. Besides, even if all the reinforcements he requested had been started in his direction without delay, it was altogether unlikely that they could arrive — even from North Alabama, let alone elsewhere — in time to help him meet the crisis now at hand. Two days later, midway through the ice storm, a follow-up circular warned that it was "highly probable that we will fight a battle before the close of the present year." Corps commanders were told to look to their defenses and line of retreat; Lee, who had the center, was cautioned to "select all good points in rear of his right and left flanks, and fortify them with strong self-supporting detached works, so that, should it become necessary to withdraw either of the corps now upon his flanks, the flank thus becoming the right or left flank of the army may be in condition to be easily defended." Furthermore, so important did Hood consider resumption of work on the outlying strongholds, all three lieutenant generals were urged to supervise their construction in person, "not leaving them either to subordinate commanders or engineer officers."

He did what he could, ice-bound as he was, and three days later, while the thaw converted the sleet to slush and the frozen earth to slime, word came that Thomas had crossed his cavalry from Edgefield, over the Cumberland, to Nashville. He was massing behind his works there, spies reported, for an all-out attack on the Confederate left, where dirty and fair weather had combined to prevent completion of the vital redoubts. Hood warned Stewart to "give Chalmers such assistance as you think necessary, keeping in communication." Next day, December 14, with the roads beginning to dry a bit, corps commanders were able to begin complying with orders to "send all their wagons, except artillery, ordnance, and ambulances, to the vicinity of Brentwood," five miles in their rear. At the same time, previous instructions regarding the hoarding of ammunition — in limited supply because of the transportation breakdown — still applied: "Not a cartridge of any kind will be burned until further orders, unless the enemy should advance upon us."

✗ 4 ✗

Thomas intended to do just that: advance: but he was determined not to do so, despite prods and threats from his Washington and City Point superiors, until he felt that his army was in condition to accomplish the annihilation Hood had been inviting ever since he took up his present position, in front of the Tennessee capital, two weeks back. Numerically, the blue force assembled to oppose him had reached that stage before the end of the first week; Thomas by then had gathered 71,842 soldiers under his command, "present for duty, equipped." Of these, 9000 were at Murfreesboro and about the same number were garrison troops, two thirds of them posted at Nashville and the other third at such outlying points as Johnsonville and Chattanooga, whose complements had been stripped to skeleton proportions. The rest — some 54,000 of all arms — were available as a striking force, and that was the use their commander had in mind to make of them as soon as he judged the time was ripe. A. J. Smith's 12,000 arrived by transport from Missouri while the battle raged at Franklin, and next morning Schofield marched in with his own 10,000 and Stanley's 14,000 survivors, now under Wood. Steedman came by rail from Chattanooga, that day and the next, with 6000 more, including a number of veterans who had returned from re-enlistment furloughs too late to march with Sherman to the sea. Finally there was the cavalry, 12,000 strong, though more than a third lacked horses and the others were badly frazzled after a week of contesting Hood's advance from Duck River to the Harpeth and beyond.

This necessity for resting and refitting his weary troopers, while trying to find mounts for the 4000 Wilson had had to leave behind when he rode out to join Schofield at Columbia, was the principal cause of delay, at least at the outset. In response to a pair of wires from Grant, December 2, urging him to "move out of Nashville with all your army and force the enemy to retire or fight upon ground of your own choosing," Thomas stressed his need for "a cavalry force sufficient to contend with Forrest," who had "at least 12,000" veteran horsemen. That was close to twice the Wizard's actual strength, and roughly six times the number he left with Hood when he departed for Murfreesboro next morning; but Thomas accepted the estimate as a figure to be matched, or at any rate approximated, before he undertook Hood's destruction. His main problem, even with all of Kentucky at his back, was the procurement of remounts, which were in short supply after more than three years of a war that had been about as hard on horses as it was on men, and broke them down at an even faster rate. Some measure of his difficulty was shown by the response George D. Prentice, the Union-loyal editor of the Louisville *Courier*, received when he complained to Military Governor Andrew Johnson about the use to which the army had put a $5000 investment he had made in cotton down in Nashville. The bales had been commandeered for installation as part of the capital fortifications; he wanted them back, he wrote Johnson, with something less expensive put in their place. But there was nothing the Vice President-elect could do for him in the matter, having himself just had a fine team of carriage horses seized for conversion to cavalry mounts. Others suffered similar deprivations, including a traveling circus, whose bare-back riders were left poised in mid-air, so to speak, and the city's street-car line, which had to suspend operations throughout the crisis for lack of mules to draw its cars. All within reach, of whatever crowbait description, were sent across the Cumberland to Edgefield, where Wilson was reorganizing and getting his troopers in shape for their share in the deferred offensive against the rebels intrenched southward, in plain view from Capitol Hill and the high-sited forts that rimmed the city in that direction.

All this required time, however, and time was the one thing his superiors did not consider he, or they, could afford at the present critical juncture; especially Grant. Halleck kept warning Thomas that their chief was losing patience, but the Virginian's files contained by then a sheaf of dispatches that made only too clear the City Point general's feelings in that regard. "You will now suffer incalculable injury upon your railroads if Hood is not speedily disposed of. Put forth, therefore, every possible exertion." "Hood should be attacked where he is. Time strengthens him, in all probability, as much as it does you." "Attack Hood at once, and wait no longer for a remount of your cavalry. There is great danger of delay resulting in a campaign back to the Ohio River." "Why not attack at once? By all means avoid the contingency of a foot race to see which, you or Hood, can beat to the Ohio." Thus Grant fumed through the first week of the Tennessee stalemate. Thomas's replies, over that same span — in which he spoke of his "crippled condition" and promised to move out, first, "in a few days," then within "less than a week," and finally by December 7, "if I can perfect my arrangements" — only goaded his chief into greater exasperation. Moreover, Halleck by now was warning that continued inaction might lead to his removal. Thomas replied that he regretted Grant's "dissatisfaction at my delay in attacking the enemy. I feel conscious that I have done everything in my power.... If he should order me to be relieved I will submit without a murmur." That was on December 9, and he closed with a weather report that seemed to him to rule out, at least for the present, any further talk of an advance. "A terrible storm of freezing rain has come on since daylight, which will render an attack impossible until it breaks."

He also passed news of this to Grant. "I had nearly completed my preparations to attack the enemy tomorrow morning, but a terrible storm of freezing rain has come on today, which will make it impossible for our men to fight to any advantage. I am, therefore, compelled to wait for the storm to break and make the attempt immediately after." And he added: "Major General Halleck informs me that you are very much dissatisfied with my delay in attacking. I can only say I have done all in my power to prepare, and if you should deem it necessary to relieve me I shall submit without a murmur." Alas, the reply he received that night was, if anything, even more chill and grudging than the others. "I have as much confidence in your conducting a battle rightly as I have in any other officer," Grant informed the Rock of Chickamauga, "but it has seemed to me that you have been slow, and I have had no explanation of affairs to convince me otherwise.... I telegraphed to suspend the order relieving you until we should hear further. I hope most sincerely that there will be no necessity for repeating the order, and that the facts will show that you have been right all the time."

Thomas was hard put to comprehend how Grant, five hundred miles away in front of Richmond — stalemated himself, not for a week but for the past six months — could presume to say what was practicable for a conglomerate army, so hastily and recently assembled under a man who was a stranger to more than half its members. However, his chief of staff, Brigadier General William Whipple, an old-line West Pointer, had a theory that someone hereabouts was "using the wires to undermine his commander" in Washington or City Point or both. At first he suspected Andrew Johnson, but on being informed that the governor was too brusque and aboveboard for such tactics, he shifted to Schofield as a likelier candidate for the Judas role. Sure enough, a prowling staffer picked up at the telegraph office the original of a recent message from the New Yorker to Grant: "Many officers here are of the opinion that General Thomas is certainly slow in his movements." Thomas read it with considerable surprise, then turned to James Steedman, who was with him at the time. "Steedman, can it be possible that Schofield would send such a telegram?" Steedman, whose share in the glory of Chickamauga had been second only to his chief's, replied that he must surely be familiar with his own general's writing. Thomas put on his glasses and examined the message carefully. "Yes, it is General Schofield's handwriting," he admitted, and asked, puzzled: "Why does he send such telegrams?" Steedman smiled at the Virginian's guileless nature, uncorrupted by twenty-four years of exposure to army politics. "General Thomas," he presently asked, "who is next in command to you in case of removal?" Thomas hung fire for a moment. "Oh, I see," he said at last, and shook his head at what he saw.

In point of fact, there was more behind Grant's exasperation, and a good deal more had come of it, than Thomas or anyone else in Tennessee had any way of knowing. Prodded by Stanton, who translated Lincoln's trepidation into sneers at "the McClellan and Rosecrans strategy of do nothing and let the rebels raid the country," Grant said later, in confirmation of earlier testimony by his aide: "I was never so anxious during the war as at that time." Indeed, under pressure of this anxiety, he lost his accustomed military balance. His fret, of course, was not only for Slow Trot Thomas, out in Nashville; it was also for Sherman, who had not yet emerged from his trans-Georgia tunnel, and for Butler, who continued to resist being hurried down the coast to Wilmington. Worst of all, he saw the possibility of the war being turned around just at the moment when he believed it was practically won. "If I had been in Hood's place," he afterwards declared, "I would have gone to Louisville and on north until I came to Chicago." Taking counsel of his fears, he had told Halleck on December 8: "If Thomas has not struck yet, he ought to be ordered to hand over the command to Schofield." Old Brains replied that if this was what Grant wanted he would have to issue orders to that effect. "The responsibility, however, will be yours, as no one here, so far as I am informed, wishes General Thomas's removal." Grant drew back: "I would not say relieve him until I hear further from him." But there was no let-up in the telegraphic goading. "If you delay attack longer," he wired the Virginian on December 11, three days into the ice storm, "the mortifying spectacle will be witnessed of a rebel army moving for the Ohio River, and you will be forced to act, accepting such weather as you find. . . . Delay no longer for weather or reinforcements."

Thomas's reply, delivered the following morning — "I will obey the order as promptly as possible, however much I may regret it, as the attack will have to be made under every disadvantage. The whole country is covered with a perfect sheet of ice and sleet, and it is with difficulty the troops are able to move about on level ground" — exhausted what little patience Grant had left. "As promptly as possible" was far from a commitment, and the rest of the message seemed to imply that the blame for any failure, when and if the attack was launched, could not properly be placed on a commander who had done his best to resist untimely orders. Grant reacted by concluding that the hour was at hand for a change in Middle Tennessee commanders.

As it happened, John A. Logan was visiting City Point headquarters at the time, on leave from his corps, which had reached the outskirts of Savannah two days ago; he was still celebrating the national election, which he had helped the Administration win, and he still was trying to digest the disappointment he felt at not having been appointed to succeed McPherson as permanent head of the Army of the Tennessee. George Thomas had been instrumental in keeping him from receiving that reward, so there was a certain poetic justice in what Grant now had in mind; which was to make Logan the Virginian's own successor. He told him so next day, December 13, when he gave him a written order to that effect, along with verbal instructions to proceed at once by rail to Nashville, going by way of Washington and Louisville. If by the time he reached the latter place Thomas had attacked, Logan was to remain there and get in touch with Grant by telegraph. Otherwise he would proceed to Nashville and take over, as directed in the order.

Logan had no sooner left than Grant began to fret anew. Black Jack was unquestionably a fighter; indeed, that was why he had been chosen; plus, of course, the fact that he was handy at the time. But perhaps, as Sherman had indicated by passing him over for Howard after the Battle of Atlanta, he lacked other qualities indispensable in the commander of an army and a department; in which case personal supervision was required. That day, that night, and most of the day that followed — December 14; Ben Butler had finally departed for Wilmington and the powder-boat explosion he believed would abolish Fort Fisher — Grant pondered his way to a decision he reached by sundown. "I am unexpectedly called away," he told Meade in a last-minute note, and got aboard a fast packet for Washington, where he expected to catch the first train west. Arriving next morning he read a telegram Thomas had sent Halleck the night before: "The ice having melted away today, the enemy will be attacked tomorrow morning." Grant decided the best thing to do was suspend his journey and await the outcome, which he would learn from Logan at Louisville or Nashville, or from Thomas himself, before the day was over.

Accordingly, he checked into Willard's to wait in comfort; but not for long. Presently there was word from Halleck that Old Slow Trot had advanced as promised, with conspicuous success, although the battle was still in progress. "Well, I guess we won't go to Nashville," Grant remarked, passing the message to an aide, and then composed for Thomas an order so characteristic that it scarcely needed a signature: "Push the enemy and give him no rest until he is entirely destroyed. . . . Do not stop for trains or supplies, but take them from the country as the enemy has done. Much is now expected."

Much was expected. In downtown Nashville, five days ago, the Virginian had said more or less the same thing to his chief subordinates when they assembled in his quarters at the St Cloud Hotel on December 10, midway through the ice storm, to receive preliminary instructions for the attack they would launch as soon as the rebel-occupied hills to the south unfroze enough for climbing. Close to twenty miles of intricate Federal intrenchments stretched from bend to bend of the Cumberland, including seven that ran in a secondary line a mile behind the first-line right and center, manned by the 8000 garrison and service

troops under Chief Quartermaster J. L. Donaldson, a fifty-year-old
West Pointer who had been awarded the brevet rank of brigadier.
When the jump-off came, these would move forward and take over the
works in their front, simultaneously guarding against a counterstroke
and freeing well over half the 54,000 combat soldiers now arrayed in a
long arc, east to west, under Steedman, Schofield, Wood, A. J. Smith,
and Wilson, for the assault and the pursuit that was to follow the dislodgment. First off, Steedman would feint against the enemy right,
drawing Hood's attention away from the main effort, which would
then be made against his left by Smith and Wood in a grand left wheel,
with Wilson's troopers shielding the outer flank and Schofield's two
divisions waiting in reserve to be committed in either direction. Thus,
with Donaldson's and Steedman's men employed on the defensive and
the remaining 48,000 available for offensive use against barely half their
number, Thomas had been able to plan something more than the usual
massing of troops for a breakthrough at a single point. Instead, his line
of battle would be of practically equal strength throughout its length
as it swung forward gatelike, south and southeast, inexorably crunching
whatever it encountered. In this way, once a thaw set in, the ponderous
Virginian intended not only to defeat Hood, there on the ground where
he stood, but also to destroy him in the process.

West Pointers all, except the battle-tested Steedman, the six
lieutenants gave full approval to the plan, although Schofield expressed
some disappointment at the comparatively minor role assigned his corps
in the attack. He had nothing to say, however, regarding another matter
that came up when Thomas told of the pressure being exerted on him
to advance before he judged his cavalry was ready or the ground was
fit for maneuver. Speaking first, as was customary for the junior at such
councils, Wilson quickly protested any suggestion of a commitment until the ice had melted from the pikes and hillsides. "If I were occupying
such an intrenched line as Hood's with my dismounted cavalrymen,
each armed with nothing more formidable than a basket of brickbats,"
he declared, "I would agree to defeat the whole Confederate army if it
should advance to the attack under such circumstances." Four of the
other five generals (Donaldson and Smith, fifty and forty-nine respectively, were older than their chief, while Steedman and Wood, at forty-
seven and forty-one, were younger) were similarly outspoken on the subject of untimely haste, and Schofield, who was thirty-three, concurred at
least to the extent of keeping silent. With that, the conference adjourned; whereupon Thomas, after asking Wilson to remain behind —
ostensibly for further instructions, but actually to thank him for his
exuberant support — confided sadly: "Wilson, the Washington authorities treat me as if I was a boy." Thus, for the first and only time,
the stolid Virginian, reported to be as ponderous of mind as he was of
body, demonstrated some measure of the resentment he felt at being

prodded and lectured by Grant and Halleck, neither of whom was within five hundred miles of the scene of the action they kept insisting was overdue. Having said as much, even if only in confidence to a subordinate barely three months past his twenty-seventh birthday, he seemed to experience a certain lift of spirits. "If they will just let me alone, I will show them what we can do. I am sure my plan of operations is correct, and that we shall lick the enemy if only he stays to receive our attack."

There was little to fear on the last count, however, since the condition of the roads precluded a Confederate withdrawal quite as much as it did a Federal advance. Thomas received confirmation of this when, two days later — in partial compliance with Grant's telegraphic order the day before: "Delay no longer for weather or reinforcements" — he had Wilson begin the movement of his troopers across the river from Edgefield. Rough-shod though they were for surer footing, a considerable number of horses slipped and fell on the icy bridge and cobbled streets, injuring their riders as well as themselves in the course of the crossing by the four divisions to take position in rear of A. J. Smith on the far right. "The Yankees brought their weather as well as their army with them," Nashvillians were saying, watching men and mounts topple and thrash about on the sleety pavement, with much attendant damage to knees and dispositions. Thomas was watching, too, as the freeze continued into its fourth day. An aide told how the thick-set army commander, glumly stroking his gray-shot whiskers and brooding under his massive overhang of brow, "would sometimes sit by the window for an hour or more, not speaking a word, gazing steadily out upon the forbidding prospect, as if he were trying to will the storm away."

He seemed to have succeeded the following day, December 13, when a warm rain began melting the sleet that rimed the hills and caked the hollows. Indeed, he seemed to have known he would succeed; for only last night he had passed out written orders for the attack, explaining that it would be launched as soon as a thaw provided footing for the troops. Each man was to be issued three days' rations and sixty rounds of ammunition, while supply and ordnance wagons were to be fully loaded and double-teamed, ready to roll at a moment's notice. Next morning the sun came out, glittering on what little ice remained, and even began to dry the roads a bit. At 3 o'clock that afternoon Thomas reassembled the corps commanders in his quarters and discussed with them the details of his plan. By way of revision, Steedman was told to convert his feint into a real attack, if he found reason to believe one would succeed, and Schofield was placated with assurance that his veterans were only being required to stay their hand for delivery of the knockout blow, which would be landed as soon as the enemy had been set up for the kill. Reveille would sound at 4 a.m. in all the camps, allowing time for the designated units to breakfast and be poised for the jump-off two hours later, at first light; "or as soon thereafter as practicable," the orders read.

That night, having sent a wire to Halleck announcing tomorrow's long-deferred attack, Thomas left a call at the St Cloud desk for 5 o'clock, and when it came — an hour before dawn, two hours before sunrise, December 15 — went down to the lobby, checked out, and after handing his packed suitcase to an orderly mounted his horse for the three-mile ride to the front: specifically to Lawrence Hill, a high salient jutting out from the left of Wood's position in the center. This was to be the pivot for the "grand left wheel," and it also would afford him a clear view of most of the field, including Montgomery Hill, a somewhat lower eminence directly opposite, where the rebels had established a matching salient less than half a mile away.

It would have afforded a view, that is, except for the fog that rose from the warming earth to hold back the dawn and obscure the sun when it came up beyond Steedman's position, an hour past the time originally scheduled for the attack to open there. Still another hour went by before the first shots broke the cotton-wrapped stillness on the left; but Thomas did not fret at the delay. He was convinced there would be time enough, despite the brevity of mid-December daylight, to accomplish all he had in mind. Besides, he did not need to see the field to know it, having studied it carefully in the past from this same observation post, as well as on maps in the small-hours quiet of his room. Four of the eight main thoroughfares, radiating spokelike from the city in his rear, were open or scantly obstructed; the Lebanon and Murfreesboro turnpikes on the left, the Charlotte and Harding turnpikes on the right, were available for use by the superior blue force in moving out to strike the flanks of Hood's four-mile line of intrenchments, which covered the other four main-traveled roads, the Nolensville Pike on his right, the Hillsboro Pike on his left, and the Franklin and Granny White pikes between, running nearly due south in his rear. If Thomas could sweep wide around the rebel flank to seize and hold the latter two, meantime pinning his adversary in position on the hills confronting the Union fortifications, he could then, with better than twice as many troops and something over three times as many guns, destroy him at his leisure. That was just what he intended to do, once the delays were overcome and the crunch got under way.

It seemed however, at least for a time, that there would be no end to the delays, caused first by the fog, which held up the advance on the left till 8 o'clock, two hours behind schedule, and then by the initial attack there, which stalled almost as soon as it got started. Cheatham's corps, posted on Rains Hill, beside the Nolensville Pike, and on to a steep-banked railway cut beyond, held firm against repeated assaults by Steedman's three brigades, each about the size of a Con-

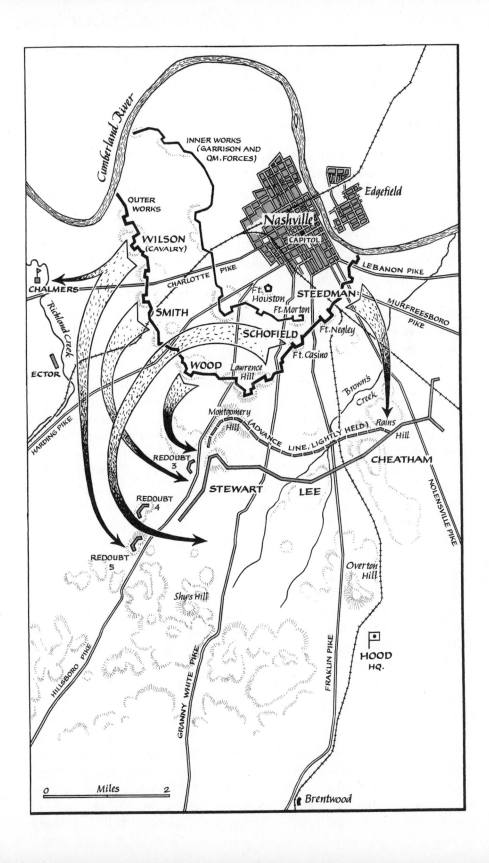

federate division. Two were composed of Negro troops, the first to be committed offensively in the western theater since the bloody repulse at Port Hudson, nearly twenty months ago — and the outcome here was much the same, as it turned out. Crossing Brown's Creek, whose banks were shoe-top deep in mud, they encountered the remnant of Granbury's Texas brigade of Cleburne's division, well dug in but numbering fewer than 500 survivors, and were badly cut up in a crossfire. They fell back "in a rather disorderly manner," one regimental commander admitted; then came on again. This continued, with much the same result, for two hours. Thomas, watching from his command post now that the mist had thinned and drifted off in tendrils, was not discouraged by the failure to gain ground with what had been intended as a feint in any case. Steedman apparently had not drawn Hood's reserves eastward to meet the threat, but at least he was keeping Cheatham occupied with only about an equal number of men — which helped to stretch the odds at the opposite end of the line, where the main effort was to be exerted. Hopefully, Thomas looked in that direction: only to find that, on the right as on the left, a snag had delayed the execution of his well-laid plan.

Beyond Wood's right, in rear of Smith and beyond his right in turn, Wilson's troopers awaited the signal to advance. A third of them, still without horses, would fight dismounted — supplementary infantry, so to speak — while the other 9000, armed to a man with the new seven-shot carbine repeater, comprised a highly mobile strike force. But Thomas no sooner ordered them forward, around 8.30, than the horsemen found both turnpikes blocked by one of Smith's divisions, which he was unexpectedly shifting eastward, across their front, for a closer link with Wood. For more than an hour Wilson fumed and fretted, champing at the bit until at last the slow-trudging foot soldiers cleared his path and let him get on with his task of rimming the "grand wheel." It was close to 10 o'clock by the time he moved out the Harding and Charlotte pikes to take position in Smith's front and on his outer flank.

The last wisps of fog had burned away by then, and well in rear of the advancing columns, along and behind the lofty fortress-studded double curve of intrenchments, spectators crowded the hilltops for a panoramic view of the show about to open on the right. Three years ago, before the occupation that followed hard on the fall of Donelson to Grant, Nashville had had a population of less than 30,000. Now it had better than three times that many residents: "nearly all of whom" — despite this triplicate influx of outsiders — "were in sympathy with the Confederacy," a Federal general observed. When he looked back and saw them clustered wherever the view was best, anticipating carnage, it crossed his mind that any applause that might come from those high-perched galleries was unlikely to be for him or the blue-clad men he rode among. "All the hills in our rear were black with human beings watching the battle, but silent. No army on the continent ever played on any field to so large and so sullen an audience."

What followed was still preliminary, for a time at any rate. Wilson and Smith, with a combined strength of 24,000 sabers and bayonets in their seven divisions, had small trouble driving Rucker's and Ector's outpost brigades — respectively from Chalmers' and French's divisions, and containing fewer than 2000 men between them, mounted and afoot — down the two pikes and over Richland Creek, where they could offer little or no resistance to the massive wheeling movement soon in progress across their front. By noon, so smoothly did the maneuver work once it got under way, the two blue corps were beyond the Harding Pike, confronting the mile-long extension of Hood's left down the Hillsboro Pike from the angle where his line bent sharply south in rear of Montgomery Hill. A low stone wall afforded cover for the division of graybacks crouched behind it on the east side of the road, and three unfinished redoubts bristled with guns on the side toward the Federals, who were massing to continue their advance across the remaining stretch of muddy, stump-pocked fields. Half the daylight had been used in getting set for the big push designed to bring on Hood's destruction. Now the other half remained for its execution.

Moreover, Thomas had another 24,000 standing by under Wood and Schofield, whose five divisions made up the other half of his right-wing strike force, awaiting orders to double the weight of the mass about to be thrown against Hood's left. These were the men who had stood fast at Franklin, and Wood, who had succeeded there to command of the army's largest corps when Stanley took a bullet through the neck, wanted nothing so much as he did an opportunity to wipe out the stain that had marred his record ever since he complied with instructions to "close up on Reynolds" at Chickamauga, thereby creating the gap through which Longstreet's troops had plunged. Still a brigadier, despite the mettle he had proved at Missionary Ridge and Lovejoy Station, he wanted above all a chance to show what he could do on his own. And here at Nashville he got it, just past noon, when word came down for him to execute his share of the grand wheel. All morning he had stood on Lawrence Hill, the pivotal center, obliged to contribute nothing more to the battle than long-range artillery fire, while Steedman and Wilson and Smith moved out, flags aflutter, on the left and on the right. Now that his turn had come, he was determined to make the most of it by storming the enemy works on Montgomery Hill, just opposite his command post.

This was by no means as difficult an undertaking as it appeared to be from where he stood. Five days ago, screened by the blinding fall of sleet, Hood had had Stewart withdraw his main line half a mile rearward, from the brow to the reverse slope of Montgomery Hill, leaving no more than a skeleton crew to man the works established on his arrival, two weeks back. Old Straight had only two full divisions on hand there anyhow, since one of French's three brigades was Ector's, on outpost duty two miles west, and another had been detached to guard the mouth of Duck River, lest Union gunboats penetrate the region in Hood's rear. French himself, a victim of failing eyesight, had departed just that morning, leaving only his third brigade, under Brigadier General Claudius Sears, posted between Walthall's division on the left and Loring's on the right. Stewart thus had barely 4800 men in the path of the 48,000 earmarked by Thomas for the execution of his grand left wheel.

Shortly after 12.30 Loring's pickets looked out from the all-but-abandoned trenches along the crest of the hill, midway between the two main lines of battle, and saw Wood's infantry coming toward them, out of the intervening valley and up the hillside. "The sharp rattle of fifty-caliber rifles sound[ed] like a canebrake on fire," one of the handful of defenders was to say. He and his fellows gave the advancing throng a couple of volleys, then scuttled rearward. Wood, peering intently from his command post on the far side of the valley, was impressed by what he saw. "When the grand array of troops began to move forward in unison," he would write in his report, "the pageant was magnificently grand and imposing. Far as the eye could reach, the lines and masses of blue, over which the national emblem flaunted proudly, moved forward in such perfect order that the heart of the patriot might easily draw from it the happy presage of the coming glorious victory." What pleased him most, apparently, was the progress made by the lead brigade of his old division, now under Brigadier General Samuel Beatty. Recalling its surge up the hillside in advance of all the rest, he waxed Homeric. "At the command, as sweeps the stiff gale over the ocean, driving every object before it, so swept the brigade up the wooded slope, over the enemy's intrenchments; and the hill was won."

What was won in fact was the crest of the hill and a line of empty trenches, not the new main line resistance, half a mile beyond, which held firm under the follow-up attack. Hood, having avoided being drawn off balance by the secondary effort against his right, saw clearly enough his adversary's true over-all intention, and on hearing from Stewart that his portion of the line — the critical left, already menaced by masses of bluecoats, north and west — was "stretched to its utmost tension," did what he could to reduce the lengthening odds in that direction. Stephen Lee, whose corps had scarcely fired a shot from its central position, was told to send Johnson's division to bolster the left, and similar orders went to Cheatham, who was having little trouble containing Steedman's effort on the right, to send Bate's division there as well. Whether they would arrive in time was another matter; Wood's assault had no sooner been launched against Stewart's front than Smith and Wilson resumed their combined advance upon his flank. Hard on the heels of this, moreover, Thomas passed the word for Schofield to join in the attack, bringing the total right-wheel commitment to just under 50,000 of all arms. That was better than twice the number Hood had on hand in his entire command, and roughly ten times as many as Stewart would have in his depleted corps until reinforcements reached him.

One unit had arrived by then as a reinforcement, albeit a small one: Ector's 700-man brigade, which came in from the west around 11 o'clock, after being driven back across Richland Creek by Smith and Wilson. Appealed to by the occupants of one of the redoubts short of the Hillsboro Pike, who urged them to join in its defense, the winded veterans replied: "It can't be done. There's a whole army in your front," and kept going, taking position on the left of Walthall, whose three brigades were strung out behind the stone wall running south along the far side of the pike. Such words were far from encouraging to the troops in the three redoubts, each of which was built on rising ground and contained a four-gun battery, manned by fifty cannoneers and supported by about twice that number of infantry lodged in shallow trenches alongside the uncompleted breastworks. These miniature garrisons had been told to hold out "at all hazards," and they were determined to do so, knowing they were all that stood between Hood's unshored left flank and the Federals who soon were massing to the west and northwest after completing the first stage of their grand wheel. Between noon and 1 o'clock, while Wood's attack exploded northward beyond the loom of Montgomery Hill, Wilson and Smith opened fire with their rifled batteries at a range of just under half a mile. The defenders replied as best they could with their dozen smoothbores, but hoarded their energy and ammunition for the close-up work that would follow when the dark blue mass, already in attack formation and biding its time through the bombardment, moved against them.

As it turned out, these three redoubts, numbered 3 and 4 and 5 — 1 and 2 lay northward, east of the pike, where Stewart's line bent south — held up the next stage of the wheeling movement, here on the Federal right, even longer than fog had delayed the jump-off on the left. For close to an hour the Union gunners made things hot for the clustered graybacks, who could do little more than hug their shell-jarred works and wait their turn. This came around 1.30 when the iron rain let up and the multiwaved assault rolled within range of their 12-pounders. Flailed ragged along its near edge by double-shotted canister, the blue flood paused in front of Redoubts 3 and 4, but not for long in front of Redoubt 5, which was unsupported on its outer flank, three quarters of a mile beyond the end of Walthall's line. Wilson's rapid-firing troopers, charging dismounted — somewhat awkwardly, it was true, for no one had thought to tell them to leave their low-slung cavalry sabers behind — rushed past it on the left and right and swamped it from the rear. They had no sooner done so, though, than they received a high-angle salvo from Redoubt 4, next up the line, where Captain Charles Lumsden's Alabama battery was supported by a hundred Alabama infantry. Lumsden, a V.M.I. graduate and one-time commandant of cadets at the University of Alabama, had already notified Stewart that he and his men, with a combined strength of 148, were likely to be swept away in short order, once the enemy pressed the issue. Old Straight's reply: "Hold on as long as you can," was followed to the letter. Firing front and flank with their brass Napoleons and rifles, the Alabamians held fast against the menace of a dozen regiments from Smith and four from Wilson. In the end, nearly three hours past the opening of the preliminary bombardment, the attackers came tumbling between the fuming guns, bayonets flashing, carbines a-clatter. "Take care of yourselves, boys!" Lumsden called out, and the survivors trotted back to the main line, half a mile rearward, prepared to join in its defense against the final stage of the blue assault.

Two of Johnson's brigades had arrived by then from Lee's corps in the center, and Old Clubby was on the way with the other two, while Bate hurried westward from the far right, sent by Cheatham on orders from Hood to help shore up the hard-pressed left. Even if both divisions arrived in time, however, they would do little to reduce the odds; Schofield had come up, across the way, and was taking position on Smith's right to overlap Stewart's extension of his line down the Hillsboro Pike. It was now past 3 o'clock. While the Federal batteries displaced forward, beyond fallen Redoubt 4, to try their hand at knocking down the stone fence Walthall's men were crouched behind, Smith's left division, commanded by Brigadier General John McArthur, advanced upon and captured Redoubt 3. Taken promptly under fire by Redoubt 2, across the pike, McArthur — a Scotch-born former blacksmith who had prospered as the proprietor of a Chicago ironworks and had served with bristly distinction in most of the western campaigns — stormed and took the companion work as well, turning its guns on nearby Redoubt 1, already under heavy pressure from two of Wood's divisions.

If this went, all went: Stewart knew that, and so did Wood, who had ordered two six-gun batteries advanced to bring converging, almost point-blank fire to bear on the angle where Sears's brigade was posted, hinge-like, between Walthall and Loring. Then at 4 o'clock, after a good half hour's pounding by these dozen guns, Wood told Brigadier General Washington Elliott — Wagner's replacement after Franklin — to assault the rebel salient with his division "at all costs." At 4.30, angered by the delay, which Elliott claimed was needed to give Smith's corps time to come up on his right, Wood passed the word for Kimball to make the strike instead. Kimball did so, promptly and with what his superior later called "the most exalted enthusiasm." As his troops entered the works from the northeast, followed closely by the tardy Elliott's, McArthur's flank brigade came storming in from the west to assist in the reduction, together with the capture of four guns, four stands of colors, and "numerous prisoners."

Mainly these last were laggards or members of the forlorn hope, left behind to cover the withdrawal of the main body of defenders. Stewart, foreseeing disaster — both on his left, which was considerably overlapped by Schofield, and in his center, where the hinge was about to buckle under pressure from Wood and Smith — had just ordered a pull-back to a new position shielding the vital Granny White Pike, a mile in rear of the line that now was crumbling along the Hillsboro Pike and the near slope of Montgomery Hill. Despite the panic in certain units, what followed between sunset at 4.45 and full darkness, one hour later, was not a rout. Johnson's two advance brigades, posted in extension of Walthall's left before the fall of Redoubt 4, came unglued when the Federals charged them, and Ector's brigade was cut off from the rest of Stewart's corps, northward beyond the gap their flight created. Elsewhere, though, Walthall's and Loring's veterans responded in good order to instructions for disengagement. Up in the critical angle, under assault from two directions, Sears managed to pull most of his men out, avoiding capture, but as they fell back he turned to study the lost post with his binoculars and was struck in the right leg by a well-aimed solid, perhaps from one of his abandoned guns. He fell heavily, then was hustled off to an aid station, where surgeons removed his mangled leg that night. Meantime Stewart, reinforced at last by Bate and Johnson's other two brigades, got his two divisions realigned in a southward prolongation of Lee's unshaken left, helped by the jubilant confusion of the Federals, who were about as disorganized by their sudden twilight victory as his own troops were by their defeat.

Hood was there, too, intent on shoring up this battered third of his army. He had lost 16 guns today, along with some 2200 soldiers, more than half of them made prisoner in the collapse of his left wing, the rest killed or wounded here and on the right, which had stood firm. Meeting Ector's peripatetic brigade as it fell back from its second cut-off position, across the Hillsboro Pike from Redoubt 5, he spoke briefly to the men and led them nearly a mile eastward to a hill that loomed just short of the Granny White Pike. Four of the six regiments were one-time Texas cavalry outfits, long since dismounted for lack of horses and down to about a hundred men apiece.

"Texans," he said, "I want you to hold this hill regardless of what transpires around you."

They looked at the hill, then back at Hood, and nodded. "We'll do it, General," they told him.

★　　★　　★

Union and Confederate, the lines ran helter-skelter in the dusk. Still on Lawrence Hill, Thomas watched his army's campfires blossom where rebel fires had burned the night before. Except for unexpected delays — caused first by the fog, then by Smith's last-minute adjustment of his front, which held up the start of the grand wheel, and finally by the prolonged resistance of the flimsy enemy redoubts west of the Hillsboro Pike — he was convinced he would have achieved the Cannae he had planned for, and expected, until darkness caught up with the attackers before they could complete the massive turning movement he had designed to cut off Hood's retreat. In any case, not being much given to dwelling on regrets, he perceived that the best course now was for all units to bivouac where they were, in preparation for taking up their unfinished work tomorrow, well rested from the day-long exertions that had put them where they were tonight, practically within reach of the only two unseized turnpikes leading south. Just how far they would have to go, before the battle was resumed, would depend on what progress Hood's beaten troops could make on the muddy roads toward Franklin and the Harpeth — if, indeed, they were in any condition to move at all — before daylight and better than 50,000 Federals overtook them.

Returning to Nashville for a good night's sleep in a proper bed, Thomas got off to Halleck at 9 o'clock a telegram that somehow managed to be at once both ponderous and exuberant. "I attacked the enemy's left this morning and drove it from the river, below the city, very nearly to the Franklin Pike, a distance [of] about eight miles.... The troops behaved splendidly, all taking their share in assaulting and carrying the enemy's breastworks. I shall attack the enemy again tomorrow, if he stands to fight, and, if he retreats during the night, will pursue him, throwing a heavy cavalry force in his rear, to destroy his trains, if possible." A reply from Edwin Stanton himself, sent three hours later, hailed "the brilliant achievements of this day" as "the harbinger of a decisive victory that will crown you and your army with honor and do much toward closing the war. We shall give you a hundred guns in the morning." From Grant there came two wires, sent fifteen minutes apart, between 11.30 and midnight. "Much is now expected," the first ended, and the second had rather the nature of an afterthought — a brief correction of, if not quite an apology for, a lapse in manners. "I congratulate you and the army under your command for today's operations, and feel a conviction that tomorrow will add more fruits to your victory."

Closer at hand, there were those who did not share this conviction. Receiving after dark Thomas's order, "which was in substance to pursue the retreating enemy next morning," Schofield took alarm at the thought that such evident overconfidence, in addition to costing the army its half-won victory, might also expose it to defeat. He had supplied the crowning blow today, coming in hard around the crumpled rebel left at sunset, but he was by no means convinced that what had been delivered was a knockout punch, as his superior seemed to think. In fact he did not believe for a minute that Hood was in retreat. For all he knew, his former roommate was even then planning a first-light strike at one of the Union flanks: most likely his own, though both were more or less exposed. "He'll hit you like hell, now, before you know it," he had warned Sherman when Hood first took over, down around Atlanta five months ago, and it seemed to him, from the order just received, that Thomas needed reminding of that danger. Accordingly, he called for his horse and rode through the darkness to headquarters, back in Nashville, where he found the Virginian about to retire for the night. "You don't know Hood," he protested earnestly. "He'll be right there, ready to fight you in the morning."

Thomas knew Hood a good deal better than Schofield seemed to think; but even so this warning gave him pause. And having paused he acted in revision of his plans. Previously he had alerted his cavalry for a fast ride south at the first glimmer of the coming day, his purpose being to cut the retreating graybacks off, or anyhow bring them to a halt before they crossed the Harpeth, and thus expose them to slaughter without the protection of that river barrier, which might oblige the blue pursuers to fight a second Franklin, in reverse. Now instead he sent word for Wilson to "remain in your present position until it is satisfactorily known whether the enemy will fight or retreat." That would help cover his right, where the troopers had drawn rein at nightfall, and by way of further insurance he had A. J. Smith send one of his three divisions to reinforce Schofield on that flank, in case Hood really was planning the dawn assault his one-time roommate feared. This done, Thomas at last turned in for the good night's sleep he had prescribed for his whole army.

There was little or no rest, however, for the gray-clad troops across the way: not because they were on the march, as Thomas had presumed, but because they were digging — digging in. Schofield was right, at least in part: Hood had chosen to stay and fight, if only on the defensive. The crumpling of his left today, while the other two thirds of his army stood firm, had by no means convinced him that the enemy host, for all its heavy numerical advantage, was capable of driving him headlong from the field: whereas a Federal repulse, here at the capital gates, might still afford him an opening for the counterstroke on which his hopes were pinned. Moreover, the position he retired to, just under two miles south, was so much stronger than the first — especially in man-saving compactness, though it covered only two of the eight converging turnpikes — that the wonder was he had not occupied it at the outset, when he came within sight of Nashville, two weeks ago tomorrow.

Despite the confusion attending the sunset collapse of his defenses along the Hillsboro Pike and across Montgomery Hill, the nighttime withdrawal to this new line was accomplished in good order. Lee's corps, which had scarcely been engaged today except for part of Johnson's division, simply fell back two miles down the Franklin Pike to Overton Hill, east of the road, where the new right flank was anchored. The left was just over two miles away, beyond the Granny White Pike, and its main salient was the hill on which Hood had posted Ector's brigade at twilight (Shy's Hill, it would afterwards be called for young Lieutenant Colonel William Shy, who would die on its crown tomorrow at the head of his Tennessee regiment); Cheatham, whose losses had also been light today, occupied this critical height, his flank bent south around its western slope. In the center, disposed along a range of hills between the outer two, Stewart's diminished corps took position and began to prepare for the resumption of the battle, as the others were doing on the right and left, by scraping out shallow trenches and using the spoil to pile up breastworks along that low range lying midway between Brentwood, less than four miles south, and the Nashville fortifications. Like Ector's Texans, who by now had been joined by Bate's division on its arrival from the right, they were determined to give Hood all he asked of them, though they had trouble understanding why he did so with two turnpikes leading unobstructed to the crossing of the Harpeth, barely a dozen miles in their rear.

Dawn found them settled in, weary from their all-night toil but confident, as one division commander said, that their improvised works were "impervious to ordinary shots." Extraordinary shots presumably would have to be taken as they came, but at any rate Chalmers had combined his two brigades in Cheatham's rear, where his troopers were in position to help fend off a repetition of yesterday's overlapping assault upon that flank. Still, for all his determination not to be hustled into disorderly retreat, Hood knew the odds he faced and was quite aware of what they might portend. Accordingly, he ordered all wagons to proceed at first light to the Harpeth, clearing the narrow gorges in his rear, and soon afterwards, at 8 o'clock, sent warning notes to all three corps commanders, specifying that "should any disaster happen to us today," Lee would hold fast on the Franklin Pike, until Stewart had moved down it, and Cheatham would take the Granny White Pike, his withdrawal covered by Chalmers. Minor adjustments were made in the line, which was only half as long as the one the day before, but most of the morning was spent in idle waiting by the graybacks for the shock that would come when Thomas resumed his effort to destroy them where they stood.

The slowness of the Federals in getting back to grips with their opponents was due to the scattered condition of the army when it bedded down the night before. On the right, Wilson and Schofield

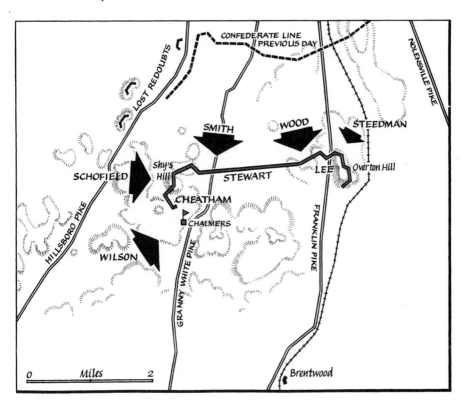

were in reasonable proximity to Cheatham on Shy's Hill, and so presently, on the left, was Steedman in relation to Lee, whose skirmishers he encountered as he approached Overton Hill, east of the Franklin Pike, around midmorning. It was in the center, in particular the right center, that the worst delays occurred; Smith and Wood were at right angles to each other, and neither knew, when the day began, whether the rebels had pulled out in the night, or, if not, what position Hood had chosen for another stand. By the time they found out, and got their troops aligned for the confrontation, noon had come and action had opened on the left. This was as it had been the day before, except that at no stage of the planning was Steedman's effort, reinforced by one of Wood's divisions, intended as a feint. His orders called for the Confederates to be "vigorously pressed and unceasingly harrassed," for if Hood's right could be turned and "his line of retreat along the Franklin Pike and the valley leading to Brentwood commanded effectually," Thomas would succeed today in bringing off the Cannae he had intended yesterday. The result, here on the Union left, was the bloodiest fighting of the two-day battle.

Two of Lee's divisions, under Major Generals Henry Clayton and Carter Stevenson, not only had scarcely been engaged the day before, they had not even taken part in the assault at Franklin, and their conduct here today, astride the Franklin Pike and on the crest of Overton

Hill, gave some notion of what Hood's whole army might have accomplished at the gates of Nashville, just over two weeks later, if it had been spared the late-November holocaust that cost it 6000 of its best men, including Pat Cleburne and a dozen other brigade and division commanders. At full strength, both in numbers and morale, these five brigades — reinforced by a sixth from Johnson, whose division was on their left, adjoining Stewart's corps in the center — stood off, between noon and 3 o'clock, a series of combined attacks by Wood and Steedman, whose persistence cost them dearly. Suffering little themselves, despite massed incoming artillery fire that Wood pronounced "uncommonly fine" and one defender said "was the most furious I ever witnessed," they inflicted such heavy punishment on the attackers that finally, after three hours of surging up and stumbling down the muddy slopes of the hill on the far Confederate right, the blue flood receded. Steedman's losses were especially cruel. One unit, the 13th U.S. Colored Infantry, suffered 221 casualties in all, the greatest regimental loss on either side. "After the repulse," Wood later reported, "our soldiers, white and colored, lay indiscriminately near the enemy works at the outer edge of the abatis."

When this attack first opened, threatening to turn his right and cut the Franklin Pike, Hood ordered Cheatham to send three of the four brigades from the division on his left — formerly Cleburne's, now under its senior brigadier, James A. Smith — to reinforce the opposite flank. As it turned out, this was a serious mistake. Lee not only needed no help, but by the time Smith's men reached him, around 3.30, the attack had been suspended. Worse, there wasn't time enough for them to return to their former position below Shy's Hill, which they had no sooner left than they were sorely missed. Stewart had been watching in both directions from his command post in the center, east of the Granny White Pike, and had seen trouble coming: not on the right, though the Overton Hill assault was even then approaching its climax, but on the left, where the situation was uncomfortably similar to the one he himself had faced the day before, when his had been the corps on that flank. "Should Bate fall back," he said in a hastily-written 2 o'clock note to Walthall, whose division adjoined Bate's on Cheatham's right, "keep your left connected with him, falling back from your left toward right and forming a new flank line extending to hills in rear."

There was more to this than a generally shared mistrust of Bate, whose three brigades had not done well in recent operations. All morning, though none of the five blue infantry divisions arrayed in a nearly semicircular line confronting Shy's Hill from the north and west had so far come to grips with the defenders, Wilson, fighting with two divisions dismounted while the other two ranged wide, had been pressing Chalmers' horsemen back on their supports. By noon, as a result, the Granny White Pike was firmly in Union possession to the south, no longer a possible rebel escape route, and Cheatham's left was bent in the shape of a fishhook. Hood pulled Ector's troops back from the crest of the hill to help Smith's remaining brigade hold off Wilson's attackers, whose repeaters gave them a firepower out of proportion to their already superior numbers. This caused Bate to have to extend his line still farther westward in taking over the works Ector's men had occupied, and worst of all, now that the rapid-firing blue troopers had pushed within carbine range, this part of the line was taking close-up fire not only from its front and flank but also from its rear. "The Yankee bullets and shells were coming from all directions, passing one another in the air," a butternut private would recall.

By 3 o'clock, when the blue attack finally sputtered out on the Confederate right, a good part of the night-built breastworks on Shy's Hill had been flattened or knocked apart — small wonder; one of Schofield's batteries, for example, pumped 560 rounds into the hill before the day was over — by well-aimed shots from artillery massed north and west and south. A cold rain had begun at midday, and the defenders could do little, under the fall of icy water and hot metal, but hug the earth and hope for a let-up that did not come, either of raindrops or of shells. It was more or less clear to everyone here, as it was to Stewart in the center, that the position now being pounded by close to a hundred guns could not be held much longer than it took the commanders of the three Union corps — one in its front, one on its flank, one in its rear — to stage the concerted push the situation called for.

Thomas, though he still declined to be hurried in his conduct of the battle — not even by a midday wire from the Commander in Chief, in which, after tendering "the nation's thanks for your good work of yesterday," Lincoln ended on a sterner note, as if on cue from Grant: "You made a magnificent beginning. A grand consummation is within your easy reach. Do not let it slip" — saw clearly enough what was called for, and was moving even now to bring it off. About the time the Overton Hill attack subsided he set out from his Franklin Pike command post and rode westward through the pelting rain in rear of the extension of Wood's line, on beyond the Granny White Pike, where A. J. Smith had his two remaining divisions in position, and then around the southward curve of front to Schofield's headquarters, due west of Shy's Hill. Wilson was there, remonstrating against Schofield's delay in giving the prearranged signal he and Smith had agreed would launch the converging assault by all three corps. The cavalryman had sent a series of couriers urging action for the past two hours, ever since he gained the rebel rear, and now at last — within an hour of sunset — had come in person to protest, although with small effect; Schofield wanted another division from Smith before advancing, on grounds that to attack high-sited intrenchments without a greater advantage in numbers than he now enjoyed would be to risk paying more in blood for the hill than it was worth. Thomas heard him out, then said dryly: "The battle must be fought, if men *are* killed." He looked across the northwest slope of the fuming hill, where it seemed to him that McArthur, adjusting his line for a closer take-off, was about to slip the leash. "General Smith is attacking without waiting for you," he told Schofield. "Please advance your entire line."

Here at last was a direct order; Schofield had no choice but to obey. He did so, in fact, so promptly that Wilson, riding happily south to rejoin his troopers in rear of the blue-clamped rebel left, did not get back in time to direct their share of the three-sided push that drove the defenders from Shy's Hill. So sudden indeed was the gray collapse that Hood himself, watching from horseback in rear of his left center, said later that he could scarcely credit what he saw. "Our forces up to that moment had repulsed the Federals at every point, and were waving their colors in defiance, crying out to the enemy, 'Come on, come on.' " With the crisis weathered on his right and sunset barely an hour away, he planned to withdraw after nightfall for a dawn assault on the Union right, which he believed was exposed to being turned and shattered. Alas, it was his own flank that was shattered as he watched. "I beheld for the first and only time" — he had not been on Missionary Ridge with Bragg, just over a year ago — "a Confederate army abandon the field in confusion."

Old Straight had seen disaster coming two hours before, and it came as he had warned. Assailed by Smith and Schofield on both sides of the angle, all the while taking fire from Wilson's dismounted horsemen in their rear, Bate's three brigades gave back from their enfiladed works, fought briefly, and then for the most part fled, although some units — the Tennesseans under twenty-five-year-old William Shy, for instance, whose fall gave the lost hill its future name — resisted till they were overrun. By that time, the attack had widened and the panic had infected Stewart's corps, along with the rest of Cheatham's; "The breach once made, the lines lifted from either side as far as I could see," Bate would report. All three of his brigade commanders were captured, and so was Edward Johnson when the break extended beyond the center, under pressure from Smith and Wood, and spread to his division on Lee's left. Everywhere to the west of there, eastward across the rear of what had been the Confederate left and center, butternut veterans were in headlong flight for the Franklin Pike, the one remaining avenue of escape. They wanted to live: perhaps to fight another day, but certainly not here.

"It was more like a scene in a spectacular drama than a real incident in war," a colonel on Thomas's staff would note. "The hillside in front, still green, dotted with boys in blue swarming up the slope, the dark background of high hills beyond, the lowering clouds, the waving flags, the smoke rising slowly through the leafless treetops and drifting

across the valleys, the wonderful outburst of musketry, the ecstatic
cheers, the multitude racing for life down into the valley below — so
exciting was it all that the lookers-on instinctively clapped their hands
as at a brilliant and successful transformation scene; as indeed it was.
For in those few moments an army was changed into a mob, and the
whole structure of the rebellion in the Southwest, with all its possibilities,
was utterly overthrown."

But that was to overstate the case, if not in regard to the eventualities, then at any rate in regard to the present dissolution of Hood's
army. On Overton Hill, in the final moments before the opposite flank
gave way, Stephen Lee observed that his troops were "in fine spirits
and confident of success," congratulating themselves on their recent
repulse of Wood and Steedman. Then out of nowhere came the collapse, first of Cheatham's corps, then Stewart's, and the blue attack
rolled eastward to engulf them; Johnson's division wavered and broke,
its commander taken, and Stevenson's, next in line, seemed about to
follow. East of the Franklin Pike, in rear of Clayton's division, Lee
spurred his horse westward, taking the fences on both sides of the turnpike, and drew rein amid the confusion behind his center, crowded
now with graybacks who had bolted. He leaned down and snatched a
stand of colors from a fugitive color bearer, then brandished it from
horseback as he rode among the panicked veterans, shouting hoarsely at
them: "Rally, men, rally! For God's sake, rally! This is the place for
brave men to die!"

Some few stopped, then more. "The effect was electrical," one
among them was to write. "They gathered in little knots of four or
five, and he soon had around him three or four other stands of colors."
They were not many, but they were enough, as it turned out, to cause
the attackers — confused as much by their abrupt success today as they
had been at the same late hour the day before — to hesitate before moving forward again through the smoky, rain-screened dusk that followed
hard upon sunset. By that time Clayton, unmolested on the right, had
managed to withdraw his division from Overton Hill and form it in some
woods astride the Franklin Pike, half a mile below. When Lee fell back
to there, the same observer noted, "he was joined by a few pieces of
artillery and a little drummer boy who beat the long roll in perfect
time." Stevenson's fugitives rallied too, in response to this steady
drumming, and together the two divisions comprised a rear guard that
kept open, well into darkness, the one escape route still available to
the army.

This was of course no help to the men already rounded up in their
thousands on the field of battle, including Johnson — he had just been
exchanged in October, five months after his previous capture at Spotsylvania — and all three of Bate's brigade commanders, Brigadier Generals
Henry Jackson and T. B. Smith and Major Jacob Lash. Old Clubby,

still crippled from the leg wound he had suffered at McDowell, two and a half years ago, was taken while trying to limp away from his shattered line, and it was much the same with Jackson, a forty-four-year-old former Georgia lawyer-politician, who found the rearward going slow because of the mud that weighted down his boots. He had stopped, and was trying to get them off with the help of an aide, when a blue-clad corporal and three privates came upon him by the roadside.

"You're a general," the corporal said accusatively, spotting the wreathed stars on his prisoner's collar.

"That is my rank," Jackson admitted.

"Captured a general, by God!" the Federal whooped. He took off his flat-topped forage cap and swung it round and round his head. "I'll carry you to Nashville myself."

Smith and Lash on the other hand were taken on Shy's Hill itself, along with most of their men, when their lines were overrun. Imprisoned, Lash would not receive the promotion he had earned by surviving his superiors, but Smith's was a crueler fate. A graduate of the Nashville Military Institute and a veteran of all the western battles, he had risen from second lieutenant, over the years, to become at twenty-six the army's youngest brigadier; which perhaps, since his youth and slim good looks implied a certain jauntiness in happier times, had something to do with what presently happened to him. While being conducted unarmed to the Union rear he was slashed three times across the head with a saber by the colonel of the Ohio regiment that had captured him, splitting his skull and exposing so much of his mangled brain that the surgeon who examined his wounds pronounced them fatal. He did not die, however. He survived a northern prison camp to return to his native state when the conflict was over, then lived for nearly another sixty years before he died at last in the Tennessee Hospital for the Insane, where he spent the last forty-seven of his eighty-five years, a victim of the damage inflicted by the Ohio colonel. This was another face of war, by no means unfamiliar on either side, but one unseen when the talk was all of glory.

It was not the face Thomas saw when, completing a sunset ride from the far right, he urged his horse up Overton Hill, which had just been cleared, and looked out over the field where his troops were hoicking long columns of butternut captives to the rear. He lifted his hat in salute to the victors in the twilight down below, exclaiming as he did so: "Oh, what a grand army I have! God bless each member of it."

Such hilltop crowing was uncharacteristic of the Rock of Chickamauga, however well it might suit him in his new role as the Sledge of Nashville, but in any case both salute and blessing were deserved. His army captured here today an additional 3300 prisoners, bringing its two-day haul, as a subsequent head-count would show, to 4462 rebels of all ranks. Moreover, another 37 pieces of artillery were taken, which made 53 in all, one more than R. E. Lee had captured throughout the Seven Days to set the previous battle record. Thomas's loss in killed, wounded, and missing, though twice heavier today than yesterday, barely raised his overall total above three thousand: 3061. Hood lost only half as many killed and wounded as he had done the day before, but his scant loss in those two categories — roughly 1500 for both days, or less than half the number his adversary suffered — only showed how readily his soldiers had surrendered under pressure, thereby lifting his loss to nearly 6000 casualties, almost twice as many as he inflicted. Thomas of course did not yet know these comparative figures. All he knew was that he had won decisively, more so tactically perhaps than any general in any large-scale battle in this war, and that was the cause of his exuberance on Overton Hill and afterwards, when he came down off the height and rode forward in the gathering darkness.

Normally mild of speech and manner, practically never profane or boastful, he continued to be quite unlike himself tonight: as was shown when he spotted his young cavalry commander riding back up the Granny White Pike to meet him. He recalled what he had told him in private on the eve of battle, and he greeted him now, the other would note, "with all the vehemence of an old dragoon" and in a voice that could be heard throughout this quarter of the rain-swept field. "Dang it to hell, Wilson!" he roared, "didn't I tell you we could lick 'em? Didn't I tell you we could lick 'em?"

Southward, the disorderly gray retreat continued. Lee's rear guard task was eased by having only Wood's corps to contend with; Steedman had stopped, apparently from exhaustion, and Smith and Schofield had been halted to prevent confusion when their two corps came together at right angles on Shy's Hill. Below there, Wilson's remounted troopers were opposed by Ector's surviving handful of infantry and Rucker's cavalry brigade, assigned by Chalmers to keep the bluecoats off the Franklin Pike, which was clogged with fugitives all the way to Brentwood. Rucker managed it, with the help of Ector's veterans and the rain and darkness, though at the cost of being captured — the fourth brigade commander in the past two hours — when he was shot from his horse in a hand-to-hand saber duel with two opponents. Lee meantime withdrew in good order, two miles beyond Brentwood to Hollow Tree Gap, where he set up a new rear-guard line by midnight, six miles short of Franklin and the Harpeth.

In this way, from sunset well into darkness, when they finally desisted, the Federals were kept from interfering with the retreat of the army they had routed. But neither could that army's own leaders interfere with its rearward movement, though they tried. "It was like trying to stop the current of Duck River with a fish net," one grayback was to say. Not even Ben Cheatham, for all the fondness his men had for him, could prevail on them to pause for longer that he could fix them with his eye. He would get one stopped, and then when he turned to appeal to another, the first would duck beneath the general's horse and continue on his way. Even so, he had better luck than did some younger staffers who tried their hand. One such, hailing a mud-spattered infantryman headed rearward down the turnpike, ordered him to face about and meet the foe. "You go to hell — I've been there," the man replied, and kept on trudging southward in the rain. None among them had any way of knowing that the war's last great battle had been fought. All they knew was they wanted no more of it; not for now, at any rate.

Hood was no better at organizing a rally short of Brentwood than the least of his subordinates had been. He tried for a time, then gave it up and went with the flow. A bandaged Tennessee private who had seen and pitied him earlier, just before the break — "How feeble and decrepit he looked, with an arm in a sling and a crutch in the other hand, trying to guide and control his horse" — felt even sorrier for him tonight when, seeking him out to secure "a wounded furlough," he came upon the one-legged general near Hollow Tree Gap, alone in his headquarters tent beside the Franklin Pike, "much agitated and affected" by the events of the past six hours "and crying like his heart would break." His left arm dangling useless at his side, he ran the fingers of his right hand through his hair in a distracted gesture as the tears ran down his cheeks into his beard, golden in the light of the lantern on the table by his chair. Unabashed — after the manner of Confederates of all ranks, who respected their superiors in large part for the respect they knew they would receive in turn if they approached them — the bullet-nicked private entered, asked for, and received his furlough paper, then went back out into the darkness and the rain, leaving Hood to resume his weeping if he chose. "I pitied him, poor fellow," the Tennessean wrote long afterward, remembering the scene. "I always loved and honored him, and will ever revere and cherish his memory.... As a soldier, he was brave, good, noble, and gallant, and fought with the ferociousness of the wounded tiger, and with the everlasting grit of the bulldog; but as a general he was a failure in every particular."

For all its harshness, Franklin and Nashville had confirmed and reconfirmed this assessment, so far at least as most of the Kentucky-born Texan's critics were concerned, before it was made: not only because he fought them with so little tactical skill, offensive or defensive, but also because he fought them at all. Within a span of just over two weeks, these two battles had cost him 12,000 casualties — better than twice the number he inflicted — and in the end produced a rout as complete as the one a year ago on Missionary Ridge. Pat Cleburne had saved Bragg's retreat then with his defense of Ringgold Gap, and though the Arkansan now was in his grave in St John's churchyard, Stephen Lee performed a similar service for Hood next morning at Hollow Tree Gap, which he held under pressure from Wilson and Wood while the rest of the graybacks crossed the Harpeth. Outflanked, he followed, burning the bridge in his wake, and took up a covering position on Winstead Hill, three miles south of Franklin, where Hood had had his command post for the attack that cost him the flower of his army. To-day's defense only cost him Lee, who was wounded there and had to turn his corps over to Stevenson when he fell back that evening to take up a new position near Spring Hill, another place of doleful memory.

By the following morning, December 18, Cheatham had reas-sembled enough of his corps to assume the duty of patrolling rain-swollen Rutherford Creek, which the pursuers could not cross, once the turnpike bridge was burned, until their pontoon train arrived. The resultant two-day respite from immediate blue pressure (for the train, having been missent toward Murfreesboro by a clerical error, then re-called, was obliged to creak and groan its way by a roundabout route over roads hub-deep in mud) was heartening to the graybacks plodding down the Columbia Pike. But the best of all news, especially for Chal-mers' drooping horsemen, was the arrival last night of one of the four detached brigades of cavalry, followed today by another, which brought word that Forrest himself would soon be along with the other two. Sure enough, he rode in that night. Ordered by Hood to fall back from Murfreesboro through Shelbyville to Pulaski, he had decided instead to rejoin by a shorter route, through Triune, and had done so: much to his superior's relief. Hood's plan had been to call a halt along Duck River and winter in its lush valley, much as Bragg had done two years ago, but he saw now there could be no rest for his ground-down command short of the broader Tennessee, another seventy miles to the south. Ac-cordingly, having begun his withdrawal across the Duck, he was all the more pleased by Forrest's early return, since it meant that the Wizard and his veteran troopers, lately conspicuous by their absence, would be there to hold off the Federals while the rest of the army went on with its dangerous task of crossing a major river in the presence of a foe not only superior in numbers, warmly clad, and amply fed, but also flushed with victory and clearly bent on completing the destruction begun three days ago at the gates of Nashville.

In taking over this rear-guard assignment — for which he had about 3000 cavalry whose mounts were still in condition for hard duty, plus 2000 infantry under Walthall, roughly a fourth of them bare-foot and all of them hungry, cold in their cotton tatters, and close to exhaustion from two days of battle and two of unrelieved retreat — Forrest combined his usual inventiveness with a highly practical applica-tion of the means at hand, however slight. Part of the problem was the weather, which changed next day from bad to worse. Alternate blasts of sleet and rain deepened the mud, stalled the supply train, and covered the roads and fields with a crust of ice that crunched and shattered under foot and made walking a torture for ill-shod men and horses. He solved the immobilized wagon dilemma by leaving half of them parked along the pike and using their teams to double those in the other half, which then proceeded. Because of the drawn-out Federal delay, first in clearing brim-full Rutherford Creek and then the more formidable Duck, four miles beyond, there was time for the doubled teams to haul the first relay far to the south and then return for the second before the pursuers bridged and crossed both streams. As for the infantry crippled for lack of shoes, Forrest solved that problem by commandeering empty wagons in which the barefoot troops could ride until they were called on to jump down and hobble back to their places in the firing line. "Not a man was brought in contact with him who did not feel strengthened and invigorated," one among them was to say of the general who thus converted shoeless cripples into horse-drawn infantry.

Not until the night of December 21, with their pontoons up and thrown at last, did the first Federals cross Duck River to begin next day at Warfield Station, three miles beyond Columbia, a week-long running fight that proceeded south across the frozen landscape in the earliest and coldest winter Tennesseans had known for years. Outflanked, Forrest fell back, skirmishing as he went, and at nightfall took up a new position at Lynnville, twelve miles down the line. Here he staged a surprise attack the following morning, using Walthall's men to block the pike while his troopers slashed at the Union flanks, then retired on the run before his pursuers recovered from the shock, bringing off a captured gun which he employed next day in a brisk Christmas Eve action on Richland Creek, eight miles north of Pulaski, where Buford suffered a leg wound to become the twenty-first Confederate brigade, division, or corps commander shot or captured in the course of the campaign. By then the main body, unmolested since Forrest took over the duty of guarding its rear, was well beyond the Alabama line, approaching the Tennessee River, and next day the head of the column pulled up on the near bank opposite Bainbridge, just below Muscle Shoals. It was Christmas, though scarcely a merry one, and a Sunday: five weeks, to the day, since Hood left Florence, four miles downstream, on the expedition that by now had cost him close to 20,000 veterans killed, wounded, or missing in and out of battle, including one lieutenant general, three major generals, and an even dozen brigadiers, together with five brigade commanders of lesser rank. Of these, moreover, only two — Lee and Buford — were alive, uncaptured, and had wounds that would permit an early return to the army that had set out for Middle Tennessee in such high spirits, five weeks back, with twice as many troops and guns as were now in its straggled ranks.

Forrest too was over the Alabama line by then, holding Wilson off while the gray main body bridged the river with the pontoons he had saved by doubling their teams. Gunboats, sent roundabout by Thomas from the Cumberland and the Ohio, tried their hand at shelling the rickety span, but were driven off by Stewart's artillery and Rear Admiral Samuel P. Lee's fear of getting stranded if he ventured within range of the white water at the foot of Muscle Shoals. Hood finished crossing on December 27; Forrest's cavalry followed, and Walthall's forlorn hope got over without further loss on the 28th, cutting the bridge loose from the northern bank. Thomas — whose own pontoons were still on the Duck, seventy miles away, and whose infantry had not cleared Pulaski — declared the pursuit at an end next day. Hood's army, he said, "had become a disheartened and disorganized rabble of half-naked and barefooted men, who sought every opportunity to fall out by the wayside and desert their cause to put an end to their sufferings. The rear guard, however, was undaunted and firm," he added, "and did its work bravely to the last."

Schofield was more generous in his estimate of the defeated army's fighting qualities, especially as he had observed them during the long-odds Battle of Nashville, where fewer than 25,000 graybacks held out for two days against better than 50,000 bluecoats massed for the most part of their flank. "I doubt if any soldiers in the world ever needed so much cumulative evidence to convince them they were beaten," he declared. This was not to say they weren't thoroughly convinced in the end. They were indeed, and they showed it through both stages of the long retreat: first, as one said, while "making tracks for the Tennessee River at a quickstep known to Confederate tactics as 'double distance on half rations,'" and then on the follow-up march beyond, after Hood decided his troops were no more in condition for a stand on the Tennessee than they had been when they crossed the Duck the week before. By way of reinforcing this assessment, Thomas would list in his report a total of 13,189 prisoners and 72 pieces of artillery captured on and off the field of battle in the course of the forty days between Hood's setting out, November 20, and his own calling of an end to the campaign, December 29. Moreover, weary as they were from their 120-mile trek over icy roads in the past two weeks, the butternut marchers themselves agreed that the better part of valor, at least for now, would be to find some place of refuge farther south, if any such existed. "Aint we in a hell of a fix?" one ragged Tennessean groaned as he picked himself up, slathered with mud from a fall on the slippery pike. "Aint we in a hell of a fix: a one-eyed President, a one-legged general, and a one-horse Confederacy!"

Their goal, they learned as they slogged west across North Alabama toward the Mississippi line, was Tupelo. There, just thirty months ago this week, Braxton Bragg had taken over from Beauregard after the retreat from Corinth, and there he had given them the name they made famous, the Army of Tennessee, first in Kentucky, then back again in Middle and East Tennessee and Georgia. Bragg's tenure had ended soon after Missionary Ridge, and so would Hood's after Nashville, a comparable rout; there was little doubt of that, either in or out of the army. "The citizens seemed to shrink and hide from us as we approached them," a soldier would recall, and the reaction of his comrades was shown in a song they sang as they trudged into Mississippi and the New Year. The tune was the banjo-twanging "Yellow Rose of Texas," but the words had been changed to match their regret, if not their scorn, for the quality of leadership that had cost them Pat Cleburne and so many others they had loved and followed down the years.

> *So now I'm marching southward,*
> *My heart is full of woe;*
> *I'm going back to Georgia*
> *To see my Uncle Joe.*
> *You may talk about your Beauregard*
> *And sing of General Lee,*
> *But the gallant Hood of Texas*
> *Played hell in Tennessee.*

✗ 5 ✗

Back at City Point after breaking off his intended western trip, Grant had the familiar hundred-gun victory salute fired twice in celebration of the Nashville triumph. "You have the congratulations of the public for the energy with which you are pushing Hood," he wired Thomas on December 22, adding: "If you succeed in destroying Hood's army, there will be but one army left to the so-called Confederacy capable of doing us harm. I will take care of that and try to draw the sting from it, so that in the spring we shall have easy sailing." He sounded happy. One week later, however, on learning that Hood's fugitives had crossed the Tennessee and Thomas had ordered his erstwhile pursuers into winter quarters to "recuperate for the spring campaign," Grant's petulance returned. "I have no idea of keeping idle troops in any place," he telegraphed Halleck, who passed the word to Thomas on the last day of the year: "General Grant does not intend that your army shall go into winter quarters. It must be ready for active operations in the field."

Grant's fear, throughout the two weeks leading up to the thunderous two-day conflict out in Tennessee, had been that Old Tom's balkiness would allow the rebels to prolong the war by scoring a central breakthrough all the way to the Ohio, thereby disrupting the combinations he had devised for their destruction. Yet this fear had no sooner been dispelled, along with the smoke from the mid-December battle, than another took its place; namely, that this same "sluggishness," as he called it during the two weeks following the clash at the gates of Nashville, would delay the over-all victory which now at last seemed practically within his grasp, not only because of the drubbing given Hood, whose survival hung in the balance until he crossed the Tennessee River, but also because of other successes registered elsewhere, at the same time, along and behind the butternut line stretching west from the Atlantic. A sizeable budget of good news reached City Point while Thomas was failing to overtake his defeated adversary, and every item in it only served to whet Grant's appetite for more. That had always been his way, but it was even more the case now that he saw the end he had worked so hard for in plain view, just up the road.

Chief among these simultaneous achievements was the occupation of Savannah, eleven days after Sherman's arrival before it at the end of his march from Atlanta. Having stormed and taken Fort McAllister on December 13, which enabled the waiting supply ships to steam up the Ogeechee, he proceeded with a leisurely investment — or near investment — of the city just over a dozen miles away. Within four days he had progressed so far with his preparations that he thought it only fair to give the defenders a chance to avoid bloodshed by surrendering. He was "prepared to grant liberal terms to the inhabitants and garrison," he said in a message sent across the lines; "but should I be forced to resort to assault, or to the slower and surer process of starvation, I shall then feel justified in resorting to the harshest measures, and shall make little effort to restrain my army, burning to avenge the national wrong which they attach to Savannah and other large cities which have been so prominent in dragging our country into civil war." The rebel commander replied in kind, declining to surrender, and in closing dealt in measured terms with Sherman's closing threat. "I have hitherto conducted the military operations intrusted to my direction in strict accordance with the rules of civilized warfare, and I should deeply regret the adoption of any course by you that may force me to deviate from them in the future. I have the honor to be, very respectively, your obedient servant, *W. J. Hardee*, Lieutenant General."

Hardee, with barely 15,000 regulars and militia — two thirds of them lodged in the city's defenses, the rest posted rearward across the Savannah River to cover his only escape route, still menaced by Foster near Honey Hill — had appealed to Richmond for reinforcements to help him resist the 60,000 newly arrived bluecoats closing in from the east and south. Davis conferred with Lee at Petersburg, then replied on December 17 — the day of Sherman's threat to unleash his burning veterans on Savannah when it fell — that none were available; he could only advise the Georgian to "provide for the safety of your communications and make the dispositions needful for the preservation of your army." This authorized the evacuation Beauregard had been urging from his headquarters in Charleston, a hundred miles up the coast. With a bridgeless river at his back and no pontoons on hand, that seemed about as difficult as staying to fight against six-to-one odds, but Old Reliable found the answer in the employment of some thirty 80-foot rice flats, lashed together endwise, then planked over to provide a three-section island-hopping span from the Georgia to the Carolina bank. It was finished too late for use on the night of December 19, as intended, so a circular was issued for the withdrawal to begin soon after dark next evening — by coincidence, the fourth anniversary of South Carolina's secession from the Union — preceded by daylong fire from all the guns, which would not only discourage enemy interference but would also reduce the amount of surplus ammunition to be destroyed, along with the unmovable heavy pieces, when the cannoneers fell back. Wagons and caissons would cross the river first, together with the light artillery, and the men themselves would follow, filing silently out of their trenches after moonset. "Though compelled to evacuate the city, there is no part of my military life to which I look back with so much satisfaction," Hardee was to say. And the fact was he had cause for pride. The operation went as planned from start to finish, despite some mixups and much sadness, especially for long-time members of the garrison, who thus were obliged to turn their backs on what had been their home for the past three years. "The constant tread of the troops and the rumblings of the artillery as they poured over those long floating bridges was a sad sound," one retreater would presently recall, "and by the glare of the large fires at the east of the bridge it seemed like an immense funeral procession stealing out of the city in the dead of night."

Sherman was not there for the formal occupation next morning, having gone up the coast to confer with Foster about bringing in more troops from Hilton Head to block the road to Charleston; the road over which, as it developed, Hardee marched to safety while the conference was in progress. When the Ohioan returned the following day, December 22 — chagrined if not abashed by the escape of 10,000 rebels he had thought were his for the taking — he found his army in possession of Savannah and quartermaster details busy tallying the spoils. These were considerable, including more than 200 heavy guns and something over 30,000 bales of cotton, negotiable on the world market at the highest prices ever known. Most of the guns had been spiked, but the rich haul of cotton was intact, not only because there had been no time or means to remove it, but also because, as Hardee explained to his superiors, it was "distributed throughout the city in cellars, garrets and warehouses, where it could not have been burnt without destroying the city." A U.S. Treasury agent was already on hand from Hilton Head, reckoning up the profit to the government, and when the red-haired commander bristled at him, as was his custom when he encountered money men, the agent turned his wrath aside with a suggestion that the general send a message, first by ship to Fort Monroe and then by wire to the White House, announcing the fall of Savannah as a Christmas present for Lincoln. "The President particularly enjoys such pleasantry," he pointed out. Sherman considered this a capital notion, and at once got off the following telegram, composed before the tally was complete.

> To his Excellency President Lincoln,
> Washington, D.C.
>
> I beg to present you, as a Christmas gift, the city of Savannah, with 150 heavy guns and plenty of ammunition; also about 25,000 bales of cotton.
>
> W. T. Sherman
Major General.

He was, as usual, in high spirits after a colorful exploit — and this, which reached its climax with the taking of Savannah and would afterwards find its anthem in the rollicksome "Marching Through Georgia," had been the most colorful of all. Partly because of that scare-head aspect, lurid in its reproduction in the memory of participants, as well as in the imagination of watchers on the home front, the march achieved a significance beyond its considerable military value, and though the risk had turned out slight (103 killed, 428 wounded, 278 captured or otherwise missing: barely more, in all, than one percent of the force involved) even Sherman was somewhat awed in retrospect. "Like a man who has walked a narrow plank," he wrote his wife, "I look back and wonder if I really did it." In effect, after seven months of grinding combat at close quarters, he and his bummers had broken out of the apparent stalemate, East and West, to inject a new spirit of exuberance into the war. You could see the feeling reflected in the northern papers brought to headquarters by the navy, first up the Ogeechee, then the Savannah. "Tecumseh the Great," editors called him now, who had formerly judged him insane, and there was a report of a bill introduced in Congress to promote him to lieutenant general so that he and Grant could divide control of the armies of the Union. His reaction to this was similar to his reaction four months ago, at the time of the Democratic convention in Chicago, when there was talk of nominating him for President. "Some fool seems to have used my name," he wrote Halleck from his position in front of besieged Atlanta. "If forced to choose between the penitentiary and the White House . . . I would say the penitentiary, thank you." So it was now in regard to this latest proposal to elevate him. "I will accept no commission that would tend to create a rivalry with Grant," he informed his senator brother. "I want him to hold what he has earned and got. I have all the rank I want." As if to emphasize this conviction, he presently re-marked to a prying inquirer, in a tone at once jocular and forthright: "Grant is a great general. I know him well. He stood by me when I was crazy and I stood by him when he was drunk. And now, sir, we stand by each other always."

In point of fact, the general-in-chief was standing by him now, even to the extent of deferring to his military judgment: and that, too, was part of the cause for his red-haired exuberance. He had just made Georgia howl. Now he was about to make the Carolinas shriek.

Originally — that is, in orders he found waiting for him when he reached the coast — Grant had intended for Sherman and his Westerners to proceed by water "with all dispatch" to Virginia, where they would help Meade and Butler "close out Lee." He was to es-tablish and fortify a base near Savannah, garrison it with all his cavalry and artillery, together with enough infantry to protect them and "so threaten the interior that the militia of the South will have to be kept at home," then get the rest aboard transports for a fast ride north to the Old Dominion. "Select yourself the officer to leave in command, but you I want in person," Grant told him, adding: "Unless you see objections to this plan which I cannot see, use every vessel going to you for the purpose of transportation."

Sherman did have objections, despite the compliment implied in this invitation to be in on the kill of the old gray fox at Petersburg, and was prompt to express them. He much preferred a march by land to a boatride up the coast for the reunion, he replied, partly because of the damage he could inflict en route and the effect he believed an extension of his trans-Georgia swath would have on the outcome of the war. Besides, there was a certain poetic justice here involved. "We can punish South Carolina as she deserves, and as thousands of people in Georgia hoped we would do. I do sincerely believe that the whole United States, North and South, would rejoice to have this army turned loose on South Carolina, to devastate that state in the manner we have done in Georgia." He was convinced moreover, he said in closing, that the overland approach "would have a direct and im-mediate bearing upon the campaign in Virginia," and he went into more detail about this in a letter to Halleck, invoking his support. "I attach more importance to these deep incursions into the enemy's country," he declared, "because this war differs from European wars in this par-ticular: We are not only fighting hostile armies, but a hostile people, and must make old and young, rich and poor, feel the hard hand of war, as well as their organized armies. I know that this recent movement of mine through Georgia has had a wonderful effect in this respect. Thousands who have been deceived by their lying newspapers to be-lieve that we were being whipped all the time now realize the truth, and have no appetite for a repetition of the same experience." In short, he told Old Brains, "I think the time has come when we should attempt the boldest moves, and my experience is that they are easier of execution than more timid ones.... Our campaign of the last month, as well as every step I take from this point northward, is as much a direct attack upon Lee's army as though we were operating within the sound of his artillery."

To his surprised delight, Grant readily agreed: so readily, indeed, that it turned out he had done so even before his friend's objections reached him. In a letter written from Washington on the same date as Sherman's own — December 18: he was about to return to City Point: Fort McAllister had fallen five days ago, and Savannah itself would be taken in three more — the general-in-chief sent his congratulations "on the successful termination of your campaign" from Atlanta to the Atlantic. "I never had a doubt of the result," he said, though he "would not have intrusted the expedition to any other living commander." Then he added a few sentences that made Sherman's ears prick up. "I did think the best thing to do was to bring the greater part of your army here, and wipe out Lee. [But] the turn affairs now seem to be taking has shaken me in that opinion. I doubt whether you may not accomplish more toward that result where you are than if brought here, especially as I am informed, since my arrival in the city, that it would take about two months to get you here with all the other calls there are for ocean transportation. I want to get your views about what ought to be done, and what can be done.... My own opinion is that Lee is averse to going out of Virginia, and if the cause of the South is lost he wants Richmond to be the last place surrendered. If he has such views, it may be well to indulge him until we get everything else in our hands.... I subscribe myself, more than ever, if possible, your friend."

This reached Sherman on Christmas Eve, three days after the occupation of Savannah, and lifted his spirits even higher. Here, in effect, was the go-ahead he had sought for himself and his bummers, whom he described as being "in splendid flesh and condition." Promptly that same evening he replied to Grant at City Point, expressing his pleasure at the change in orders; "for I feared that the transportation by sea would very much disturb the unity and morale of my army, now so perfect.... In about ten days I expect to be ready to sally forth again. I feel no doubt whatever as to our future plans. I have thought them over so long and well that they appear as clear as daylight."

Chief among those "other calls ... for ocean transportation" were the ones that had secured for the Butler-Porter expedition, whose mission was the reduction of Fort Fisher, the largest number of naval vessels ever assembled under the American flag. Packed with 6500 troops in two divisions, Butler's transports cleared Hampton Roads on December 13, and five days later joined Porter's fleet of 57 ironclads, frigates, and gunboats at Beaufort, North Carolina, ninety miles up the coast from their objective. Next morning, December 19, they arrived off Wilmington to find bad weather making up and the surf too rough for a landing. This obliged the transports to return to Beaufort for shelter, but the warships remained on station, riding out the storm while the admiral studied the rebel stronghold through his telescope. Unlike prewar forts, which mostly were of masonry construction, this one had walls of sand, piled nine feet high and twenty-five thick, designed to withstand by absorption the fire of the heaviest guns afloat, and was laid out with two faces, one looking seaward, close to 2000 yards long, and the other about one third that length, looking northward up the narrow sand peninsula, formerly called Federal Point but renamed Confederate Point by the secessionists when they began work on the place in 1861. Defended by a total of 47 guns and mortars, including a battery posted atop a sixty-foot mound thrown up at the south end of the seaward face to provide for delivering plunging fire if the enemy ventured close, the fort seemed all but impossible to reduce by regular methods; nor could the ships run past it, as had been done at New Orleans and Mobile, since that would merely cram them into Cape Fear River, sitting ducks for the rebel cannoneers, who would only have to reverse their guns to blow the intruders out of the water. Porter however had in mind a highly irregular method in which by now he placed great faith. This was the ingenious Butler's powder ship, brought along in tow from Norfolk and primed at Beaufort for the cataclysmic explosion the squint-eyed general claimed would abolish Fort Fisher between two ticks of his watch.

Porter was inclined to agree, though less emphatically, having made a close inspection of the floating bomb. She was, or had been, the U.S.S. *Louisiana*, an overaged iron gunboat of close to three hundred tons, stripped of her battery and part of her deckhouse to lighten her draft and make her resemble a blockade runner. In a canvas-roofed framework built amidships, as well as in her bunkers and on her berth deck — all above the water line, for maximum shock effect — 215 tons of powder had been stored and fuzed with three clockwork devices, regulated to fire simultaneously an hour and a half after they were activated. The plan was for a skeleton crew to run the vessel in close to shore, anchor her as near as her eight-foot draft would allow to the seaward face of the fort on the beach, set the timing mechanisms, then pull hard away in a boat to an escort steamer that would take them well offshore to await the explosion; after which the fleet, poised twelve miles out for safety from the blast, would close in and subject what was left of the place to a heavy-caliber pounding, while troops were being landed two miles up the peninsula to close in from the north. Some said the result of setting off that much powder — which, after all, was more than fifty times the amount used near Petersburg, five months ago, to create the still-yawning Crater — would be the utter destruction of everything on or adjoining Federal or Confederate Point. Others — mainly demolition "experts," who as usual were skeptical of anything they themselves had not conceived — discounted such predictions, maintaining that the shock would probably be no worse than mild. "I take a mean between the two," Porter declared judiciously, "and think the effect of the explosion will be simply very severe, stunning men at a distance of three or four hundred yards, demoralizing them completely, and making them unable to stand for any length of time a fire from the ship. I think that the concussion will tumble magazines that are built on framework, and that the famous Mound will be among the things that were, and the guns buried beneath the ruins. I think that houses in Wilmington [eighteen miles away] will tumble to the ground and much demoralize the people, and I think if the rebels fight after the explosion they have more in them than I gave them credit for."

In the fort meantime, during what turned out to be a three-day blow, the garrison prepared to resist the attack it had known was coming ever since the huge assembly of Union warships bulged over the curve of the eastern horizon. Determined to hold ajar what he termed "the last gateway between the Confederate States and the outside world," Fort Fisher's commander, Colonel William Lamb, had at first had only just over 500 men for its defense, half the regular complement having been sent to oppose Sherman down in Georgia. Blockade runners kept coming and going all this time, however, under cover of the storm, and on December 21 — when four of the swift vessels made outward runs after nightfall, all successful in slipping through the cordon of blockaders off the coast — some 400 North Carolina militia showed up, followed two days later by 450 Junior Reserves, sixteen to eighteen years of age. This total of 1371 effectives, most of them green and a third of them boys, were all Lamb would have until the arrival of Hoke's division, which had begun leaving Richmond two days ago, detached by Lee in the emergency, but was delayed by its necessarily roundabout rail route through Danville, Greensboro, and Raleigh.

The gale subsided on the day the Junior Reserves marched in, December 23, and though the wind remained brisk all afternoon, the night that followed was clear and cold. Despite the heightened visibility, which greatly lengthened the odds against blockade runners, the fast steamer *Little Hattie*, completing her second run that month, made it in through the mouth of the Cape Fear River, shortly before midnight, and soon was tied up at the dock in Wilmington, unloading the valuable war goods she had exchanged in Nassau a week ago for her outbound cargo of cotton.

Although no one aboard knew it, she had overtaken and passed the *Louisiana* coming in, and the signals flashed from Fort Fisher in response to those from the *Hattie* were of great help to the skeleton crew on the powder ship, groping its way through the darkness toward the beach. Encouraged by improvement in the weather, Porter had ordered the doomed vessel in at 11 o'clock that night, and had also sent word to Beaufort for the transports to return at once for the landing next day. Lightless and silent, the *Louisiana* dropped anchor 250 yards offshore, just north of the fort, and her skipper, Commander A. C. Rhind — told by the admiral, "You may lose your life in this adventure, but the risk is worth the running.... The names of those connected with the expedition will be famous for all time to come" — started all three clockwork fuzes ticking at precisely twelve minutes short of midnight. Finally, before abandoning ship, he set fire to half a cord of pine knots piled in the after cabin on instructions from Porter, who had little faith in mechanical devices; after which Rhind and his handful of volunteers rowed in a small boat to the escort steamer waiting nearby to take them (hopefully) out of range of the explosion, due by then within about an hour. Now there was nothing left to do but wait.

Twelve miles out, crews of the nearly sixty warships watched and waited too, training all available glasses on the starlit stretch of beach in front of the rebel earthwork. Started at 11.48, the ticking fuzes should do their job at 1.18 in what by now was the morning of Christmas Eve; or so the watchers thought, until the critical moment came and went and there was no eruption. By then, however, the pinpoint of light from Rhind's fire in the after cabin had grown to a flickering glow, and Porter felt certain all 215 tons of powder would go as soon as the flames reached the nearest keg. He was right, of course, though the wait was hard. 1.30: 1.35: 1.40: then it came — a huge instantaneous bloom of light, so quickly smothered in dust and smoke you could almost doubt you'd seen it. Just under one minute later the sound arrived; a low, heavy boom, a *New York Times* reporter was to say, "not unlike that produced by the discharge of a 100-pounder." Moreover, there seemed to be no accompanying shock wave, only the one deep cough or rumble, and a colleague aboard the press boat saw a gigantic cloud of thick black smoke appear on the landward horizon, sharply defined against the stars and the clear sky. "As it rose rapidly in the air, and came swiftly toward us on the wings of the wind," he later wrote, "[it] presented a most remarkable appearance, assuming the shape of a monstrous waterspout, its tapering base seemingly resting on the sea. In a very few minutes it passed us, filling the atmosphere with its sulphurous odor, as if a spirit from the infernal regions had swept by us."

If this was anticlimactic — which in fact was to put the measure of Porter's disappointment rather mildly — what followed, over the course of the next two days, was even more so. Subsequent testimony would show that, while there were those who claimed to have felt the

shock as far away as Beaufort, the monster explosion had done the fort
no damage whatever, producing no more than a gentle rocking motion,
as if the earth had twitched briefly in its sleep. A sentinel on duty at the
time made a guess to the man who relieved him that one of the Yankee
ships offshore had blown her boiler. Many in the garrison, veterans and
greenhorns alike, said later that they had not been awakened by the
blast, though this was denied by one of the boy soldiers, captured next
day in an outlying battery. "It was terrible," he said. "It woke up nearly
everybody in the fort." Daylight showed no remaining vestige of the
Louisiana, but Fort Fisher was unchanged, its flag rippling untattered
in the breeze. Only in one respect did Butler's experiment work, even
approximately, and that was in the disguise he had contrived for the
vanished powder vessel. Lamb recorded in his diary that morning: "A
blockader got aground near the fort, set fire to herself, and blew up."

Porter spent the morning absorbing the shock of failure, then
steamed in at noon to begin the heaviest naval bombardment of the war
to date. Capable of firing 115 shells a minute, his 627 guns heaved an
estimated 10,000 heavy-caliber rounds at Fort Fisher in the course of the
next five hours, to which the fort replied with 622, though neither
seriously impaired the fighting efficiency of the other. Ashore, two guns
were dismounted, one man killed, 22 injured, and most of the living
quarters flattened, while the fleet lost 83 dead and wounded, more than
half of them mangled by the explosion of five new hundred-pounder
Parrotts on five of the sloops and frigates. Near sunset, Butler finally
showed up with a few transports. The rest would soon be along, he
said: much to Porter's disgust, for the day by then was too far gone for
a landing. Disgruntled, the admiral signaled a cease fire.

As the ships withdrew, guns cooling, the fort boomed out a single
defiant shot, the last. "Our Heavenly Father has protected my garrison
this day," Lamb wrote in his diary that night, "and I feel that He will
sustain us in defending our homes from the invader."

By 10.30 next morning — Christmas Day and a Sunday — the
fleet was back on station, lobbing still more thousands of outsized projectiles into the sand fort. Three hours later, three miles up the way,
just over 2000 soldiers were put ashore under Major General Godfrey
Weitzel, second in command to Butler, who observed the landing from
his flagship, a sea-going tug which he kept steaming back and forth in
front of the beach while the troops were moving southward down it,
capturing a one-gun outwork when they got within a mile of Fort
Fisher's landward face. Porter maintained a methodical fire — mainly
to make the defenders keep their heads down, since he believed he had
done all necessary damage to their works the day before. Reports from
Weitzel, however, showed that this was far from true. Approaching the
fort, his men received volleys of canister full in their faces, and it soon
developed that the final hundred yards of ground was planted thickly

with torpedoes wired to detonator switches which rebel lookouts could throw whenever they judged an explosion would be most effective. Moreover, prisoners taken on the approach march bragged that Hoke's division, 6000 strong, was expected to arrive at any minute on the road from Wilmington, hard in the Federal rear. Butler weighed the evidence, along with signs that the rising wind would soon make it impossible for boats to return through the booming surf, and promptly ordered a withdrawal by all ashore. "In view of the threatening aspect of the weather," he signaled Porter when two thirds of Weitzel's men had been reloaded — the other third, some 700 wet and cold unfortunates for whom this holy day was anything but merry, were stranded when the breakers grew too rough for taking them off — "I caused the troops with their prisoners to re-embark." Seeing, as he said, "nothing further that can be done by the land forces," he announced: "I shall therefore sail for Hampton Roads as soon as the transport fleet can be got in order."

Fairly beside himself with rage at this unceremonious abandonment of the supposedly joint effort, Porter kept up a nightlong interdictory fire to protect "those poor devils of soldiers," whose rifles he could hear popping on the beach. Next afternoon, when the wind changed direction, he managed to get them off, thereby limiting the army's loss to one man drowned and 15 wounded — a total clearly indicative of something less than an all-out try for the fort's reduction. Butler by then was on his way to Norfolk, however, and the admiral had no choice except to retire as well, though only as far as Beaufort, withdrawing his ships a few at a time, that night and the following morning, so that Fort Fisher's defenders would not be able to claim a mass repulse.

Nevertheless: "This morning, December 27, the foiled and frightened enemy left our shore," Lamb wired Wilmington, where Hoke's veterans were at last unloading from their long train ride. The garrison had in fact had a harder time than Porter knew, losing 70 men in the second day's bombardment, which, though less intense, had been far more accurate than the first. "Never since the foundation of the world was there such a fire," a Confederate lieutenant testified. "The whole interior of the fort . . . was one 11-inch shell bursting. You can now inspect the works and walk on nothing but iron." Lamb began repairing the damage without delay, knowing only too well that the Yankees would soon return, perhaps next time with an army commander willing to press the issue beyond pistol range of the sand walls.

That was just what Porter had in mind now that his fleet was reassembled at Beaufort, replenishing its stores and ammunition. Moreover, he could see at least one good proceeding from the abortive Yuletide expedition. "If this temporary failure succeeds in sending General Butler into private life, it is not to be regretted," he wrote

Welles, "for it cost only a certain amount of shells, which I expend in a month's target practice anyhow."

Grant was of the same opinion in regard to the need for a change when the effort against Fort Fisher was renewed, as he certainly intended it to be. "The Wilmington expedition has proven a gross and culpable failure," he informed Lincoln on December 28, adding: "Who is to blame I hope will be known." A wire to Porter, two days later, indicated that he had already decided on a cure. "Please hold on where you are for a few days," he requested, "and I will endeavor to be back again with an increased force and without the former commander."

His concern was based on a number of developments. First, because it had been determined that Sherman would march north through the Carolinas, Grant saw Wilmington as an ideal place of refuge, easily provisioned and protected by the navy, in case the rebels somehow managed to gang up on his red-haired friend. Second, he believed that a full report on the recent fiasco would provide him with excellent grounds for getting rid of Ben Butler, whose political heft was unlikely to stand him in nearly as good stead with the Administration now that the election had been won. Third — and no one who knew Grant would think it least — he was no more inclined than ever to accept a setback; especially now, when so many welcome reports were clicking off the wire at City Point from all directions, indicating that the end of the struggle was by no means as far off as it had seemed a short while back.

One of the most welcome of these came from George Stoneman, exchanged since his late-July capture down in Georgia and recently given command of all the cavalry in Northeast Tennessee. Anxious to retrieve his reputation, he set out from Knoxville on December 10 with 5500 troopers in an attempt to reach and wreck the salt and lead mines in Southwest Virginia, so long the object of raids that had come to nothing up to now. Beyond Kingsport, three days later, he brushed aside the remnant of Morgan's once-terrible men, still grieved by the loss of their leader three months before, and pressed on through Bristol, across the state line to Abingdon, where he drove off a small force of graybacks posted in observation by Breckinridge, whose main body, down to a strength of about 1200, was at Saltville, less than twenty miles ahead. Stoneman bypassed him for a lunge at Marion, twelve miles up the Virginia & Tennessee Railroad, obliging Breckinridge to back-pedal in an effort to save the vital lead works there and at Wytheville. This he did, by means of a fast march and a daylong skirmish on December 18; but while the fighting was in progress Stoneman sent half his horsemen back to undefended Saltville, with instructions to get started on the wreckage that was the true purpose of the expedition. Reuniting his raiders there next day, after giving Breckinridge the slip, he spent another two days completing the destruction of the salt works, then withdrew on December 21. Back in Knoxville by the end of the year, he could report complete success. Salt had been scarce in the Old Dominion for two years. Now it would be practically nonexistent, leaving the suppliers of Lee's army with no means of preserving what little meat they could lay hands on for shipment by rail or wagon to the hungry men in the trenches outside Petersburg and Richmond.

Sheridan too had not been idle during this period of stepped-up Federal activity, coincident with Thomas's pursuit of Hood and Sherman's occupation of Savannah. While the greater part of his army continued its impoverishment of the people in the Shenandoah region by the destruction of their property and goods — a scourging process he defined as "letting them know there is a God in Israel" — he launched a two-pronged strike, by three divisions of cavalry, at military targets beyond the rim of his immediate depredations. Torbert, with 5500 horsemen in two divisions, would aim for Gordonsville and the Virginia Central, east of the Blue Ridge, while Custer diverted attention from this main effort by taking his 2500-man division south up the Valley Pike for a raid on Staunton, which if successful could be continued to Lynchburg and the Orange & Alexandria. Both left their camps around Winchester on December 19, Torbert riding through Chester Gap next morning to cross the Rapidan two days later at Liberty Mills. Apparently Custer had decoyed Early's troopers westward from their position near Rockfish Gap, just east of Staunton, for there was no sign of them as the blue column approached Gordonsville after dark. There was, however, a barricade thrown up by local defenders to block a narrow pass within three miles of town, and Torbert chose to wait for daylight, December 23, before deciding whether to storm or outflank it. Alas, he then found it would be unwise to attempt either. Warned of his approach, Lee had detached a pair of veteran brigades from Longstreet, north of the James, and hurried them by rail to Gordonsville the night before. "After becoming fully satisfied of the presence of infantry," Torbert afterwards reported, "I concluded it was useless to make a further attempt to break the Central Railroad." Instead, he withdrew and made a roundabout return march, through Madison Courthouse and Warrenton, to Winchester on December 28.

Custer by then had been back five days, having done only too good a job of attracting Early's attention. In camp the second night, nine miles from Harrisonburg, he was attacked before reveille, December 21, by Rosser's cavalry division, which Early had sent to intercept him a day's march short of Staunton. Driven headlong, Custer kept going northward down the pike, abandoning the raid, and returned to his starting point next day. Between them, he and Torbert had lost about 150 killed or wounded or captured, exclusive of some 230 of Custer's men severely frostbitten during their fast rides out and back. He would have stayed and fought, he informed Sheridan — he would never be flat whipped till Little Big Horn, twelve years later — except for a shortage of rations and "my unprepared state to take charge of a large body of wounded, particularly under the inclement state of the weather. In addition," he said, straight-faced, "I was convinced that if it was decided to return, the sooner my return was accomplished the better it would be for my command."

Grant was not inclined to censure anyone involved: least of all Sheridan, who had exercised his aggressive proclivities in weather most generals would have considered fit for nothing but sitting around campfires, toasting their toes and swapping yarns. Moreover, hard as the two-pronged raid had been on Union horseflesh, not to mention the blue riders' frost-nipped hands and feet and noses — 258 of Torbert's mounts had broken down completely in the course of his ten-day outing — it had no doubt been even harder on the scantly clad Confederates and their crowbait nags, which would be that much worse off when spring unfroze the roads and northern troopers came pounding down them, rapid-fire carbines at the ready. That too was a gain, perhaps comparable in its future effect to Stoneman's descent on Saltville, and the two together fit nicely into the year-end victory pattern whose larger pieces were supplied by Thomas and Sherman, in Tennessee and Georgia, as well as by Pleasonton and Curtis out in the Transmississippi, where the last of Price's fugitive survivors came limping into Laynesport this week, in time for a far-from-Merry Christmas.

Now that all these pieces were coming together into a pattern, West and East, even those who had cried out loudest against Grant as "a bull-headed Suvarov" — a commander who relied on strength, and strength alone, to make up for his lack of military talent — could see the effects of the plan he had devised nine months ago, before launching the synchronized offensive that had re-split the South and was now about to go to work on the sundered halves.

★   ★   ★

With mounting excitement, though not without occasional stretches of doubt and fret at the lack of progress in front or back of Richmond, Atlanta, and Nashville, Lincoln had watched the pattern emerge with increasing clarity, until he saw at last in these year-end triumphs the fruits of the hands-off policy he had followed in all but the times of greatest strain. Sherman's wire — "I beg to present you, as a Christmas gift, the city of Savannah" — reached Washington on Christmas Eve, and the President released it for publication Christmas morning, pleased to share this gift with the whole country. Next day, when John Logan called at the White House, back from Louisville and on his way down the coast to resume command of his XV Corps, Lincoln gave him a letter for delivery to Sherman, expressing his thanks for the timely gift and restating his intention not to interfere with the actions or decisions of commanders in the field.

"When you were about leaving Atlanta for the Atlantic coast, I was anxious, if not fearful," he admitted, "but feeling that you were the better judge, and remembering that 'nothing risked, nothing gained,' I did not interfere. Now, the undertaking being a success, the honor is all yours; for I believe none of us went further than to acquiesce. And taking the work of General Thomas into the count, as it should be taken, it is indeed a great success. Not only does it afford the obvious and immediate military advantage, but in showing to the world that your army could be divided, putting the stronger part to an important new service, and yet leaving enough to vanquish the old opposing force of the whole — Hood's army — it brings those who sat in darkness to see a great light. But what next? I suppose it will be safer if I leave General Grant and yourself to decide."

Other duties, more clerkly in nature, had continued to require his attention as Commander in Chief throughout this final month of the year. One was the approval of a general order, December 2, removing Rosecrans from command of the Department of the Missouri and replacing him with Grenville Dodge, who had recovered by then from the head wound he had suffered near Atlanta in mid-August. Old Rosy had enjoyed no more success than his predecessors had done in reconciling the various "loyal" factions in that guerilla-torn region, and now he was gone from the war for good. Another departure, under happier circumstances, was made by Farragut, who left Mobile Bay aboard the *Hartford* about that same time, and dropped anchor December 13 in the Brooklyn Navy Yard. Like his flagship, soon to go into dry dock, the old man was in need of repairs, having declined command of the Fort Fisher expedition on a plea of failing health. "My flag [was] hauled down at sunset," he informed Welles a week later. As it turned out, he and the *Hartford* ended their war service together, though there was no end to the honors that came his way. Two days later, on December 22, Congress passed a bill creating the rank of vice admiral, and Lincoln promptly conferred it on the Tennessee-born sailor, who thus became the nation's first to hold that rank, just as he had been its first rear admiral. To crown his good with creature comforts, a group of New York merchants got up and presented to him, on the last day of the year, a gift of $50,000 in government bonds. "The citizens of New York can offer no tribute equal to your claims on their gratitude and affection," an accompanying letter read. "Their earnest desire is to receive you as one of their number, and to be permitted, as fellow citizens, to share in the renown you will bring to the Metropolitan City."

Two other events of a more or less military nature, widely separated in space but provoking simultaneous reactions, engaged the attention of the public and the President at this time. One was a late-

November attempt by a group of eight Confederate agents, operating out of Canada, to terrorize New York City by setting fire to a score of hotels with four-ounce bottles of Greek Fire, similar to those used at St Albans the month before. In the early evening of November 25, nineteen fires were started within a single hour, but they burned with nothing like the anticipated fury, apparently because the supposedly sympathetic local chemist had concocted a weak mixture, either to lengthen his profit or, as one agent later said, to "put up a job on us after it was found that we could not be dissuaded from our purpose." In any case, firemen doused the flames rather easily, except at Barnum's Museum, a target of opportunity, where bales of hay for the animals blazed spectacularly for a time. All the arsonists escaped save one, who was picked up afterwards in Michigan, trying to make it back to Toronto, and returned to Fort Lafayette for execution in the spring. Though the damage was minor, as it turned out, the possibilities were frightening enough. Federal authorities could see in the conspiracy a forecast of what might be expected in the months ahead, when the rebels grew still more desperate over increasing signs that their war could not be won on the field of battle.

The other semi-military event occurred four days later in the Colorado Territory, 1500 miles away. Indians throughout much of the West had been on the rampage for the past three years, seeing in the white man's preoccupation with his tribal war back East an opportunity for the red man to return to his old free life, roving the plains and prairies, and perhaps exact, as he did so, a measure of bloody satisfaction for the loss of his land in exchange for promises no sooner made than broken. When John Pope took over in Minnesota two years ago, hard on the heels of his Bull Run defeat, he put down one such uprising by the Santee Sioux, in which more than 400 soldiers and settlers had been killed, and had the survivors arraigned before a drumhead court that sentenced 303 of them to die for murder, rape, and arson. Reviewing the sentences, despite a warning from the governor that the people of Minnesota would take "private revenge" if there was any interference on his part, Lincoln cut the list to 38 of "the more guilty and influential of the culprits." Hanged at Mankato on the day after Christmas, 1862, wearing paint and feathers and singing their death song with the ropes about their necks, these 38 still comprised the largest mass execution the country had ever staged. Now two years later, farther west in Colorado, there was another — a good deal less formal, lacking even a scaffold, let alone a trial, but larger and far bloodier — in which the President had no chance to interfere, since it was over before he had any way of knowing it was in progress.

Colonel John M. Chivington, a former Methodist preacher and a veteran of the New Mexico campaign, rode out of Denver in mid-November with 600 Colorado Volunteers, raised for the sole purpose, as he said, of killing Indians "whenever and wherever found." The pickings were rather slim until he reached Fort Lyon, sixty miles from the Kansas border, and learned that 600 Cheyennes and Arapahoes were camped on Sand Creek, forty miles northeast. They had gathered there the month before, after a parley with the governor, and had been promised security by the fort commander on their word, truthful or not, that they had taken no part in recent depredations elsewhere in the territory. Chivington did not believe them, but it would not have mattered if he had. "I have come to kill Indians," he announced on arrival, "and believe it is right and honorable to use any means under God's heaven to kill Indians." Asked if this included women, he replied that it did. And children? "Nits make lice," he said.

He left Fort Lyon early the following evening, November 28, reinforced by a hundred troopers from the garrison, on a wintry all-night ride that brought the 700-man column and its four mountain howitzers within reach of the objective before dawn. Two thirds of them squaws and children — most of the braves of fighting age were off hunting buffalo, several miles to the east — the Indians lay sleeping in their lodges, pitched in a bend of the creek at their back. They knew nothing of the attack until it burst upon them, aimed first at the herd of ponies to make certain there would be no horseback escape in the confusion soon to follow. It did follow, and the slaughter was indiscriminate. The soldiers closed in from three sides of the camp, pressing toward the center where the terrified people gathered under a large American flag that flew from the lodgepole of a Cheyenne chief, Black Kettle, who had received it earlier that year, as a token of friendship and protection, from the Commissioner of Indian Affairs. He displayed it now, along with a white flag raised amid the smoke of the attack. Both were ignored. "It may perhaps be unnecessary for me to state that I captured no prisoners," Chivington would report. He claimed between four and five hundred killed, all warriors; but that was exaggeration. A body count showed 28 men dead, including three chiefs, and 105 women and children. The attackers lost 9 killed and 38 wounded, most of them hit in the crossfire. By way of retaliation, or perhaps out of sheer exuberance, the soldiers moved among the dead and dying with their knives, lifting scalps and removing private parts to display as trophies of the raid. Then they pulled out. Behind them, the surviving Indians scattered on the plains, some to die of their wounds and exposure, others to spend what remained of their lives killing white men.

This too — the Sand Creek Massacre — was part of America's Civil War, and as such, like so much else involved, would have its repercussions down the years. For one thing, Chivington's coup discredited every Cheyenne or Arapahoe chief (and, for that matter, every Sioux or Kiowa or Comanche) who had spoken for peace with the white man: including Black Kettle, who, in addition to the bright-striped flag, had been given a medal by Lincoln himself for his efforts in that direction. Moreover, when the buffalo-hunting braves returned and saw the mutilations practiced by the soldiers on their people — fathers and sons, mothers and daughters, wives and sisters — they swore to serve their enemy in the same fashion when the tables were turned, as they soon would be, in the wake of a hundred skirmishes and ambuscades. Nor was that the only emulation. There were those in and out of the region who approved of Chivington's tactics as the best, if not indeed the only, solution to the problem of clearing the way for the settlers and the railroads: Sheridan, for example, who took them as a guide, some four years later, in pursuing a policy summed up in the dictum: "The only good Indian is a dead Indian."

News of these and other late-November developments found Lincoln hard at work on the year-end message his secretary would deliver at a joint meeting of the House and Senate on December 6, the day after Congress began its second session. Otherwise, much of the month that followed his reëlection — the first ever won by a free-state President — was spent in putting his political house in order. In addition to paying off, as best he could with the limited number of posts at his disposal, the debts he had contracted in the course of the campaign, this meant a clearing up of administrative business that had hung fire while the outcome was in doubt, including the retirement and replacement of a long-time cabinet member, as well as the appointment of a new Chief Justice.

The cabinet member was Attorney General Edward Bates, a septuagenarian old-line Democrat of a type still fairly common in Washington, but getting rarer year by year as the new breed of office-holders settled in. For some time now the Missourian had been feeling out of step with the society around him, out of place among his radical cohorts, and out of touch with the leader who had summoned him here, four years ago, to play a role he found increasingly distasteful. Decrying the "pestilent doctrines" of the ultras, right and left, and complaining in a letter to a friend of "how, in times like these, the minds of men are made dizzy and their imaginations are wrought up to a frenzy by the whirl of events," Bates believed he saw the cause of the disruption: "When the public cauldron is heated into violent ebullition, it is sure to throw up from the bottom some of its dirtiest dregs, which, but for the heat and agitation, would have lain embedded in congenial filth in the lowest stratum of society. But once boiled up to the top they expand into foam and froth, [and] dance frantically before the gaping crowd, often concealing for a time the whole surface of the agitated mass." He was disillusioned, he was disillusioned and bitter; he was, in short, a casualty of this war. He had to go, and on December 1, the election safely over, he went. Lincoln found a replacement in another Border State lawyer-politician, James Speed of Kentucky. Now only

Seward and Welles remained of the original cabinet slate drawn up in Springfield.

Another source of disappointment for Bates, now on his way home to Missouri, was Lincoln's rejection of his application to succeed Roger Taney as Chief Justice, and it was no great consolation that others with the same ambition —Montgomery Blair and Edwin Stanton, for two— were similarly passed over in favor of still a fourth one-time cabinet member: Salmon Chase. The eighty-seven-year-old Taney — appointed as John Marshall's successor by Andrew Jackson in 1836, nine Presidents ago — died in mid-October, following a long illness. Hated as he was by abolitionists for his Dred Scott decision, and scorned by most liberals for several others since, when he fell sick and seemed about to pass from the scene ahead of James Buchanan, Ben Wade prayed hard that he would live long enough for Lincoln to name his successor. As a result, the Marylander not only survived Buchanan's term, he seemed likely to outlast Lincoln's. "Damned if I didn't overdo it," Wade exclaimed. Then in October, perhaps in answer to supplementary prayers sent up on the eve of what might be a victory for McClellan, the old man died. Chase was the party favorite for the vacant seat at the head of the Court, his views being sound on such issues as emancipation, summary arrests, and a number of controversial financial measures he had adopted as Treasury chief; but Lincoln took his time about naming a replacement. The election was less than four weeks off, and delay ensured Chase's continued fervent support — as well as Blair's. Moreover, here was one last chance to watch the Ohioan squirm, a prospect Lincoln had always enjoyed as retribution for unsuccessful backstairs politics. "I know meaner things about Mr Chase than any of these men can tell me," he remarked after talking to callers who objected to the appointment on personal grounds. One day his secretary brought in a letter from Chase. "What is it about?" Lincoln asked, having no time just then to read it. "Simply a kind and friendly letter," Nicolay replied. Lincoln smiled and made a brief gesture of dismissal, saying: "File it with his other recommendations." All the same, and with the uncertain hope (in vain, as it turned out) that this would cure at last the gnawing of the presidential grub in Chase's bosom, he sent to the Senate on December 6, four weeks after election, his nomination of "Salmon P. Chase of Ohio, to be Chief Justice of the Supreme Court of the United States vice Roger B. Taney, deceased." He wrote it out in his own hand, signing his name in full, as he only did for the most important documents, and the Senate confirmed the appointment promptly, without discussion or previous reference to committee.

On that same day, the President's fourth December message was read to the assembled Congress. Primarily a report on foreign relations and the national welfare, about which it went into considerable diplomatic and financial details furnished by Seward and Fessenden, the text made little mention of the war being fought in the field, except to state that "our arms have steadily advanced." But in it Lincoln spoke beyond the heads of his immediate listeners — albeit through the voice of Nicolay, who delivered it for him at the joint session — to the people of the South, much as he had done at his inauguration, just under four years ago, when he addressed them as "my dissatisfied countrymen." Now he had reason to believe that their dissatisfaction extended in quite a different direction, and he bore down on that, first by demonstrating statistically the emptiness of all hope for a Federal collapse or let-up. Pointing to the heavy vote in the recent election, state by northern state, as proof "that we have more men now than we had when the war began; that we are not exhausted, nor in process of exhaustion; that we are gaining strength, and may, if need be, maintain the contest indefinitely," he declared flatly that the national resources, in materials as in manpower, "are unexhausted, and, as we believe, inexhaustible." So, too, was the resolution of the northern people "unchanged, and, as we believe, unchangeable," to an extent that altogether ruled out a negotiated settlement. Previously he had avoided public reference to Jefferson Davis, making it his policy to pretend that the Mississippian was invisible at best. Now this changed. He spoke openly of his adversary, though still not by name, referring to him rather as "the insurgent leader," and pronounced him unapproachable except on his own inadmissable terms. "He would accept nothing short of severance of the Union," Lincoln pointed out: "precisely what we will not and cannot give. His declarations to this effect are explicit and oft repeated. He does not attempt to deceive us. He affords us no excuse to deceive ourselves. . . . Between him and us the issue is distinct, simple, and inflexible. It is an issue which can only be tried by war, and decided by victory. If we yield, we are beaten; if the Southern people fail him, he is beaten. Either way, it would be the victory and defeat following war." This did not mean, however, that those who followed Davis could not accept what he rejected. "Some of them, we know, already desire peace and reunion," Lincoln said. "The number of such may increase. They can, at any moment, have peace simply by laying down their arms and submitting to the national authority under the Constitution. After so much, the government could not, if it would, maintain war against them."

He spoke in this connection of "pardons and remissions of forfeiture," these being things within his right to grant, but he added frankly that there was much else "beyond the Executive power to adjust," including "the admission of members into Congress, and whatever might require the appropriation of money." Nor did he sugar his offer, or advice, with any concession on other matters: least of all on the slavery issue. Not only would the Emancipation Proclamation stand, he also urged in the course of his message the adoption of a proposed amendment to the Constitution abolishing slavery throughout the United States. It had nearly passed in the last session, and would surely pass in the next, whose Republican majority had been increased by last month's election; "And as it is to so go, at all events, may we not agree that the sooner the better?" Above all, he wanted to speak clearly, both to his friends and to his present foes, and he did so in a final one-sentence paragraph addressed to those beyond the wide-flung line of battle: "In stating a single condition of peace, I mean simply to say that the war will cease on the part of the government whenever it shall have ceased on the part of those who began it."

All this he said, or Nicolay said for him, on December 6. The next ten days were crowded with good news: first from Georgia, where Sherman reached the coast at last, so little worn by his long march that he scarcely paused before he stormed Fort McAllister to make contact with the navy waiting off the mouth of the Ogeechee: then from Middle Tennessee, where Thomas crushed Hood's left, in front of Nashville, and flung him into full retreat with the loss of more than fifty guns. Lincoln responded by tightening the screws. In late November the War Department had done its part by lowering the minimum standard height for recruits to "five feet, instead of five feet three as heretofore." Now the Commander in Chief followed through, December 19 — Sherman by then had closed in on Savannah, which Hardee would evacuate next day — by issuing another of his by now familiar calls for "300,000 more," this time presumably including men who were not much taller than the Springfields they would shoulder. Privately, moreover, Stanton assured Grant that still another 200,000 troops would be called up in March if those netted by the current proclamation did not suffice to "close out Lee."

Success, as usual, fostered impatience and evoked a sense of urgency: especially in Lincoln, who had read with pleasure a message Grant sent Sherman after the fall of Atlanta, just under four months ago: "We want to keep the enemy pressed to the end of the war. If we give him no peace whilst the war lasts, the end cannot be distant." Sherman then had marched to the sea, eastward across the Confederate heartland, and after taking Savannah, bloodlessly though at the cost of having its garrison escape, obtained approval for a follow-up march north through the Carolinas. He was preparing for it now. "I do not think I can employ better strategy than I have hitherto done," he wrote Halleck on the last day of the year: "namely, make a good ready and then move rapidly to my objective, avoiding a battle at points where I would be encumbered by my wounded, but striking boldly and quickly when my objective is reached." Lincoln liked the sound of that, much as he had enjoyed Grant's hustling tone in the Atlanta dispatch. But when Stanton set out the following week, on a trip down the coast to confer with the red-haired commander, it occurred to the impatient President that if the Westerners were to come up hard and fast to join in putting the final squeeze on Lee, there had perhaps not been enough stress on the advantage of an early start. Accordingly, he got off a reminding wire to that effect. "While General Sherman's 'get a good ready' is appreciated, and is not to be overlooked," he told the Secretary, "*Time,* now that the enemy is wavering, is more important than ever."

His advice to the southern people, tendered in the December message to Congress, had been more grim than conciliatory; they need only reject their "insurgent leader ... by laying down their arms," and he would do what he could for them in the way of "pardons and remissions." Since then, however, the news from Nashville and Savannah had encouraged him to believe that the hour was near when they would no longer have any choice in the matter, if only he could provoke in his generals the sense of urgency he was convinced would end the rebellion in short order, and he said as much in the wire that followed Stanton down the coast. Now that their adversary was "on the downhill, and somewhat confused," he wanted the Secretary to impress on Sherman the importance of "keeping him going."

LIST OF MAPS

*Maps drawn by Rafael Palacios, from originals
by the author. All are oriented north.*

BIBLIOGRAPHICAL NOTE

The following bibliographical note was included with the full text of
THE CIVIL WAR: A Narrative—Red River to Appomattox.

So there now. Twenty years have come and gone and I can say with
Chaucer, "Farwel my book and my devocion." All through the second of
these two decades—the drawn-out time it took to write this third and
final volume—my debt to those who went before me, dead and living, continued to mount even as the Centennial spate diminished to a trickle and
then ran dry. Previous obligations were enlarged, and new ones acquired,
on both sides of the line defining the limits of the original material: especially on the near side, where the evidence was assembled and presented in
general studies, biographies, and secondary accounts of individual campaigns. Chief among these last, to take them in the order of their use, were
the following: *Red River Campaign* by Ludwell H. Johnson, *Lee's Last
Campaign* by Clifford Dowdey, *Autumn of Glory* by Thomas L. Connelly,
Jubal's Raid by Frank E. Vandiver, *The Decisive Battle of Nashville* by
Stanley F. Horn, *Sherman's March Through the Carolinas* by John G. Barrett,
and two recitals of the Appomattox chase, *An End to Valor* by Philip Van
Doren Stern and *Nine April Days* by Burke Davis. Similarly, my long-term
obligation to works on naval matters was extended by Virgil Carrington
Jones's *Civil War at Sea: The Final Effort* and Edward Boykin's *Ghost Ship
of the Confederacy.*

No one who has read or even scanned these books can fail to see my
debt to them, as well as to the biographies cited earlier, two of which had
concluding volumes that came out just as the need for them was sorest:
Hudson Strode's *Jefferson Davis: Tragic Hero* and Bruce Catton's *Grant
Takes Command.* Having had them, I cannot see how I could have managed
without them, and the same applies to J. G. Randall's *Lincoln the President,*

completed after his death by Richard N. Current in *Last Full Measure,* and Jim Bishop's *Day Lincoln Was Shot.* Clifford Dowdey's *Lee* brought his subject into sharper focus, and T. Harry Williams filled a sizeable gap with his *Hayes of the Twenty-third,* as E. B. Long did many others with *The Civil War Day by Day: An Almanac.* Nash K. Burger's and John K. Bettersworth's *South of Appomattox* helped get me down to the wire, and Kenneth M. Stampp, who was with me at the start in *And the War Came,* was also with me at the finish in *The Era of Reconstruction,* another old friend among the many I know only through their work.

To all these I am grateful, as I was and am to those mentioned in the end notes to the first two volumes of this iliad, most of whom continued their contribution through the third. Originally I intended to list my obligations in a complete bibliography here at the close of the whole, but even this chore has been spared me—along with a considerable added bulkiness for you—by Ralph G. Newman and E. B. Long, whose 1964 pamphlet, *A Basic Civil War Library,* first published in the *Journal of the Illinois State Historical Society,* enumerates by category the 350-odd books I owe most to, old and new and in and out of print. Other such compilations are readily available, including a much fuller one in Long's own *Almanac,* yet this one is to me the best in its inclusion of the works I mainly relied on, at any rate up to its date of issue. While I hope I have acknowledged my heaviest contemporary debts in this trio of notes, there are two I would like to stress in particular. One is to Bruce Catton, whose *Centennial History of the Civil War* was finished in time for its third volume, *Never Call Retreat,* to be available, together with his earlier *Stillness at Appomattox,* as a source and guide all through the writing of my own third volume. I was, as Stonewall Jackson said in another connection on his deathbed, "the infinite gainer" from having him thus meet his deadline even as I was failing to reach mine. My other chief debt is to the late Allan Nevins, whose close-packed *Organized War to Victory,* the last in his four-volume *War for the Union,* was similarly available during the past two years. Both gave me a wealth of useable material, but at least as valuable was their example of dedication and perseverance, double-barreled proof that such an undertaking could be carried to a finish. In that sense my debt to them is personal, though not as much so, nor as large, as the ones I owe my editor, Robert Loomis, and my wife, Gwyn Rainer Foote, both of whom bore with me all the way.

Perhaps in closing I might add that, although nowhere along the line have I had a "thesis" to argue or maintain—partly no doubt because I never saw one yet that could not be "proved," at least to the satisfaction of the writer who advanced it—I did have one thing I wanted to do, and that was to restore a balance I found lacking in nearly all the histories composed within a hundred years of Sumter. In all too many of these works, long and short, foreign and domestic, the notion prevailed that the War was fought in Virginia, while elsewhere—in an admittedly large but also rather empty region known vaguely as "the West"—a sort of running skirmish wobbled back and forth, presumably as a way for its participants, faceless men with unfamiliar names, to pass the time while waiting for the issue to be settled in the East. I do not claim that the opposite is true, but I do claim that it is perhaps a little closer to the truth; that Vicksburg, for example, was as "decisive" as Gettysburg, if not more so, and that Donelson, with its introduction of Grant and Forrest onto the national scene, may have had more to do with the outcome than either of the others had, for all their greater panoply, numbers, and documentation. In any case, it was my hope to provide what I considered a more fitting balance, East and West, in the course of attempting my aforesaid purpose of re-creating that war and making it live again in the world around us.

So, anyhow, "Farwel my book and my devocion," my rock and my companion through two decades. At the outset of this Gibbon span, plunk in what I hope will be the middle of my writing life, I was two years younger than Grant at Belmont, while at the end I was four months older than Lincoln at his assassination. By way of possible extenuation, in response to complaints that it took me five times longer to write the war than the participants took to fight it, I would point out that there were a good many more of them than there was of me. However that may be, the conflict is behind me now, as it is for you and it was a hundred-odd years ago for them.

—S.F.

INDEX

ABOUT THE AUTHOR

Shelby Foote was born in Greenville, Mississippi, and attended school there until he entered the University of North Carolina. During World War II he served in the European theater as a captain of field artillery. In the period after the war he wrote five novels: *Tournament, Follow Me Down, Love in a Dry Season, Shiloh,* and *Jordan County.* He was twice awarded a Guggenheim fellowship. A longtime resident of Memphis, Tennessee, he died in 2005 at the age of 88.